Alfred North Whitehead:

The Man and His Work

THE JOHNS HOPKINS UNIVERSITY PRESS   BALTIMORE AND LONDON

Victor Lowe

Whitehead

The Man and His Work

Volume II: 1910–1947

Edited by J. B. Schneewind

The Johns Hopkins University Press
701 West 40th Street, Baltimore, Maryland 21211
The Johns Hopkins Press Ltd., London

Illustration Credits

Photographs of Whitehead and his family and colleagues, courtesy of Mrs. T. North Whitehead.
Sketches from Whitehead's letters, courtesy of Special Collections Division, Milton S. Eisenhower Library, Johns Hopkins University.

The paper used in this publication meets the minimum requirements of American National Standard for Information Sciences—Permanence of Paper for Printed Library Materials, ANSI Z39.48-1984.

Library of Congress Cataloging-in-Publication Data

Lowe, Victor, 1907–1988
   Alfred North Whitehead : the man and his work.
   Includes bibliographies.
   Contents: v. 1. 1861–1910 — v. 2. 1910–1947.
   1. Whitehead, Alfred North, 1861–1947. 2. Philosophers—England—Biography. 3. Mathematicians—England—Biography. I. Title.
B1674.W354L57 1985   192   84-15467
ISBN 0-8018-2488-5 (v. 1 : alk. paper)
ISBN 0-8018-3960-2 (v. 2 : alk. paper)

For Allie

Contents

Preface

Victor Lowe died on November 16, 1988, leaving behind the unfinished manuscript of the second volume of his life of Whitehead, of
which the Johns Hopkins University Press had published the first volume in 1985. Some years earlier Victor had appointed me his literary
executor. We talked occasionally about his progress in the intervening
years, but he gave little indication of how far he had gotten on the
project and said little about his plans for the unwritten portions. It was
clear that he was working as hard and as continuously as his health
would allow, and that his main hope in life was to finish the book. As a
second best, he wanted to be sure that what he had written would be
published.

The condition of the manuscript was as follows. Up through Chapter XI it was written and footnoted, essentially ready for publication.
Chapter XII had been begun, and what was written, though scant, was
fairly polished. Beyond that there was nothing: no rough drafts, no
sketches, and very little in the way of written or printed material for the
later chapters. In our last conversation Victor said he had written nothing about *The Adventures of Ideas,* and I have found nothing about any of
the other books and papers Whitehead wrote after *Process and Reality.* A
transcription of Whitehead's letters to his son and daughter-in-law had
been made, and the appendix on the second edition of *Principia Mathematica* had been written. Victor planned other appendices, but neither
they nor material for them could be found. In effect, Whitehead's biography from 1910 through 1929—the years of his most creative philosophical activity—had been completed and the period beyond that
barely touched.

Victor planned to end the book with a new assessment of Whitehead's philosophy as a whole. He asked me to say that while he still
thought the interpretation he had given in his earlier *Understanding
Whitehead* was sound, he wanted to amplify it in parts and to add to it.
At the time of his death he had written nothing of this assessment for the
book. He had, however, written an essay for the collection edited by
Ernest Wolf-Gazo, *Process in Context* (Bern: Peter Lang, 1988). Pro-

fessor Wolf-Gazo kindly sent me a copy, and I have used that, with the kind permission of the publisher, as the final chapter.

The only other addition I have made is a very brief conclusion to Chapter XII, chronicling Whitehead's years after the publication of *Process and Reality*. I have made no attempt to go beyond the few materials—newspaper clippings and other ephemera—which I found in Victor's files. The years from 1929 to 1947 do not seem to have been especially eventful ones in Whitehead's outer life. Victor might have corrected that judgment; but only he could have written the missing chapters.

Thus the book is incomplete, as Victor feared it might be; but I hope not too seriously so. Thanks to his exhaustive investigations we know as much as it is possible to know about the life of a man who had the bulk of his papers destroyed. And for the understanding of Whitehead's work, what is missing is surely not as important as the part Victor wrote.

I do not know who the people are whom Victor would have thanked had he lived to complete the biography. I am sure he would have repeated and added to the list of those to whom he expressed gratitude in the Preface to the first volume, and on his behalf I thank all those who contributed the reminiscences and other material that went into the making of this one. Particular thanks are again due two people who cannot receive them, T. North Whitehead and Jessie Whitehead, who in 1965 gave Victor blanket permission to collect and use whatever material he could find that he judged useful for the biography they knew he was working on, and who gave him access to the letters from Whitehead that form Appendix B, as well as to numerous family photographs from which the ones published here were selected.

I do know that there were many people who helped me make this second-best outcome possible. Mrs. Bennett Gold, Victor's secretary, helped me sort out Victor's files and papers, and located a good deal of indispensable material. Peter Batke of the Johns Hopkins University Computing Center retrieved whatever was in the by now aged-looking computer Victor used, thereby finding the only copy of a whole section of one chapter. Sue McElvaney put most of the manuscript into the maws of a more up-to-date computer in record time and with astonishing accuracy; and what she did not do, Edna Ford did with equal skill. Cynthia Requardt is an admirable and helpful custodian of the Whitehead material Victor entrusted to the Special Collections Division of the Milton S. Eisenhower Library, the Johns Hopkins University. The letters and photographs reproduced in this volume are on temporary loan to the Special Collections Division. Nancy Thompson checked the transcription of the letters from Whitehead to his son and daughter-in-law against the originals in the Special Collections Division, and managed to decipher some of the more intractable bits. Jennifer Welchman checked the page references in the footnotes and endnotes, making corrections where necessary.

At a time when Victor felt that there was more to be done than he could finish, he found a research assistant, Dr. Leemon B. McHenry, now of the Philosophy Department at Central Michigan University. Dr. McHenry was the principal author of Chapters V and VI, and Victor wanted to record his gratitude for Dr. McHenry's able work.

Two other philosophers gave a great deal of time and thought to answering questions and making suggestions about the manuscript. George L. Kline and Donald W. Sherburne generously brought their unsurpassed expertise in Whitehead to the assistance of a non-Whiteheadian. They helped from beginning to end in assessing the general state of the manuscript, in ironing out matters of detail, and in making some important decisions about the final shape of the book. I have not always taken their advice, but it is only thanks to their assistance that I have some hope that the book has been made as worthy of its predecessor as it could have been.

To Jack Goellner and the staff of the Johns Hopkins University Press I am most grateful for the expedition and skill with which they have handled all the many tasks connected with actually publishing the manuscript. Penny Moudrianakis, who edited the manuscript with sensitivity and unfailing good sense, has my special gratitude.

Finally, my thanks go to Alice Lowe. Her determination to see the book published and her generosity in facilitating the preparation of the manuscript continued the care she gave Victor while he was working on it. Victor wished the book to be dedicated to her. She more than anyone else made it possible for him to complete as much of it as he did.

J. B. SCHNEEWIND

ALFRED NORTH WHITEHEAD:

THE MAN AND HIS WORK

Whitehead's First Years in London

I n the summer of 1910 Alfred North Whitehead, D.Sc., F.R.S., Fellow of Trinity College, Cambridge, moved from Cambridge to London with his wife, Evelyn, and their children, North, Jessie, and Eric. He had resigned his Senior Lectureship in Mathematics at Trinity College late in April, without lining up an academic position in London; he had not found one since. During the academic year 1910–11 he was unemployed.

Alfred and Evelyn Whitehead had been angered by the action of the Trinity College Council in promptly accepting their good friend Andrew Forsyth's resignation of his fellowship. Although indignation triggered the Whiteheads' move, it was far from being their only motive. At Cambridge, Alfred was in a groove. Possibly he talked to friends about some other job there, but I think that if he did, he was half-hearted about it. London was an infinitely larger, more varied world. The students there, to whom he would teach mathematics and mathematical physics as soon as he could, were bound to be very different from Cambridge students. It was terribly important that they receive a sound scientific education that would fit them for the modern world. Teaching was always as essential a part of Whitehead's life as mathematical research. London gave him a new teaching opportunity and a challenge. Also, the idea of life in London appealed strongly to his wife; she had had enough of Cambridge.[1]

Evelyn found a satisfactory house for them in Chelsea, at 17 Carlyle Square. This was not considered a good address; several decades later Chelsea became fashionable, but in 1910 it was run down. As the children were no longer small, a good neighborhood was not essential. To turn the interior of a Chelsea house that "seemed impervious to beauty"[2] into something strikingly beautiful was the sort of challenge that Evelyn delighted in. As she was restless, and happiest as an interior decorator, in the course of the Whiteheads' fourteen years in London they moved four times. Except for three years in South Kensington, they always moved to another Chelsea address.

Whitehead believed that the future of England depended heavily on the quality of the education provided for the masses in her great cities. Rote learning dominated the teaching of his subject, mathematics. Instead, the teacher ought to concentrate on the basic general ideas behind the formulas. He should present only the minimum number of ideas, with their interrelations, but do this with a rigor that was absent from the textbooks. The power of these ideas could be shown by throwing them into fresh combinations, and by work on a *few* of their most important applications to natural phenomena. The goal should be to develop in the student a sense of the great value of abstract mathematical ideas. Before Whitehead left Cambridge he had sketched out an introduction to mathematics that led the reader to understand the subject by gaining a precise grasp of its elementary great ideas in these ways.

There was now an opportunity to flesh out this sketch into a small book. The London publishing house of Williams and Norgate was bringing out a large series of small, inexpensive books, "The Home University Library of Modern Knowledge." It was aimed at those members of the general public who were eager to read authoritative accounts of Parliament, the Stock Exchange, Shakespeare, the Renaissance, evolution, philosophy, mathematics, et cetera, et cetera. The general editors were H. A. L. Fisher, Gilbert Murray, J. Arthur Thomson, and W. T. Brewster. The volumes were sometimes called "shilling shockers," for their authors were mainly scholars or public figures who had just achieved reputation or leadership. J. Ramsay Macdonald, M.P., wrote *The Socialist Movement,* John Masefield *William Shakespeare,* G. E. Moore *Ethics,* Bertrand Russell *The Problems of Philosophy.* Many of the volumes have become classics. The earliest, a large batch, came out in 1911.[3] One of them, No. 15 in the series, was *An Introduction to Mathematics,* by A. N. Whitehead. He had not been idle in his year of unemployment. Indeed, he never learned how to be idle.

All students of Whitehead's thought will profit from an examination of this book. His explanations of the nature and importance of mathematics contain short statements of philosophical doctrines, not intended to be such, but therefore all the more revealing of the selective emphases and the natural bent of Whitehead's thought in his—so-called—prephilosophical period.

In his short first chapter, "The Abstract Nature of Mathematics," Whitehead writes that his object is "not to teach mathematics, but to enable students from the very beginning of their course to know what the science is about, and why it is necessarily the foundation of exact thought as applied to natural phenomena." He constantly emphasizes the goal of understanding nature; this little book is as much an introduction to mathematical physics as an introduction to mathematics. The idea of a vector, which Whitehead calls "the root-idea of physical science," appears early on.[4] Chapter XII is entitled, "Periodicity in Nature." Whitehead makes no fundamental distinction between pure and applied mathematics.

The book achieved its stated purpose, and achieved it beautifully. Gilbert Murray wrote to Bertrand Russell on July 14, 1911, "I enjoyed Whitehead's Mathematics immensely. It seemed to tell me just what I always wanted to know and what my masters never told me." Russell found the book "absolutely masterly."[5] The historian of science, George Sarton, called it "very elementary but very wise."[6]

The writing will come as a delightful surprise to readers of Whitehead who know only the passages in earlier or later books in which he is working out his own mathematical or philosophical conceptions. *An Introduction to Mathematics* is clear, succinct, and lively. Here are a few examples. The second chapter, "Variables," begins, "Mathematics as a science commenced when first someone, probably a Greek, proved propositions about *any* things or about *some* things, without specification of definite particular things." In the chapter on the symbolism of mathematics Whitehead uses as an example "$x + y = y + x$," translates it into words, and says, "This example shows that, by the aid of symbolism, we can make transitions in reasoning almost mechanically by the eye." He continues with this vigorous comment:

> It is a profoundly erroneous truism, repeated by all copy-books and by eminent people when they are making speeches, that we should cultivate the habit of thinking of what we are doing. The precise opposite is the case. Civilization advances by extending the number of important operations which we can perform without thinking about them. Operations of thought are like cavalry charges in a battle—they are strictly limited in number, they require fresh horses, and must only be made at decisive moments.[7]

Whitehead has here dramatically expressed a valuable insight. But there is a flaw in the passage, one that frequently appears in his writings. He had a keen eye for the important facts that blind obedience to a truism can blind us to. In his opposition to received doctrines, he often says that the precise opposite is the case. To make his point, he did not need to say that here. In everyday life, the habit of not thinking of what you are doing is the habit of absent-mindedness. Whitehead himself was remarkably absent-minded.

Only one scientific discovery is recounted at any length in *An Introduction to Mathematics:* Archimedes' discovery of the theory of specific gravity, which enabled him to test the purity of the gold in King Hiero's crown.[8] "This day, if we knew which it was, ought to be celebrated as the birthday of mathematical physics." Whitehead, out of his long-established habit of reflecting on the history of civilization, appends this comment:

> The death of Archimedes by the hands of a Roman soldier is symbolical of a world-change of the first magnitude: the theoretical Greeks, with their love of abstract science, were superseded in the leadership of the European world by the practical Romans. . . . No Roman lost his life because he was absorbed in the contemplation of a mathematical diagram.[9]

Throughout this book, Whitehead loses no opportunity to assert the indispensability of abstract general ideas for the advance of scientific knowledge. Of course he mentions the early use by the Chinese of the characteristic property of the compass needle, remarks that they "do not seem to have connected it with any theoretical ideas," and contrasts this with the use of mathematical ideas by Europeans from Coulomb to Maxwell, whereby electromagnetic science with its endless practical applications was created.[10] Whitehead asserts, "The really profound changes in human life all have their ultimate origin in knowledge pursued for its own sake."[11] The growth since 1911 of the history of technology makes it impossible for us to be as confident as Whitehead was on this point.

An Introduction to Mathematics includes (Chapters VI–VIII) a splendid account of imaginary numbers and of the enlargement of algebra effected by the introduction of complex quantities. The book stops short of non-Euclidean geometry. Weierstrass's elimination of infinitesimals is persuasively presented in rigorous explanations of the general idea of a function, and of the differential calculus.

Some of the diagrams in the book were badly drawn. In 1942 the Oxford University Press issued an edition revised under the direction of Whitehead's nephew, the eminent mathematician J. H. C. Whitehead; in it the diagrams were redrawn, a few inaccuracies and typographical errors were corrected, and more recent books were mentioned in the bibliography with which the original book concluded.

ii

In July 1911 Whitehead accepted a job at University College, London. He was to be the Lecturer in Applied Mathematics and Mechanics. The salary was unusually low. But this was a teaching job; the lecture subjects were familiar to him; and the college could boast of a mathematical tradition left by Augustus de Morgan and W. K. Clifford.

University College, London, was the outcome of a movement started in 1825 by Thomas Campbell, the poet, and a group of radical and liberal men. At that time Oxford and Cambridge were firmly in the grip of the Established Church; a student had to declare himself an Anglican in order to enter Oxford or to get a degree from Cambridge, and the same requirement was imposed on teachers. Surely there ought to be an English university that was open to men of all faiths and even to secularists. London, above all other cities, needed a non-residential university of this kind. What was later called University College, London, opened its doors in October 1828. It was the first modern university in Britain, for it was designed to provide an education in the sciences and modern humane studies, in contrast to the largely classical curricula of Oxford and Cambridge. Theology had no place in its curriculum. Of course University College was called "the godless institution in Gower Street." The success of the campaign to found such a teaching center owed something to the influence of Henry Brougham, and to Jewish philanthropists. Jeremy Bentham is commonly supposed to have been one of the founders of University College. He was not a founder, but he soon gave the new institution his blessing and financial support; opponents of the venture considered him its patron devil. The modernization of Oxford and Cambridge was secured by acts of Parliament much later, but in at least one respect University College, London, remained well ahead of them: in 1878 it undertook to grant degrees to women on the same terms as men.

Only a year after the launching of University College, Anglicans founded Kings' College, in the Strand, as a rival purveyor of modern knowledge to Londoners. In 1836 the two were brought together in a federal academic institution, called the University of London; it scarcely deserved to be called a university, for its business was merely to conduct examinations and confer degrees. As the Victorian age advanced, a great variety of other colleges and schools sprang up in London. There was increasing pressure to put this miscellany under one umbrella by reorganizing the University of London so that all became subject to it. On January 1, 1907, University College, by act of Parliament, ceased to exist as an independent corporation. It became a unit of the University of London, with the awkward title, "University of London: University College."* The Council that had governed the College became a committee responsible to the Senate of the University.

When Whitehead began teaching at University College in 1911, its enrollment was increasing rapidly. (It doubled in the seven years preceding 1914.) The increase was greatest in the number of women enrolled. New departments were being created, enlarged laboratory accommodations were being provided. But the income from endowments was not increasing. The college was poverty-stricken.

A most unusual web of circumstances at Trinity College, Cambridge, was responsible for the early start that Whitehead got on his teaching career in 1884.[12] Circumstances that were fairly unusual led to the beginning of his teaching in London. A friend of University College, the anthropologist Sir Francis Galton, bequeathed money in 1911 for a department of Applied Statistics and Eugenics. It was understood that his follower, the Cambridge mathematician Karl Pearson, would be appointed to the new chair. To accept it, Pearson had to resign the chair he had held for twenty-seven years at University College. This was the Goldsmid chair of Applied Mathematics and Mechanics. Upon his resignation from it in June 1911, it was decided to postpone naming his successor and to make a temporary arrangement for 1911–12. The work was reduced to mechanics and astronomy. The Lecturer on Mechanics, Assistant Professor Ebenezer Cunningham, was asked to continue his teaching and also to lecture in place of Pearson on astronomy. In July he was released to accept an offer of a mathematical lectureship at Cambridge, where he had been the Senior Wrangler in 1902. Pearson then approved and brought to the Provost—perhaps he initiated—the idea of inviting Whitehead to replace Cunningham. Whitehead accepted the invitation despite the pitifully low salary of the post, £300. He trusted his wife to manage somehow, and he did not want to spend another year without teaching.

During the interregnum year 1911–12 Whitehead was the only member of his department in the Faculty of Science at University College. He taught the most essential courses, courses he had often taught at Cambridge. His new freshmen heard him on dynamics and hydrostatics; his sophomores studied the theory of the potential and of attraction, advanced statics and advanced particle dynamics. He taught a

---

*University College Hospital and University College School (a preparatory school) continued to be independent of the University of London.

general course in astronomy; with an assistant, he scheduled a course of practical work in astronomy (so far as the atmosphere in London permitted such work to be performed). Whitehead spent the month of September 1911 near the Cambridge Observatory, preparing his lecture notes and preparing himself in astronomy.

He had with him some proofs of the second volume of *Principia Mathematica,* to wit, those for Part IV, "Relation-Arithmetic."[13] On September 20 Whitehead wrote to his collaborator:

Dear Bertie

I am awfully sorry to have kept the proofs in this unconscionable way. Every day I thought that I could get a little time. But this wretched astronomy (interesting enough in itself) has taken all my time—including the "reducing" of the observations, so that I have never been fresh enough to follow the reasoning. This relation-arithmetic is too complicated to be corrected by eye, and wants a fresh brain to manage the reasoning.

The continuation of this passage affords an example of the admiration that Whitehead in his letters to Russell often bestowed on his hungry former pupil: "As usual the notation (e.g. ★182) struck me as beautiful. You have surpassed yourself."

Whitehead hoped to be seriously considered for the chair that Karl Pearson had vacated. In mid-March 1912 his hopes were abruptly destroyed. The final decision was in the hands of the Professorial Board, comprising the heads of the departments in the Faculty of Science at University College. They were to act on a report that had been made to the Registrar of the University of London by a Board of Advisors on Friday, March 15.* On Saturday the Registrar communicated it to the Provost of the College, who at once called a special meeting of the Professorial Board for Monday afternoon to hear and consider it. In one crucial respect the Advisors had not followed customary procedure: according to their report, they had not advertised the professorial vacancy. They had considered seven names of persons they thought suitable, and decided to recommend Dr. L. N. G. Filon. Filon, who when

---

*The Board of Advisors consisted of the Vice-Chancellor of the university, the Provost and three professors of University College, and three professors from other universities. The Board's report, and the other sources of the information used in the remainder of the present section, are in University College, London, Professorial Board file 1884–1916, folio 151.

quite young had worked under Pearson, was in his eighth year as Assistant Professor in the Department of Pure Mathematics at University College; he was a competent mathematician and a most conscientious teacher, a safe man to appoint.* The Professorial Board approved the Advisors' report, and before Monday afternoon ended the Academic Council of the University Senate made Filon's appointment official. Thus Whitehead's hope of getting the long-vacant chair was swept away in one extended weekend.

We have to notice two letters that were sent to the Provost of the College, T. G. (later Sir Gregory) Foster, on Saturday, March 16. One was an angry letter from Karl Pearson. He deeply regretted that no public announcement had been made of the vacancy in the chair, since without it no real knowledge of possible candidates and of what each would say for himself could be reached. Pearson protested that what was done was contrary to the spirit of the College's founders as evidenced in their regulations for professorial appointments, and declared that the College would be harmed if procedures like this became customary. He also said that his opinion had not been sought and he would not attend Monday's special meeting.

The other Saturday letter was from Whitehead.† As acting head of Applied Mathematics, he was a member of the Professorial Board, and so had just received from the Provost the report of the Board of Advisors. His consternation is easy to imagine. In haste he wrote a job letter to the Provost, "for communication to the Professorial Board." After referring to the Provost's assurance, written to him on August 12, 1911, "that my temporary position would not debar me from being a candidate for the permanent post," Whitehead described his mathematical goals and his qualifications for the post; he urged that similar statements be sought from all men who were being considered, since otherwise "all those whose lines of work are by chance unknown to the appointing Board" would not receive due consideration. Alas, the Advisors had left no time for anything of the sort. In fact, Whitehead's was one of the seven names the Board had considered; University College records are silent on the question of whether the list of seven was drawn

---

*So I infer from G. B. Jeffery's obituary notice of Filon, in *Obituary Notices of Fellows of the Royal Society* 2, No. 7 (January 1939): 501–7.

†I am indebted to the Secretary of University College, London, for permission to quote from Whitehead's letter, and to Mrs. J. Percival, the College Archivist, for calling it to my attention. I published the entire letter, with detailed comment, in "A. N. Whitehead on His Mathematical Goals: A Letter of 1912," *Annals of Science* 32 (1975): 85–101.

up at a meeting of the Advisors on February 16, or not until the day of their decision, March 15. In any case, Whitehead had not been given a chance to speak for himself. This was a pity. Everyone knew of his collaboration with Russell on *Principia Mathematica,* the first volume of which had come out a year earlier. Few Englishmen knew his other work, and almost no one knew what *his* long-term mathematical goals were. Whitehead's letter to the Provost described these goals,* emphasized his experience in teaching applied mathematics, and indicated how he would organize that teaching at University College. In connection with the last, he called attention to his *Introduction to Mathematics.*†

iii

The appointment of Filon to the chair of Applied Mathematics and Mechanics left a gap in the other mathematical department at University College, that of Pure Mathematics. Whitehead was a natural choice to fill it. Filon had introduced projective geometry into the curriculum. At Cambridge, Whitehead had published a tract, *The Axioms of Projective Geometry.*[14] He was much more of an authority on geometry than Filon was. A new position was created for him: in July he was appointed Reader in Geometry. The English "Reader" is roughly equivalent to the American "Associate Professor." Filon had been Assistant Professor.

The Professor of Pure Mathematics was Micaiah J. M. Hill, four years older than Whitehead. Hill was born in India, the son of a missionary. When only sixteen he took his baccalaureate at University College, London, then went on to Cambridge. There he was Fourth Wrangler in 1879, as Whitehead was in 1883. Hill had been professor at University College since 1884. He was something of an authority on Euclid's *Elements,* but he had little time for mathematical research. Like Whitehead, he devoted himself to his students. Academic administration absorbed most of his other energies. After many years on the University Senate, he served from 1909 to 1911 as Vice-Chancellor of the University. Hill was always conscientious; every problem was a major problem. By all accounts, he was a modest, beloved, but essentially colorless person. He was well disposed to Whitehead, and I think Whitehead respected him.

When Whitehead failed to get Pearson's chair, he scouted around in

---

*For Whitehead's description of his mathematical goals, see Section iv below.
†See Section i above.

hopes of finding some job better than that of Lecturer in Applied Mathematics and Mechanics. That he decided to be content with his new position under Hill appears from the reply he wrote on November 8, 1912, to a well-wishing good friend. Ralph Hawtrey* had written to suggest that he apply for a high administrative position that had just opened up within the University of London. His letter, like others that Whitehead received while in England, is not extant. When I visited Hawtrey in 1968, he could no longer remember what the position was, but he gave me Whitehead's reply to him. This does not name the position, but the content shows that it must have been that of principal of King's College, London.†

Although King's had been founded by Anglicans in rivalry to University College, its theological side was left alone when the rest of King's College became a unit of the University of London on January 1, 1910. The appointment of the principal was now placed in the hands of the Crown.

In his reply to Hawtrey, Whitehead said:

> I do not think Asquith would appoint me. The traditions of the place are clerical; and though the work is now formally separated, yet, even for the lay part, he will for the first appointment probably look for a "persona grata" to the Church-people.

In January Asquith appointed a good churchman, the classical scholar R. M. Burrows. Whitehead was realistic; Hawtrey, eighteen years younger and inclined to rate Whitehead higher than most people did, may have been a bit naive. Whitehead wrote to Hawtrey that he was "very happy and comfortable" in his "present post":

> Of course if a really big job—like the one now suggested—came my way, I should naturally accept it gladly, very gladly. But the authorities here are doing all they can to make themselves agreeable. And I must not meet them with a succession of efforts to get away. . . . I shall settle into my present post without looking on it as a merely temporary job.

---

*Hawtrey read mathematics at Trinity College, Cambridge, first came to know Whitehead intimately when elected to the Apostles in 1900, and took a keen interest in the project of *Principia Mathematica*. (He was given a presentation copy of its first volume.) Since 1904 Hawtrey had been at the Treasury. He stayed there until 1945, was knighted, and wrote several books on economic theory.

†The London *Times* on October 31, 1912, reported the resignation of A. C. Headlam (later Bishop of Gloucester) from the principalship.

Whitehead spent only two years as Reader in Geometry; then he left University College for the Imperial College of Science and Technology. In those two years he taught advanced projective geometry and standard courses in plane coordinate geometry, the differential and integral calculus, and solid geometry. But he also gave two courses that were not standard. One, given in 1912–13, reflected his interest in diverse conceptions of "space"; he called it "Geometrical Theory and Speculation." A course he gave in 1913–14 was announced as "A course on Mathematical Logic with applications to Geometry."

There were a good many student clubs that welcomed the participation of faculty members. Whitehead enjoyed doing this. For two years he was president of the Mathematical and Physical Society. A quite different club was the Critical Society. Of the several occasions on which Whitehead was active in it, I mention two because they show that he was more than a mathematician. In 1913 he read a paper, "The Role of Exact Reasoning in Practical Affairs." (This was scheduled for May 15, but postponed because Whitehead came down with a quite serious case of influenza.) Early in 1914 he spoke to this society on "Philosophy and Science in Poetry." Julia Bell, a young mathematician who was assistant to Karl Pearson, wrote to me about this meeting; she said of Whitehead, "One could have listened to him all night."[15] She added that Pearson came to hear Whitehead and "tremendously enjoyed" the lecture.

Late in August 1912 the Fifth International Congress of Mathematicians met in Cambridge. Bertrand Russell was one of its Secretaries. He was now living in rooms at Trinity College, where he was Lecturer on Logic and the Principles of Mathematics. The Cambridge University Press had published the second volume of Whitehead and Russell's *Principia Mathematica* in the spring. Since the thesis it attempted to demonstrate, and the most controversial ideas in it, were originally Russell's, almost everyone interested in the work tried to talk to him. Whitehead attended the Congress, but was less active. His official part in its program was in its Educational Section. He read there a fine paper (to be discussed, along with his other papers on education in mathematics, in Chapter III below): "The Principles of Mathematics in Relation to Elementary Teaching." He had become much more concerned with reforming the teaching of mathematics than with the foundations of its branches, other than geometry. He had done some work on what was meant to be Volume IV, "Geometry," of the *Principia,* for which he alone would be responsible. In the Congress he took part, with Peano, in the discussion of E. V. Huntington's important paper, "A Set of

Postulates for Abstract Geometry, Expressed in Terms of the Simple Relation of Inclusion." But Whitehead was quite happy to leave the defense of the finished parts of *Principia* to Russell. He himself had little polemical interest in his work once it was done.

Russell had invited the American logician and philosopher Josiah Royce to the Congress, but Royce was not well enough to come. Whitehead's personal acquaintance with American logicians did not begin until he came to Harvard in 1924.

iv

By 1913 it was evident that the number of mathematicians and philosophers interested in mathematical logic was great enough to justify an international congress for them. The First Congress of Mathematical Philosophy, sponsored by the Société Française de Philosophie and the editors of the *Encyclopédie de Sciences Mathématique,* was held in Paris from April 6 to April 8, 1914. In the paragraph on this congress in Whitehead's "Autobiographical Notes," written when he was eighty, he said, "It was crammed with Italians, Germans, and a few English including Bertrand Russell and ourselves."[16] In fact, Russell was not there; he was at Harvard, lecturing on logic in its Philosophy Department and giving Lowell Lectures in Boston. But Russell had been active in planning the congress.

On April 8 Whitehead delivered a paper on the relational theory of space. To understand the nature of his interest in this subject, let us attend to what, so far as I know, is the only description of his long-term mathematical goals that he ever wrote down. It occurs in the letter he sent to the Provost of University College on March 16, 1912. There Whitehead said:

> During the last twenty-two years I have been engaged in a large scheme of work, involving the logical scrutiny of mathematical symbolism and mathematical ideas. This work had its origin in the study of the mathematical theory of Electromagnetism, and has always had as its ultimate aim the general scrutiny of the relations of matter and space, and the criticism of the various applications of mathematical thought. . . .
>
> For some years past my investigations have turned on the necessary mathematical relations between space and matter, and this has led me back to modern electrical theories which were my original point of departure.
>
> This scheme of research of which only part is yet published, and

of which much remains yet in project, has led me in the past naturally to concentrate my teaching almost entirely on Applied Mathematics.[17]

Much of this language is vague, and the last sentence is an overstatement; Whitehead wrote hastily in the vain hope of being seriously considered for the chair of Applied Mathematics. But the "large scheme of work" cannot be dismissed. Whitehead's mathematical research began with his 1884 Trinity College fellowship dissertation on Maxwell's *Electricity and Magnetism*. In 1887 he lectured on Grassmann's Calculus of Extension, "with applications." This calculus was the most powerful of the many algebraic systems that physicists could use widely. Hamilton's quaternion theory was another. By 1890 Whitehead envisaged a comparative study of all such systems. Toward this end he wrote his first book, *A Treatise on Universal Algebra*. The final comparison would have to face the question of the dependence of these systems on the algebra of symbolic logic. Russell, in *The Principles of Mathematics,* had argued that all known mathematics could be deduced from the principles of symbolic logic. It was natural for Whitehead to give up his work on the second volume of *Universal Algebra* in order to join with Russell in writing *Principia Mathematica*.

In 1905 Whitehead sent to the Royal Society an important memoir, "On Mathematical Concepts of the Material World." In it he set out five "Concepts," each a single set of axioms and definitions embracing both the relations of the elements of space *inter se* and their relations to instants of time and to the "stuff" in space. Concept I, "the classical concept of the material world," accepts the absolute theory of space. But Whitehead indicates a preference for "Leibniz's theory of the Relativity of Space," on the ground that since "entities are not to be multiplied beyond necessity," the elements of space and those of matter should not be accepted as ultimately independent classes of entities, if a monistic alternative be possible. The Concept he recommended for consideration, Concept V, embodied a relational theory of space. Whitehead sketched a way in which this Concept might be used to set the stage for a general theory of the electromagnetic physics of that day. Alas, the memoir of 1905 was long, difficult, and written in the *Principia* notation; physicists ignored it.[18]

The completion of Whitehead's work on *Principia*'s fourth volume, "Geometry," is the one thing that we can be sure he had in mind when he wrote to the Provost of University College in 1912 that much of his scheme of research "remained yet in project." On October 1, 1913, he wrote to Russell, "I have done a lot of writing for vol IV, and now know much more about Geometry than formerly." He also said that he would like to attend the congress at Paris in April to "'air' . . . some things on Space." When on January 10 he sent Russell a rewritten draft of his paper for the congress, he wrote him:

> The paper as it stands—provided it survives your criticisms—will go nearly without change into vol IV. Meanwhile I will send it to Leon [Xavier Leon, President of the Société Française de Philosophie and founder of the *Revue de Métaphysique et de Morale*] for the Congress and the Revue de Metaph-.

It was in a special issue of this journal, edited by Leon, that the paper was published two years later—in French, as "La Théorie Relationniste de l'Espace."[19]

It is most unlikely that the paper Whitehead sent first to Russell and then to Leon was written in French. As Whitehead, unlike his wife, his daughter, or Russell, spoke French badly, he probably read the paper as he had written it, in English, and let Leon translate it for publication in his *Revue*. The English original disappeared long ago. No English version was available until 1978, when an American, Dr. Patrick J. Hurley, made a translation from the published French one.[20]

Time and motion are not discussed in this paper—only space. Einstein's special theory of relativity is not mentioned, nor is Minkowski's union of space and time. Whitehead will deal with their work in his book of 1919–22 on the philosophy of natural science. Talking to me in May 1941, he said, "Minkowski's paper was published in 1908, but its influence on me was postponed approximately ten years." "Ten" may be an overstatement by one to three years.

Whitehead had long favored the relational theory of space, and never favored the absolute theory.[21] But, unlike Russell, he was slow to commit himself in print. In his article "The Axioms of Geometry," published in 1910 in the eleventh edition of the *Encyclopaedia Britannica,* he had expressed the opinion, "No decisive argument for either view has at present been elaborated." The situation, as he saw it in 1914, was that almost every physicist disavowed the absolute theory but tacitly used it; relative motion was habitually treated as differential motion within absolute space. But if there is no absolute position, the relational theory is mere verbiage apart from definitions of points in terms of relations between objects. Whitehead perceived that more than one way of doing this should be possible. He worked out one way for presentations to the congress. In the memoir of 1905 he had developed his "Theory of Interpoints," by which points were defined in terms of relations between proposed ultimate material entities. In the four years after 1914 he mounted a broad, new attack on the traditional presuppositions of physics, and presented a detailed construction of the exact concepts of space and time out of the data of perception; *An Enquiry Concerning the Principles of Natural Knowledge* was published in 1919. In it he named his constructive procedure "the method of extensive abstraction." It was a broader application, beginning with different data, of the technical procedure he used in 1914. "La Théorie Relationniste de l'Espace" has to be accounted a transitional work; I think it is also his most poorly written work. I shall therefore postpone my account of the method of extensive abstraction until I come to the *Enquiry*.

In the 1914 paper Whitehead said of the relational theory of space:

> The fundamental order of ideas is first a world of things in relation, then the space whose fundamental entities are defined by means of these relations and whose properties are deduced from the nature of these relations.[22]

Accordingly, the base from which Whitehead starts is a class of relations. He denotes this class by the symbol σ, and calls the relata of these relations σ-objects. He uses the *Principia Mathematica* notation for relations and their properties. The work of defining "point" begins with the attribution of certain properties to the relations between σ-objects that he calls the "inclusion" of one within another. At one stage he introduces the hypothesis that two objects which stand in the same relations to all other objects are identical, and notes that this is practically Leibniz's doctrine of the identity of indiscernibles.

As a necessary introduction to his subject, Whitehead distinguishes four meanings of the word "space," as currently used. In this he seems to me to cover the ground very well for his purpose. He draws a primary distinction between apparent space and physical space. The former is the place of objects as they appear to us. Within apparent space, Whitehead distinguishes between immediate apparent space—what an individual perceives at a moment—and complete apparent space, in which the perceptions of different individuals are adjusted to one another. In ordinary conversation about the perceived world, "space" means "complete apparent space." Physical space is something else; it is the space not of apparent objects but of the physical objects that correspond to them and are customarily thought of as causing our perceptions; it is the space of physical science, the space in which electrons and molecules move and act on one another, and in which our sense organs are excited. The exact analysis of the relation between apparent objects and physical objects, Whitehead says, is "a fundamental scientific problem" which he will "set aside."[23]

None of these meanings of "space" fits the subject of geometry as a deductive science. That science is wholly abstract; it deals with *any* entities whose interrelations satisfy the geometer's axioms. Such entities form an "abstract space." Whitehead is not now interested in it.

He is interested in defining the idea of "being at a point," for complete apparent space and for physical space; Whitehead addresses himself to both, and so deals with two kinds of δ-objects. In his expositions he usually begins with complete apparent space, then turns to physical space. Points are defined in the same way in both cases.

It is in connection with physical space that Whitehead finds the ultimate import of the relational theory. The theory forbids us to consider physical bodies "as existing first in space, then acting on one another, directly or indirectly." Rather,

> They are in space because they act on one another, and space is none other than the expression of certain properties of their interaction. A book of geometry, insofar as it is treated as a science applicable to physical space, is none other than the first part of a treatise of physics. Its subject is not "the prolegomena to physics"; it is part of physics.[24]

In dealing with the relations between physical objects, Whitehead views all direct relations as causal. He asserts that the only kind of fact physical science has to consider is, how the state of the physical universe during a certain lapse of time determines the future states. His only discussion of that kind of fact in "La Théorie Relationniste de l'Espace" is a preliminary examination of the idea of action at a distance. He begins it by noticing three common-sense axioms in physics: an object cannot be entirely in two places at the same time, two objects cannot be in the same place at the same time, and two objects at a distance cannot act on one another. Physicists who hold that action between distant objects takes place through a continuous medium must face the fact that any two points in the medium are separated by a distance. As smaller and smaller separations are considered, may we say that when the distance becomes infinitesimal the action begins? No, Whitehead declares; Weierstrass abolished the infinitesimal. There are no infinitely small volumes, and no two points are contiguous. After stating and dismissing other relevant possibilities, Whitehead leaves the question of how physical objects act on one another unresolved. The moral of the discussion is the importance of trying to define points instead of taking them as undefined geometrical entities. If "point" is undefined, "location at a point" is undefined.

The paper ends when the author reaches his definition of "occupation of a point." This concludes many pages in the symbolism of *Principia Mathematica*.

V

At the beginning of October 1910 the Whitehead's older son, North, like his father thirty years earlier, went up to Trinity College, Cambridge. In August 1908 he had contracted scarlet fever in Switzerland; it was then a much more serious disease than it is now. His parents treated him as a semi-invalid for more than a year. Being consequently short of time, he went to a "crammer," who enabled him to pass the entrance examination. North's interests were scientific, but he did not read for the Mathematical Tripos. There was a new Tripos in Economics, which involved no previous study of the subject; his reading of Thomas Nixon Carver's *The Distribution of Wealth* and the Minority Report of the Royal Commission on the English Poor Law gave him an initial enthusiasm for economics. This did not last; in his unpublished autobiography North wrote, "I was one of Maynard Keynes' less promising students." He was just good enough to graduate in 1913 with third-class honors in economics. That autumn he enrolled in University College, London, to study the subject he loved: mechanical engineering. He lived with his parents in Chelsea. Whitehead loved all his children, but his relationship with North was always the closest.

The daughter, Jessie, was sixteen in 1910. She was always lively and highly intelligent, but she stammered badly. North told me that she had done so since she was three.[25] Whitehead's friend Dr. Henry Head, and perhaps others, were consulted. On August 23, 1910, Whitehead began a letter to Bertrand Russell about their *Principia Mathematica* with the news, "Jessie's stammer is *cured*. Isn't it splendid. She does not go back to school till half-term for fear of a relapse." The stammer was not cured, nor was it cured at other times when it seemed to be. Although it was sometimes absent, the stammer continued as long as Jessie lived.

During Whitehead's first years in London, Russell continued to be his closest friend. They had to meet frequently in order to see *Principia* through the press. Russell's relations with Evelyn Whitehead took a new turn late in March 1911, when Bertie discovered that he was passionately in love with Lady Ottoline Morrell, the beautiful wife of Philip Morrell, M.P. The Whiteheads were among the very few friends to whom Russell said anything about this; secrecy was imperative. Early in his collaboration with Whitehead, Russell had ceased to care for his wife, Alys, and fallen in love with Evelyn Whitehead. She was fond of him but did not return his love.[26] Gradually she became the confidante in his emotional life. Bertie and Alys miserably kept up a nominal marriage for nine years, until he declared his love to Lady Ottoline. He wanted Ottoline to devote herself to him, but she was strongly attached to her husband and daughter. He asked her to call on Mrs. Whitehead. Ottoline did so and was able to explain her feelings, which Russell had been unable to grasp. The two women did not care for each other, but Evelyn wanted to do what she could for Bertie in his *affaire*. Alys, abetted by her brother, Logan Pearsall Smith, was causing trouble. Evelyn disliked Alys but was seeing her; she kept Bertie *au courant*. She also let the lovers meet in her house when her servants and children were not there. At one point Evelyn undertook to find a safe flat in Chelsea.

Whitehead's way of helping Russell was intellectual. In August 1911 Russell sent him a typed copy of *The Problems of Philosophy*, which he had just finished writing for the Home University Library. One of the editors of this series, Russell's friend Gilbert Murray, had invited him to write it, assuring him that he could surely produce a splendid "message to the shop-assistants about philosophy."[27] Although Russell had published three books on philosophies *of*—of geometry, Leibniz, mathematics—this was his first book on *general* philosophy. It dealt mainly with theory of knowledge. Russell began by asking what we can know with certainty, and how we can know it; he went on to the kinds of knowledge, and their limits. The book was written with Russell's usual clarity, and has been used more in colleges than any other book he wrote.

When Whitehead thanked him for the typescript on August 23, he called the book "really excellent," but said that some arguments in it did not convince him; he would write to Bertie about them. Three days later Whitehead sent off fourteen pages (in his large hand) of critical notes, along with a short letter in which he said,

What I recognize as distinctively yours, seems to me to be excellent. But where (in my ignorance) I guess that you are repeating received ideas, I cannot follow. You seem to me to lack self-confidence (or rather, time) to systematize philosophy afresh, in accordance with your own views.

. . . As a "Message", I cannot praise too highly.

Whitehead pulled no punches in his critical notes; he could not have thought of doing so with his intimate friend and collaborator. Russell in his first chapter, "Appearance and Reality," took the position that the certainty on which knowledge is based is the sensing of sense-data: I sense brownness, touch hardness, and *infer* that I am perceiving a brown, hard table. Whitehead commented, "Such inferences are quite beyond plain people like myself. I perceive *objects,* and want to know about the reality of the objects I perceive." Although Whitehead's views changed in the next decade, he never gave up his disagreement with Russell's 1911 view that belief in the table is an *inference* from sense-data. Russell in his second chapter undertook to refute solipsism. Whitehead wrote, "Your confutation of the solipsist seems to me to be entirely fallacious." Whitehead never thought solipsism needed to be argued against.

The longest critical discussion was of Russell's eighth chapter, which was meant to demolish Kant's theory of a priori knowledge. Whitehead concluded, "It seems to me that Chapter VIII is not within a hundred miles of Kant's position." I omit mention here of Whitehead's objections to passages in three more chapters.*

From Russell's correspondence with Murray about the text of *The Problems of Philosophy,* it seems very likely that he turned in his final typescript before he received Whitehead's critical notes. We cannot say with certainty that he took no account of them when he read proof in November 1911, since the proof-sheets no longer exist; but we can give a negative answer with high probability. Russell would have had to notice and judge positions opposed to his own; in the book as published all of the very many passages that Whitehead objects to appear unchanged. In the second printing (September 1913) a footnote was inserted in Chapter VIII; I read it as providing what Russell thought a sufficient short answer to Whitehead's defense of Kant. In later printings no notice is taken of any of Whitehead's other criticisms. In the original Preface, never changed, Russell wrote that he had "derived

---

*The complete text of Whitehead's critical notes and of his two letters to Russell, along with a fuller commentary than I can offer here, was published in my paper, "Whitehead's 1911 Criticism of *The Problems of Philosophy.*" *Russell* (the journal of the Bertrand Russell Archives) 13 (Spring 1974): 3–10.

valuable assistance from unpublished writings of G. E. Moore and J. M. Keynes"—from Moore on "the relations of sense-data to physical objects"; and he thanked Murray for "criticisms and suggestions." He did not mention Whitehead.

In the letters Whitehead wrote to Russell when they were writing *Principia Mathematica,* he habitually overemphasized his own incompetence in philosophy. Although he generally left it to Russell to attack the philosophical problems that arose, his criticisms are an essential part of the story of their collaboration, and sometimes Russell accepted them.[28] What Whitehead in criticizing Russell's view of 1911 failed to realize was the strength of his attachment to them. On December 19, 1912, Russell, writing to his American friend Lucy Donnelly about the favorable reception of *The Problems of Philosophy* in America, said, "I feel myself that it is rather an achievement! I attained a simplicity of thought beyond what I had thought possible"; and "I feel as if I had just discovered what philosophy is and how it ought to be studied." Whitehead felt, as he felt ever after, that the simplicity was deceptive.

In a letter to me, dated July 24, 1960, Russell wrote that he could say of Whitehead, "definitely and with certainty," that "before 1918, he had no definite opinions in philosophy and did not actively combat mine." Protective memory?

vi

In the summer of 1910 the Whiteheads, besides settling into a house in Chelsea, found a small cottage in Wiltshire that was for rent. It was in the hamlet of Lockeridge (pronounced Lock-e-ridge), near Marlborough and off the main road from London to Bath. Beyond the woods lay Wansdike, a prehistoric dike. Stonehenge was a little more than twenty miles away. The cottage went by the magnificent name, "Sarsen Land." (Sandstones were scattered nearby.) The Whiteheads were there for at least the last month of this summer.

Throughout their twenty years of marriage Alfred, always devoting himself to mathematical teaching, research, and writing, had let Evelyn take the lead in practical matters; he usually went along with her decisions. Now the owner of Sarsen Land was willing to sell it. Evelyn bought it, with the idea that it would be their permanent country home as long as Alfred worked in London. They would spend almost half of each year there, since the English academic year takes up only twenty-six weeks. She immediately more than doubled its size. What had been a humble thatched cottage became a handsome house, with a beautiful long drawing room. Whitehead's study was on the ground floor of the original cottage. The house is now known as "Piper's Plot."*

The Whiteheads often saw Lytton Strachey, for he lived nearby in Lockeridge.

Friends often came for weekends, or longer. The Whiteheads' friends were mostly, like themselves, non-religious liberals. On one weekend in March 1913 Josiah Wedgwood, M.P. (later Baron Wedgwood), was a guest with his daughters, Helen and Frances. An amusing entertainment was provided for them on the Sunday. Helen Wedgwood, then nearly eighteen, was later the Honorable Mrs. H. B. Pease. On September 8, 1968, she wrote out for me her recollection of this entertainment:

> Mrs. Whitehead said, "The servants are all out for the afternoon, so Alfred, Jessie and North are going to act a 'mystery play.'" A. N. W., North and Jessie entered the room arm in arm carrying a football.† (A. N. W. made a most paternal and benevolent God the Father). ANW said, "I've had a wonderful new idea. Let's put something alive on this ball." Action of putting things on it, with comments on the Creation. Then they stood watching it and tutt tutting over the deplorable goings on on Earth. Son (North) and Pigeon (Jessie) appeared to be a bit doubtful whether the Creation *was* such a good idea after all!! A. N. W. said, "I am sorry, Son, but you must really go down there and see if you can do something about it." After some argument North gathered up a portmanteau and rugs and reluctantly left the room. ANW and Jessie continued to observe the Ball and commented suitably (and wittily) on the Son's career on Earth. (I cannot unfortunately remember what they said—it was all quite harmless.) Finally North returned in a somewhat dishevelled condition. "Oh I have had an *awful* time. I won't ever go there again." They continued to watch the Ball. ANW shook his head sadly. "And it hasn't done a bit of good. They are worse than ever! Oh, *bother* the thing!" A vigorous kick sent the ball into the corner of the room and the Trinity went out arm in arm.

This parody of simple Christian theism shows the Whiteheads' cheerful despair of the redeemability of mankind by Christianity, in 1913. At that time it was relatively easy for educated Englishmen of good will to pursue their social ideals without religious faith. Steady

---

*I do not know whether the Whiteheads or some later owner first gave this name to Sarsen Land.

†The ball was a Rugby football, which is more like a soccer ball than an American football.

progress by reform, not by force (except in Ireland) seemed to be the order of the day, and was what the Whiteheads believed in.

How did Evelyn manage the family finances? Their house at 17 Carlyle Square, Chelsea, was only rented, not bought; nor were any of their other London residences bought. I think she got help to buy and enlarge Sarsen Land in the same way in which she got money in Cambridge to enable her to add a room to the old Mill House and to live in style without skimping on anything for Alfred or the children. There, Bertrand Russell was the donor, without Alfred's knowledge.[29]

Even before that, the Whiteheads had begun to have a close relationship with the family of an immensely wealthy banker, Henry R. Beeton, who was one of the Governors of University College, London, and took an interest in what intellectuals were doing. His daughter, Mary, had studied mathematics at Girton with Whitehead, who told her she would do well in the Tripos of 1897 (she did), but that her score would make no difference to his opinion that she knew her work well and understood it most thoroughly. Mary Beeton was often a guest for lengthy periods at the Mill House, sometimes with her brother Alan. She was an interesting woman with a social conscience, and Whitehead's affectionate friend all his life. Alan Beeton had a nervous breakdown while an undergraduate at Cambridge. Whitehead got in touch with the father; the result was that Alan did what he really wanted to do; he went to Paris to study art, and subsequently became a painter. In the summer of 1908, when North Whitehead was stricken by scarlet fever in Switzerland, his parents wired Alan, who was then in England, asking him to join them and North there; he did, and was helpful, for three weeks. A diary kept by Mrs. H. R. Beeton[30] shows that during the Whiteheads' last two years in Cambridge, Evelyn on trips to London frequently went shopping and to the theater with her, was a guest at meals in the Beeton house, and often stayed overnight. In some academic vacations all the Whiteheads stayed for many days at the Beeton's country house in Berkshire. The two families were close friends until the Whiteheads left for America in 1924. I cannot believe that Evelyn never dropped a hint about her financial problems to Harry Beeton, who had much more money than he knew what to do with.

Another way that Evelyn used to make ends meet consisted in taking on as a paying guest someone who was studying or working in London and who was the child of a friend with means. Mrs. Norah Nicholls told me that when she was a young woman working at one of the London hospitals in the early 1920s she was a paying guest for fourteen

months, longer than anyone else. She was one of the daughters of Sir
Arthur Schuster.

Impulsive generosity was another part of Evelyn Whitehead's complex character. In 1914 she lent the Lockeridge house to Hugh Dalton
for his honeymoon. She did the same for Ralph Hawtrey in April 1915.

Evelyn could not rest content for long with any of the beautiful
homes she created. She sold this house in 1917. Having to move all his
books, papers, and work in progress was a perennial burden in Whitehead's life with her.

CHAPTER II

1914–1918

A t the age of fifty-three, Whitehead finally secured a professorship. It was in applied mathematics at the Imperial College of Science and Technology, in South Kensington, London. It paid £800.

His old friend Andrew Forsyth traveled for quite a while after leaving Cambridge in 1910. Early in 1913 he gained a chair that was newly created at the Imperial College—Chief Professor of Mathematics.[1] The Imperial College had come into existence in 1907 as an amalgam of three quite different colleges: the Royal College of Science, the City and Guilds Engineering College, and the Royal School of Mines. There were departments of mathematics at the first two, but it was not a principal subject in either one. Forsyth's appointment was a step in the gradual change of the amalgam of the three colleges, each jealous of the others, into a union; he was placed in charge of mathematics for the Imperial College as a whole. Although his creative work was over, he was the first eminent mathematician to be appointed there, and he had had much administrative experience; his job was to modernize the teaching, and expand the program, in mathematics. Among the recommendations that he submitted to the Governors in February 1914 was the request that a second mathematical professor be appointed; this had been considered when Forsyth was appointed, but held in abeyance pending his recommendations. He now asked for a man of recognized scientific eminence who, under him, would take applied mathematics as his domain. (Forsyth was primarily a pure mathematician.)

Forsyth is likely to have had Whitehead in mind for this post. But the special committee that the Governors of Imperial College set up to choose the incumbent did not proceed in the quick, improper way of the Board of Advisors at University College in 1912, by which Whitehead lost his chance of a professorship there.[2]

The Imperial College committee advertised the post in the *Times,* in *Nature,* and in the *Cambridge University Reporter.* Whitehead read the advertisement in *Nature,* asked for particulars of the post, and applied for it in a letter dated June 16, 1914. In the letter he mentioned his "practical experience in lecturing, chiefly in Applied Mathematics and Geometry," and his "theoretical researches into the ultimate nature of Mathematical and Physical ideas." In listing his books, Whitehead called attention to the wide sale of his *Introduction to Mathematics;* he avowed that he could "interest a body of students, diverse both in their ability and in the courses of Physical Science which are occupying their attention." (London was not like Cambridge!) To the recital of his administrative positions Whitehead could now add that of being a member of the Council of the Royal Society.

There were eleven candidates for this professorship; Whitehead and four others were seriously considered. He was interviewed on July 1. The diverging interests of the three colleges gave the special committee much trouble on all the candidates. It was pointed out that Whitehead had never taught engineering mathematics. Nevertheless, on July 10 the committee recommended to the Governing Body that he be appointed Professor of Applied Mathematics under the direction of the Chief Professor of Mathematics as of September 1, 1914. This was immediately approved, and on July 15 University College, London, allowed Whitehead to resign his position as Reader in Geometry.

ii

Whitehead's pleasure in his election to a professorship at the Imperial College was followed, in the second half of July, by worry about what the nations of the Continent were doing. He had no idea that when he was to assume his duties, England would be four weeks into a war against Germany, and his son North would be in Flanders with the British Expeditionary Force.

Whitehead eventually came round to the view that the Great Powers blundered into the First World War. But at the time, he believed that England, at least, had no choice but to take part. Bertrand Russell, still his closest friend, emphatically disagreed. On August 28 Whitehead wrote from Lockeridge:

Dear Bertie,

. . . I am miserable at differing from you on so great a question. I cannot see what other course was open to us than the one which we actually took. I have read the White Paper carefully and have formed the conclusions (1) that Grey and our Government did everything in their power to preserve the peace of Europe, (2) that, if the German Government meant to

make an unprovoked attack on France and Russia at a favourable moment, they could not have acted in any other way than
that in which they actually did act.

Also, granting such an unprovoked attack, it seems to me
that it would have been national suicide for us to stand out.

You must remember that the Germany which would emerge
victorious is not the Germany of Goethe and Helmholtz, but
the Germany of the Kaiser, Bernhardi, and Treitschke. . . .

Our immediate task is to save Western Freedom, as exemplified in England and France. . . .

Of course we were not legally bound to Belgium. If you
like, it was a "pretext". I should prefer to say "a test case".
Germany showed thereby that, given the occasion and the
power, she would not consider herself bound to respect either
treaties or weaker nations. This governed the whole situation.

It appears that Whitehead took the Government's White Paper at face
value.

I do not know whether Evelyn read the White Paper. She did not
need to do so in order to declare to Bertie, "the bully must be stopped,"
for she had been anti-German since childhood. Many liberals, Russell
among them, were distressed that England was on Russia's side; Whitehead was not happy about it. On August 4, before England's midnight
declaration of war, Evelyn wrote to Bertie, "Germany is a greater
menace to Europe, and we cannot sit still and see France smashed."

North Whitehead was spending the summer working at the large
British Thomson Houston Electrical Works in Rugby. On the day after
England's declaration he went to the recruiting sergeant there and tried
to enlist. He was told that if he wanted to be a soldier, he should have
thought of that before: "There is a war on now; we haven't time for raw
recruits like you." North went to London, then to the War Office in
Whitehall, accompanied by his father and mother and by his Uncle
Henry, who, as a Bishop in the Established Church, introduced them to
War Office officials. A commission as second lieutenant was secured.
North was assigned to mechanical transport in the Second Division of
the B.E.F. On August 21 his parents saw him off.

None of the Whiteheads felt the exultation which masses of unthink-
ing Britons displayed as they sent their sons away to fight. Years later
Evelyn expressed contempt for a Belgian scholar who boasted of having kept his son out of the war by hiding him under the hay in a cart
going across the border. To her, there was glory in being a soldier in a
righteous war. But she felt no happiness in the necessary participation

of North and a host of other young men. To Alfred, there was no glory, only necessity. He began the letter to Russell, from which I quoted, with the exclamation, "What a nightmare!" His feeling was the exact opposite of that expressed by Rupert Brooke in the lines,

Now God be thanked Who has matched us with His hour
And caught our youth, and wakened us from sleeping.

North once told me that his father "hated war so." Whitehead knew from his wide reading in the history of Europe that the progress of civilization is punctuated with sharp setbacks, but he had not anticipated a ghastly setback in his lifetime. The guns of August shattered his world.

                    iii

When the Whiteheads left Cambridge in 1910, they sold the lease on their house at 11 Cranmer Road to William Julius Mirrlees. He was a Scot with an inventive turn of mind, interested in almost everything. He had done well in South Africa, and wanted to live in Cambridge because his daughter Hope (later a distinguished scholar) was at Newnham. His wife was one of the women Whitehead had in mind when he wrote, "uneducated clever women, who have seen much of the world, are in middle life so much the most cultured part of the community."[3] She and her husband soon became, and remained, devoted friends of the Whiteheads.

The Mirrleeses frequently entertained the intellectual aristocracy of Cambridge. In July 1914 they were hosts for a few days to two interesting Americans that Hope knew: Gertrude Stein and Alice Toklas. (Gertrude Stein had come to London to see her publisher, John Lane.) At dinner they met the Whiteheads.

Whitehead and Gertrude Stein, both great readers of history, talked easily. Evelyn at first looked down her nose at Gertrude and her companion. Then she discovered that Gertrude personally knew various painters in Paris. Thereafter the four were on excellent terms with each other.[4] Soon the Whiteheads had Stein and Toklas to dinner in Carlyle Square. From there, on July 29, Whitehead wrote, "Dear Miss Stein, We are immensely looking forward to seeing you and Miss Toklas on Friday afternoon [July 31] at our Wiltshire Cottage." He told her what train to take, then said, "Please excuse my wife for not herself writing; we are in the agony of changing our London houses."

In *The Autobiography of Alice B. Toklas* Stein wrote that when they arrived they found several other houseguests, and that there was not much concern about imminent war. On the next day, Germany was at war with Russia and France was mobilizing. It was impossible for Stein and Toklas to return to Paris. Evelyn urged them, and they agreed, to stay in the Lockeridge house instead of a London hotel. Thus what was meant to be a weekend visit lasted six weeks.

Whitehead and Gertrude Stein took many country walks together; they talked about the meaning of the war, and philosophically about the course of Western civilization. From their first meeting, she thought he was a genius. She has Alice Toklas say that although Toklas at one time or another met several great people, she knew only "three first-class geniuses"; she saw their quality at once, before it was generally recognized.[5] The other two, naturally, were Picasso and Gertrude Stein. Whitehead thought that Stein was a lively woman with new ideas about literary expression. On the question of how well he understood her writing, I have no evidence, and shall make no conjecture.

Soon after England became fully involved in the war, Stein and Toklas made a trip to London to get money and their trunks. Evelyn went with them, to find out what she could do to help Belgian refugees. In mid-October, when the visitors went back to Paris, Evelyn again went with them, this time because North had left his overcoat at home. She was determined that he should have it, and got papers from the War Office that enabled her to deliver it to British authorities in Paris. In an undated letter to Whitehead from 27 Rue de Fleurus, Gertrude Stein told him that Evelyn was staying with them and was very well.

After the war was over Jessie Whitehead, working in Paris, used to lunch with Gertrude Stein almost weekly. When Stein, become quite famous, made a lecture tour of the United States in 1934, she did not visit the Whiteheads, then in Cambridge, Massachusetts. Alfred was ill much of that year. There may have been another reason for the non-visit. *The Autobiography of Alice B. Toklas* had been published the year before. It contained a false statement that made Evelyn indignant: "Mrs. Whitehead was terribly worried lest he [North] should rashly enlist."[6] Of course Evelyn was proud of North for trying to enlist at Rugby on August 5, 1914; and, unlike her husband, she did not readily forgive.

Gertrude Stein was enthusiastic about the work of an unappreciated Irish painter who had come to Paris, Harry Phelan Gibb. He gave a fairly successful show in Dublin in 1913, when he was forty; he was not doing well in Paris. Shortly after the war began he came to London, where he entered into the Whiteheads' lives as Gertrude Stein's legacy to them. At Christmastide he was in their Lockeridge house.

Gibb had run through a fortune and taken to drinking heavily. Evelyn had a habit of helping people who were down and out. She let him live in the Whiteheads' Chelsea house. He was never sober, but he did not make passes at the maids or otherwise cause trouble. Although Whitehead abhorred drunkenness, he accepted Gibb's presence; the man was in trouble, art was art, and Whitehead, always in his study or at the Imperial College, would tolerate anything if Evelyn wanted it. After three years of this, Gibb married a woman who straightened him out. He and his paintings became less interesting. His letters to Gertrude Stein from 1917 to 1925 lament the continued failure of the art critics to recognize him. He was still unrecognized when he died in 1946. In the early 1920s Evelyn acquired a Gibb painting that I have seen; it reminds one of Augustus John.

iv

In 1914 more than a hundred thousand Belgians, fleeing from the German troops, came to Britain. The generosity with which they were received is one of the bright spots in British history. The Whiteheads' Wiltshire house in Lockeridge was made available for a time.

Although the number of students enrolled at the Imperial College was much reduced after the war started, the courses required for a diploma had still to be taught; as some of Whitehead's colleagues were in military service, he had a somewhat heavier teaching load than was normal. Nevertheless, he undertook to write the important book he called *An Enquiry Concerning the Principles of Natural Knowledge,* which I shall discuss in Chapter VI.

Letters from North made Whitehead aware that calculating the path of a shell fired at a high angle took too much time. On November 20, 1917, the Royal Society received his paper, "Graphical Solution for High-Angle Fire."[7] Except for two papers in 1889 on the motion of viscous fluids, this was the only paper in applied mathematics that he ever published.[8] In it he worked out the equations of motion from which, he thought, a skilled draftsman, using the Army's gunnery tables and a few well-known empirical formulas, could construct graphs that would be applicable to all projectiles and all paths. I do not know whether Whitehead's idea was practicable enough to be used by the British Army.

As the war went on, more and more young men from Cambridge University and University College, London, went into the trenches.

The casualty list tore Whitehead's heart, for he had taken a personal interest in all his pupils.

Whitehead was very much a family man. To know what his experience of the 1914–18 war was like, we must know what his children and his wife did and underwent in those years.

North was more fortunate than most Cambridge men. In the summer of 1915 he was invalided back to England, suffering from shell shock at the very least. In the autumn he was judged fit for "light home duties," and sent to a large camp in Salisbury Plain. The chief duties were participation in frequent parades. He begged to be put on the active list, and volunteered for anything that turned up. This turned out to be combat in East Africa, where the contiguous British and German colonies would be bargaining pawns if the war ended in a stalemate. Before the war, the idea of life in a colony like British East Africa had fascinated North. Like many Cantabrigians, he thought of the colonies as the places where things happened. On graduating from Cambridge in 1913 he obtained an appointment as Assistant Commissioner in British East Africa. It was because he was a year younger than a man was required to be to assume this position that, on his father's advice, he spent the academic year 1913–14 at University College, London, where he studied mechanical engineering.

The unpredictability of crucial events is a frequent theme in Whitehead's philosophy of life. I may illustrate it by the fact that his soldier son, before reaching East Africa, had as close a brush with death as any he experienced in the field. The troop ship, a captured German liner, ran into a storm in the Bay of Biscay. In his unpublished autobiography North wrote that the ship

> had some sort of stabilizing water tanks to damp down rolling. Either there was something wrong, or our people did not understand them. . . . The Captain afterwards told me that the inclinometer on the bridge had once registered a forty-five degree roll. He thought the ship had gone.[9]

But she took the troops around the Cape to Mombasa, the chief port of what is now Kenya.

In East Africa the fighting was very different from what it had been in Belgium and France. The war here was a war of movement, with no set front. It was a clean war, with good feeling between the British and German commanders (General Smuts and General von Letow-Vorbeck), and between their men. The British force was a mixed lot. Besides the English (many of them, like North, invalided from Flanders), there were Indians, Canadians, South Africans, and black Africans. North was a good officer. He never lost a man to an ambush. The chief cause of casualties was tropical disease. North suffered three attacks of malaria and more than one of dysentery. He spent much of 1917 in hospitals.

I believe that only two of the many wartime letters between North and his parents are extant. The one he wrote to his father on October 23, 1916, begins with a unique sidelight on the war in East Africa:

My darling Daddy

I was stopped in the open velde yesterday by a S. African trooper who asked me whether I was Lt Whitehead, I told him that I was & he handed me a packet of about 30 letters from you all! . . . My C. O. happened to see this trooper & finding that he was travelling in my direction gave him my mail. We were over 100 miles apart & the trooper had travelled for 6 days.

After a final hospital stay in Capetown, North was sent home in the spring of 1918. He was pronounced unfit for further service overseas, and given the duty of inspecting electrical and mechanical machinery, first in Birmingham and then in London, where he lived with his parents.

Jessie Whitehead had entered Newnham College, Cambridge, in the autumn of 1913. When the war broke out she joined her mother in doing various things to help Belgian refugees. In the autumn she did not go back to Newnham, but got a job as a clerk in the Secretariat of the Foreign Office, where she worked on matters concerned with England's blockade of Germany. Her feeling about the war was the same as her mother's.

Evelyn, like other ladies of her class, took some part, though not as much as ladies of "society," in arranging benefit performances for war victims. When North was on active service, she frequently sent him packages of the very best non-perishable foods. Evelyn's social life was only a little curtailed; Mrs. Beeton's diary continued to record trips to the theater with her. From North I learned that at one time, when there was a shortage of shells, his mother made the heroic gesture of going to work in a munitions factory. She was so ill fitted for steady work of this kind that it lasted only a few weeks.

V

The war's heaviest blow to the Whiteheads fell in March 1918. Here
is the dedication of the *Enquiry,* which Cambridge published in 1919:

> To Eric Alfred Whitehead / Royal Flying Corps / November 27,
> 1898 to March 13, 1918 / Killed in action over the Forêt de Go-
> bain / giving himself that the city of his vision may not perish / The
> music of his life was without discord, / perfect in its beauty.

Eric had been admitted to Westminster School in the spring of 1914;
he left it three years later, and was admitted to Balliol College, Oxford,
for 1917. Instead of planning to go there, in May he took a commission
in the Royal Flying Corps. After he gained his pilot's wings, he was
employed as an instructor in England. In February 1918 he was sent to
France at his own request. On March 13 he was flying on patrol in a
single-seater, and was last seen diving at a German two-seater; then his
wings were seen to break.[10] North told me that his father's response on
receiving the news that Eric had been shot down was "a sickly smile."
Writing to Bertrand Russell on April 1, Evelyn said, "I cannot tell you
about Alfred, he looks much older."

Eric was quite unlike North and Jessie in character. They were both
strong individuals; he was not one. They had good Whitehead brains,
though Jessie often refused to use hers in the ways that other people
wanted her to use them; Eric was not brainy. Nor a particularly good
student; his record at Westminster School was mediocre. But he was a
dear and lovely person. North told me that he himself would sometimes "go off the rails." Jessie early fell into the habit of going off the
rails. Eric, by contrast, was almost always on them. His behavior was
impeccable; he did what, and only what, was expected of a young
gentleman. A brother officer wrote to his father of Eric's "cheerfulness,
devotion to duty, and the unusual cleanliness of his thoughts and
ways."[11]

Eric was his mother's favorite. North sometimes, and Jessie often,
ignored her wishes or tried to thwart them; he never did. Whitehead's
grief over his son's death was more than doubled by his empathy with
Evelyn's sorrow.

vi

For almost fifteen years before the war, Bertrand Russell had been
like one of the family. He was Whitehead's most brilliant pupil, then his
collaborator for more than ten years. He was very fond of Evelyn, and

she of him. And he was fond of all three Whitehead children. He had been especially close to the oldest, North. For example, early in 1907 he had taken North on a walking tour in the Lake Country. Early in the summer vacation of 1911 North was Russell's companion on a walking tour of the Malvern hills; in the evenings Bertie read him some chapters from the manuscript of *The Problems of Philosophy,* which he had begun to write.* In July 1913 Russell took North and Eric around Cornwall.

Russell's passionate denunciation of the war cooled his friendship with the Whiteheads, but did not break it. On January 30, 1915, North wrote to him, "I am begging for a letter from you." On February 15 North thanked Bertie for his letter, and sent him a cheery one in return. Writing to him on March 17, North described life at the front; he had just taken off his boots for the first time in a week.

In 1915 Russell began to work with the most active of the anti-war organizations, the No-Conscription Fellowship. Conscription was new to Britain, the freest of the civilized nations. Northcliffe had plumped for it from the start of this war; on December 28, 1915, the cabinet agreed to it in principle; on February 9 it became law. When Russell asserted his opposition to it in a letter to Whitehead,† Whitehead replied on April 16:

> Dear Bertie, I had meant to avoid discussion with you—where feeling is acute, and divergence deep, discussion among intimates is often a mistake. Your letter necessitates an explanation. . . .
>
> I hold that the State has the right to compulsion both in taxes and in personal service. Here I agree with all the great liberal statesmen, e. g., Cromwell, the French Revolutionary Statesmen, Lincoln, J. S. Mill, etc. You used to admire these men; I never suspected your fundamental divergence.
>
> Similarly as to the use of force by the State against enemies, external and internal. Compulsion involves punishment for non-compliance. The forcing of conscience is always an evil. I would therefore exempt men who by a previous course of conduct had made evident their adherence to some code of thought which involves burdens as well as exemptions. For this reason Quakers can be exempted. I would not exempt men who produce their conscientious objections ad hoc. It is a grave evil, but it is impossible to discriminate.

---

*In August Russell sent North's father the typescript of this book. See Chapter I, Section v, for Whitehead's critical comments on it.

†Not extant. Whitehead did not keep letters.

This evil, though grave, is not comparable to the awful evil involved in the breakup of a state—in particular, not comparable to the
horrors through which the world is now passing. . . .

I am not greatly impressed by men who ask me to be shocked that
they are going to prison, while ten thousand men are daily being
carried to field hospitals, . . . Frankly, the outcry is contemptible.
Of course where I can testify to good cause for exemption, on first
hand knowledge, I am glad to do so. It mitigates the necessary evil of
the times. I have already done so for Norton.* But on the whole,
men who refuse military service are avoiding a plain, though painful
moral duty.

Russell's attacks on the Government were unremitting—in countless speeches, pamphlets, and articles.† His sharp, cool analyses of
its actions, his passionate opposition to warfare, and his growing reputation as a philosopher combined to make him a formidable opponent.
In May 1916 the Government reluctantly decided to prosecute him
under the Defence of the Realm Act, in connection with the Everett
case.

One Edward Everett was exempted from combat service as a conscientious objector, but refused to report for non-combat service, and
was sentenced to two years at hard labor. Russell wrote a leaflet that
called for vigorous defense of those who were fighting for liberty of
conscience. Six members of the No-Conscription Fellowship who had
distributed the leaflet were sentenced to a month in jail. Russell thereupon wrote a letter to the *Times* (printed May 17) to say that he was its
author and that if anyone were prosecuted, he should be.

Russell did not want to be acquitted. He was enjoying his campaign
against the war-waging Government enormously, and only lacked the
glory of martyrdom. Pleading his own case in the Court of the Lord
Mayor of London, he made a superb speech, cutting and passionate in
defense of freedom from governmental coercion. Evelyn, who was
present, admired it. But the Mayor found him guilty, and fined him
£100 *or* 61 days imprisonment. His friends, by buying his library and
some other possessions, met the fine.

I sympathize with both Russell and Whitehead. Russell had been
right in opposing Britain's entry into the war and the Government's

---

*H. T. J. Norton, a Fellow of Trinity College and one of Russell's Cambridge pupils.

†Early in 1916 he gave voice to both his repugnance and his idealism in a series of
lectures, "Principles of Social Reconstruction," which were considered mischievous.
(They were published with that title in England, but in America as *Why Men Fight*.).

persistent refusal to seek an end to the carnage except by outright victory; Whitehead was wrong on both counts, though it is much easier for us to see this than it was in 1914–16. Russell was wrong about the adoption of conscription, because there was plainly no way to keep on fighting the war without it. And he was wrong about a state's right to draft men who were not genuine conscientious objectors, for the reason Whitehead gave in his letter of April 16.

When Whitehead was seventy he recalled that, although he had generally voted in the reforming minority of Englishmen, the causes he supported were sooner or later adopted. "I have never, never been at final variance with the bulk of my countrymen."[12] At public school he had acted with his fellow students, and for them as Head Boy. He was within the English socio-political world. Russell was outside it, always passionately condemning the beliefs and actions of his countrymen with the fervor of a modern-day Hebrew prophet; he was the philosopher who possessed a higher standard of morality than theirs and a rationality they could not begin to emulate. Compromise, a virtue to Whitehead, was almost always a sin to him. How impossible, in retrospect, was his grandmother Russell's vision of him as a future prime minister! What was he, then? Simply Bertrand Russell—intellectual, writer, and adored or hated public storm center. Because Russell was so fanatically devoted to his pacifist cause, he could only condemn the Whiteheads' attitude toward the war as savage.[13] He was not easily tolerant of people whose convictions opposed his. When he wanted to be indignant, he put away his sense of objectivity into some other compartment of his mind. Whitehead seldom did that.

Russell appealed his conviction, but lost. Thereupon the Council of Trinity College, which had the power to dismiss from the College anyone convicted of any crime, dismissed Russell from his lectureship there.* The vote, on July 11, 1916, was unanimous, but did not truly reflect the opinion of the Fellows of Trinity. The younger Fellows, some of whom had been in the war, were less pro-war than the older ones who made up the Council. F. M. Cornford, with help from James Ward, collected twenty-two signatures to an unemphatic protest that was sent to the Council in January:

> The undersigned, Fellows of the College, while not proposing to take any action in the matter during the war, desire to place it on

---

*This was a five-year renewal of the five-year lectureship to which he had been elected on Whitehead's urging in 1910.

record that they are not satisfied with the action of the College in depriving Mr Russell of his Lectureship.

The signatories included two members of the Council who had not been in Cambridge on July 11, many young Fellows who later achieved high reputation (e.g., G. H. Hardy, J. E. Littlewood, A. S. Eddington, C. D. Broad, and a future Master of Trinity, E. D. Adrian)—and Whitehead. In a friendly letter to Russell on September 14, Whitehead mentioned a pamphlet on him which he wrote to the Fellows of Trinity in July.[14]

Everyone knew that Russell had set aside his philosophical research to devote himself to his pacifist cause; but he had been giving his scheduled lectures at Trinity. Council's action against an eminent philosopher was deplored by quite a few scholars elsewhere. Gilbert Murray, the philosopher Samuel Alexander, and many professors in America as well as in Britain, felt that Russell's ouster, however legal, was contrary not only to the best interests of Trinity College but to the ideal of completely free criticism of anything and everything, which ought to be maintained in the British academic world. (The German government had tried to get a pacifist critic removed from the faculty at the University of Munich, but Munich stood its ground.)

Late in 1917 Russell began to think his pacifist propaganda ineffective, and wanted to take up philosophy again. Among the pupils who studied logic with him at Cambridge before the war, one, Ludwig Wittgenstein, had become intellectually more intimate with him than Whitehead or anyone else. Russell, wanting to revise his philosophy of logic in the light of Wittgenstein's ideas, announced a series of eight lectures with the title, "The Philosophy of Logical Atomism." He gave them in London, early in 1918.

Before Russell finished these lectures, Lloyd George's government began action against him. All through 1917 he had been editing, and every week writing an article for, the weekly newspaper, the *Tribunal,* put out by the No-Conscription Fellowship. His successor being ill, Russell hastily wrote an article for the issue of January 3, 1918. Because one sentence cast an aspersion on the American Army ("capable of intimidating strikers"), Russell was charged with having made in print statements "likely to prejudice His Majesty's relations with the United States of America." He was found guilty and sentenced to six months' imprisonment in the Second Division, that is, with ordinary convicts. Thanks to the intervention of Gilbert Murray and other friends, along with Arthur Balfour, the Home Office changed his sentence to the First Division.[15] This meant special privileges, such as receiving more visitors and—most important to Russell—being allowed to read and write as much as he liked, provided he did no pacifist propaganda. The writing of his *Introduction to Mathematical Philosophy* was only the first item in the quantity of philosophical work Russell did under these circumstances.

He was in Brixton Prison by May 6, 1918, and, being given credit for good conduct, was freed on September 11. In this period his brother Frank (second Earl Russell) arranged for his visitors, conveyed messages to friends, and in many ways made his life easy. Evelyn Whitehead drew up a list of French Revolutionary memoirs; they were got from the London Library for Bertie's reading. Whitehead was among his early visitors; writing to Frank on May 16, Russell said, "It was maddening having so little time to talk shop with Whitehead." I suppose that this shoptalk was about points in the *Introduction to Mathematical Philosophy*. To Frank on July 1 Russell wrote:

> I find seeing Whitehead an immense stimulus, please tell him. I have been thinking a great deal about matters he and I discussed, and there seems to me a lot of interesting work to be done on Facts, Judgment, and propositions.

I doubt that Whitehead got much stimulus for his own thinking from these brief discussions in Brixton. He was writing his *Enquiry*, containing his philosophy of physics; in later writings and in his lectures at Harvard (begun in 1924) he never praised either the philosophy of logical atomism or *The Analysis of Mind* (which Russell was sketching at this time).

Russell's opposition to the war did not affect the Whiteheads' convictions about it in the least. On January 8, 1917, Whitehead sent Russell a clipping from the *Times* of January 7 which reported a protest in Paris against the deportation of Belgians and French to Germany, and asked, "What are *you* going to do to help these people?"

But the Whiteheads felt that Bertie had a right to express his honest convictions, and were grieved by the Government's prosecutions of their old friend. On May 17, 1916, Evelyn wrote him:

> We have just seen your letter in the Times, do write or come if you do not feel it too painful, we are thinking of you a great deal and missing you.
>
> I cannot see why a difference of point of view must create a

breach, friends even intimate ones cannot agree on all essentials.
Surely the test of friendship comes in one's capacity for leaving
contentious points out, if we cannot bear to mention them.

On June 4 Whitehead wrote,

Let me know if and how I can help or show any office of friendship—
you know well enough that the mere fact that I think your views of
state policy and of private duty in relation to it are mistaken, does not
diminish affection.

Three months later, when the Government excluded Russell from certain parts of the country, Whitehead wrote him, "what asses the authorities are making of themselves in worrying you in the way they
are. . . . I am awfully sick at their action."

On April 2, 1918, North sent Russell a letter: "I am writing to tell
you how sorry I am that you are in trouble, and to tell you what a warm
feeling of friendship I feel for you."

Evelyn wrote many affectionate letters to Russell in 1916 to 1918.
She often urged him to visit them, but he seldom did so. He preferred to
work at the office of the No-Conscription Fellowship; and to relax at
Garsington Manor, where his former mistress, the brilliant Lady Ottoline Morrell, made people with pacifist sympathies feel at home. On
January 10, 1917, Evelyn sent Russell a letter complaining of his neglect
of her, even when she was ill; the letter is full of self-pity, which is not
obscured by her saying that her husband resented this neglect (which he
probably did).

On February 9, 1918, Evelyn wrote a good letter to Russell. He was
lecturing on the philosophy of logical atomism, and had been sentenced
to prison. After urging him to devote himself to philosophy, she said:

If at any time we can do anything to mitigate, or to make the present
more endurable, let us know it at once. However passionately we
may disagree with your present views to us, you are you, the friend
we value, whose affection we count on, the friend whom our boys
love, & in many ways still our Infant Prodigy.

The fact that Russell's friendship with the Whiteheads was not
broken should be credited primarily to them.

CHAPTER III

Whitehead on Education

i/First address on education, 1911. Whitehead's
experience as educator. Style of his educational
writings. His denunciation of uniform external
examinations.

ii/Purpose of education, to stimulate and guide pupil's
self-development. Protest against inert ideas.

iii/Main themes in "The Aims of Education": Need for
both culture and expert knowledge. Discovering the
power of general ideas. The child's mind not a
passive instrument. Reason for teaching quadratic
equations. Need for a connected curriculum.
Supreme importance of the present.

iv/"The Place of Mathematics in a Liberal Education."
Training in logical reasoning. "The Principles of
Mathematics in Relation to Elementary Teaching."
Need to avoid reconditeness. Whitehead on the
value for philosophical thought of the ideal
mathematical training. Author's interpretation.

v/Desirability of technical education being organically
related to science and literature. Whitehead's view of
the pursuit of science. Enjoyment, not knowledge,
essential in the study of literature. The Benedictine
ideal of work. Summary of Whitehead's philosophy
of mathematics and mathematical education.

vi/Need for ideals that are definite. Whitehead's
patriotism. Happiness in helping others. The
teaching of science in a general education.

I n the course of Whitehead's years in London, 1910–24, he published ten addresses and two essays on education. His first publication on this subject appeared in the opening number, November 1911, of the short-lived *Journal of the Association of Teachers of
Mathematics for the Southeastern Part of England*. This journal was
devoted to the teaching of elementary mathematics in schools of every
type. The chairman of the association was a Cambridge-trained mathematician who was teaching at the public school in Tonbridge, Kent. His
editorial in the first issue expressed the hope that by bringing together
people with good teaching experience and people with some knowledge of modern views of what mathematics is, something might be
done to narrow the chasm between professional mathematicians and
teachers of elementary mathematics. It was natural to choose as the first
president of the association the man of Kent who wrote *Universal Algebra* and co-authored *Principia Mathematica*. Whitehead entitled his inaugural address (given at Tonbridge), "The Place of Mathematics in a
Liberal Education."

Whitehead's interest in schools began before he became a school
pupil; he was taught at home by his father, Alfred Whitehead, until he
was fourteen. As a small boy he often accompanied his father on daily
visits to his three parochial schools—for boys, for girls, and for small
children.[1] At his public school, Sherborne, he became Head Boy, responsible for all discipline outside the classroom. Thirty years at Cambridge University followed. When he lived in the nearby village of
Grantchester he was on the local School Committee.

In his years at London Whitehead was deeply involved in the problems of many educational institutions in the metropolitan area. It was of
this London period that he wrote, in a two-page preface to an unpublished collection of his essays on education:

> It has been my fortune to be concerned with almost every type of
> educational institution, either as a member of the staff, or as an active
> governor, or at least as an official inspector. I have been chairman of
> governing committees of a crèche, of a school of art, of technical and

secondary schools and of colleges and universities. Also I have inspected a nunnery applying for affiliation to a university.*

Whitehead also said in this preface, "I have never passed beyond my own personal observation." The preface does not mention any of the doctrines that have been maintained by writers on education. What is more, apart from some concern with Plato's teaching and a brief comment on the Montessori system, nowhere in his many essays does Whitehead take up any familiar doctrine about education. Nor does he deal with the isms under which theories about education are habitually classified. It is wholly unnecessary to prepare to read Whitehead on education by brushing up on these isms. That would only distract attention from what Whitehead has to say. He did not care about the isms. Nor did he care how his own views on education might be classified, so long as they were carried out in practice.

Another paragraph of the preface to the projected collection reads:

> Though the occasions of some of the addresses are casual, the substance embodied involves some intimate experience or recollection on which I have been brooding at the time of composition. They illustrate various phases of a life activity engaged in education.

It is with this in mind that one should read Whitehead's essays on education.

His positive views are relevant to every place and time in any civilized country, and his criticisms are all too relevant to Britain and America in the twentieth century.

Whitehead's English writings on education are easier to read than any of his writings on philosophy or mathematics. Their style is quite different from that of his scientific writings. He is not making investigations, he is expressing his strong convictions about education as he found it in English schools, and as it should be. He tries to be realistic, and he takes care to give credit where credit is due, but he does not rein in his feelings.

Whitehead was a good denouncer, but he was wholly unsuccessful in his repeated all-out attacks on the custom of imposing uniform external examinations on students in different schools. In his very first educa-

---

*Whitehead gave me a copy of this unused preface in March 1941. It may be assumed that almost all the essays he meant to include in the projected volume were reprints of those in *The Organisation of Thought* (1917) or *The Aims of Education* (1929), or were subsequently reprinted in Part III, "Education," of *Essays in Science and Philosophy* (1947).

tional address he told the teachers of mathematics in southeastern England that the association they had formed

> enables the results of first-hand experience to acquire the authority of a collective demand capable of constraining the nameless Furies who draw up our schedules of examinations.[2]

In the original form of his best-known address, "The Aims of Education," he said,[3]

> The devil in the scholastic world has assumed the form of a general education consisting of scraps of a large number of disconnected subjects; and, with the artfulness of the serpent, he has entrenched himself behind the matriculation examination of the University of London, with a wire entanglement formed by the Oxford and Cambridge schools' examination.

Instead,

> Every school should grant its own leaving certificates based on its own curriculum. The standards of these schools should be sampled and corrected. But the first requisite for educational reform is the school as a unit with its approved curriculum based on its own needs, and evolved by its own staff.

A. D. Lindsay praised this recommendation in a two-page Foreword to the 1950 English reprint of *The Aims of Education*. He lamented, "I have never heard it discussed seriously as a practicable reform in educational administration." He thought it was time to do so. (Lindsay aptly called Whitehead "an educational Congregationalist.")

On the other hand, the historian H. A. L. Fisher* observed that Whitehead had not sufficiently appreciated "the difficulty of carrying on the work of a modern democratic State without external examinations."[4]

British educational reformers had protested against the examination system since the 1880s. Whitehead was unique among them. A mathematical scientist of some distinction, he was not concerned to take a stand for character building against book learning; he dealt only with education on its intellectual side, and first of all with the teaching of mathematics.

Whitehead cannot have been happy about the American reliance on

---

*Fisher was in the Cabinet as President of the Board of Education from 1916 to 1922. He broadened and liberalized free public education.

the Educational Testing Service. Probably because he was conscious of being a visitor, he made no comment on this in the four educational essays he wrote in America.

ii

Whitehead's positive doctrines about education rest on this "main idea," which he calls a "premiss": "The students are alive, and the purpose of education is to stimulate and guide their self-development."[5] This, he told the British Association for the Advancement of Science in 1919, was "the one fundamental principle of education."[6] Transmission of the most valuable achievements of a culture to the next generation is a worthy purpose, but unless the pupil makes them his own the result is hollow. The same must be said of something Whitehead much desired—turning out young people whose trained intelligence would serve England well.

The students being alive,

> It must never be forgotten that education is not a process of packing articles into a trunk. Such a simile is entirely inapplicable. It is, of course, a process completely of its own peculiar genus. Its nearest analogue is the assimilation of food by a living organism.[7]

All historians of education are aware of other advocates of the principle of self-development. One thinks of John Dewey, Froebel, Herbart, Pestalozzi, and Rousseau. Whitehead says nothing about any of them. Nor does he refer to what John Adams (later Sir John Adams) was calling "the new teaching," which focused on the pupil's interests more than on the subject taught.[8] Whitehead must have heard about this as Adams was Professor of Education in the University of London. The only addition I would make to Whitehead's statement that he was writing solely from his own experience concerns his wife. Evelyn seemed to believe ardently in the principle of self-development, and to believe that every individual is different from every other individual. Her possessiveness sometimes got in the way of action on these beliefs, but Whitehead was not possessive. He could assert them from his heart, and enjoy her fervent agreement and her praise of his punch-lines.

Whitehead made many statements about what education is, but did not offer a formal definition of the word. Closest perhaps is "Education is the acquisition of the art of the utilization of knowledge."[9] He commented, "This is an art very difficult to impart." Bits of knowledge can easily be learned; what matters is their *use*. Whitehead disclaimed reverence for knowledge as such. In his philosophical writings there are many disparaging remarks about the learned world.

An appropriate title for his unpublished collection of educational writings would have been, "Protest against Inert Ideas." By "inert ideas" he meant "ideas that are merely received into the mind without being utilised, or tested, or thrown into fresh combinations."[10] It is only in these activities that ideas can make lasting contributions to the self-development of the student's mind. In Whitehead's English essays on education, protest against inert ideas is a recurrent theme.

iii

Among all his educational essays, the one we ought to read if we were compelled to choose is "The Aims of Education"; it is also far and away the best-known one. I shall devote this section to it, then return to the shorter ones, on the teaching of mathematics, which preceded it.

"The Aims of Education," too, is about the teaching of mathematics: in fact, it was Whitehead's presidential address, given in January 1916, to the Mathematical Association.* Its subtitle was "A Plea for Reform."† Only a few of the many commentators on it take into account the fact that Whitehead was talking to mathematicians about reform in the teaching of their subject. Much of what he said in the address applies to education in general, but that does not excuse the critics who complain that it does not present a complete philosophy of education.‡

The 1929 text begins with the famous sentence, "Culture is activity of thought, and receptiveness to beauty and humane feeling."[11] This statement, which was not meant to be an inclusive definition, seems to me profoundly true. What Whitehead meant to exclude appears from his next sentence: "Scraps of information have nothing to do with it."

---

*The members of this association were teachers of mathematics, mainly in schools. It had developed out of the Association for the Improvement of Geometrical Teaching, founded back in 1871.

†Whitehead first published it in *The Organisation of Thought* (1917). The book in which my reader is most likely to find it is *The Aims of Education and Other Essays,* first published in 1929. There, the following are omitted: the subtitle, a page-long illustration that included formulae, the first two paragraphs (they were about England's situation in 1916), and the three paragraphs after them. There are no other alterations. The omissions reduce the essay to what was significant to English and American readers in 1929.

‡A classic example is the article by M. J. Langeveld, "On Whitehead's 'Aims of Education,'" in *Educational Forum* 31 (1966–67): 157–66. At that time Langeveld was Director of the Institute of Education at the University of Utrecht (Holland).

He goes on to say that the educator should aim at producing not merely well-informed persons but persons who have both what he called culture and expert knowledge in some special direction. "Their expert knowledge will give them the ground to start from, and their culture will lead them as deep as philosophy and as high as art." Whitehead was *not* thinking of philosophy as a body of expert knowledge, but as a mode of thought.

Whitehead explains that insistence on both culture and expert knowledge of a special subject does not require two separate courses of study, one general and one special. Good teachers are always bringing the two together. The pupils are interested in various special studies; their elimination would kill vitality. Also, the sense for style, by which one achieves his end most simply and without waste, can arise only in a specialist.[12]

Many of the recommendations in this essay can be thought of in terms of the contrast between understanding and information. We today do best to leave information to computers; they are designed to retrieve it. Understanding must be living. It is approached as the pupil relates one idea to another and to more general ideas, and explores an idea's applications. The applications are what make an intellectual education worth having.

> From the very beginning of his education, the child should experience the joy of discovery. The discovery which he has to make, is that general ideas give an understanding of that stream of events which pours through his life, which is his life.[13]

At this point an extended quotation will show, as nothing else could, what Whitehead was trying to do, and the spirit and manner in which he dealt with the aims of education.

> I appeal to you, as practical teachers. With good discipline, it is always possible to pump into the minds of a class a certain quantity of inert knowledge. You take a text-book and make them learn it. So far, so good. The child then knows how to solve a quadratic equation. But what is the good of teaching a child to solve a quadratic equation? There is a traditional answer to this question. It runs thus: The mind is an instrument, you first sharpen it, and then use it; the acquisition of the power of solving a quadratic equation is part of the process of sharpening the mind. Now there is just enough truth in this answer to have made it live through the ages. But for all its half-truth, it embodies a radical error which bids fair to stifle the genius of the modern world. I do not know who was first responsible for this analogy of the mind to a dead instrument. For aught I know, it may

have been one of the seven wise men of Greece, or a committee of the whole lot of them. Whoever was the originator, there can be no doubt of the authority which it has acquired by the continuous approval bestowed upon it by eminent persons. But whatever its weight of authority, whatever the high approval which it can quote, I have no hesitation in denouncing it as one of the most fatal, erroneous, and dangerous conceptions ever introduced into the theory of education. The mind is never passive; it is a perpetual activity, delicate, receptive, responsive to stimulus. You cannot postpone its life until you have sharpened it. Whatever interest attaches to your subject-matter must be evoked here and now; whatever powers you are strengthening in the pupil must be exercised here and now; whatever possibilities of mental life your teaching should impart, must be exhibited here and now. That is the golden rule of education.[14]

Whitehead goes on to give his answer to the question, why quadratic equations should be taught; because of their part in algebra, which is essential to understanding the quantitative aspects of the world. The teacher must first decide what quantitative aspects of the world are simple enough for his pupils to explore. He should then engage them *concurrently* in two kinds of study, not to be confused with each other. One is the theoretical study of such essential algebraic ideas as the variable, function, rate of change, equations and their solution; the exposition of these ideas should be short and simple, but strict and rigid as far as it goes. The other is the study of a few important applications. Throughout, all recondite detail should be omitted.

What the best procedure will be, cannot be prescribed; there are many different types of teenage students and many differences between their prospects in life; also, much depends on the peculiar ability of the teacher. It is because of these differences, Whitehead remarks, that the uniform external examination is so deadly. "We do not denounce it because we are cranks, and like denouncing established things."[15] He allows that such examinations "have their use in testing slackness." But he believes that successful accomplishment of the educational task "depends on a delicate adjustment of many variable factors."[16] Here, as so often, Whitehead's intuition was sound.

The discussion of algebra is followed by a discussion of geometry on similar principles. "Every proposition not absolutely necessary to exhibit the main connection of ideas should be cut out, but the great fundamental ideas should all be there."[17] Of course, for many secondary schools surveying and maps are the natural applications.

Whitehead, along with some other reformers, was concerned that the curriculum in every school should be a connected one in which algebra, geometry, history, geography, foreign languages, and English literature are related to each other. "The problem of education is to make the pupil see the wood by means of the trees."[18]

Another of his concerns was the educator's attitude toward the passage of time. "The only use of a knowledge of the past is to equip us for the present. No more deadly harm can be done to young minds than by depreciation of the present." Whitehead continues with two sentences that I regret—they have been so frequently misunderstood. "The present contains all that there is. It is holy ground; for it is the past, and it is the future."[19] Here Whitehead had added a moral injunction—to consider as supremely important the question of what one faces and does in the present moment—to a truism. No one doubts that it is merely truistic to say, as he does a few lines later, "The communion of saints is a great and inspiring assemblage, but it has only one possible hall of meeting, and that is, the present." But many critics wrongly thought that Whitehead was denigrating the study of the past. When H. L. Mencken reviewed *The Aims of Education* he called Whitehead's attitude toward the present "John Bullish."[20] Whitehead was clearer when, recurring to his point in the final paragraph of the essay, he said, not that the present "is" the past, but that it holds the past within itself. I read Whitehead's identification of the future with the present as hyperbole in reminding his audience that the future depends on what one does *now*.

One page from the end of the essay, Whitehead lets go:

> When one considers . . . the broken lives, the defeated hopes, the national failures, which result from the frivolous inertia with which [the education of a nation's young] is treated, it is difficult to restrain within oneself a savage rage.

A call to arms follows. "In the conditions of modern life the rule is absolute, the race which does not value trained intelligence is doomed."[21] Whitehead then embraces the old notion that education should be religious, that is, should inculcate duty and reverence. He explains that duty arises because ignorance "has the guilt of vice" whenever attainable knowledge could have changed the outcome, and that reverence rests on the perception that the present moment is everything. In respect to both duty and reverence, one must agree.

iv

Let us return to Whitehead's first educational address, "The Place of
Mathematics in a Liberal Education."[22] It was given in 1911, under the
circumstances noted in the first paragraph of the present chapter. The
address is concerned with the education of boys up to the age of nine-
teen. Although the phrase "liberal education" appears in the title of no
other piece by Whitehead, in *all* of the many essays he wrote about how
mathematics should be taught his concern was with mathematics as an
essential part of a liberal education.

At the beginning of this essay, more than in any other, Whitehead
dealt with the fact that an educational revolution was going on. Every
large change in our intellectual outlook has to be followed by such a
revolution, though inertia and vested interests may delay it for a generation.[23] Secondary education that is dominated by the classics, as
Whitehead's was, is doomed, for classical literature, which he respects,
no longer provides a sufficient store of ideas for a liberal education;
science has quite altered our world and our ways of thinking. (The
injection of science into English school curricula began decades earlier.
Too often instruction in science was simply added to a classical curriculum; lack of time nullified all such "reforms.")

Whitehead went on to describe, in this essay, the way in which
elementary algebra should be studied, and studied for its own sake, not
as a mere preliminary to higher mathematics. It should be studied as a
group of abstract ideas whose logical relations are shown in trains of
reasoning which use them. Instead of drilling his students in the learning of a great many mathematical formulae, the teacher should aim at
getting them to understand mathematical ideas. This requires the application of the ideas to examples. "By examples," said Whitehead, "I
mean important examples. What we want is one hour of the Caliph
Omar, to burn up and utterly destroy all the silly mathematical problems which cumber our text-books."[24]

To prepare students for the abstract ideas of the variable and of a
function, Whitehead proposed that they be asked to construct graphs
from statistical data on natural phenomena and on social phenomena;
graphs of the latter will make history vivid. In "The Aims of Education" Whitehead repeated this proposal, noting that graphs had become
fashionable, but were being used without enough attention to the algebraic ideas involved.[25]

On the teaching of geometry, Whitehead noted that not much benefit had resulted from the disuse of Euclid's *Elements* as a textbook.
Students were incorrectly told that the initial propositions in geometry

must be accepted as self-evident. Worse, logical sloppiness had crept in.[26] Whitehead held that one main object of mathematical teaching should be to develop in the student the power of logical reasoning, so that he becomes able to spot unprecise ideas and unwarranted conclusions, and able to know what is being assumed.[27] This does not at all mean that he should learn logic as a logical primer presents it. Rather, work that concentrates on the most important propositions in Euclid is desired.

The "essential principle" behind Whitehead's reform of mathematical teaching, as he says in the conclusion of this first address, is: "simplify the details and emphasize the important principles and applications." Insistence on this is repeated, with illustrations, in all his subsequent writings on the subject.

The next one was the paper he read at Cambridge in August 1912 in the Educational Section of the Fifth International Congress of Mathematicians. Its title was "The Principles of Mathematics in Relation to Elementary Teaching." Here he described the object of a mathematical education as acquisition of the powers of analysis, of generalization, and of reasoning.[28] The training in analysis and generalization, if it is to achieve thereby a grasp of an abstract idea, must not begin with the refined result of analysis and generalization, but with the idea as it exists in the child's mind.

> The schoolmaster is in fact a missionary, the savages are the ideas in the child's mind; and the missionary shirks his main task if he refuse to risk his body among the cannibals.[29]

Whitehead declared that a mathematical education is a failure if the student does not acquire the ability to reason precisely.[30] The only principles that are presupposed in mathematical reasoning, he said, are the logical principles that make deduction possible. This is Bertrand Russell's logicist thesis, which *Principia Mathematica* was written to demonstrate. Without naming that work, Whitehead said that between those logical principles and the supposedly fundamental truths of arithmetic and geometry "there is a whole new world of mathematical subjects concerning the logic of propositions, of classes, and of relations." But that world, he concluded, is too abstract to be useful in training students to reason precisely about abstract ideas.[31]

Whitehead attacked the notion that there is any value in teaching the differential calculus to engineers and physicists without attending to its logic. "What is of supreme importance in physics and in engineering is a mathematically trained mind." The training consists in leading the student to make the initial ideas of the calculus precise and the proofs adequate.[32]

In March 1913 Whitehead delivered a presidential address to the London Branch of the Mathematical Association. His title was "The Mathematical Curriculum,"* and he laid out the ideal curriculum as he conceived it. He harped on the avoidance of whatever is recondite. By that word he did not mean "difficult," but intricate and highly specialized in use. Mathematics, viewed as a whole, *is* a recondite subject, to the delight of mathematicians; but this reconditeness destroys the utility of mathematics in a liberal education. And whereas the study of Latin culminates in the reading of Horace and Virgil, the traditional study of mathematics culminates in knowledge of such things as the properties of the nine-point circle. That is ridiculous.[33] On the other hand, Euclid's fifth book was omitted. "It deals with ideas, and therefore was ostracised."[34] Whitehead argued for the inclusion of selected parts of it.

He always had the applications of mathematics in mind. On the teaching of trigonometry, he urged that scores of formulae be omitted, and attention be concentrated on the simplest propositions needed to express periodicity and wave motion.[35] Mathematics must not be taught as a mechanical discipline, but as a useful one to understand.

In all his essays on mathematical education, Whitehead insisted on the need for much practice in precise reasoning. In this address he generalized:

> The art of reasoning consists in getting hold of the subject at the right end, of seizing on the few general ideas which illuminate the whole, and of persistently marshalling all subsidiary facts round them. Nobody can be a good reasoner unless by constant practice he has realised the importance of getting hold of the big ideas and of hanging on to them like grim death.[36]

Whitehead observed that educational reforms are always hard to effect, and paid tribute to the teachers who had achieved some reorganization of mathematical instruction. He urged a continuation of their efforts that would make the elements of mathematics offer not only a training in logical method but "an acquisition of the precise ideas which lie at the base of the scientific and philosophical investigations of the universe."[37]

---

*The address was published as Chapter IV in *The Organisation of Thought* and reprinted as Chapter VI in *The Aims of Education*.

What is the significance of this assertion, so far as philosophical investigations are concerned? Whitehead did not say "the physical universe," but "the universe," which is a short way of referring to the totality of existence. Earlier in "The Mathematical Curriculum" he had made a stronger remark; after saying that the ideas that are studied in the mathematical curriculum of a school are the abstract ideas of spatial relations and relations of quantity and number, and insisting on the need to devote years of work to these ideas and their applications, so that the student understands them precisely, he asserted:

> Such a training should lie at the base of all philosophical thought. In fact elementary mathematics rightly conceived would give just that philosophical discipline of which the ordinary mind is capable.[38]

The adjective *all* in the first sentence does not absolutely prevent us from thinking that Whitehead would have acknowledged the right of *some* philosophical thought to go beyond the domain of space, number, and quantity, for we do not know how at this time he thought of the connections between different permissible kinds of philosophic thought. But these references to philosophy do imply that a philosopher who lacks a precise understanding of spatial, numerical, and quantitative relations has an inadequate basis for saying anything about the universe.

In Whitehead's many years at Trinity College, Cambridge, he had heard much of the philosophy he here disparages from McTaggart, Ward, and others. And we know that in 1913 he did not believe in God, let alone in Christianity.* In the metaphysics that he wrote in America many years later, he conceived of God as "one aspect" of "the universe," but there is no evidence that in 1913 he held any world-view that was antagonistic to materialism.

Another explanation of the remarks about philosophy that we are discussing is that Whitehead was in close touch with Bertrand Russell and knew that he was philosophizing within the limits mentioned in these remarks. (Russell published his results the next year, in *Our Knowledge of the External World as a Field for Scientific Method in Philosophy*.)[39] It was Whitehead's habit to speak well of Russell's work, and I think that this was a factor in leading him to insert the remarks about philosophy in "The Mathematical Curriculum." But it would be far-fetched to suppose that this was the only reason for them, and that

---

*For a dramatic illustration of this, see Chapter I, Section vi.

Whitehead himself did not believe what he said. At the very least, he was in sympathy with what Russell was doing.

V

Since Whitehead always considered applied mathematics to be as important as pure mathematics, it is not surprising that he took a keen interest in technical education. It was the topic of his second presidential address to the Mathematical Association, given in January 1917.[40] The ongoing war with Germany made Englishmen aware of the great need for good technical education. At the beginning of this address Whitehead asserted that "it is unpractical" to discuss the conditions for successful technical training without framing the ideal toward which we should work. That is what Whitehead tried to do, and is what gives the address most of its permanent value.

Whitehead took technical education to be mainly a training in the art of using knowledge to manufacture things or to make aesthetic objects. He warned against identifying it, as many did, with training a youngster early on to be a specialized workman; that ability can be picked up on the job. He himself thought of technical education as an ingredient in the complete development of ideal human beings; there should be something that one knows well, and something that one can do well. I believe he came to think of his son North as a good example of this.

The full title of this address was, "Technical Education and Its Relation to Science and Literature." Whitehead argued that, although one of these three must receive the dominant emphasis in a particular student's curriculum, something of the other two should be infused.[41]

The outcome of a scientific education should be skill in observing natural phenomena* and knowledge of the causal laws in two or three allied sciences, along with skill in deducing consequences of the laws. The causal knowledge is likely to be a permanent acquisition if the student has used his technical knowledge to set up the experimental situation. "If you want to understand anything, make it yourself, is a sound rule."[42] Generally speaking, without technical education the student's scientific knowledge is in danger of becoming a set of empty formulae.

---

*When he speaks of science Whitehead always refers to natural science. What we have come to call the social sciences were severally important to him, though he never discussed them as a group.

Without contradicting this educational view, Whitehead affirms a conception of the pursuit of science that he always maintained, and that sets him apart from holders of instrumentalist philosophies of science: "science is almost wholly the outgrowth of pleasurable intellectual curiosity."[43] Whitehead does not want us to think of this curiosity as a purely mental faculty. It is doubtful that there is any such thing. In this address he calls the antitheses between mind and body, and between thought and action, "disastrous" to the theory of education.[44] Thought that is not mere fantasy naturally passes into action disciplined by thought. According to Whitehead action, in a broad sense of the word, enters into all scientific thought, however abstract: the scientist "does not discover in order to know, he knows in order to discover." His discovery yields "the enjoyment which arises from successfully directed intention."[45] Of course the artist enjoys the same pleasure in another form. You may call this elementary psychology; that does not keep it from being a truth that is sometimes forgotten.

Whitehead put a high value on literature, and a low one on literary knowledge:

> Literature only exists to express and develop that imaginative world which is our life, the kingdom which is within us. It follows that the literary side of a technical education should consist in an effort to make the pupils enjoy literature. It does not matter what they know, but the enjoyment is vital.[46]

Although this presidential address to the Mathematical Association is not nearly so well known as the one ("The Aims of Education") that Whitehead gave the year before, it contains vigorous expressions of his views that no one who is interested either in education or in his general philosophy ought to miss. In addition to the views that I have already noticed, there is strong criticism of "the mean view of technical training,"[47] which assumes that ideal aims other than technical ones have no relevance to it. There is also a passing affirmation of the desirability of using art "as a condition of healthy life." "It is analogous to sunshine in the physical world."[48]

In this address, unlike his others, Whitehead was concerned with students of all ages. (At this time he was one of the governors of the Borough Polytechnic, in Southwark; most of its students were working men and women who enrolled in evening courses.) He dwelled on the importance of work being enjoyable, both for workers and for employers. That is part of the ideal of technical education, and is what the nation needs. The employer's enjoyment that he had in mind was not that of making money, but that of being enterprising, of trying out new ideas and methods.* As for the workers, we have to remember that Whitehead wrote before assembly lines had made almost all factory work boring. That, however, makes his insistence, in this address, on the need for a modern version of the Benedictine ideal of work more urgent.[49] Was Whitehead here a dreamer? I think not. He was recognizing the reality of the curse laid on mankind to live by the sweat of its brow, and saying that apart from some intellectual and moral vision, work is bound to be wearisome.

Let me close this section by quoting from Whitehead's fine summary of his philosophy of mathematics.[50]

> The essence of mathematics is perpetually to be discarding more special ideas in favour of more general ideas, and special methods in favour of more general methods. We express the conditions of a special problem in the form of an equation, but that equation will serve for a hundred other problems, scattered through diverse sciences. The general reasoning is always the powerful reasoning, because deductive cogency is the property of abstract form.

However,

> We shall ruin mathematical education if we use it merely to impress general truths. . . . After all, it is the concrete special cases which are important. Thus in the handling of mathematics in your results you cannot be too concrete, and in your methods you cannot be too general.

Whitehead was ardent in his dedication to improving mathematical teaching, but he was not a foolish optimist.

> This exhibition of the general in the particular is extremely difficult to effect, especially in the case of younger pupils. The art of education is never easy. To surmount its difficulties, especially those of elementary education, is a task worthy of the highest genius. It is the training of human souls.

This passage is a good specimen of Whitehead's style. He does not say that the exhibition of the general in the particular is very hard to carry out; he says that it is "extremely difficult to effect." The shorter words would have been precise enough; the longer ones convey Whitehead's

---

*Whitehead remarked, "There is much more hope for humanity from manufacturers who enjoy their work than from those who continue in irksome business with the object of founding hospitals" (*AE,* pp. 69–70).

meaning with absolute precision. Their use, and the tenor of the passage, suggest that the author is Victorian, as Whitehead was. Bertrand Russell, who was not a Victorian, would have expressed the thought differently. The phrase, "the training of human souls," would have been natural in the mouth of an educator who was a Roman Catholic. But Whitehead was still an atheist.[51] The death of so many of his pupils in the war may have begun to soften his atheism.

vi

Recall that in the address I have just discussed Whitehead said it was unpractical to talk about technical education without framing its ideal. The need for ideals is emphasized in all his writings on education, and also in his philosophical books. But there is another notion to which, with his realistic mind, he always gives equal emphasis: the notion of definiteness. "Ideals which are not backed by exact knowledge are mere fluffy emotion, and often lead to disastrous action." This is true in technical education, and in human life generally: "do not be content with vague aspirations. Always push on to definite knowledge."[52]

These quotations are from the last page of an address Whitehead gave in London on February 1, 1919, to the pupils at the Stanley Technical Trade School; its title was "The Functions of Technical Schools." It added little on that subject to what I noticed in Section v. But it included a strong repetition of his doctrine that the purpose of education is to stimulate and guide the pupil's self-development. He said:

> Whatever creates a disinterested curiosity for knowledge, or an appreciation of beauty, enlarges the mind and causes it to expand by its own free inward impulse. . . . You are not pieces of clay which clever teachers are modelling into educated men.[53]

Whitehead's love of England was manifest in this address; he felt that, Germany having been defeated, England faced a radically new situation, one in which her future depended entirely on the pluck, the wisdom, and the education of her youth. Whitehead's patriotism dominated a speech he made in the dark days of February 1917, on the occasion of giving prizes to pupils at the Borough Polytechnic Institute in Southwark.* His patriotism was firm and unyielding; he could have

---

*The speech was published, under the title "A Polytechnic in War-Time," in OT (1917). It is the first of Whitehead's educational writings that was not primarily about the teaching of mathematics.

mentioned the fact that in December Germany had sent the Allies a note saying that the Central Powers were prepared to negotiate, but he did not. (In any event, England refused.)

Whitehead's patriotic writing is sincere but not exceptional, and his rhetoric is undistinguished. What I like best in the prize-giving speech is what Whitehead said after he declared that success in earning your living is wholly worthy of respect:

> But if you steer your lives by the compass which points steadily to the North Pole of personal success, you will have missed your greatest chances in life. The genial climate is in the south.
>
> What I mean is this: you must make up your mind to find the best part of your happiness in kindly helpful relations with others. . . . The fortunate people are those whose minds are filled with thoughts in which they forget themselves and remember others.[54]

This sounds like Rotary. In Whitehead's mouth it is authentic, and significant to us because it describes his own attitude perfectly.

I want next to notice a paper of 1921 on "Science in General Education," which Whitehead read to the Second Congress of Universities of the Empire. In it, following a practice that by then had become customary in England, he assumed that schools would concentrate on general education until the pupil reached sixteen years of age, and thereafter devote most of the time to some special subjects. The general education would be pretty much the same for all.[55] In designing the scientific part of it, Whitehead warned, we must avoid "the fallacy of the soft option." For general education in science, the soft option would limit the teaching to the most interesting facts and most exciting generalizations. Whitehead argued that lasting knowledge requires plenty of hard work at definite tasks.[56] He remarked that the enthusiasm of educational reformers easily leads them to forget this fact, and to dwell on "the rhetoric of education."[57] Whitehead was always a hard-headed reformer.

In this paper he made the point that the study of a subject should be concerned not so much with producing knowledge as with forming habits.[58] In science, these are the habits of seeking causes, of classifying by similarities, and of knowing what to look for in making exact observations.[59]

Whitehead paid attention to the effect on character which the study of science should have.

> Literary people have a way of relegating science to the category of useful knowledge, and of conceiving the impress on character as gained from literature alone.[60]

The study of science should discipline a pupil's imagination in ways not otherwise to be had. In another aspect, science

> is the systematization of supremely useful knowledge. In the modern world men and women must possess a necessary minimum of this knowledge, in an explicit form, and beyond this, their minds must be so trained that they can increase this knowledge as occasion demands.[61]

vii

In the preface that Whitehead composed for the never-published collection of his essays on education,* he wrote, "The last chapter, 'Genius,' was composed in 1919." All of this that appeared in print consists of what he said about genius when he opened the "Discussion upon Fundamental Principles in Education," in Section L (Education) of the Eighty-seventh Meeting of the British Association for the Advancement of Science, which was held at Bournemouth in 1919.[62] I shall devote this section to his assertions about genius.

Whitehead began with the striking statement, "All education is the development of genius," but continued:

> Genius is the divine instinct for creation, incident throughout life, a certain quality of first-handedness accompanying and directing activity. An education mainly devoted to the development of genius is the best education for eliciting common sense. The three factors of genius are the habit of action, the vivid imagination, and the discipline of judgment.

By *genius* Whitehead evidently meant disciplinable creativity.

> The acquisition of knowledge "is the ultimate *substratum* of education" [italics added]. Knowledge and genius are the twin factors of effective personality, and the true ultimate problem before the educator is how to impart knowledge so as to stimulate genius.

Whitehead concluded:

> It is the demand of genius that it lives its own life in its own way. It is the function of education to supply criticism and knowledge.

Two years later, toward the close of the paper that I discussed in the last section, Whitehead touched again on the education of genius: "Un-

---

*See Section i of this chapter.

less we are careful, we shall organize genius out of existence; and some measure of genius is the rightful inheritance of every man."[63]

Genius, as the disciplinable creativity that inheres not only in great men but in every man, was a topic dear to Whitehead's heart. In his regular lectures at Harvard he sometimes expatiated on it. It was the sole topic in his next-to-last lecture there, on May 6, 1937. My notes of that lecture show him asserting, just as he had in 1919, that genius is the divine instinct for creation, and that education for genius is the best education for eliciting common sense. By common sense, Whitehead said, he meant the somewhat rare power of dealing sanely with the interrelations of everyday life; its opposite is routine thought. So construed, common sense is itself a form of genius. Whitehead possessed it in a high degree, whereas the brilliant Bertrand Russell did not.

Before 1919, Whitehead had written of school children as having creative potentialities that education should actualize, but he had not called this quality genius. His son Eric, as I described him in Section v of the last chapter, was a dear but untalented young man. When Eric, fighting for England, was killed in 1918, it became natural for Whitehead to think of him and all young men like him as geniuses, that is, as carriers of a disciplinable creativity.

viii

Whitehead expounded what may be called a psychology of the stages of educative processes. The premise of this psychology was the truism, "different subjects and modes of study should be undertaken by pupils at fitting times when they have reached the proper stage of mental development."[64] A pupil's progress with a subject, he held, is not naturally uniform; it is naturally cyclical. A cycle begins with free exploration, initiated by wonder; Whitehead called this "the stage of romance." Next comes the acquirement of technique and detailed knowledge—"the stage of precision." It reaches fruition in a final stage of romance, marked by the free application of what has been learned—"the stage of generalisation." Each kind of study has its own cycle; thus the stage of precision in language studies normally occurs while the study of science is still in its first romantic stage. Whitehead's name for his general idea was "the rhythm of education." He gave an address so entitled to the Training College Association in 1922.

Whitehead emphasized the plurality of cycles, cycles early and late, cycles within cycles, cycles in phase and out of phase with one another. If we believe it is essential that pupils be interested in their work,

Whitehead's doctrine of the rhythm of education is not speculative; it states an ideal pattern that is based on the premise stated above and on the fact of periodicity in life (most obvious in the alternations of work and play, activity and sleep). "The pupils must be continually enjoying some fruition and starting afresh."[65] In fact, this rhythm is not an alien pattern; it reflects the natural cravings of the pupil's mind.

Whitehead's conception of the rhythm of education shows some similarity to the one which T. Percy Nunn, of the University of London, expounded from 1905 on. Nunn called Whitehead's conception independent of his.[66] As Whitehead had been attending to cycles in the work in mathematics and mathematical physics which he began in 1884,* it was natural for him to look for them elsewhere. He did not discuss Nunn on the subject.

With this doctrine Whitehead repudiated two conventional assumptions: that the pupil's progress should be uniformly steady, and that the easier subjects should precede the harder ones. He countered the second assumption by noting the enormous difficulty of the infant's first task, that of acquiring spoken language; also, in mathematics it is harder to understand the elements of algebra than to understand what follows.

Whitehead warned against supposing that he was advocating a method that could be learned and applied on schedule by any teacher to any group of pupils. "Education," he often insisted, "is a difficult problem, to be solved by no one simple formula."[67] Romance must be present at every stage, or interest dies. Whitehead attributed the success of the Montessori system to its recognition of the dominance of romance in early childhood; but no one could be more insistent on the need for disciplined learning later on.[68] Indeed, all three—romance, precision, generalization—should be present at all times; the cycles are alternations in their dominance. The mistake of traditional teachers is their assumption that only the stage of precision counts.

Whitehead held that whereas the area of romantic interest is scarcely definable, it is important that the teacher carefully determine just what must be precisely learned.

He applied his doctrine of rhythm to the pair of contrasting necessities in education: freedom and discipline.† At the beginning of this section the adjective *free* was used in the description of the first and third

---

*This is the year of his Trinity College fellowship dissertation at Cambridge, on Clerk Maxwell's theory of electricity and magnetism.

†He did this a year later in an article, "The Rhythmic Claims of Freedom and Discipline," published in the *Hibbert Journal* and reprinted as Chapter III in *AE* (1929).

stages of a cycle. "An education which does not begin by evoking initiative and end by encouraging it must be wrong."[69] Discipline should dominate the second stage, that of precision. Here "the watchword is pace, pace, pace. Get your knowledge quickly, and then use it. If you can use it, you will retain it."[70] But the grasp of ideas will be hindered if the teacher imposes a discipline of precision "before a stage of romance has run its course in the growing mind."[71]

But what if different pupils are in different stages at the same time? I suppose that they had better be in different types of schools. Whitehead said nothing about this in his published essays, but did so in a letter he wrote to North's wife, Margot, from the American Cambridge on September 14, 1924. Her problem was to find the best type of school for her son. In this letter Whitehead made the point that there are two types of children. Some, which he called Type A, are very quick and facile at picking up the details of what they are taught; they need to be pushed on into problems that will make them think. Others (Type B) are slow to acquire precise details, and so are in danger of discouragement; some of these will always be slow to grasp ideas, but many will not, and need encouragement in coordinating the ideas they have; they will gradually acquire knowledge and technique, which should not be forced upon them early. "Progressive" schools seem to be better for Type B children, more traditional schools for Type A.

Whitehead rightly held that the only kind of discipline that is important for its own sake is self-discipline.[72] Obviously this can grow only in the exercise of freedom.

He realized that "there are more topics desirable for knowledge than any one person can possibly acquire." But there is something else that can be attained but may be missed: wisdom. It is "vaguer but greater" than knowledge.[73] It concerns the handling of knowledge. The wise person concentrates on the key issues in a situation, acts on principles that he understands well, and thereby adds value to immediate experience.

In his address at the Borough Polytechnic in 1917, Whitehead said something that I did not mention in Section vi: he devoted two pages to the value of including art in the activities of a school. This was, I believe, the first comment on art in his writings.[74] Six years later, he concluded his discussion of the rhythmic claims of freedom and discipline with two pages on the importance of art for postwar England, saying,

In these days of economy, we hear much of the futility of our educational efforts and of the possibility of curtailing them. . . . It would, however, require no very great effort to use our schools to produce a population with some love of music, some enjoyment of drama, and some joy in beauty of form and colour.[75]

In the second half of the nineteenth century music and art were part of the education of boys from affluent families in public schools (like Sherborne). Whitehead was talking about the education of the masses in the English school system. His point was taken for granted a few decades after he spoke; in 1923 it needed to be made. (His own enjoyment of music and the arts was not great; his sense of their importance was augmented by his life with Evelyn.) Two years later, Whitehead in *Science and the Modern World* affirmed the necessity for art in a civilized society. His context then, "scientific materialism," was quite different.

Some philosophers maintain that a sound understanding of Whitehead on education requires us to consider the philosophy he developed in that book and those which followed it. I shall postpone this question to my last chapter, believing that my account of Whitehead on education is intelligible on its own.

ix

In 1915 Herbert Dingle enrolled in a three-year course, Statics and Dynamics, that Whitehead taught at the Imperial College of Science and Technology. What I learned about Whitehead's teaching when I interviewed Professor Dingle in 1965 should not surprise the reader of the preceding sections. At the first few lectures, Dingle was flummoxed: Whitehead was always generalizing as he went along. At the end of the first term the students had got very little; but those who stayed with Whitehead, as Dingle did, came to understand the subject better than those who were conventionally taught, though they would not pass examinations as easily; Whitehead was a poor examination coach. He taught without a text; after telling the class to read Routh's treatises on dynamics, he lectured on the subject without attending to those treatises. To my question, "Did Whitehead *succeed* in encouraging originality?" Dingle's answer was an unqualified "Yes."

Whitehead showed his absent-mindedness by occasionally forgetting to go from his office to the lecture-room at the appointed hour. Sometimes he lectured past the appointed time; then he would say to the class, "You should have reminded me."

Dingle told me that most of Whitehead's students at the Imperial College were in physics or mathematics, not in engineering. By 1917–

18 Dingle was both an advanced student and a member of the staff.
From 1918 onward he was a member of the Physics staff, and went to all
of Whitehead's lectures that he could. In 1919–20 these included a
lecture course of postgraduate standard, "Relativity and the Nature of
Space"; this started Dingle's lifelong interest in the theory of relativity.
Whitehead encouraged him to write *Relativity for All.*[76]

Another student at that time, L. C. Martin, wrote to me that Whitehead "spared no pains to help his pupils."[77] A little later an undergraduate in engineering, Kelvin Spencer, audited Whitehead's lectures on
relativity.* He remembered that Whitehead treated the pupils as his
intellectual equals, which they were not.[78] Recollections of Whitehead's teaching that I have gleaned from other students at the Imperial
College are in accord with those I have set down.

X

Mathematics was the first subject whose teaching Whitehead tried to
reform. In 1916, the year of his "Aims of Education," he as President of
the Mathematical Association and A. W. Siddons as the Chairman of its
Teaching Committee sent a letter to the editor of the *Mathematical
Gazette.*† It stated the Association's general position on the teaching of
mathematics in schools. It is entirely in accord with Whitehead's views
on this subject, as set forth in Sections i–v of this chapter. As a statement of the position of the chief organization of mathematical teachers,
the letter had some effect, but probably not what it deserved. In the war
years so many schemes of educational reform were being advocated
that none had much chance of being fully accepted.

A wide reform which Whitehead supported got accepted in the
1920s and 1930s. In April 1916 liberal educationists, at a conference
called by the Teachers' Guild, founded the Education Reform Council.
Its program, issued in November, called for secondary education for all
to age sixteen. Whitehead, along with Nunn, Gilbert Murray, and
others, signed it.[79]

In general, Whitehead's English essays on education have had too
little influence on practice in his own country. Substantial specific influ-

---

*Spencer eventually became Chief Scientist in the Ministry of Power, and was
knighted.

†This joint letter—it is only half a page long—is not listed in the Bibliography. It was
printed in *Mathematical Gazette* 9, No. 127 (January 1917): 14.

ence has depended on the chance that a headmaster was so impressed that he brought about some realization of Whitehead's ideals in the face of the uniform examination system. That system has flourished, with variations, to the present day, despite continued attacks on it, such as that of the classical scholar Sir Richard Livingstone in his *On Education*.[80] Whitehead's doctrine that the aim of education should be the self-development of the pupil had many English supporters from Whitehead's time on, but none like him. From 1911 through the twenties Edmond Holmes, who had been H.M. Chief Inspector of Schools, argued for a shift in elementary education from "the path of obedience" to "the path of self-realisation";[81] far from being a scientist, he was a poet and a student of Buddhism. Keith Evans's excellent survey published in 1985, *The Development and Structure of the English School System*, did not mention Whitehead. There were echoes of Whitehead's protest against inert ideas in the official Hadow Reports of 1926, 1931, and 1933. Recently, the Cockcroft Report, *Mathematics Counts* (1982) urged, as Whitehead had, that teachers of mathematics give their pupils less detail and more understanding. Whitehead's English addresses on education had a moderate degree of *diffuse* influence. On balance, however, John Dewey had a greater effect than Whitehead in moving English school education away from its traditional practices.

The school system in England and Wales has not been such as to favor Whiteheadian influence. The Education Act of 1902 got the system started; the 1944 Act made secondary education compulsory. Since then, education has been a national service that is centrally guided but locally provided and administered. The central guidance has reflected shifts between Conservative and Labor governments, but both have insisted on examining pupils at age eleven and again at sixteen, when their educational and vocational futures were largely determined. In comparison with the United States, school education in England has been a straitjacket for pupils. Reform has been more concerned with education as social policy than with education itself.

Whitehead's ideal of technical education was largely ignored in England. Emphasis was placed on something he warned against—catching the young early on and training all but those in the top social class for a particular kind of job. Under the Thatcher government, the needs of the economy have taken priority over those of education; central oversight of the training of ordinary teenagers has to a considerable degree been assigned to a non-education agency, the Manpower Services Commission in the Department of Employment.

In the United States, Whitehead's *Aims of Education* enjoyed wide general influence. And it inspired many teachers, not so much in public schools as in private ones. A notable example was the Shady Hill School in Cambridge, Massachusetts. This was a primary school, from kindergarten through the ninth grade; it also trained apprentice teachers. From 1921 to 1949 Katherine Taylor was its Director. Her educational policy was largely founded on Whitehead's "Aims of Education." Her successors, Edward Youmans and Joseph Segar, continued Miss Taylor's policy.[82] The school continually had to fight the Secondary Schools Admission Test, composed, administered, and graded by the Education Testing Service. Mr. Segar told me of being proudly shown a school in which the day's activities were programmed and fed into an electronic device which sent the commands through the school building. The mechanization of schools is a formidable barrier in the United States to the humanizing influence of Whitehead's philosophy of education.

Perry Dunlap Smith, when Headmaster at the North Shore Country Day School in Winnetka, Illinois, tried to apply Whitehead's ideas; later he spread the gospel while teaching education at Roosevelt College in Chicago. The teaching at Germantown Friends School and the New Canaan (Connecticut) Country School also were influenced by Whitehead. There must be other examples that have not come to my attention.

In discussions of curricula at American colleges, the common-core movement benefited from the influence of Whitehead's educational writings.

His ability to coin striking epigrams was most exercised in those writings, and his influence in the United States—in contrast to Dewey's influence—owes much to this.* The popularity of an epigram can be unfortunate. In America Whitehead's "protest against inert ideas" was sometimes misconstrued as a protest against ideas that have no immediate practical use.

Whitehead's *Aims of Education* has been translated into many languages, even into Tamil. I cannot assess its influence outside England and America. Certainly the school systems of France, Germany, and Italy were less receptive to Whitehead's ideas.

---

*Let me add two to those I have already quoted. "There is only one subject-matter for education, and that is life in all its manifestations" (*AE*, p. 10). "Moral education is impossible apart from the habitual vision of greatness" (ibid., p. 106).

xi

In 1923 Whitehead published an article, "The Place of Classics in Education"; I shall discuss it in the next chapter. After he went to Harvard in 1924 he wrote no more about school education, but dealt with various aspects of college and university education. I shall briefly consider his chief ideas about higher education in Chapters VIII and XI. However, his 1928 essay, "Universities and Their Function," will be noticed now, in order to round out "Whitehead on Education."

This essay was an address to a meeting of the American Association of the Collegiate Schools of Business. Whitehead began it with praise for graduate schools of business, and discussed their ideals; but more than half of the address was about the ideal that should inspire university education generally. The main point was that "the proper function of a university is the imaginative acquisition of knowledge."[83]

> Education is discipline for the adventure of life; research is intellectual adventure; and the universities should be homes of adventure shared in common by young and old. For successful education there must always be a certain freshness in the knowledge dealt with. . . . Knowledge does not keep any better than fish.[84]

Thus, "the whole point of a university, on its educational side, is to bring the young under the intellectual influence of a band of imaginative scholars."[85] Apart from this, knowledge might be acquired—at less expense—from books alone.[86]

CHAPTER IV

Last Years in England

i/The University of London. Whitehead, Dean of its Faculty of Science and Chairman of its Academic Council. Creation of a department on the history and philosophy of science. Promotion of a plan to aid "external" students. Promotion of the Convent of the Sacred Heart. Whitehead on academic rules.

ii/Goldsmiths' College, in South London. Whitehead's work for it. Reason for naming a new science building after him in 1970. His address at the dedication of the War Memorial in 1921.

iii/Whitehead's work on behalf of the Borough Polytechnic, in Southwark; as a Governor of another polytechnic. An academic obligation in Surrey.

iv/Prime Minister's Committee on the Place of Classics in the English Educational System. Dame Dorothy Brock's memories of Whitehead on this committee. His article "The Place of Classics in Education." A minority report?

v/A house in Surrey. Relations with Bertrand Russell. Arthur Schuster. North's marriage, and work for the Admiralty. Whitehead's social life. Evelyn and Bloomsbury people. Whitehead's custom when lunching alone. R. B. Haldane. Mark Barr. Friendships with children. Visit to Bryn Mawr College in 1922.

Whitehead's academic activities multiplied after October 30, 1918, when he was elected Dean of the Faculty of Science in the University of London, a post he held for four years. In March 1919 he became a member of the University's deliberative body, the Senate;[1] he remained a Senator until he moved to Harvard in 1924. There were about sixty persons in the Senate; leadership was provided by its Academic Council. Soon Whitehead was a member of the Academic Council,[2] and its chairman from 1920 to 1924.

Whereas the University of Cambridge, in Whitehead's time there, consisted of seventeen colleges, the University of London was a confederation of more than sixty institutions of many different kinds. In addition to University College, King's College, and the Imperial College of Science and Technology,* mention should be made of the important London School of Economics and Institute of Historical Research. Though most of the colleges were co-educational, some had been founded for women and were still women's colleges. There was also a College of Household Science, and, for training school teachers, the London Day Training College.† I have given only a small sample of what existed under the umbrella called the University of London.‡

Plainly, a professor who was both Dean of the Faculty of Science and Chairman of the Academic Council of the Senate could not carry on any research of his own; but Whitehead did, as we shall see in Chapter VI.

In January 1919 the national Association of Science Teachers called for the creation of a Consultative Council, composed of equal numbers of school and university teachers of science, in order to keep under review the higher work of schools and its relation to the work of univer-

---

*The first two were described in Chapter I, Section iii; the third in Chapter II, Section i.

†In 1932 this became the Institute of Education.

‡In his *Universities: American, English, German* (New York: Oxford University Press, 1930), Abraham Flexner confessed himself unable to understand in what sense the University of London was a university at all (p. 231). *Per contra*, it should be said that this "university" grew up to meet the needs of the population of Greater London, and did so.

sities with respect to science. Whitehead was appointed to represent the University of London on this Council.[3] Thus his addresses on education, whatever their effect in reforming school teaching, brought more work for him.

Education in science was one of his foremost concerns. The war with Germany had caused Britain to give increased attention to science. Whitehead was anxious that this should not be tapered off after the war, but enhanced. He worked for the establishment of a new program in the Faculty of Science at the University of London. University College had initiated some lectures in scientific method and in the history of science. Whitehead had long been convinced of the value of knowing the history of science; it did not become a prestigious academic subject until decades later. In 1922 the University created a new department at University College, History and Methods of Science, with a professor of Logic and Scientific Method as its head.[4] Whitehead and other members of the committee that recommended this action had preferred the broader title "History, Principles, and Methods of Science." Whitehead never adhered to the dogma that fidelity to the experimental method of science was all that the advance of science required. Breadth, if not precision, was gained in 1946, when the names of the department and chair were changed to "History and Philosophy of Science."[5]

Until 1858 the University of London was only an examining and degree-granting body. That was still its function for "external" students. "Internal" students did their work for the London degree at one of the many units (also called internal schools) of the University, for example, University College or King's. External students were enrolled, if anywhere, in one of the even more numerous institutions that were only affiliated with the University. In 1922 Whitehead, as Chairman of the Academic Council, and Ernest Graham-Little, as Chairman of the External Council, proposed that an advisory service be provided for external students; for a nominal fee, they would be provided with study-schemes furnished by professors in the units of the University. Serious opposition arose; many Senators feared that this would cut down enrollment at the internal schools. Graham-Little later recalled, "Whitehead's immense influence with the Academic Council and with the Senate carried the proposal."[6] As the internal schools were generally more expensive than the external ones, I am sure that one of Whitehead's motives was desire to help financially poor students get the best education possible.

Of course many institutions that were not affiliated with the University of London wanted to become so. In Section i of the last chapter I quoted from Whitehead's summary of his educational experience: "Also I have inspected a nunnery applying for affiliation to a university." This was the very small Convent of the Sacred Heart, in Hammersmith. In 1920 it applied for the third time. The Academic Council asked Whitehead and two others to inspect its research, teaching, and equipment.[7] The inspectors recommended that "if, on general grounds the Senate decide that a Catholic Convent College can suitably become a School of the University, a final decision with regard to its admission be deferred" pending the Senate's receipt from the Convent of a complete scheme for its organization as a College in the Faculty of Arts.[8] Presumably a considerable expansion of the Convent's academic work was desired. There was no teaching of science—a fact which could not have pleased Whitehead, for one.

I turn now to a sample of Whitehead's action on a different kind of administrative problem. The question was what the Imperial College should do about a request, made early in 1924, that one of its part-time lecturers receive from the University the title "Recognized Teacher in the University of London." Lecturers were appointed by the units of the University—in this case, by the Imperial College; recognition was the University's certificate of approbation, given to about one-third of the teachers. On making inquiries, Whitehead learned that the man was a member of the staff at the Air Ministry and only occasionally a lecturer in the relatively new Department of Aeronautics at the Imperial College. He then wrote a letter to the Registrar of the College to "strongly advise the *withdrawal* of the application before it reaches the University." He "could not support the application on the University Committees which deal with these matters."[9] His view was that academic rules and customs, once adopted, should not be closed in exceptional circumstances; in a postscript he suggested that if it should be desirable that this applicant be appointed as the responsible teacher for a graduate student, the University could "recognize him for *that purpose* in each individual case as it comes up."[10]

Whitehead always had it in mind that some men who lack academic qualifications may be excellent teachers of technology because of their special experience. At a meeting of the Imperial College's Board of Studies* back in 1915 he had remarked, "Many of the best teachers in Polytechnics come from the workers."[11]

The impact of the University of London extended far beyond aca-

---

*Composed of the professors in the College.

demic matters. In a letter that Whitehead wrote to his son North on July 19, 1925, he said, "My experience on the Senate of the University of London was one of almost continual influence on the policy of governmental bodies." He had been struck by the absence of this sort of influence in the United States at that time.

ii

At New Cross in South London there is a flourishing educational institution known as Goldsmiths' College. Its science building is named after Whitehead.[12]

The Goldsmiths were one of the great Livery Companies of London. In 1891 they opened at New Cross an institute to promote "technical skill, knowledge, health and general well-being among men and women of the industrial, working and artisan classes."[13] In 1905 they presented their land and buildings to the University of London. Thereafter the University effected a general supervision of Goldsmiths' College through a Delegacy, while its management was in the hands of a Warden appointed by the University Senate.[14] In 1919 Whitehead was appointed to the Delegacy, which included six Senators of the University (one of whom was its chairman), two men nominated by the Goldsmiths' Company, two nominated by the London County Council, and one each from the County Councils of Kent, Surrey, and Middlesex. As most of the students planned to be teachers, the (teacher) Training Department was the largest one in Goldsmiths' College; hence the Board of Education for the United Kingdom made grants to the College.

In July 1920 the University Senate appointed Whitehead Chairman of the Delegacy; it renewed this appointment annually until July 1924, when he left for Harvard; Graham Wallas then succeeded him.

Goldsmiths' students received the Bachelor of Arts degree on passing the University of London examination. There was no program leading to a B.Sc. degree. That was what young persons who planned to teach science in schools wanted. It was established in 1923; half a century later, the College was one of the chief sources of supply for science teachers in English schools.[15] In 1968 the Warden, Sir Ross Chesterman, came to the conclusion that it must have been Whitehead, as Senator and Chairman of the Academic Council of the University, who persuaded the Senate to establish a degree program in science.[16] Hence the naming of the new science building after him.

Sir Ross very kindly went over the minutes of the Delegacy's meetings during Whitehead's chairmanship, looking for indications of Whitehead's other activities. He found that he had started some valuable developments which the College only achieved many years later.[17] The complicated arrangements between the College and the University were burdensome. Thus, on March 8, 1922, Whitehead, as Chairman of the Delegacy, had to write a letter to the Chairman of the Finance Committee of the University in answer to that committee's complaint that the College had raised fees without obtaining the consent of the Senate. The letter* was detailed and convincing, not written by an other-worldly mind. Whitehead pointed out that the College had no other option, that the Finance Committee was not set up so as to include anyone charged with "knowledge of the special and complex circumstances of the College," and that the College's action was in accordance with precedent in its dealings with the University. (Sir Ross wrote me that Whitehead's "grasp of complicated University matters" was "noteworthy.")[18] In conclusion, Whitehead said that the only cause for financial anxiety lay in the possibility of drastic economies by the Government, which he had mentioned "in the course of a speech at the last meeting of the Senate." Another Senator at that time, W. R. Matthews, later recalled that Whitehead *read* his speeches to the Senate, word by word.[19] When Whitehead was preparing to leave for the simpler environment provided by Harvard, he was leading a fight against the Board of Education's reductions in its grants to Goldsmiths' College.[20]

On October 29, 1921, when the College War Memorial was unveiled, Whitehead gave the address.† The only personal note in it is Whitehead's memory of the first Warden of the College, William Loring, as a young man at Cambridge; Loring had died at Gallipoli. I quote enough of the address to show how Whitehead expressed his feeling about democracy and education, youth and death.

> It is but a superficial rendering of the truth when we say, "Time in its ever-rolling stream bears all its sons away." Fix your minds on the deeper thought of a greater writer. "Seeing that we are compassed round with so great a crowd of witnesses let us worthily run the race that is set before us. . . ."
> The presence in College of this Memorial . . . should generate in us a constant feeling of reverence for the average capacities and inherent worth of our countrymen. Democracy, if it is worth anything, means reverence for the intrinsic character of humanity. Of all

---

*Sir Ross kindly supplied me with a copy of this letter.
†It was never published, but Sir Ross sent me a copy.

ages a democratic age should share that feeling in the highest degree. Also it is the right feeling for those of us who are engaged, or are about to be engaged, in education. Each pupil should be for us a jewel of the most precious worth, the final product of the age-long toil of spiritual forces.

We dedicate [this Memorial] to men who have enriched life with a worth which is eternal and who forever rest among the victors.

This fine address contains no reference to personal immortality or to God. It reminds me of what Whitehead said in 1919 about every man's genius.* What is new here is the vague reference to "age-long toil of spiritual forces."

iii

The Borough Polytechnic, in Southwark, was older than Goldsmiths' College, and was independent of the University of London. Most of its students were working men and women enrolled in evening classes. The contrast with Cambridge colleges could scarcely have been greater. But Whitehead desired opportunities to guide England's education of her masses.† Students did not have to be teenagers to evoke his interest in their education and his sympathy with them. Before his first year in London ended, he agreed to be one of the Governors of the Borough Polytechnic.‡

There were about two dozen Governors. Whitehead was a co-optative Governor, that is, one chosen by the governing body itself, not a representative of any other body. His interest in education must have become known soon after his arrival in London. Publication of his *Introduction to Mathematics* early in 1911 established his reputation wherever the teaching of that subject was taken seriously. The Principal of Borough Polytechnic in 1911–12, C. T. Millis, consulted Whitehead about the courses in mathematics which Millis was planning for the curriculum. Whitehead was made a member of the most important

---

*See Chapter III, Section vii.

†See Volume I, pages 317–18, and Whitehead's own description, in Abiog. Notes, of the problem of higher education in London.

‡At that time English polytechnics were private institutions peculiar to London. The Stanley Technical Trade School, where Whitehead gave the prize-giving speech I dealt with in Section vi of Chapter III, was then run by the Governors of the Borough Polytechnic; after becoming independent, it was called the Norwood Technical College.

committee of the governing body, the Education Committee, and remained a member of it until 1920, when his connection with the Borough Polytechnic ended. He did not serve on any other committee of
the Governors, but Evelyn was a member of two of their advisory
committees, that on dressmaking and that on ladies' tailoring.*

It seems to me likely, though I cannot confirm, that the Whiteheads'
particular interest in the Borough Polytechnic owed something to their
friendship with the Beeton family.† When some of Alan Beeton's
paintings were hung in the Governors' room, there was a row, and
Whitehead had to soothe feelings.

For three years Whitehead was a Governor of another polytechnic in
London, the South Western Polytechnic Institute, now the Chelsea
College of Science and Technology. It seems to have been of less importance to him. In June 1918 he was elected a co-optative member of
its Governing Body for one year, and served on its Finance and General
Purpose Committee.[21] He was re-elected a co-optative Governor for
six years, that is, to June 1925, but because of non-attendance he ceased
to be a Governor, and resigned as of February 1, 1922.[22] Probably this
resignation, and the ending in 1920 of his connection with the Borough
Polytechnic, were due to the demands on his time entailed by the
chairmanship of the Academic Council at the University of London and
his duties at the Imperial College of Science and Technology.

At least one of his duties took him outside London proper. In July
1921 the Imperial College nominated Whitehead to represent the College on the Surrey Education Committee, which reported to the Surrey
County Council; this was approved. Whitehead was to replace an Imperial College professor who reported that he found it difficult to attend
meetings. Of course the Surrey Education Committee had subcommit-
tees; Whitehead was to serve on the one on scholarships and the one on
educational reports. He was also made a member of the Surrey County
Council's Standing Committee on Higher Education, which dealt with
everything from curricula to lavatories. Whitehead's attendance record
to March 1924 was bad: nine out of seventy-two possible meetings.‡

---

*These facts about the Borough Polytechnic are due to J. E. Garside, its Principal in
1965, who kindly looked over the annual reports for me in August of that year. Unfortunately he died that autumn.

†See Chapter II, Section vi.

‡The information in the last three sentences was given to me by Professor Brian
Hendley, in a letter of September 21, 1983.

iv

Whitehead's administrative position in the educational world of London involved him in a host of committees set up for specific purposes. I have not tried to compile a list of them, and will be content to mention one. In 1919 the Faculty of Science at the University of London undertook to consider the detailed report of a committee that had been appointed by the Prime Minister to inquire into the position of natural science in the British educational system. The Faculty of Science then resolved to appoint a small committee, consisting of the Dean of the Faculty (Whitehead), its Secretary, and two others, to consider what questions, raised by this report, the Faculty should discuss.[23]

The committee that took up more of Whitehead's time than any other in his life was a committee appointed by the Prime Minister on November 27, 1919, to inquire into the position of classics in the nation's educational system. This committee did a thorough job, interviewing hundreds of witnesses in the course of its eighty-five meetings. The last meeting was on June 7, 1921; the committee's report, running to more than three hundred pages, was published later that year.[24] The chairman was a Liberal statesman, the Marquess of Crewe; his main contribution was to preside with complete fairness. Roughly half of the eighteen members were Greek or Latin scholars of some distinction, like Gilbert Murray, Richard Livingstone, and the Cambridge scholar T. R. Glover. Except for Sir Henry Hadow, who later issued the Hadow Reports,* the others were mainly school administrators, heads of colleges, or classics teachers. There was one Fellow of the Royal Society: Whitehead. It was a good committee.

One of its younger members was Dorothy Brock (later Dame Dorothy), a successful schoolteacher of Latin and Greek. On April 30, 1968, she wrote to give me her memories of Whitehead in the committee meetings.

> I have been vainly looking for papers. . . . From 1921 to 1968 is a long time. . . . But one thing I *can* say is that Professor Whitehead was an outstanding member of the Committee. . . . My memory of him is of someone who had no axe to grind, who was seeking truth, who didn't talk much, but when he *did* every word meant something.

In an interview two months later, Dame Dorothy recalled Whitehead's way with witnesses, saying that he drew them out well. When a witness

---

*See Chapter III, Section x.

talked nonsense, he would cut through the nonsense with the utmost courtesy; "he never squashed a witness." This is of a piece with what people at Harvard said about Whitehead: "He might disagree with you, but he never made you feel a fool."* Dame Dorothy, who never saw him before or later, also perceived something about him that I have come to think was central: "I felt he was remote." I should say, impersonal, detached. He kept his emotions under firm control.

Dame Dorothy remembered that the committee members often went out to lunch in small groups, and that when she was taken out to lunch they regaled her with their unfavorable reactions to the opinions expressed by other committeemen. Whitehead was different; he usually went off by himself for lunch. I assume that he sometimes had a private talk with one other member; that was his strategic weapon.

Of course the Committee's Report upheld education in the classics. There would be no point in going over the Report here. Most of it was written by the Secretary to the Committee, in Civil Service English. Dame Dorothy told me she wished Whitehead had written it. In the twenty-page introduction, however, two pages on language as symbolism strike me as Whiteheadian in thought, vocabulary, and style. So do the recommendations that Greek science be studied, and the suggestion that teachers of classics and of science consult one another.

The Committee's work finished, Whitehead wrote an article, "The Place of Classics in Education," which was published in January 1923.[25] In it he made only one reference to the meetings of the Committee:

> it was my misfortune to listen to much ineffectual wailing from witnesses on the mercenary tendencies of modern parents. I do not believe that the modern parent of any class is more mercenary than his predecessors. When classics was the road to advancement, classics was the popular subject for study. Opportunity has now shifted its location, and classics is in danger.[26]

Whitehead adds that in his experience, scientists are not hostile to classics.

Whitehead spends most of his article on the reasons for teaching Latin to youngsters. Not to enable them to read Roman authors in the original; very few of them will ever do that. One good reason is to train them to think. Discipline in logic should begin by analyzing familiar

---

*Bertrand Russell was often called "the great Destroyer." Whitehead saw no point in destruction.

English sentences, going on to French sentences, then to Latin ones.* "Every language embodies a definite type of mentality."[27] The mentality that is embodied in Latin is important for grasping the foundation of Western civilization in, or funneled through, Rome; this is the second good reason for studying Latin. Some reading of Roman authors in the original, and more in translation, will introduce students to the unity of Western civilization, and should replace the dry political history of the Republic and the Empire. "When you come to think of it, the whole claim for the importance of classics rests on the basis that there is no substitute for first-hand knowledge."[28]

No member of the Prime Minister's Committee on Classics wrote a minority report. Should we interpret the article just discussed as one, though Whitehead did not so label it? There are some differences, but I do not think them sufficient to justify this conclusion. Nor did Dame Dorothy Brock.[29] Her memory of the Committee's meetings was that Whitehead "did not come out with startling divergencies of opinion."[30]

v

After Evelyn sold the house in Lockeridge the Whiteheads took one in Oxted, Surrey. It was only a little more than twenty miles by train from London, yet in the country. In 1919 they let their flat in London from May into September. On May 13, when Evelyn invited Bertie Russell for a weekend, she wrote, "Our woodland is full of blue bells, and the new green is too lovely for words, the nightingale sings day and night." There was a croquet lawn, on which Whitehead played with North and with visitors.

I know of no evidence that Russell accepted Evelyn's invitation, and think acceptance unlikely. Russell was living sometimes in London with his pacifist friend Clifford Allen and sometimes at the Morrell's Garsington Manor. Most of his friends were not friends of the Whiteheads. Alfred, busy with the foundations of physics, had in 1917 stopped showing Bertie his work in progress.† Russell, when not trying to get in touch with Wittgenstein, was working out the ideas which were published in 1921 as *The Analysis of Mind*. The paths of the former collaborators had separated. Whitehead still believed that Bertie would do brilliant work in philosophy, and was one of the signers of an appeal,

---

*This is not presented as an alternative to the discipline in thinking that a good teacher of algebra or geometry can give. That was discussed in Chapter III, Section iv.

†See Volume I, page 229.

issued by Gilbert Murray in the fall of 1918, for funds that would enable Russell to write.[31]

In 1918 the Whiteheads became close friends of the Arthur Schusters. Schuster, ten years older than Whitehead and son of a wealthy German family, had studied physics under Helmholtz and Kirchhoff. He moved to Manchester in 1869 and became a British subject in 1875. He performed significant experiments in spectroscopy,* and advanced the study of periodicities. But he is most important in the history of science as an organizer, beginning with the productive Manchester school of physics.† Schuster participated in several scientific expeditions for the observation of eclipses. His wealth enabled him to do for national and international science the things that governments do today. The British Association for the Advancement of Science recognized Schuster's leadership by making him its President in 1915; he was already a Secretary of the Royal Society, and from 1920 to 1924 served as its Foreign Secretary. He was knighted in 1920.

A few years after he left Manchester, Schuster bought an estate, Yeldahl, at Twyford in Berkshire. He admired Evelyn, and the Whiteheads often visited Yeldahl. In the 1920s Evelyn had many more social engagements with the Schusters than with her other wealthy friends, the Beetons. One of the four Schuster daughters, Margaret,‡ married North on November 3, 1920. She was a war widow with two children, Roy and Sheila Dehn. The Schuster daughter who studied medicine and lived with the Whiteheads for a time, Norah, was mentioned earlier.§ As Schuster was generous with his money, it is probable that when Evelyn was short of cash he came to the rescue.

North told me that his father and Schuster found that they had little to say to each other. And Whitehead did not even play bridge. The contrast between the quiet man of ideas and this successful organizer of scientific advance reminds me of the earlier contrast between Whitehead and Herbert Hall Turner.‖

Jessie Whitehead, who had been a secretary in the Foreign Office in

---

*It was Schuster who coined this word.
†Bohr, Moseley, and Rutherford worked there.
‡Evelyn called her Margot, and the name stuck.
§See Chapter I, Section vi. Her diagnosis of Evelyn's heart trouble as pseudo-angina was set forth in Volume I, page 240.
‖See Volume I, page 121. In fairness to Schuster, I add that besides being a good experimenter, he entertained some advanced scientific ideas, notably the idea of anti-matter.

the war, worked during the peace conference at Paris as a précis-writer, drafting news releases for the press. Shortly after his marriage North was appointed Assistant Scientific Officer to the Admiralty, and later Scientific Officer.[32] When not aboard a ship, he worked at the National Physical Laboratory just outside London; it was like the National Bureau of Standards in the United States.

At one time, after the war but before his marriage, Lady Ottoline Morrell invited North to her house. Her friends were mostly Bloomsbury people; the Whiteheads, especially Evelyn, disliked them. Much later, Norah Schuster told me what happened to this invitation: Evelyn said to her, "I soon put a stop to that. I wasn't going to have him going into that milieu." North was almost thirty years old. I doubt that Whitehead would have done this, but Evelyn tended to bully North and Jessie all their lives.

In 1919–22, when Kelvin Spencer* was a student at the Imperial College, he used to lunch cheaply at an A.B.C. Teashop next to South Kensington station. According to Sir Kelvin,

> Frequently Whitehead lunched there too. A distinguished-looking man, but dowdily dressed, often with an old raincoat and a Homburg hat much the worse for wear. He customarily confined himself to a poached egg on toast. He sat . . . at a crowded marble-topped table, with off-hand waitresses, and was unaccompanied by any of his University peers.[33]

Evelyn arranged Whitehead's social life; she believed, rightly, that if left to himself he would spend all his time reading, writing, and performing academic duties. The Whiteheads were at home to friends on Thursday evenings. These included some old Cambridge friends, like Charles Sanger and his wife, and some philosophers, for Alfred had joined the Aristotelian Society in 1915. A non-professional philosopher whom they saw about once a month was the statesman R. B. Haldane, who had influenced the structure of the University of London. Norah Schuster (later Mrs. Norah Nicholls) told me that Haldane tended to avoid Evelyn, as he liked to talk deep. In 1921 he published *The Reign of Relativity;* Whitehead helped him with the mathematics of Einstein's theory. Once, when Norah Schuster was living with the Whiteheads, they gave a party for Haldane, Maynard Keynes, Bertie Russell, and a fourth; she and Evelyn were supposed to stay upstairs, while Whitehead received the guests in the basement.[34]

---

*See Chapter III, Section ix, of this volume.

Mark Barr and his wife were often at the Whiteheads'. He was an electrical engineer who had invented a calculating machine. Three years younger than Whitehead, he was British but at home in New York as well as in London. Barr will come into the story of Whitehead's move to Harvard in 1924.*

One of the Whiteheads' neighbors in Chelsea was the actress Sybil Thorndike. When I interviewed Dame Sybil in 1970, she had a vivid memory of Whitehead as an old gentleman taking walks on the street. Besides being amiable to everyone, he made friends of all the neighborhood children.†

In academic vacations the Whiteheads no longer traveled in Europe, as they had before the war. However, they accepted an invitation to cross the Atlantic in April 1922. They had never been in America. The occasion was a festival to honor Charlotte Angas Scott on her retirement as Professor of Mathematics at Bryn Mawr College. She was English, had been at Bryn Mawr since 1885, and had published some mathematical books and papers. She had studied at Girton, where the day in 1880 when Cambridge announced that she had made a score in the Mathematical Tripos equal to that of the Eighth Wrangler was celebrated. (As Cambridge did not give degrees to women, her B.Sc. and D.Sc. were from the University of London.) Whitehead conveyed the greetings of Girton's staff and read a paper, "Some Principles of Physical Science," dedicated to Miss Scott; it was reprinted as Chapter IV of his *Principle of Relativity*. The Whiteheads returned to London as soon as the festival ended, but they had fallen in love with America.

vi

Whitehead was quite versatile in his mathematical teaching at the Imperial College. Thus in 1921–22 he lectured on the Tensor Theory in its application to mathematical physics, on electromagnetic theory, and on elasticity. In 1915 Whitehead's lectures at the Imperial College had included some on the theory of the motion of aeroplanes. A student who heard those lectures, H. Bradley, went into the Royal Flying Corps. Upon returning to the Imperial College in 1919, he told Whitehead that when learning to fly he had noticed behavior in accordance with the theory.[35] Whitehead remarked that he was not including that

---

*See Chapter VII, Section i.

†For a delightful example of Whitehead's absorption in children's activities, see the second paragraph of his letter to North on July 19, 1925, in Appendix B.

in his lectures anymore.[36] I do not know whether his main reason was Eric's death or the fact that Aeronautical Engineering had become the province of a new department in the College.

Whitehead was always ready to pinch-hit for a colleague. In September 1918 Forsyth's wife was stricken with cancer. Whitehead gave Forsyth's scheduled lectures for him.

After the war, enrollments at the Imperial College rose mightily. By the autumn of 1923 the staff of the Department of Mathematics had increased to twenty-six. Forsyth had just retired; Whitehead took his place as Head of that big department. He did not enjoy the endless attention which he was supposed to give to details.

For many years relations between the Imperial College and the University of London were strained. To get their diplomas, students had to pass both the College's final examinations and the University's. One of Whitehead's last tasks in London was to draw up, with Professor L. N. G. Filon of University College, a substantial memorandum on a sensible solution of this problem.[37]

A radical solution had been urged. The Annual Report of the Governing Body of the College for the year that ended August 31, 1923, spoke well of the idea that the College withdraw from the University of London and be reconstituted as the Imperial University of Science and Technology that the British Empire needed.* Scientists and engineers wanted a bigger place in the sun. This Report of the College's Governing Body approved of the claims made by the alumni comprising the Imperial College Association

> that Science has so far outgrown other branches of learning, and has so varied an outlook, that it provides a special culture of its own, and that students would be attracted to an Imperial University of Science and Technology who are not specially attracted to a *College* or to the University of London.

But Whitehead (in 1917) had argued that technical education, though absolutely necessary and unduly neglected, should be organically related not only to science but to literature.† North Whitehead, himself an engineer, told me he thought his father did not give education in science the dominant position that the twentieth century required it to

---

*In 1919 the Senate of the University had noticed such proposals, and taken no positive action.

†See Chapter III, Section v.

have. In fact Whitehead never forgot that the values of human experience range far beyond the sciences and their applications.

In 1967 T. G. Henderson published a fine short article, "For a Biographer of Whitehead."[38] Tom Henderson was a Canadian graduate student of philosophy at Harvard who became an intimate friend of Alfred and Evelyn. In this article he told of an incident which he was unable to document but related because it "has to do with the sort of thing that could have happened, even though it might be not literally true." Evelyn was undoubtedly its source. As Henderson told it,

> Whitehead was offered the Vice-Chancellorship of the University of London. This offer had to be accepted or rejected at short notice. Whitehead found the decision most difficult, . . . he worried about whether he should assume broader administrative responsibilities than his already held Deanship of the Faculty of Science in the same University, or whether he should concentrate on his teaching and writing. The evening before the answer had to be given, and during the sleepless night, he struggled within himself. Throughout breakfast he discussed the pros and cons with his wife. Finally, without being able to make up his mind, he left the breakfast table to do his current work. As went out of the room he delegated the decision to Mrs. Whitehead and asked her to pass it on by telegraph to the proper authority. But a few minutes later he poked his head through the door and said, "Remember dear, it's God or Mammon."[39]

I have heard the "God or Mammon" story from several people. They did not all agree in identifying the high administrative position offered to Whitehead. But if I understand the man at all, he would in the end have chosen to concentrate on his teaching, thinking, and writing.

Geoffrey C. Lowry, who was later (1934–58) Secretary of the Imperial College, became a member of its staff in the academic year 1923–24. He has recalled that in that year about a dozen professors used to forgather after lunch in a small Common Room.

> Day after day Whitehead held court, and dilated on a tremendous variety of subjects of general interest. Whenever he was present and in the mood to talk, everyone seemed hypnotized by his magnetic personality, and quite content to listen. . . . I never heard of anyone complaining of being bored by Whitehead's monologues.[40]

When Whitehead talked to pupils, he drew them out first of all. With colleagues, he could freely express his views on the subjects that interested him. Almost everything did. He read widely, but never simply to kill time; whether he read fiction or nonfiction, he was in the habit of making a thoughtful response, intellectual and emotional. His interests in his London years became increasingly philosophical. The next two chapters will show how, from 1915 on, he dealt with problems in the philosophy of physics.

vii

By 1920 Whitehead had acquired enough fame to become a recipient of an honorary degree. His highly mathematical *Enquiry Concerning the Principles of Natural Knowledge,* published the year before, had shown that he was much more than the co-author of *Principia Mathematica.* At the University of Manchester, the distinguished mathematician Horace Lamb* presented him for an honorary D.Sc.

In 1922 St. Andrews did the same. Whitehead's friend from his undergraduate days at Trinity College, Cambridge, D'Arcy Thompson,† was Professor of Natural History there. He was also a first-rate classical scholar. And he was unusually knowledgeable in mathematics; his *On Growth and Form* (1917) was epoch-making in what the author called his "heresies," which consisted in treating growth and form in mathematical terms.

When Whitehead, accompanied by Evelyn, came to St. Andrews to receive the honorary degree, they stayed in Thompson's house. It was unfortunate for the development of Whitehead's thought that Thompson was away from St. Andrews. So was his wife. Their sixteen-year-old daughter, Ruth, looked after the guests.‡

In 1923 an honor came to Whitehead in London. He was elected a member of the Athenaeum, under a rule which sanctioned the election of very distinguished persons.

On February 2, 1924, Whitehead's mother died. The funeral was at Ramsgate on February 4. Sarah Buckmaster Whitehead§ was ninety-one, and had been a widow since 1898. In those years she lived occasionally with her son Charles, but mostly with her widowed daughter,

---

*See Volume I, note on page 94.

†See Volume I, pages 82–83.

‡Miss Thompson was terrified of Evelyn, who seemed "grande dame" to her. All she could think of to feed the Whiteheads was salmon. When they left, Evelyn said to her, "Thank you, my dear. I have never eaten so much salmon in my life!" (Ruth D'Arcy Thompson to Victor Lowe, February 21, 1969).

§See Volume I, page 26.

Shirley Blanch; never with Alfred and Evelyn, for wife and mother disliked each other. Whitehead's own relation to her was never close.

He was now nearing retirement, although not facing it. The regulations of the Imperial College required that a faculty member's retirement be considered when he reached the age of fifty-nine, and annually thereafter; at sixty-five, retirement was compulsory. On September 14, 1919, Whitehead wrote to North; "I have two years certain at my post, and in *all probability* another five beyond that." His health had been good, despite an attack of influenza in 1918. In March 1920, when he had just turned fifty-nine, he was informed that he would not be retired at the close of the session in which he reached sixty, that is, on August 31, 1921.[41] He received similar notices about the two following academic years.

It is commonly believed that in 1924, when Harvard offered Whitehead a professorship in philosophy, he had just been retired from his mathematical professorship at the Imperial College. Not so. On June 29, 1923, the Secretary of the College wrote to him that

the College Authorities do not propose to ask you to retire on your reaching the age of sixty-three years. The matter will be again considered a year hence.

As Whitehead would be sixty-three on February 15, 1924, he could have spent the academic year 1924–25 at the Imperial College, had he chosen to do so. But he might, or might not, have found himself retired at its end; or at the end of the session 1925–26; after that, only the making of an extraordinary exception could have staved off his retirement, one year at a time. It was an unhappy situation for a man like Whitehead, who worried easily, enjoyed lecturing, and felt that he had many years of work still in him.

CHAPTER V

First Philosophical Publications

i/London Aristotelian Society. Whitehead's encounter with G. E. Moore at a Joint Session.

ii/Purpose of Whitehead's Pre-speculative Epistemology, 1915–17; preliminaries to Volume IV of *Principia Mathematica*. Progress of the work on Geometry between 1905 and 1914.

iii/"Space, Time, and Relativity," "The Organisation of Thought," "The Anatomy of Some Scientific Ideas." The empirical basis for natural knowledge. The rough world and the smooth world.

iv/Whitehead's analyses of scientific ideas. Method of solving fundamental question of scientific philosophy.

In his "Autobiographical Notes" Whitehead writes: "My philosophic writings started in London, at the latter end of the war. The London Aristotelian Society was a pleasant centre of discussion, and close friendships were formed."[1] Actually Whitehead had already delivered two philosophical papers to the British Association for the Advancement of Science and re-read them to the Aristotelian Society, published these papers along with his educational essays in *The Organisation of Thought,* and was well under way with *An Enquiry Concerning the Principles of Natural Knowledge* by the end of the First World War. If Whitehead himself considered his *Enquiry,* published in 1919, to mark the onset of his philosophical career he might have had in mind the cumulation of his views during the war years. But in the period 1915–17 one finds a quite distinct period in which Whitehead's philosophical ideas began to take shape.

The London Aristotelian Society for the Systematic Study of Philosophy was founded in 1880 with the ideal of "studying philosophy not as an academic subject, but as the story of the development of human thinking." Although the forum of discussion was centered in London, the Society also merged once a year with the Mind Association and the British Psychological Society for the Joint Session at some specified location in the United Kingdom.

When Whitehead joined the Aristotelian Society in 1915, Russell and G. E. Moore had already been active members since 1896. Other prominent members during Whitehead's time included T. P. Nunn, C. Lloyd Morgan, H. Wildon Carr, C. D. Broad, D'Arcy Thompson, Lord Haldane, Norman Kemp Smith, and Samuel Alexander. The Synoptic Index to the Minutes of the Proceedings* from 1915 to 1924 shows Whitehead as a frequent participant, and holding the chair on numerous occasions. Although Whitehead was still a professional mathematician, judging from the variety of philosophical topics listed

---

Principal author, Leemon B. McHenry.

*The actual minutes of the Society from this time did not survive the German bombings of London during the Second World War.

in the Index, the Aristotelian Society would have been appealing to Whitehead the Apostle. During this time Whitehead read seven papers on the philosophical presuppositions of natural science. These papers, along with later papers on science and metaphysics, were republished as *The Interpretation of Science* on the occasion of the hundredth anniversary of Whitehead's birth.[2]

Some of the younger members of the Society remember Whitehead's response to their papers as gentle and encouraging. He always spoke warmly of their efforts, but with the same gentle enthusiasm rebuked what he thought was in error. When Whitehead read a paper I suppose he expected the same courteous treatment, but different philosophic temperaments are bound to clash.

In one quite famous and somewhat amusing incident in a Joint Session, held in Manchester in 1922, Whitehead was the attempted target of one of Moore's rages. Whitehead was reading a paper entitled "The Philosophical Aspect of the Principle of Relativity." In the discussion which ensued, Moore became furious at what he took to be an evasion in Whitehead's answer to the old question of *what* is bent when the stick in water looks bent. Moore advanced excitedly from his seat to the front of the speaker's desk and shook his fists practically in Whitehead's face. But Whitehead simply repeated his answer "the pattern of the molecules,"* and, unperturbed by Moore's raving, continued with his account.[3] Finally, with a gesture of despair, Moore stood with his head in his hands and retreated to his seat.

Although some members present thought Whitehead's behavior a bit mischievous, this seems in perfect keeping with his way of handling heated polemic. In his later philosophical works this becomes evident in that he never thought the progress of thought depended so much on polemic as on the elucidation of premises. In fact Whitehead saw that polemic was in danger of becoming the chief occupation of philosophers. Professor L. J. Russell's memory of the episode with Moore was

---

*A plausible explanation of Whitehead's reply to Moore is contained in his 1917 paper, "The Anatomy of Some Scientific Ideas." In developing his theory of sense-objects of perception, Whitehead says that the thought-objects of perception are "the rock upon which the whole structure of commonsense thought is erected." "But when we consider the limits of its application," he continued, "the evidence is confused" (*AE*, p. 197)— sticks appear bent half in and half out of water. The pattern of molecules *is* bent—namely, the difference between the stick half in and half out of water. Since common sense is deceived we must rely on the disintegration of perception into smaller thought-objects for an adequate explanation.

that even though Whitehead had left quite a few present in the dark, he emerged with "a seraphic smile of triumph."[4]

Moore's obsession with being exactly right, regardless of how tedious the process of getting there, sometimes resulted in a tendency to show outright anger for what he thought to be obscurity or intellectual error. At least this was true insofar as the notion under consideration did not cohere with his common-sense realism. I suspect that another part of the story is the difference between Moore's Edwardian character and Whitehead's thoroughly Victorian manner. Later in this chapter, we shall see that the difference between Whitehead and the Moore-Russell line of thought is more than just one of temperament.

ii

The second phase of Whitehead's work begins with his investigations in the philosophy of natural science. The papers of 1915, 1916, and 1917—entitled, respectively, "Space, Time, and Relativity," "The Organisation of Thought," and "The Anatomy of Some Scientific Ideas"—are the first pieces of writings that would ordinarily be called "philosophical." They are published in *The Organisation of Thought, Educational and Scientific* (1917), and republished with slight omissions* in *The Aims of Education and Other Essays* (1929). In these papers, he has come to questions that are immediately of interest to scientists as a group and to philosophers, not only to mathematicians and logicians.

The early philosophical writings can be characterized generally in terms of the attempt to formulate a pre-speculative epistemology. *Pre-speculative* is a key term here. It signifies a thoroughly empirically based inquiry. Whitehead's central concern is to give an answer to the question of how the evident model of clear and precise knowledge of the world of mathematical physics is arrived at. The resulting epistemological study is one in which logical construction, and physical and psychological knowledge, are all relevant.

Although tempting, it would be a fundamental error to view these works as epistemological preparation undertaken for the construction of Whitehead's later metaphysical system. Reflecting back on his early philosophical writings, he said to me that his works on the foundations of physics were all preliminaries to Volume IV of *Principia Mathe-*

---

*Upon republishing these essays, Whitehead eliminated some technical detail for the non-specialist in mathematics.

matica.[5] His philosophical interests thus grew out of initial motives to provide a logical analysis of space for *Principia.*

Whitehead never completed the *Principia* Geometry, even though he had intended to do so even after he went to Harvard.[6] Six of his letters to Russell, written between 1905 and 1914,[7] document his progress on Volume IV. The completed parts, however, must be presumed to have been destroyed along with the other manuscripts and correspondence after his death. The letters written on April 27, 29, and 30, 1905, show considerable progress in Whitehead's attempt to set out the mathematical foundations of the principles of Geometry, despite some disagreement between him and Russell over how to proceed. Published works by Veblen and Pieri are discussed, and it appears that while Whitehead and Russell were developing the *Principia Mathematica* treatment of relations, they had in mind its application to space. Whitehead has proposed to adopt Veblen's view of Geometry as the study of a single many-termed relation;[8] his immediate task is to develop a notation for triadic, tetradic, and beyond that to *n*-adic relations.

Over five years later, in a letter of September 22, 1910, Whitehead wrote to Russell: "The beginning of Geometry is going beautifully," and reported work on sections ★500 ("Associated Symmetrical and Permutative Triadic Functions"), ★502 ("Associated Relation of a Triadic Function"), ★504 ("Axioms of Permutation and Diversity"), and ★505 ("Axioms of Connection"). Although we cannot discover, from the content of this letter, just exactly how the Geometry developed proposition by proposition, it is likely, given the procedure of the earlier three volumes, that Volume IV began with a Prolegomena to Geometry at ★400.

As late as October 1913, Whitehead's work on the *Principia* Geometry was still proceeding at a steady pace, and in a letter to Russell on October 13th he claimed to have found out what the science is about:

> The whole [subject] depends on the discussion of the connective properties of multiple relations. This is a grand subject. It merges into the discussion of Cl _,* where _ is a cardinal number, preferably inductive. I call such things "multifolds."

Whitehead's reference to "a grand subject" might signal that his conception of the Geometry was becoming very ambitious. In fact, the task

---

*[Victor Lowe's drawing of a mathematical symbol here and after "where" was illegible. —Ed.]

that he set for himself enlarged in a few years well beyond logical foundations to include investigations of the necessary mathematical relations between space, time, and matter.

As far as I know, the last extant letter concerning *Principia* Geometry is dated January 10, 1914, when Whitehead proposed to include his paper "La Théorie Relationniste de l'Espace" in Volume IV.* At this point there is no indication of his plan of an excursion into the philosophy of physics, but quite clearly the whole conception of Geometry as the logical analysis of space required rethinking in light of the Special Theory of Relativity. Whitehead was greatly affected by the revolution in physics that had taken place in the first decade of the twentieth century, but for him the physicist's conception of the interrelations of space, time, and matter that emerged was far too narrow. So, I take it, nothing was more natural than to postpone the completion of the *Principia* in order to "lay the basis of a natural philosophy which is the necessary presupposition of a reorganized speculative physics."[9] For the time, the more interesting and challenging question was, What are the foundations of geometry, considered not as a purely mathematical, but as a physical science?

Whitehead had long held the conviction that mathematics is about the world of things and events. For him, the truth sought in pure mathematics is necessary truth about the world, though we are compelled to express it hypothetically. Russell, on the other hand, dropped a youthful Victorian belief that applied mathematics was superior to pure mathematics because it could make the world better, in favor of the view that the devotee of pure mathematics escapes from the sordid actual world to "a pluralistic, timeless world of Platonic ideas."[10] He held this view, with more or less intensity of feeling, throughout his collaboration with Whitehead. But there is no hint of it in any of Whitehead's writings of that time, and much against it later.[11] His persistent interest was in mathematical theory as applicable to the world, and as the *Principia* Geometry developed he seems to have been pursuing this conviction.

We can be sure that the convulsion of the war was no help to Whitehead's work on the Geometry. In 1959, Russell wrote: "after [Whitehead] had done a lot of the preliminary work, his interest flagged and he abandoned the enterprise for philosophy."[12] But to a group of Harvard students in April 1931, Whitehead attributed his failure to complete the

---

*See Chapter I, Section iv, this volume.

fourth volume in the post-war years to his participation in administrative affairs at the University of London. Even after he had completed *Process and Reality* with its own theory of extension in Part IV, he had hoped, vainly, to return to the fourth volume of *Principia*. But his thought was always pushing on to breaking new ground; he would have had little patience with what would have amounted to backtracking.

The customary division between Whitehead's first mathematical phase and his second phase devoted to the philosophy of natural science is linked by his aim of understanding the nature of mathematics as the most general science of the physical world. Rudiments of this developing position go back as far as his unpublished study of Maxwell's *Electricity and Magnetism* in 1884 and his carefully worked out views in "On Mathematical Concepts of the Material World." But to the large scheme of mathematical work, Whitehead now adds the question of the empirical basis of our knowledge of space, time, and matter. Thus begins the expansion of his enterprise into philosophy. His point of departure concerns the desirability of conducting discussions of relativity on a broad basis, in which the points of view of psychology and of axiomatic foundations of mathematics should be joined to the physical point of view.

iii

While the lengthy paper "The Anatomy of Some Scientific Ideas" appears in *The Organisation of Thought* for the first time, the other two philosophical papers, "Space, Time, and Relativity" and "The Organisation of Thought" were each read to the British Association and the Aristotelian Society. Taken separately these papers reveal slightly different aims. Following the line of thought developed in "La Théorie Relationniste de l'Espace," "Space, Time, and Relativity" attempts to defend the merits of a Leibnizian relational theory of space over a Newtonian or Kantian position, but now brings together problems of space and time. "The Organisation of Thought," on the other hand, attempts to analyze scientific propositions in terms of the generalizations of logical theory; it contains a masterful summary of *Principia Mathematica*. And in "The Anatomy of Some Scientific Ideas," Whitehead is mainly concerned to develop the "fundamental principles of mental construction according to which our conception of the external physical world is constructed."[13] It is particularly noteworthy for its short exposition of the method of extensive abstraction.

Each of these papers is important, but since it would be tedious to analyze each in turn, I shall discuss these works in terms of their common philosophical viewpoint, that is, what I have called "the pre-speculative epistemology."

The central problem with which Whitehead began his epistemological study focuses on the foundations of geometry grounded in our perception of things extended in space. How do we arrive at the precise definitions of geometrical entities—"points," "lines," and "planes," or their temporal analogues "instants" and "intervals of time"—those deceptively simple concepts of space and time in terms of which all exact natural science is expressed? This problem had occupied Whitehead for quite some time before. For instance, on December 10, 1908, he wrote to Russell, "I find that I cannot move a step in Metrical Geometry, until I have clearly settled in my mind the fundamental nature of Geometrical entities."

In "Organisation of Thought" his procedure involved filling the gap between the rough world of our fragmentary individual experiences and the smooth world of science by what he calls an "inferential construction." As he develops the nerve of the epistemological thought, he writes:

> I insist on the radically untidy, ill-adjusted character of the fields of actual experience from which science starts. To grasp this fundamental truth is the first step in wisdom, when constructing a philosophy of science. This fact is concealed by the influence of language, moulded by science, which foists on us exact concepts as though they represented the immediate deliverances of experience. The result is, that we imagine that we have immediate experience of a world of perfectly defined objects implicated in perfectly defined events, which as known to us by the direct deliverance of our senses, happen at exact instants of time, in a space formed by exact points, without parts and without magnitude: the neat, trim, tidy exact world which is the goal of scientific thought.
>
> My contention is, that this world is a world of ideas, and that its internal relations are relations between abstract concepts, and that the elucidation of the precise connection between this world and the feelings of actual experience is the fundamental question of scientific philosophy.[14]

In the same way that we "construct" the things of everyday experience from perceptual data, Whitehead suggests that by a process of refinement, the properties of extension in time and space are narrowed down to the abstractions of scientific thought. Once the analytic knife begins work on the rough, fragmentary perceptual data given to us in immediate experience, the smooth, exact world of science is cut and shaped into "points" and "instants." Such abstractions are the archetypes of the mind's own making; yet they are derived from certain types of relatedness discerned in the perceptual flux.

For all those who concern themselves with the relation of experience to scientific concepts, Whitehead's doctrine of "the rough world and the smooth world" is of utmost importance. It shows how his position is connected, on the one hand, with his examination of geometry and a physical science, and on the other hand, with the criticism of abstractions—what his critics call his "anti-intellectualism"—which dominates *Science and the Modern World*. Notice that there is nothing here that the author of *Process and Reality* need reject. In fact, it does not take much to see the doctrine of the rough world and the smooth world as an early formulation of his later notion of the "Fallacy of Misplaced Concreteness," that is, the error of mistaking the abstract for the concrete, or in the present case, the error of assuming that the smooth properties of geometrical entities are the starting point of science.

In Volume I, I briefly mentioned Russell's recollection of an argument with Whitehead over their different views of the nature of reality.* Russell's rejection of the Hegelian world-view resulted in his seeing the world as a "heap of shot"; each separate shot was as hard and precise a boundary as a Hegelian Absolute, but *externally related* to every other shot in the universe. This was the doctrine that liberated Russell and Moore from the Monistic Idealism that was thought to shackle the advance of science. But Whitehead, says Russell, was the "serpent in this paradise of Mediterranean clarity." Whitehead was all too aware of the vague, ill-adjusted character of our experience of the actual world. It is, he says, more like what one experiences "in the early morning when one first wakes from deep sleep" than "fine weather at noon day." Russell thought this remark horrid until Whitehead showed him

> how to apply the technique of mathematical logic to his vague and higgledy-piggledy world, and dress it up in Sunday clothes that the mathematician could view without being shocked.[15]

Before this encounter, Russell said that his revolt into pluralism led him to believe "that points of space and instants of time were actually existing entities, and that matter might very well be composed of actual

---

*Volume I, pages 292–93.

elements such as physics found convenient."[16] But after 1910 Russell says that he followed Whitehead's lead with new applications of Occam's razor whereby "one could do physics without supposing points and instants to be part of the stuff of the world."[17] Since points and instants could be seen as routes of approximation constructed on the basis of perceptual experience, one need not assume the smooth world to be the world of our perceptual experience. Whitehead makes this abundantly clear when he says that

> fragmentary individual experiences are all that we know, and that all speculation must start from these *disjecta membra* as its sole datum. It is not true that we are directly aware of a smooth running world, which in our speculation we are to conceive as given. In my view the creation of the world is the first unconscious act of speculative thought; and the first task of a self-conscious philosophy is to explain how it has been done.[18]

By calling attention to this problem Whitehead did not mean to imply that our intellectual constructions correspond to no facts.[19] On the contrary, our concepts of geometrical entities are the indispensable subject matter of theoretical physics. But he is quite insistent that we must not make the mistake of "assuming that we are comparing a given world with given perceptions of it." "The physical world," he writes, "is in some general sense of the term, a deduced concept."[20] To pursue Whitehead's procedure for bridging the gap between our perceptual experience and scientific concepts, between the rough world and the smooth world, takes us well into his method of extensive abstraction. Although the full treatment of this procedure must be reserved for the following chapter, where discussion of *The Principles of Natural Knowledge* will be taken up, we should take note of his early formulation expounded in "The Anatomy of Some Scientific Ideas." Here the discussion of the definition of a point will serve as the representative of all "ideal entities" of space and time.

Instead of viewing points as existing in their own right, as entities radically different from anything known in experience (such as defined by Euclid as without parts or magnitude), Whitehead replaces this notion with the definition of a point as an ideal simplicity of converging series of extensive regions. In our sense-perception we may observe lampposts converging to a vanishing point in some crude linear order. But to arrive at the concept of the mathematical point requires considerable abstraction from the given data.

Whitehead begins his procedure by defining "things" in terms of perceptual data, then space in terms of whole-part relations between things. This method is significantly modified in his later works. White-head here takes the sense-object as the particular existent doing the work of both "object" and "event" in *The Principles of Natural Knowledge* and *The Concept of Nature*. A thought-object of perception, on the other hand, is the "thing" built up on the basis of sense-objects. For example, an orange is constructed out of certain associated sense-objects such as shape, color, and scent. This is an actual thought-object of perception. But he proceeds to hypothetical thought-objects of perception which are further constructed by disintegration into smaller parts. These are the thought-objects of science, that is, molecules, atoms, and electrons.

Further abstraction is now required to reach finally the concept of points. Whitehead distinguishes between sense-time and sense-space, and thought-time of perception and thought-space of perception. The former are actually observed time-relations and space-relations between sense-objects. They are discontinuous, fragmentary, and have no points other than a "few sparse instances, sufficient to suggest the logical idea."[21] The latter are the time and space relations which hold between thought-objects of perception. They are continuous rather than fragmentary. With this distinction in mind he now defines the point in terms of thought-objects of perception related together by whole-and-part relations, that is, enclosure, considered as either a time-relation or a space-relation. From the observed fragmentary relations we proceed in thought through a series of successively contained parts toward an ideal simplicity by the law of convergence. A first crude thought-object of perception (i.e., one conceived as in the present of a short duration) takes on the space-relations of its component sense-objects. And it is from this first crude thought-object of perception that Whitehead conceives his method of extensive abstraction to start, but derivatively from the sense-objects.

Proceeding through a series of successively contained parts to an ideal simplicity is at best a route of approximation. But with regard to points, all that is needed is a universal definition of this at-a-point-ness, or punctuality, which stands for an ideal exactness in the determination of spatial position. This gives meaning to the physicist's use of such concepts as "force *at a point*" or "configuration *at an instant.*"

iv

When Whitehead read "Space, Time, and Relativity" to the Aristotelian Society in 1916 he referred to himself as "an amateur" in the science of philosophy, and said that there was no reason to ascribe to his summary of the problems of space and time "any importance except that of a modest reminder."[22] In this first address to professional philosophers, Whitehead seems well aware of his venturing into a new territory where the likes of Carr, Alexander, Russell, and Moore had been reading papers for over twenty years. And from this point of view, it seems natural that his suggestions as to solutions to philosophical problems were made with some reservation. But I doubt whether he lacked confidence in his work. His excessive modesty was more likely to have been a matter of professional courtesy.

What is most interesting about the philosophical views Whitehead developed between 1915 and 1917 (and beyond) is that he seems to have arrived at them independently of the current orthodoxy. This is not to say that he was not influenced by some of the outstanding leaders in the contemporary thought of his time. His anti-Idealist views were in much accord with the dominant neo-Realists, who rejected Idealism as an adequate foundation for the special sciences. But Whitehead's background in mathematics gave him his own line to develop in philosophy. Not only did he have a technical advantage in his approach to certain philosophical problems; he was also spared from being ensnared by the current philosophical language.

Some of the more salient characteristics of his early philosophy now call for attention. As noted above, Whitehead claimed that the elucidation of the precise connection between the world of exact thought and the feelings of actual experience is "the fundamental question of scientific philosophy." My exposition of Whitehead's method of solving this problem will take account of both his affinities and contrasts with some of his contemporary milieu. This is particularly important with regard to his differences with Russell, since the latter had taken up the same problem in *Our Knowledge of the External World*. Of course Russell's language is not quite the same, but his ideas are better known than Whitehead's, even though it was Whitehead who pioneered the techniques Russell used in this work.

Whitehead's method is built around five central ideas.

(1) His point of departure for a discussion of the data of science is an acceptance of the characteristic starting point of British empiricism. In fact he contends that the actual world is none other than

> the relations which exist within that flux of perceptions, sensations, and emotions which forms our experience of life. The panorama yielded by sight, sound, taste, smell, touch, and by more inchoate sensible feelings, is the sole field of activity.[23]

Individual experiences are *all* that we *know*. Both science and metaphysics must start from this same given groundwork, even though they "proceed in opposite directions on their diverse tasks."[24] For the purpose of science, however, Whitehead is especially interested that the formulation of basic concepts (such as life, heredity, matter, molecule, energy, space, time, and number), and the laws which state the relations connecting the various parts of the universe, have their origin in sense-experience.

As already noted in this chapter, Whitehead emphasized the fragmentary, vague, and somewhat disorderly character of our experience of the actual world. This is what we referred to as the "rough world." But by making such a claim about the nature of experience he was not committing himself to an atomistic ontology; nor was he expounding an epistemological theory in the fashion of Hume. For the moment he is excluding the broader metaphysical considerations and asking only about the observational basis of science.

The most fundamental units of his empiricism are the sense-objects. This much of his theory does have an affinity to Hume. For example, Whitehead views percepts such as objects of redness, or the mewing of the cat, to combine in various ways to form our perceptions of the thought-objects. He says sense-objects are distinguished as separate by recognition of either: (i) differences of sense-content, or (ii) time-relations between them other than simultaneity, or (iii) space-relations between them other than coincidence. They arise essentially from recognition of contrast in one way or other within our complete stream of sense-presentation.[25] We must, however, keep in mind that the sense-objects and the thought-objects of perception have a practical function in Whitehead's epistemology, namely, as elements necessary in defining the scientific and geometrical entities of the world of exact thought.

Even though we discern individual sense-objects and thought-objects in our perceptual field, Whitehead makes it clear that there is nothing in isolation. In fact, as he puts the point,

> The perception of red is of a red object in its relations to the whole content of the perceiving consciousness. . . . What we perceive is redness related to other apparents. Our object is the analysis of the relations.[26]

The role of relations in nature occupies a prominent place in all of Whitehead's later thinking. The crucial difference for his metaphysics, however, turns on the distinction between relations and their terms and the "relatedness" of nature in terms of the process of events. On this issue he was never in much sympathy with the type of empiricism espoused by Hume or by Russell and Moore.

(2) Whitehead, conscious of his empiricism, is now committed to a relational theory of space and time. The full treatment of space as the expression of certain properties of the interaction of bodies was worked out in his 1914 paper.* Points are never encountered in perceptual experience. All that we observe are various properties of things in space. But to this he now adds: "It needs very little reflection to convince us that a point in time is no direct deliverance of experience. We live in durations, and not in points."[27] Points of space and time are both deductions from experience, and are definable in terms of relations between material bodies. Like the point, the instant is no longer assumed as a primitive and undefined concept.†

(3) His third idea proposes an independence of science and metaphysics, and it is on this score that his method approaches the narrow "scientific empiricism" of the positivists. This idea will come as something of a surprise to readers of Whitehead's later works, but it is not altogether different from the claim put forth in *The Concept of Nature* that "nature is closed to mind." The central concern of science is the nature of the external world quite apart from the peculiar standpoint of the individual psychology. It is purely matter-of-fact and must by necessity exclude values. Of course this is, in itself, an implicit acknowledgment of the merits of a realist metaphysic, and indeed Whitehead's views here accord quite well with those of Nunn, Lloyd Morgan, and Alexander, but his reasons for excluding all judgments of value, and ontology generally, have a heuristic motive.

Whitehead contends that science cannot wait for the end of the metaphysical debate to determine its own subject matter. It must get on with the data at its immediate disposal, that is, "the facts which form the field of scientific activity,"[28] and not inquire as to how our perceptions relate to some true reality. All that is required is that science gather up these perceptions into a determinate class and add to them "ideal perceptions of an analogous sort, which under assignable circumstances would be obtained."[29] Once this has been satisfied and debated in due course, we can come to some agreement, whereas in metaphysics debate has hith-

---

*See Chapter 1, Section iv, for a full account of "La Théorie Relationniste de l'Espace."

†The treatment of time as "exactly on four legs with that of space" had been a topic of keen interest to Whitehead since 1911, when he was working on the Geometry. See Volume I, page 299.

erto accentuated disagreement. Whitehead imagines that if in some distant generation men arrive at unanimous conclusions on ontological questions, the roles of science and metaphysics may be reversed; but for the present "we must take the case as we find it."[30]

(4) The fourth idea is that of inferential constructions, which, in many respects, is a fresh development of Hume's principle that the connected world we take for granted is in reality a product of the habits of the imagination. Whitehead holds, as we have seen, that the world is constructed by an unconscious act of thought of which philosophy is to make us aware.[31] He adds:

> uniformity does not belong to the immediate relations of the crude data of experience. . . . the uniformity which must be ascribed to experience is of a much more abstract attenuated character than is usually allowed.[32]

The mind supplies the smooth uniformity of the world by an unconscious application of various principles of mental construction. Their origination and their present automatic operation are viewed as due to long ages of historical evolution.[33] We take ourselves to be immediately acquainted with such uniformity in experience, but it is rather inferred from the given fragmentary data. Aside from the sense-objects and various types of relations discerned within the act of experience, everything else is a construction. This is Whitehead's application of Occam's razor admirably referred to by Russell as: "Whenever possible, substitute constructions out of known entities for inferences to unknown entities."[34] This notion combines with his fifth idea to complete his procedure for defining the ideal limits of geometrical entities.

(5) Finally, with mathematical logic, which can precisely specify the conditions required for membership in a class if the class is to have certain formal properties, we can hope to exhibit *all* the concepts of science as concepts of classes of percepts. The process begins with concepts that are directly exhibited (e.g., the whole-part relation as exhibited in space-perception), and proceeds to concepts of classification and order which apply to these primary concepts, and so on, until conceptions are reached

> whose logical relations have a peculiar smoothness. For example, conceptions of mathematical time, of mathematical space, are such smooth conceptions. . . . The problem is to exhibit the concepts of mathematical space and time as the necessary outcome of these fragments by a process of logical building up.[35]

There is little doubt that Whitehead held high hopes for the class theory at this time. It would have been most unnatural to confine the exploration of its possibilities to the concepts of space and time alone.

Having now set out the ideas central to Whitehead's method of solving the fundamental question of scientific philosophy, let us focus on five more characteristics of his thought which anticipate some of his later ideas. Again, these characteristics are helpful to the extent that they define his position in contrast to that of Hume, Russell, and the logical positivists.

(1) Whitehead's attitude toward metaphysics in these early writings is not one of condemnation. Initially the plea for the independence of science and metaphysics has the goal of allowing scientific investigations to proceed without interference from larger ontological and axiological issues. But this is not a suggestion that we do away with metaphysics altogether or that metaphysical thought is merely an impoverished form of poetic expression. Instead, Whitehead recognizes that "Science only renders the metaphysical need more urgent,"[36] for quite clearly the manner in which a scientist approaches his subject matter reflects his implicit metaphysical view. One misinterpretation of these early papers is the supposition that his pre-speculative epistemology is anti-metaphysical. Development of thought in a certain region does not ultimately preclude the importance of larger questions concerning the nature of reality. Whitehead later generalized that all achievement necessitates exclusion. This is what I think he had in mind for the analysis of the perceptual basis of scientific concepts.

(2) In his epistemological study, Whitehead has not entertained any serious doubts about the ability to know the external world. In fact he seems to have completely side-stepped the issue of skepticism; it simply does not interest him. Whitehead is rather concerned with discovering just exactly how exact thought applies to the fragmentary *continua* of experience, that is, with *how* the correspondence is effected.[37] He is concerned with a method which will ultimately satisfy common sense, not contradict it.

(3) As opposed to the methods of Hume, Russell, and the Carnap of *Der logische Aufbau der Welt,* Whitehead does not attempt to construct the concepts of common sense and of science from the building up of a *public* world from *private* experiences. His theory of sense-objects and thought-objects of perception might easily lead one to believe he was working from inside out. But this is not the case. The construction of both actual and hypothetical thought-objects has the aim of the attainment of accuracy, logical smoothness, and completeness of detail. In a

few more years he will denounce the problem of building up publicity from privacy as a false one; now he seems to agree that there is a problem, and he enumerates "universal logical truths, moral and aesthetic truths, and truths embodied in hypothetical propositions" as being "the immediate objects of perception which are other than the mere affections of the perceiving subject."[38] Since his epistemological inquiry does not revolve around the antithesis between the private and the public, his subsequent move into realism will require no revolution in his ideas.

(4) Whitehead's view of the field of perception closely approximates the Jamesian concept of the specious present, and to some extent his later concept of the actual occasion. We must recall that even though the units of his empiricism—the sense-objects—are fundamental to his procedure, they occur as elements within the whole content of the perceiving consciousness. In one place Whitehead refers to the present as a duration which "includes directly perceived time-relations between events contained within it."[39] Our concept of past events is built up by means of repeated applications of a "Principle of Aggregation." Furthermore, with the rejection of the instant as the fundamental temporal unit, he anticipates his doctrine of immanence when he says,

> the present essentially occupies a stretch of time, the distinction between memory and immediate presentation cannot be quite fundamental; for always we have with us the fading present as it becomes the immediate past.[40]

Whitehead was probably acquainted with James's *Psychology* and perhaps heard much of the ingenuity of the concept of the specious present from McTaggart and others. And from this point of view it is clear that his early empiricism is more radical than atomistic; but he was developing his own theory of nature as perceived in "durations."

(5) This leads us to the last aspect of Whitehead's divergence from the standard "scientific" empiricism of his time, namely, his view regarding the *texture* of immediate experience. By *texture* we must understand him to mean not some sort of tactile sensation, but rather the web of uniform relatedness underlying experience. After describing the manner in which he proposes to arrive at "that connected infinite world in which in our thoughts we live," he comments:

> The fact that immediate experience is capable of this deductive superstructure must mean that it itself has a certain uniformity of texture.[41]

As Whitehead had maintained, uniformity does not belong to the "immediate relations of the crude data of experience"; it is rather a result of the process of inferential construction, where refined logical entities are substituted. But now he suggests that the very fact that this is possible provides evidence to believe that there must be some structure of uniform relatedness realized in the very texture of experience.

Whitehead's first philosophical publications are by no means polished works. But in these early papers there is clearly a first effort toward systematization. Aside from the absolute theory of space and time, he seems to have little interest in refuting any particular doctrine or philosopher; he is, however, concerned that any scientific or philosophic endeavor should fit the world to our perceptions, and not the other way around.[42] If we followed the latter procedure, we would be deceived by a false neatness of abstract intellectualism.

The philosophy of natural science propounded in the three important books of the 1920s is an attempt to set out these early ideas in a more precise system. But the foundations had been laid here in this attempt to grapple with the basis of scientific thought and to systematize philosophy afresh.

CHAPTER VI

"Pan-Physics": Whitehead's Philosophy of Natural Science, 1918–1922

i/Growth of reputation as a philosopher. *The Principles of Natural Knowledge, The Concept of Nature,* and *The Principle of Relativity,* Tarner Lectures at Trinity College. Purpose of the lectures.

ii/Whitehead's aims for a "pan-physics." Empirical foundation of physics. Philosophy of natural science as distinguished from philosophy of nature. Attack on the bifurcation of nature. Whitehead's realism.

iii/Events and objects; the ultimate data of science. Perception of time. The doctrine of significance. All-embracingness of reality. Address to the Royal Society of Edinburgh.

iv/The method of Extensive Abstraction. Two purposes of the method. Modifications of earlier view. Definition of the abstractive element.

v/Theory of relativity. Differences from Einstein. Stratified time-systems. Space-time as homalodial. The basis for measurement. J. L. Synge.

vi/Presidential address to the Aristotelian Society; "Uniformity and Contingency." Critique of Hume.

Whitehead gained prominence as a philosopher of science with the publication of the trio: *An Enquiry Concerning the Principles of Natural Knowledge* (1919), *The Concept of Nature* (1920), and *The Principle of Relativity* (1922). All three works were published by the Cambridge University Press.

The period between 1918 and 1922 was one of the most fruitful of Whitehead's life, despite his numerous teaching and administrative responsibilities at the Imperial College and elsewhere in the University of London. In the estimation of many followers of his thought, the philosophy of natural science expounded in these books is a high point of Whitehead's philosophical achievement even though the central idea of process, for which he is best known, is not developed here. The passage of nature is rather treated as a temporal dimension of the extensive relatedness of events.

As we saw in the preceding chapter, Whitehead's philosophical interests grew as he struggled with the question of the logical analysis of space. His *Principles of Natural Knowledge,* in fact, carries the investigation well beyond this initial problem into a much larger epistemological context. The principles developed are fundamental for all natural knowledge in the sense that they should apply not only to any particular natural science but also to everyday observation. The task of constructing such a system involved a philosopher's discernment of what is universal in our apprehension of external nature, and a mathematician's ability to develop a theoretical framework, including a theory of relativity. Whitehead was well equipped with both.

In the preface to his Tarner Lectures, *The Concept of Nature,* Whitehead says that he has been careful to avoid mathematical notation and that "the results of mathematical deductions are assumed." This work is a more polished exposition of the philosophical principles than its pre-

---

Principal author, Leemon B. McHenry.

decessor, *The Principles of Natural Knowledge,* which has mathematical physics as its primary concern. *The Principle of Relativity,* on the other hand, takes as its primary task the deduction of a General Theory of Relativity from the principles of the natural philosophy. For the purpose of this chapter I shall again discuss these works as a unit. With minor inconsistencies the three books develop essentially the same view, even though each has its own emphasis. Elaboration of technical matters in physics will be kept at a bare minimum in order to give full attention to Whitehead's central philosophical contribution.

So far as I know there is no extant correspondence concerning Whitehead's work on *The Principles of Natural Knowledge.* In the preface he says that it was thought out and written during the uncertainty of the war years, always amidst the sounds of guns and the whir of aeroplanes. Mathematical, physical, and philosophical influences all converge in this work with the aim of a new unifying concept for physical theory and research. But even though Whitehead failed to alter the path of physics in any significant sense, his work made a strong impact on the philosophical world. He became associated with the New Realism which dominated British philosophical thought at the onset of the twentieth century, much of which set out to overthrow the neo-Hegelianism of the nineteenth century. Russell, Moore, Alexander, Broad, and Nunn were the dominant figures in Britain, and Whitehead is sometimes included in this wave of thought. The only trouble is that commentators have mistakenly assumed that his views were largely shaped by Russell and Moore.[1]

The line of thought he developed and the success of the work led to his eminence in the field of the philosophy of science. Since Whitehead was still a Fellow of Trinity College, and by far the most distinguished member working in the field of the philosophy of science, he was the obvious choice for the first Tarner Lectureship in 1919.[2]

The Tarner Lectureship was founded in 1916 by George Edward Tarner, who gave Trinity College £1,000 to establish "a lectureship on the philosophy of the sciences and the relations or want of relations between the different departments of knowledge." Today, a lecturer, appointed by the College Council, is chosen about once every three years; he gives a course of public lectures in the University, under the auspices of Trinity College, and is expected to publish them afterward.[3] In Whitehead's time, the lectures were open to members of the University and to the women of Girton and Newnham colleges. Beginning on October 18 and ending on November 29, Whitehead gave seven lectures, one per week. *The Concept of Nature* follows the course of the lectures up to Chapter VIII, where two summary chapters are appended.

The invitation of the Tarner Lectureship gave Whitehead the opportunity to set the ideas of *The Principles of Natural Knowledge* in a new light and communicate his view to a much wider audience. With his central task of attempting to unify the natural sciences under one concept, the purpose of the Tarner Lectures—to explore "the Relations or Want of Relations between the different Departments of Knowledge"—perfectly suited Whitehead's aims.

ii

The term Whitehead chose to describe the scope of his enterprise was *pan-physics*. Curiously enough, he used the term only once—at the onset of *The Principle of Relativity*. It is rather inconspicuously placed, but accurate for describing his concerns. For the modern reader, however, "pan-physics" must not be confused with "physicalism," namely, the view that all is physical. Whitehead's concern here is altogether different. As he says, the philosophy he is limiting himself to "is solely engaged in determining the most general conceptions which apply to things observed by the senses.[4] It is not metaphysics, but rather the unified sciences which have nature as their common subject-matter. In *The Concept of Nature,* he says it is "the endeavour to exhibit all sciences as one science."[5] The common purpose of all three works is to replace the philosophic presuppositions of science, and especially the ancient trinity of time, space, and matter which has dominated scientific thinking, with a coherent set of meanings based on relations exhibited in sensory observation. A reorganization of speculative physics is therefore sought in the interconnection of events discriminated in perceptual experience. It is on this score that Whitehead breaks away from the British tradition. His whole project is conceived as an attempt to set out in concrete terms the status of the indispensable concepts needed in physics, but by emphasizing *relatedness* instead of disconnection between independently real and isolated bits of matter in an absolute space and time. And once physics has been set on a solid footing, the other natural sciences such as biology or astronomy should follow suit.

One of the most illuminating but neglected papers of Whitehead's philosophy of natural science is his "Time, Space, and Material: Are They, and If So in What Sense, the Ultimate Data of Science?"[6] It was delivered in an Aristotelian Society symposium in 1919, and explains in a very concise fashion the central argument of the *Enquiry.* True to form, Whitehead begins with a criticism of the received classical tradition, the concept of nature which underlies Newtonian physics. Our fundamental concept of nature as usually employed in physics has been passed on from century to century by what seems to have been the authority of science, but in reality has only been thrust upon scientific thinking by a naive common sense. Some of this has come about through the force of our practical needs and has been continually maintained by our manner of speaking, but much more to the point, Whitehead finds that the doctrine has its origin in a misconception of the metaphysical status of natural entities beginning with the Greeks.[7] Matter has been conceived as a metaphysical substratum for the properties which we perceive. It has become disconnected from the complex of immediate fact, and survives only as an abstraction of thought. "Thus what is a mere procedure of mind in the translation of sense-awareness into discursive knowledge has been transmuted into a fundamental character of nature."[8] Instead of consistently adhering to what is observed in sense-awareness, the habit of postulating a substratum has prevailed.

The main trouble with the classical view is that it does not stand up to empirical examination; it can give a coherent account of neither change nor causation. The whole conception, Whitehead says in "Space, Time, and Material," has

> every vice of a hasty systematization based on a false simplicity; it does not fit the facts. Its fundamental vice is that it allows of no physical relation between nature at one instant and nature at another instant. . . all that is left to connect nature at one instant with nature at another instant is the identity of material and the comparisons of the similarities and differences made by observant minds.[9]

Furthermore, as far as biology is concerned, the simplicity of the view does violence to the whole idea of organism. "Nothing that is characteristic of life can manifest itself at an instant."[10] The essence of an organism is that its functioning takes time. It is something with spatio-temporal spread, but this simply cannot be expressed in terms of material distribution at different instants.

In order to divest ourselves of the enormous force which the classical concept continues to exercise upon our thinking, we must return to concentrate attention on *observable* nature. The first task of a philosophy of science, according to Whitehead, "should be some general classification of the entities disclosed to us in sense-perception."[11] And if our science has any claim to be based on observation, we must consistently adhere to the empirical data, for this is the only way to shed any remnant of an illegitimate metaphysics. From this perspective, the idea of "nature at an instant" must be rejected from the start as a false abstraction.[12] We do not perceive anything at an instant. This is the warning of the psychological doctrine of the specious present; our awareness of nature rather occurs in the content of temporal slabs—"the ultimate fact for observational knowledge is perception through a duration."[13] From this building block, Whitehead substitutes a wholly different set of entities as the ultimate components of nature.

One might very well want to object to Whitehead's reorganization on the basis that all observational experience is theory-laden and that the attempt to start afresh is itself loaded with conceptual baggage. Whitehead seems not to recognize the force of this criticism. But his point is that by beginning with the ways in which the diversification of nature is interconnected in any one duration, we will be able to explain a broader and more consistently interpreted experience.

In his attempt to demarcate his concerns in constructing a pan-physics from those of metaphysics, Whitehead was quite clear that natural science must omit from consideration the relevance of the knowing mind. This is what is intended by his statement that "nature is closed to mind."[14] In metaphysics, the inclusion of mind in one's fundamental outlook is a necessity for a philosophy of nature, but in the philosophy of natural science "it blows up the whole arena."[15] The concern with nature only as an object of perceptual knowledge, as the terminus of sense-perception, does not involve us in the synthesis of knower and known.[16] Science must be able to conduct investigations and experiments without reference to the fact that what is being studied is known by a mind.

In *The Concept of Nature* Whitehead provides an argument for this position. The basis for nature's closure to mind depends largely upon the adoption of two related points: (i) his definition of nature as "that which we observe in perception through the senses"; and (ii) the realistic premise that the object of sense-observation is not thought but something which is "self-contained as against thought."[17] The first point bears little resemblance to the empiricism of Locke, Berkeley, or Hume; nor is it a simple phenomenalism. What is disclosed to the senses is nature itself, not just a datum in the mind that cannot be checked against reality. The rejection of the concept of knowledge in which the mind knows the world only mediately lies at the heart of Whitehead's protest against the bifurcation of nature. The second point secures the independence of the object of thought from thought itself. When we make an observation, we perceive something that is not mind. That is, the datum for natural science is not at all mental, for if what is perceived is considered a fact of individual psychology only, no scientific assertions about nature can be tested.[18] Science requires objectivity, that is, that its objects be separate and prior to perception and thought. Whitehead's argument here is an attempt to provide a realistic foundation for such a self-contained system of nature. But in doing so the argument "does not carry with it any metaphysical doctrine of the disjunction of nature and mind."[19] It attempts only to set up the basis upon which a limited inquiry can be carried out, namely, the investigation of the coherence of things perceptively known.

Along with his critique of matter, Whitehead delivers a blow to the doctrine that has accompanied the metaphysical substratum view. The bifurcation of nature has grown up alongside the classical concept as a supreme example of incoherence continually fostered by philosophers and scientists. It is the view of nature as partitioned into two systems of reality: a world of phenomenal appearances in the mind, and a world of objects that are the inferred causes of the appearances. More generally, Whitehead's protest is against any view in which there is a division into nature perceived and nature unperceived. The bifurcation of nature reached its peak in seventeenth-century cosmology as the representative theory of perception. Whitehead calls it the "theory of physics additions." Properties of nature are understood as furnished by the perceiving mind, while nature itself is left with elementary particles and the energy that causes the psychic additions. The result is that we end up with two systems of nature which are real in different senses. The reality of matter is never known, but only conjectured, while the reality of appearance is known but remains a dream.[20]

Whitehead argues that there is no way to establish the very distinction between our ways of knowing about the two parts of nature as thus partitioned.[21] The distinction itself is outside of natural knowledge. But science is concerned with the coherence of the known, not with the cause of the known. So any view that bifurcates nature is essentially a failure to make clear the relations between things perceptively known.

As a remedy, Whitehead proposes to view nature as one system of relations; there is no apparent nature, only nature as known in perceptual knowledge. All knowledge of nature must come from within nature. Anything else is an artificial addition.

Undoubtedly Whitehead was sympathetic to the New Realists, with whom he was closely associated, though he was by no means merely one among them. But the Idealist claim that science and metaphysics operated on different levels of reality could not have won his approval. Science was not an "ideal construction" simply because it required the isolation of its objects and external relations. Science and metaphysics are rather different aspects of one human enterprise, namely, the understanding of ourselves and the world in which we live.

The central epistemological point, that what is perceived is not just one's own mental state but a direct apprehension of nature itself, secures the basis of realism, and is not repudiated in Whitehead's later writings. But the character of his realism should have alerted his compatriots. We must see this doctrine as playing a limited role in his thinking for the sake of scientific objectivity. For the moment he is leaving out the character of the percipient event in order to concentrate attention on the perceived event. But even in the philosophy of natural science the conditions for percipience are important for understanding what is disclosed in perception.[22] Perception is considered a natural relation between percipient events and perceived events.

iii

Having given sufficient criticism to the classical view, Whitehead is now prepared to answer the question which he says has been made urgent by modern speculative physics: "What are the ultimate data of science?"[23] This takes the form of a "survey of the kinds of entities which are posited for knowledge in sense-awareness,"[24] and it is at this point that he advances his notion that within any one duration we perceive nature as a complex of events and objects. The sharp distinction between these two types of primitive entities constitutes the most prominent feature of his philosophy at this stage.

When Whitehead introduced his idea of an event in *The Concept of Nature,* he wrote:

> What we discern is the specific character of a place through a period of time. This is what I mean by an "event." We discern some specific character of an event. But in discerning an event we are also aware of its significance as a relatum in the structure of events.[25]

For the philosophy of natural science, events are the primary constituents of reality. As early as "On Mathematical Concepts of the Material World," Whitehead had been heading in this direction,* and with the

---

*See Volume I, page 302.

dematerialization of nature that was implied by the concept of vibratory energy in the field theory, the event was the most likely candidate for the basis of nature. There is no going behind events to find anything more basic or substantial; rather, all aspects of endurance and stability in nature must be explained in terms of events of varying durations. For example, Whitehead raises the point that Cleopatra's Needle on the Embankment in London may not seem to be an event by comparison with the short duration of a traffic accident. "It seems to lack the element of time or transitoriness."[26] But he argues that the abiding structure is simply a relatively stable situation in the stream of events constituting this permanence of character, and the difference between it and the traffic accident is merely one of time-span.

With Whitehead's critique of instantaneous time and his acceptance of the concept of the specious present, the impersonal time of physics and the personal time of psychology are on a closer footing. Mathematical time, like mathematical space, is simply a logical construction. As he puts the point in *The Concept of Nature*:

> Time is known to me as an abstraction from the passage of events. The fundamental fact which renders this abstraction possible is the passing of nature, its development, its creative advance.[27]

At one point he even speculates that perhaps the "alliance of the passage of mind with the passage of nature arises from their both sharing in some ultimate character of passage which dominates all being,"[28] but while noting this affinity, he does not pursue it here. He is, however, concerned to show that the conditions for empirical observation are consistent with what is actually observed as the passage of nature. The events constituting nature and the specious present of the observer both happen as temporal slabs.

Every observation of external nature reveals certain facts concerning events. Whitehead calls these facts the "constants of externality"; they are the assumptions common to all the sciences of nature and chiefly concern the relations called "extension" and "cogredience." It is important to keep in mind the primary role extension plays in understanding Whitehead's view of the passage of nature here. Extension exhibits events as actual matters of fact which issue in various spatial and temporal relations. As in the pre-speculative epistemology, this is defined by whole-part relations and is crucial to the "method of extensive abstraction." Events are nestled in one another so that overlapping and inclusion occur. Cogredience, on the other hand, is the "preservation of unbroken quality of standpoint within the duration."[29] It is the definition of a presented expanse by a percipient event, that is, how our awareness of nature occurs from within and defines our unequivocal "here."[30] The significance of the relation of cogredience is crucial to Whitehead's attempt to characterize the perception-from-a-standpoint-here-and-now for "the relativistic conclusion that individual perceptivity is the ultimate physical fact."[31]

We should return, for the moment, to consider further Whitehead's basic distinction between events and objects in the diversification of nature. Events are here and now; they happen once and do not repeat themselves. Objects, on the other hand, are the *recognita* discriminated in any one complex of events. They are the things that can happen again and retain their identity across time. Repetition of objects in the passage of nature is what makes science possible. The discovery of the laws of nature, for instance, is due to the fact that the characters of events repeat themselves in some fairly stable fashion. Whitehead distinguishes three different kinds of objects: "sense-objects" such as individual colors, sounds, or textures; "perceptual objects" such as the ordinary macroscopic bodies of perceptual experience; and "scientific objects" such as electrons and molecules. The sense-objects are the empirical building-blocks that are compounded in various ways to form the perceptual objects. The scientific objects, however, perform quite a different function in the system of natural knowledge. Although never observed directly, they are conceived as necessary for the physicist's task of obtaining a simple expression of the character of events. The scientific objects are therefore crucial to the whole basis of physical measurement: they are "the things in nature to which the formulae refer."[32]

The concept of "ingression" is introduced here and retained throughout Whitehead's later metaphysical thought. It expresses the general relation of objects to events, that is, how the object is an ingredient in and throughout some duration of nature. The different types of objects discriminated in events express different "modes" of ingression. That is, every type of object has its own peculiar relation to an event and so issues in a different mode of ingression.

The whole apparatus of events as providing the situation for objects was originally put forth to correspond to a difference evident in perception rather than as a metaphysical duality. But in making the distinction, the crucial point to keep in mind for Whitehead's epistemology is that all we know of nature is in nature itself and not bifurcated into a system in which scientific objects constitute the true reality and sense-objects have a derivative status in the mind only. As Whitehead puts the point, "the red glow of the sunset should be as much part of nature as are the molecules and electric waves by which men of science would 'explain' the phenomenon."[33]

The theory of perception which underlies Whitehead's whole philosophy of natural science contains an important distinction between what he calls, in *The Concept of Nature*, "the discerned" and "the discernible," and in *The Principle of Relativity*, "cognizance by adjective" and "cognizance by relatedness."[34] Besides the entities of the field that are directly perceived, we are aware of distant entities as mere relata. They are undiscriminated as to quality, but nonetheless must be included in order to complete the spatial relations of that which is perceived. The discernible might be something as simple as the unperceived center of a billiard ball or as complex as the spatial relations beyond our star-system.

The discerned and the discernible lie at the core of Whitehead's doctrine of significance. This is essentially his view that sense-awareness involves these two distinct but inseparable types of awareness. What is discerned is always a part of the broader field of the discernible. In fact, significance means that the events whose characters are not discerned are known through being signified, in a uniform manner, by other events. Previously, in "Space, Time, and Relativity," Whitehead had put this notion in terms of a uniform texture of immediate experience. The expansion of this ascription of "texture" into a central doctrine was probably due to his search—evident in the essays of 1915–17—for the best way to formulate the ideal or hypothetical perceptions that seemed to be necessary additions to sense-data if geometry, smooth and complete enough to be a scientific concept, was to be constructed.[35]

In a note that Whitehead appended to *The Concept of Nature* while reading proof, he removes the limitation of significance to space-relations within a duration, and argues for a wider application. There is a significance of a percipient event "involving its extension through a whole time-system [of durations] backwards and forwards," he reasons. "In other words, the essential 'beyond' in nature is a definite beyond in time as well as in space."[36] He considers this an improvement because it furthers the assimilation of time and space in one theory of extension.

The most thorough exposition of the doctrine of significance is contained in a lecture entitled "The Relatedness of Nature," delivered before the Royal Society of Edinburgh in 1922. It is reprinted as Chapter II of *The Principle of Relativity*. Aside from being thorough, it is also quite an advance over the doctrine in *The Concept of Nature*.

Whitehead began his lecture by saying that he felt some "natural diffidence" in speaking upon the theme of relatedness "in the capital of British metaphysics, haunted by the shade of Hume."[37] Instead of beginning with fact as a multiplicity of subjects qualified by predicates, Whitehead conceives of "fact as a relationship of factors" and then argues for a ground of uniformity in nature. The polyadic relations of *Principia Mathematica* which Russell once said gave thought wings now play an important role in Whitehead's treatment of nature. By "fact" he has in mind the present-whole of immediate experience, or the all-embracingness of reality, in which a multiplicity of "factors" are embedded. Factors include not only the various types of objects but also the finite events in which objects have their ingression. The process of discriminating such factors Whitehead calls "cogitation."* He distinguishes two kinds of awareness of nature: awareness "by adjective" and awareness "by relatedness."[38]

Every factor we discriminate is an abstraction from the totality of nature; the discrimination effects a limitation within that totality; the discriminated factor *signifies* factors other than itself. I can see and touch the things in the room where I sit, but I am not completely ignorant of the events now going on in the closed room next door. What I can know about those events, I know by relatedness, not by adjective. Generally speaking, I can be aware of an object by adjective and aware of its significance as a relatum, but I do not need to know all the related factors by adjective in order to see how that factor has a place in a larger system of fact.

In applying this doctrine to scientific objects, Whitehead argues that hypothetical entities such as electrons have been introduced as more precise adjectival objects which reduce the contingency of nature. The electron itself is a contingency but a much more simplified one than the sort involved in the complex relationships of sense-objects. The "historical route" of an electron is the *same* adjective qualifying events from the past to the present and on into the future. Whitehead thus conceives the aim of science as the reduction of contingency by the discovery of adjectives that explain causal relations.

---

*In his wife's copy of *The Principle of Relativity* Whitehead here wrote in the margin: "'Cogitation' is a bad term; 'Demonstration' is better; or even 'Abstraction.'"

iv

Given the overall framework of events and objects, we must now turn our attention to the ingenious logical procedure Whitehead invented for defining the elements of space and time out of the fundamental relation of extension. "Extensive Abstraction" is the name he gave to this technical instrument. It is the procedure which takes us gradually from the rough world of ragged-edged events to the smooth world of physics. Moreover, it serves as the crux of his whole system of natural knowledge, for the essential notions of "points," "lines," and "instants" must find their place within the fabric of science despite being unperceivable. The smooth world of speculative physics now receives a more precise articulation by being defined as certain logical functions of what is perceived in durations.

There are several expositions of this technical device between 1905 and 1929. Some are indeed very complex, since the range of entities requiring definition involves Whitehead in special applications of suitable abstractive classes in each case. For our purposes, however, we need grasp only a broad outline of his procedure and examine its central philosophical significance. In this section I shall focus attention on the procedure Whitehead put forth in *The Principles of Natural Knowledge,* and to some extent, his modifications in *The Concept of Nature.*

In Chapter V, I explained the basic problems with which Whitehead was concerned in developing this method. With one stroke he attempts to solve two different but related problems: (i) to give the relational theory of space and time the exact mathematical formulation its previous adherents neglected to provide; and (ii) to answer the epistemological question (of central importance for an empirical science), "How is the space of physics based on experience?" According to the relational point of view, anyone who makes a statement about a point P in physical space is really talking about a certain set of relations between extended things. But what are these relata and relations? By this formulation of the problem, the interest in "bridging the gap" between spatial experience and scientific concepts is centered upon a demand for a definition of the point of physical space, that is, the space in which natural phenomena occur, and which the mathematical physicist has in mind when he writes ordinary differential equations. Of course we require similar definitions for all "ideal" spatial and temporal entities, but if the refinement to points can be accomplished, then we can easily define all the other geometrical entities of physics as well.

The importance of the role events play in Whitehead's thought now results in a significant modification of his procedure in the 1915–17 papers. The principles of inferential construction also fade from the picture and are replaced by a more rigorous application of the logic of classes. The change in world-view, however, is the most important change to keep in mind; events with volume and duration replace sense-objects as the basic particulars within which his method operates. That is, Whitehead conceives space- and time-relations as holding between four-dimensional events instead of sense-objects or thought-objects or perceptions. This is certainly an improvement in that he escapes criticisms to which his earlier view was subject. The pre-speculative epistemology suggested to a stronger degree that all the geometrical concepts could be built up from perceptions. But if this were literally the case, our perceptions of diminishing volumes would terminate in a finite number, and points, lines, and places would never be reached. Quite clearly the properties of extension involve a conceptual element in that they are contributed by the mind rather than by sense-perception. The awareness of nature as a present-whole requires that we put these conceptual elements to work. Otherwise we should have no idea of how the parts of this whole are apprehended as extensively related events. Although Whitehead never attempted to construct the elements of space and time from pure sensa alone (as Russell did), his change of framework to events puts him on a more solid footing.

In the *Enquiry* Whitehead begins his systematic development of extensive abstraction with a set of axioms that state the fundamental properties of the whole-and-part relation of extension. The key notion is that events extend over one another either spatially or temporally or in both ways. For the sake of lucid exposition we will ignore the temporal dimension of events and substitute the term *volume* for *event*, provided that we keep in mind that the term stands not for the volumes of pure geometry but for portions of the expanse of nature displayed in perception, like the volume of the room in which we sit. Whitehead states that the relation of extending over is transitive (i.e., if *A* extends over *B* and *B* extends over *C*, then *A* extends over *C*) and asymmetrical; that its field is compact or dense (i.e., between any two volumes, one of which encloses another, there is a third which encloses the second and is enclosed by the first); that every volume encloses other volumes and is itself enclosed by other volumes; and that for any two volumes there exists a third enclosing both of them.[39] The spatial continuity of nature is further expressed by the assumption that every volume joins others. This relation of junction is defined in terms of extensions, and will make it possible to speak of two volumes as having an exact common boundary—if we have made the general assumption that volumes have exact demarcations instead of the vague ones they exhibit in perception.

The next step in the method is the definition of "abstractive sets" of volumes. This sets up the framework that makes possible a convergence to simplicity with diminution of extent. To get a clear idea of how Whitehead is proceeding at this stage we should imagine a set of spheres concentric to a certain point. But neither this notion of a point, nor that of any regular geometrical figure, enters into the definition. The abstractive set is defined by only two conditions: (i) of any two of its volumes, one encloses the other; and (ii) there is no volume which is a common part of every volume of the set. Hence each set is composed of an infinite series of successively smaller volumes that converge without arriving at a final volume. Abstractive sets are now conceived in terms of classes and types of classes such that sets which diminish in all three dimensions are distinguished from those which diminish in one or two dimensions only; thus sets which are needed to define points are separated from those which are needed to define lines and planes. In the process of convergence certain relations are excluded or simplified, but this is precisely the process whereby the ideal simplicity is reached. The "abstractive element" (point, line, plane, etc.) is defined as the class of all equivalent abstractive sets of the same type. As Whitehead puts it:

> An "abstractive element" is the whole group of abstractive sets which are equal to any one of themselves. Thus all abstractive sets belonging to the same element are equal and converge to the same intrinsic character.[40]

Having arrived at this definition, Whitehead's procedure allows us to translate any statement about points into a statement about abstractive elements. For example, the statement "points A and B are two feet apart" can be translated into the language of extensive abstraction to mean "abstractive elements A and B are such that by going down their tail-ends we can always find a volume x in A and a volume y in B such that the distance between x and y approximates two feet within any limit, however small, that we may wish to assign." The abstractive element therefore replaces the notion of a point as an entity radically different from anything known in our experience of the physical world, but believed to be an ideal limit of diminution of extensions.

Perhaps the most common error in attempting to understand Whitehead's method of arriving at points or any of the other geometrical entities is in thinking that they are actually reached as the end of the process of abstraction. We might be inclined to think of points as tiny extended entities, or as limits of diminishing volumes, but this is not the way Whitehead is thinking of them. This is, in fact, to raise the very problem he is attempting to solve: to define points without having to ascribe to them the same ontological status as perceptible volumes. Whitehead is conceiving points, lines, and planes as entities of a higher logical type which have all of the formal properties they had before, but denying them the status of real volumes. They are mere ideals of thought to which the members of the representative abstractive sets approximate more and more down toward the smaller ends. The great merit of defining the geometrical entities in this manner is that they are viewed as logical functions of extension instead of actual particulars of nature, yet they do the same mathematical work that is required.

In *The Concept of Nature* the procedure of extensive abstraction is further clarified by the introduction of quantitative series of measurements.[41] Whitehead begins by defining the successive members of the abstractive sets as

$$s - e_1, e_2, e_3, \ldots, e_n, e_{n+1}, \ldots$$

and then the quantitative expressions as

$$q(s) - q(e_1), q(e_2), q(e_3), \ldots, q(e_n), q(e_{n+1}), \ldots$$

which characterize the relations of the successive volumes. Whitehead now argues that even though s will converge to nothing (since the series is infinite), the set of quantitative expressions $q(s)$ converges to a class of limits $l(s)$. A series of quantitative measurements

$$Q - Q_1, Q_2, Q_3, \ldots, Q_n, Q_{n+1}, \ldots$$

corresponds to the members of $q(s)$ and may converge to a definite limit in the class $l(s)$. So even though an abstractive set of convergent volumes does not terminate in one final volume, but rather generates an infinite number of unobserved volumes from a finite number of observed volumes, the ideal limit is approached in the quantitative series. As Whitehead says, "the set s does indicate an ideal simplicity of natural relations, though this simplicity is not the character of any actual [volume] in s."[42]

From the methodological point of view, Whitehead's procedure is the exact opposite of that of Descartes. Instead of starting with geometry and then working to find a fit with observed phenomena, Whitehead defines the exact concepts of space and time out of the relations contained within perceptible durations. This gives him the advantage of not having to assume that the relation between experience and geometry is a solid bridge. In his view it is rather a continual process of refinement to abstraction. He says that the object of this method compares with that of the differential calculus in that "it converts a process of approximation into an instrument of exact thought."[43] But where the differential calculus determines unknown quantities from known ones, extensive abstraction begins with perceptible volumes and determines routes of approximation for geometrical entities by repeated applications of the principle of convergence to simplicity.

V

Between 1914 and 1924 Whitehead's normal teaching at the Imperial College consisted in standard courses in applied mathematics. The chief exception was lecturing on relativity, which was very close to his own research.

The theory of relativity exercised an enormous influence on Whitehead's thinking, as it did on every other live mind that had an interest in physics or the philosophy of science. As we have seen, its main effect on him was that it accelerated the application of his logical and epistemological studies on a grand scale. A comparison of *The Principles of Natural Knowledge* with his earlier writings suggests that among specific ideas, thinking about the idea of time was what the physical theory most sharply stimulated in him. He had long been peculiarly interested in relating geometry to motion, and had he not been consumed by the *Principia* collaboration and by the educational activities he plunged into afterward, he might have worked out a theory of space-time much earlier.

When he published his theory of relativity in 1922, the works of Larmor, Lorentz, Einstein, and Minkowski had been thoroughly digested by physicists. Whitehead was clearly conscious of the debt he owed these thinkers. But while he had great praise for their works, he was also acutely aware of many serious problems in the foundations of the new synthesis. As he so aptly stated at the conclusion of Part I of *The Principles of Relativity,* "the worst homage we can pay to genius is to accept uncritically formulations of truths which we owe to it."[44]

The bulk of Whitehead's criticism of the emerging scientific theory is centered on Einstein. In what follows I shall limit my discussion to three points of Whitehead's disagreement with Einstein: (i) the basis for constructing a general theory of relativity; (ii) the underlying uniformity of space-time; and (iii) the basis for measurement.

Whitehead wrote a short piece in the London *Times Educational Sup-*

plement in 1920 entitled "Einstein's Theory: An Alternative Suggestion."[45] For the general reader it is the clearest statement of his disagreements with Einstein. Whitehead, for example, argues that Einstein's
invariant property of the velocity of light is at odds with the results of
his later Theory of General Relativity. Three other papers concerning
relativity were delivered to the Aristotelian Society by Whitehead in
1922 and 1923, the most important being "The Philosophical Aspects of
the Principle of Relativity," the other two as short contributions to
discussions, "The Idealistic Interpretation of Einstein's Theory" and
"The Problem of Simultaneity: Is There a Paradox in the Principle
of Relativity in Regard to the Relation of Time Measured to Time
Lived?" The first two of these papers document Whitehead's skepticism
regarding the compatibility of the theory of relativity with philosophical idealism of the Berkeleian sort. They are certainly worth reading as
clarifications of the character of his realism at the time.

 The Principle of Relativity is virtually unintelligible apart from the
system of natural knowledge he worked out in the *Enquiry*. Unlike
Einstein's procedure of developing a General Theory from the limited
applications of his Special Theory, Whitehead's theory of relativity is
based on the results of his earlier investigations in geometry and ki-
nematics. For him, Einstein had constructed his theory upon an empirical foundation that was too narrowly restricted to laboratory operations. Whitehead thus constructs his theory without reference to
"special facts" pertaining to the measured velocity of light or to other
observations.

 The central focus of Whitehead's theory is the notion of stratified
time-systems within a four-dimensional space-time manifold. This sets
up the basis for his explanation of the relative motion of objects.

 He begins with the fundamental facts of observation, namely, durations, which are events with finite temporal and infinite spatial extension. He then postulates different families of durations to define different time-systems, and by an application of his method of extensive
abstraction arrives at the various loci of four-dimensional space-time.
The definition of parallel durations is the crucial starting point. Durations are parallel when any two are extended over by a third; otherwise
they are non-parallel. Now if we take an abstractive set of durations as
converging to a *moment*, thus defining the abstractive element, we ob-
tain a three-dimensional section as our ideal limit. The families of parallel durations and their parallel moments are understood as constituting
the succession of time in any one system. In fact, for Whitehead, time is

the abstraction of parallel moments from the sense of passage within parallel durations.

What distinguishes his theory of relativity from Newton's is the recognition of an indefinite number of families of parallel durations constituting different time-systems.[46] The parallel durations constituting any one time-system are non-interesting and define a Euclidean space. Each time-system is thus analogous to a Newtonian absolute space and time on its own. But where the different time-systems do intersect (via non-parallel moments), Whitehead is able to construct the geometry of the four-dimensional manifold. Two non-parallel moments intersect in a *level* and form an instantaneous plane in the time-system of either moment. Three moments intersect in a *rect*, or an instantaneous straight line. And four moments intersect in a *punct*, or an instantaneous point. Parallelism of levels and rects is then defined by various types of relations within a set of parallel moments, that is, within any one time-system. This establishes the continuity of the geometry across the time-systems.

Having arrived at the definition of parallelism as a type of succession in any one time-system, Whitehead now brings into focus the importance of cogredience for the basis of motion and rest in the theory of relativity. Cogredience, we recall, is the extension of a finite event throughout a duration. If we regard the duration as the content of the specious present of an observer, a cogredient event is a part of this content which lasts through the whole duration and does not change its position relative to the body of the percipient during the specious present. The finite event can be some particular body or event-particle which occupies successive positions in one time-system. A body at rest is simply the historical route intersecting the moments of our time-system in a sequence of instantaneous points. It is at rest for an observer whose specious present includes this body within the permanent space of that time-system. But relative to the space of *another* time-system, this body is moving in a straight line. The intersection of these two time-systems thus defines the perpendicular, and it is on this basis that motion and rest gain their meaning in the theory of relativity. That is, motion and rest depend on the time-system that is fundamental for the observation.[47]

By means of a complex system of event-particles, routes, stations, and point-tracks, Whitehead works out in precise manner the details of the stratified time-systems from which he defines motion and rest. The most important point of this mathematical apparatus, however, is that the whole of space-time is derived from the basis of events and that its structure is simply the underlying order of extension, of which physics investigates the contingent relations and geometry expresses its uniform relatedness.[48]

This uniform structure of space-time formed from the basis of alternative time-systems marks Whitehead's most distinctive contrast with Einstein. It also discloses the connecting thread between his system of natural knowledge and his theory of relativity.

Einstein came to the conclusion that space-time is heterogeneous, that is, that the structure varies with its contents because of peculiarities in the distribution of matter throughout the universe. For example, Einstein argues that at every point of physical space the state of matter at that point defines the metrical character of the space-time continuum. The presence of matter distorts the uniform space-time structure and results in a curved space-time. But in Whitehead's view, this is an unnecessary conclusion since it largely depends upon acceptance of the traditional concept of matter. Once the metric of space is defined in terms of objects ingredient in events, no essential connection is required with the distribution of matter. Objects in events form patterns, and the space-time of our perception is conceived as continuously uniform with the more refined space-time of scientific objects.

For Whitehead, the kind of uniform significance which lies at the base of nature is most obvious in our own specious present. That is, the manner in which any one duration includes constituent events embedded in a whole-part relatedness is considered analogous to the way in which extensive events in nature form a homalodial space-time continuum. It is on this score that Whitehead achieves a thoroughly consistent epistemology lying behind his relativity. It is also crucial for his alternative theory of measurement.

Given the sketch of Whitehead's theory of relativity presented thus far, time and space as yet have no metrical properties—only relations of order. But the uniformity central to Whitehead's non-metrical geometry is understood as presupposed in every application of metrics. For him the very possibility of measurement depends on exact congruence between regions of space. Otherwise we should not have any standard for determining what we mean by certain distances.

Whitehead argues that Einstein's heterogeneous space-time structure leads to the result that there can be no definite rules of congruence which apply in all cases. Since Einstein's theory depends on operational procedures involving the transmission of light signals, measurement depends on the contingencies of the physical field. But this being the case, there can be no conditions which remain the same for the operations of measurement. As Whitehead argues: "Practical measurement merely requires practical conformity to definite conditions. The theoretical analysis of the practice requires the theoretical geometrical basis."[49]

With the definitions of parallelism and perpendicularity in hand, he pursues his analysis of congruence in the multi-dimensional framework of alternative time-systems. Congruence applies to the comparison of spatial regions within alternative time-systems. The resulting measurement will depend on the fact that congruent geometrical elements repeat each other. For Whitehead, congruence is founded on this notion of repetition.

Whitehead's theory of relativity did not fare well with physicists. Eddington, who had done much to get Einstein's work accepted, remarked in 1933 that he could now see that in some respects the philosopher's insight had been superior, but that it had come out of season for the physicist.[50]

About 1951 the theoretical physicist John L. Synge published three lectures which he gave at the University of Maryland, *The Relativity Theory of A. N. Whitehead*.[51] In 1961 he wrote to me from the Dublin Institute for Advanced Studies:

> I was a champion for Whitehead for two reasons. First, there were some things in Einstein's theory I found obscure, and I disliked the way people discussed these matters. Secondly, I thought Whitehead had not been paid due attention, and my contribution was really to dig out his essential formula from his verbiage and to display it for physicists to view.[52]

Study of a paper by G. L. Clark, "The Problem of Two Bodies in Whitehead's Theory," tore Synge away from Whitehead, "because it seemed that his theory led to incorrect results." Synge then wrote a book on Einstein's Special Theory of Relativity, and another on the General Theory. Here is how he concluded his letter to me:

> Whitehead, ingenious as he was, is not in the same street. Perhaps I might put it this way. The further you go with Einstein, the richer the view, but with Whitehead the reverse is true.[53]

vi

In November 1922 Whitehead read his presidential address, "Uniformity and Contingency," to the Aristotelian Society.[54] Besides carrying on his philosophy of natural science, it constitutes his chief discussion in his London years of Hume's skepticism. The first of his many quotations from Hume is:

> An annalist or historian, who should undertake to write the history of Europe during any century, would be influenced by the connexion of contiguity in time and place. All events, which happen in that portion of space, and period of time, are comprehended in his design, tho' in other respects different and disconnected. They have still a species of unity, amidst all their diversity. [55]

Thus Hume accepts the reign of space and time. It is the basis of his critique of the idea of necessary connection among events. Whitehead notes that when Hume writes of the constant conjunction of events and the attendance of one event on another, those words

> must mean spatio-temporal contiguity, or else the whole point of his explanation of the idea of causation is lost. Accordingly the spatio-temporal character of nature is a presupposition of Hume's philosophy. I am not making any objection to Hume's assumption; far from it, I am claiming his support. What Hume says of the history of Europe is true of any set of events. [56]

Whitehead remarks that the expectation of the usual "is the essence of Hume's doctrine."[57] His criticism begins when he says that Hume took it for granted that the experiencing subject has been awake, not dreaming. But some dreams are usual; and a good nightmare is as vivid an experience as Hume could wish. Only the failure of the dream to fit into the uniformity of space and time proves the unreality of its content. Whitehead cites his own dreams of hovering.[58] In 1930 I heard him tell a Harvard seminar about one of those dreams: when he awoke he said, "I can definitely hover."

Hume's point, that there is nothing in the accumulation of similar instances to justify our belief in their continued recurrence, evokes this undeniable comment:

> It follows, that, if we are to get out of Hume's difficulty, we must find something in each single instance, different from every single instance, which would justify the belief. [59]

It was typical of Whitehead to say that he was not solving Hume's problem, only indicating the direction in which a solution could be found. He does not offer a description of the nature of a human experience, alternative to Hume's description, until he presents his Gifford Lectures six years later.*

In terms of the different kinds of objects he discriminates in nature, Whitehead expresses his insistence on causation by asserting that it is the very nature of perceptual objects to be controls of the ingression of sense-objects. Perceptual objects, if not knowable as adjectives of events, are knowable by relatedness, through being signified in a uniform way.

Just before he sailed for America in 1924, Whitehead wrote six short Notes for a second edition of the *Principles of Natural Knowledge*. In Note III he said that he no longer held the class-theory of perceptual objects in any form, and was trying in this book to get away from it. I think that his temporary adherence to a class-theory resulted from his collaboration with Russell on *Principia Mathematica*.

Whitehead's assessment of Hume is completely fair. The biblical reference is typical.

> The rational conclusion from Hume's philosophy has been drawn by those among the lillies of the field, who take no thought for the morrow. Hume admits this conclusion.[60]

But Hume adds that all human life must perish if lived in accordance with principles like his.

> I wonder how Hume knows this: it must be that there is some element in our knowledge of nature which his philosophy has failed to take account of.[61]

"Uniformity and Contingency" was not composed with only the eighteenth century in mind. Whitehead continues:

> Bertrand Russell adopts Hume's position. He says:—"If, however, we know of a very large number of cases in which A is followed by B and few or none in which the sequence fails, we shall in *practice* be justified in saying 'A causes B' provided we do not attach to the notion of cause any of the metaphysical superstitions that have gathered about the word."
>
> Again I should like to know how Russell has acquired the piece of information which he has emphasized by italics—"we shall in *practice* be justified, etc."

---

*But in a lecture he gave in 1927, he took issue with Hume's denial of causal efficacy; see Chapter X, Section viii.

I do not like this habit among philosophers, of having recourse to secret stores of information, which are not allowed for in their system of philosophy. They are the ghost of Berkeley's "God," and are about as communicative.[62]

Having secured the notion of causation from Hume's skepticism, Whitehead concludes "Uniformity and Contingency" with a few words in praise of John Maynard Keynes on probability and the problem of induction. Keynes had submitted a fellowship dissertation on probability to King's College in 1907, and Whitehead had been asked to judge its merit.[63] He thought that frequency theories of probability ought to have received more serious consideration than Keynes gave them. So Keynes did not receive the fellowship until later.

Migration to Harvard

On February 6, 1924, the President of Harvard University, A. Lawrence Lowell, wrote to Whitehead, asking whether he would accept an appointment as Professor of Philosophy for five years at $8,000 a year. (That was then the top salary at Harvard.) A complex story lies behind this invitation.

The first decade of the twentieth century had seen the golden days of philosophy there, with William James, Josiah Royce, George Herbert Palmer, George Santayana, and Hugo Münsterberg. (Münsterberg was primarily a psychologist; until 1934 Psychology was not a department but an appendage to Philosophy.) James retired in 1907 and died in 1910; in 1912 Santayana went to Europe for the rest of his life; Palmer reached retirement age in 1913; Royce and Münsterberg died in 1916. Late in 1919 the Professors of Philosophy—James Haughton Woods, William Ernest Hocking, and Ralph Barton Perry—undertook responsibility for finding men who could bring the Department's standing up again. Bergson, Russell, and John Dewey were sounded out.

A unique but seldom remembered merit of the old department was Royce's expertise in the philosophy of science; he had also offered courses in symbolic logic, and brought *Principia Mathematica* to the attention of graduate students. The Department would have a strong man in the philosophy of science if Whitehead could be persuaded to join it. Woods, as chairman, wrote to President Lowell about Whitehead on March 10, 1920. Lowell replied, "We must go slowly about Whitehead. . . . We must refrain rather ruthlessly from all additions that can be avoided." He feared a large deficit would be caused by a prospective raising of salaries.[1]

Nothing more was done until the fall of 1923. This time the idea of inviting Whitehead was put to Lowell by the biochemist Lawrence J. Henderson, and the necessary money was supplied by Henry Osborn Taylor.

Henderson was one of a group of about two dozen Harvard scientists who called themselves "the Royce Club." They took this name after Royce's death, for he had formed the group to meet regularly for supper and discussion of issues in the philosophy of science. On October 13 and 14 Henderson and two other members of the Royce Club, the entomologist William Morton Wheeler and the applied mathematician E. B. Wilson, were weekend guests at Taylor's estate in Cobalt, Connecticut.[2] Henderson—probably on a visit to England that summer— had learned how close Whitehead was to retirement at the Imperial College of Science and Technology.* Either Henderson or Taylor quoted Bergson as saying that Whitehead was the best philosopher writing in English.[3] All the men knew and liked some of Whitehead's work; they felt it highly desirable that Harvard should get him.[4] The upshot was that Henderson went to see Lowell. He was told that there was no money. Taylor's pledge removed Lowell's objection. Even after Harvard, at the end of 1926, changed the tenure of the appointment from five years to "without limit of time," either Taylor or his wife, Julia Isham Taylor, annually paid a sum equal to Whitehead's salary—until he retired in 1937.† The Whiteheads knew nothing of this until after Taylor's death in 1941.

Henry Osborn Taylor was not a member of any academic faculty and had not been since youth. He was well-to-do, a scholarly historian with philosophical views. (His *Medieval Mind* appeared in 1911.) When he made his pledge to Lowell, Taylor was almost seventy, childless, and a strong friend of Harvard College. The Taylors had come to know Whitehead on a visit to London, a few weeks before.[5]

In an account of Whitehead's appointment written in 1961 by Hocking, Lowell's letter of February 6 is not mentioned. Hocking wrote instead:

> On February 4, President Lowell sent by way of Taylor a formal offer to Whitehead, with the appended remark: If you cable, you can add that the professors in the Department of Philosophy are delighted with the prospect of his coming.[6]

No cable was sent, and the delivery of Lowell's letter of February 6 was delayed a week by a strike of dockworkers in Plymouth.[7]

Whitehead's friend Mark Barr,‡ living in New York at this time,

---

*For information about the Royce Club I am indebted to Hocking's excellent article, cited in note 6 of this chapter.

†Whitehead's salary was kept at the statutory limit, which was raised to $9,000 in 1927, and to $12,000 in 1930.

‡See Chapter IV, Section v.

was a confidential friend of Taylor's. Early in January Barr sounded out Whitehead, writing him that there was "a chance at Harvard"[8] of a five-year appointment. On January 13 Whitehead sent Barr a highly significant letter in reply:

> If the post should be offered to me, I should find the idea of going to Harvard for five years very attractive. The post might give me a welcome opportunity of developing in systematic form my ideas on Logic, the Philosophy of Science, Metaphysics, and some more general questions, half philosophical and half practical, such as Education. . . . I do not feel inclined to undertake the systematic training of students in the critical study of other philosophers. . . . If however I should be working with colleagues who would undertake this side of the work, I should greatly value the opportunity of expressing in lectures and in less formal manner the philosophical ideas which have accumulated in my mind.[9]

Twice in the course of his reply Whitehead wrote that he could not commit himself in response to an "unauthorized" letter. Taylor next enlisted Barr's help in an effort to nail the appointment down. On February 4 Taylor got a telegraphed assurance from Henderson: "Full agreement President and Chairman Department Philosophy." In a letter he wrote to President Lowell the next day Taylor, after mentioning the telegram, continued:

> Thereupon I saw Mr. Barr and asked him to cable Whitehead that an invitation had been mailed him for a five years professorship at Harvard. This was to prepare him and forestall accidents.

Taylor then suggested that Lowell send Whitehead the formal offer in writing at once. The President obliged with his letter of February 6, mentioned at the beginning of this chapter.

The delivery of that letter was delayed a week by a dockworkers' strike in Plymouth. Thus Taylor's trick of getting Barr to cable Whitehead that an offer had been mailed before it *was* mailed—indeed, a day before the President wrote it—had an unexpected utility.

Whitehead's forty years in academic positions, culminating in his London administrative work, had taught him—if so reticent a man needed the teaching—not to count on, or even talk about, a job offer until it came in writing from the person authorized to make it. I should be astonished if someone were to produce evidence that Whitehead talked about his Harvard offer before he had the offer in hand. The interesting question is whether he kept silence even to Evelyn. I think he did. The opportunity that fate was giving him for his old age was too special to share prematurely. Of course action on the offer would be decided with Evelyn; but she was not privy beforehand, if there is any truth in Lucien Price's account of the arrival of Lowell's letter:

> The invitation to Harvard came in 1924, a complete surprise. The letter was handed him by his wife on an afternoon which was dismal without and within. He read it as they sat by their fire, then handed it to her. She read it, and asked, "What do you think of it?" To her astonishment he said, "I would rather do that than anything in the world."[10]

Whitehead did not need to, or want to, mull over the Harvard offer, and Evelyn liked the adventure. In Whitehead's letter of acceptance to Lowell on February 24, he raised just one question: was he right "in supposing that there will be a sum allocated for the expense of moving my household from England to Cambridge?" Someone, most likely Taylor, had mentioned this to him. Lowell replied that $1,000 would be paid to Whitehead for this purpose. In his letter of April 6 Whitehead astutely said: "It will be more convenient if it can be paid into my bank account in Cambridge. If it comes to England, one-third of it will go in income-tax."

For Whitehead, the great thing about coming to Harvard as a professor of philosophy was that he would be free to do just what he most wanted to do—to develop the philosophical ideas that had accumulated in his mind, and to express them in lectures.

There was an end to his heavy load of administrative work at the Imperial College and in the University of London, and an end to teaching the mathematical subjects that he knew too well. But not an end to teacher-pupil relationships, which were always an essential part of his enjoyment of life. He said to Evelyn, "I have long wanted to teach philosophy."[11] He would not have to make any effort to maintain the freedom Harvard gave him. It was part of his welcome.

The same mail that brought President Lowell's letter of February 6, 1924, brought one sent the same day by Professor Woods.

> As Chairman of the Department, I wish to say how glad each member feels at the thought that you may decide to come. There is no difficulty in arranging the plans of the Department so that you could give your energy to the problems which interest you most.

Woods then asked whether Whitehead would like to give a lecture course on the philosophy of science, and devote one evening a week to discussion of metaphysics and logic with graduate students. These were the very subjects that Whitehead had mentioned in his January 13 letter to Mark Barr. Woods's letter ended,

> We should welcome you and Mrs. Whitehead with the utmost enthusiasm, and we shall try to protect you from everything that would interfere with the development of your thinking.

What more could he hope?

ii

Whitehead left London for Liverpool on August 15, 1924, and sailed for Boston on the SS *Devonian* the next day. He and his wife took her maid with them; Mary had come to work for them as a young, untrained girl, had been in their London house for several years, and was attached to them; she was willing to come to the American Cambridge. Bringing her along was an example of that good judgment in practical matters which Evelyn Whitehead had all her life. Mary's presence made everything easier.

Jessie Whitehead stayed in London but was expected to join them a year later.

Whitehead began and finished such an incredible amount of philosophical work in his first years at Harvard that one is tempted to suppose he must have used the twelve days of the transatlantic voyage to get a head start. He was not in a race, but he wanted, as always, to spend a couple of hours of each day thinking and writing. Unfortunately, he was not a good sailor. And he was too naturally courteous a man to shut himself off for long from other passengers. On the ninth day out he wrote to his son, North, "I have not been able to do any writing on board—either too jumpy (at the beginning), or too much desultory conversation since the fine weather." "Jumpy" is explained by what he had written four days earlier: "Intellectual operations have hitherto been reduced to the basic principle of not being seasick" in rough weather.

The *Devonian* was to reach Boston Harbor Tuesday afternoon, August 26. Instead he was writing in the middle of that afternoon:

Darling North

> Such a disappointment—just when we were off Boston harbour, about to pick up the pilot in half-an-hour, a sudden storm struck us and is still keeping it up. They say that it has come up from the Gulf of Mexico—anyhow it is a very healthy

production. It was quite smooth before lunch—our luggage
piled in the passages ready for landing, everybody tipped,
goodbyes said and cards exchanged—when suddenly the wind
began to howl, etc.—just like the stage storm in Wagner's Der
Fliegende Holländer introducing the hero—the imitation on
Nature's part is quite perfect.

America had greeted the immigrant philosopher with a summer
hurricane. It was the first in his experience. But as a boy he had grown
up beside the wicked Narrow Seas, in Ramsgate, where the harbor
works had been built to provide a haven for ships in distress between
Dover Strait and the mouth of the Thames. Nature's violence was a fact
of human life. In his letter to his son Whitehead wrote:

> One silly woman came up to apologise to us for the inclement nature
> of the American weather which was greeting us. We assured her that
> we blamed the Creator far more than the Yankees. She seemed quite
> relieved at our taking that view of it.

The *Devonian* had to contend only with the edge of this hurricane—a
liner a little farther out to sea nearly sank—and was able to anchor at the
Quarantine Station that night.

Getting off the boat and through immigration and customs the next
morning was a matter of one long wait after another. Whitehead's
account of the process in the letter he wrote to North that evening is
amusing. It will be found in Appendix B.

Although the Whiteheads knew no established Harvard people, four
persons were on the pier to greet them when they finally got off the boat
at 11:30. The four had been there since 8 o'clock.[12] Whitehead was the
sort of person for whom Americans, without being asked, went out of
their way to do things. The four were Woods, Henry Osborn Taylor
and his wife, who had come up from their home in New York City, and
Marjorie Tuppan.[13] Miss Tuppan (of Gloucester, Massachusetts) had
been in London a few years earlier as a research student (in economics)
from Bryn Mawr College. The Whiteheads had taken her into their
house one Christmas and become fond of her, and she of them.

Woods, at fifty-nine, was the oldest of the tenured philosophers at
Harvard. His teacher, William James, had suggested that he enter the
field of Indian philosophy. He became expert in it, in Far Eastern
thought, and in Greek philosophy. He is now forgotten because he
published so little. He was a Boston gentleman and scholar with an
independent income, not a member of the new breed of professional
philosophers. He was intensely proud of the Harvard Philosophy De-

partment, and raised money from outside sources to strengthen it. Woods was the one who got assurance from President Lowell that he would not veto Whitehead's appointment on grounds of age (as he had vetoed the offer of a professorship to John Dewey). Jim Woods—tall, well built, goateed—was a very fine person, with an old-fashioned kind of wit and humor. Whitehead felt more at ease with him than with anyone else in the Department. The first day in Cambridge was all that Woods needed to make Whitehead feel at home in the Harvard Yard. Thereafter Woods helped him with everything, and for many years was his most valued colleague in the Philosophy Department.[14]

iii

Everyone seemed to conspire to make the first day on American soil easy and pleasant. The twenty-five pieces of luggage, scattered in the passageways when the hurricane struck, were all together on the pier. A transfer company took the big pieces to a fine, smallish house at 116 Brattle Street. It had been engaged for the Whiteheads from September through May. The traveling luggage went with the party into two automobiles provided by Osborn Taylor.[15] The destination was an unoccupied apartment in Radnor Hall, on Memorial Drive. It belonged to another friend, the Oxford psychologist William McDougall, who had joined the Harvard faculty a few years earlier. The Whiteheads would stay there until the house was ready for occupancy. Woods then took Whitehead to the Colonial Club (predecessor of the Harvard Faculty Club) for lunch, and showed him the Yard and the rooms of Emerson Hall, where he would teach.

Whitehead liked Cambridge at once. It was more like the English Cambridge than any other American university town could be. He and Evelyn were so pleased with McDougall's riverside apartment that Evelyn tried to rent another in the same building, and succeeded. Her gamble also succeeded: a new tenant took the house on Brattle Street at once. Whitehead wrote to North on October 4, "People are rather astonished that Mummy managed to acquire simultaneously one of the most desirable small houses and one of the most desirable flats in Cambridge, things that people wait years for." This was a sample of Evelyn Whitehead's quick genius in practical matters.

The apartment at 504 Radnor Hall was perfect for them. It was an easy walk—Whitehead loved walking—to both the Harvard and Radcliffe Yards. The living room and the study were reasonably spacious, the dining room was just right for small dinners, the study was large enough to accommodate the seminary (as Harvard called seminars) that would meet there on Friday evenings, and there was a room for Jessie and one for Mary. What Whitehead liked best of all was the view down and over the Charles River. And it was easy for Evelyn to furnish the apartment graciously. The $1,000 that Harvard was paying for transporting the Whitehead household across the Atlantic was more than enough. The high American tariff* enabled them to bring from their London flat the furniture that Evelyn guessed they would want and a quantity of books: the steamship lines would rather carry such things to the United States for a pittance than sail with holds nearly empty of merchandise.

iv

"I don't understand," Whitehead had written to North, "why people go for a sea-voyage to rest; it doesn't act that way with us." His first lecture would not be until September 23. Although he had hoped to leave England in time to arrive at the beginning of August, he still had plenty of time to rest from the voyage in his comfortable flat, and to write his first lectures in philosophy.

Whitehead named the lecture course "Philosophical Presuppositions of Science." It would meet Tuesdays, Thursdays, and Saturdays at nine o'clock in Radcliffe College, then at twelve in Emerson Hall. (This was the Harvard-Radcliffe system all through Whitehead's years.)

He would have an assistant to take care of routine chores and read students' papers. For this job Woods recommended, and the Department chose, the most experienced of its untenured members, Raphael Demos, who was thirty-two and had been Instructor and Tutor in Philosophy for five years. Demos was the sort of young man Whitehead found most interesting.

Born Demetracopoulos, he had come to Cambridge as a poor immigrant eleven years before; as a graduate student he had caught Bertrand Russell's attention when Russell was Visiting Lecturer at Harvard in 1914. Demos was absorbed in metaphysics (he had once given the Department's course in it) and—like Whitehead—was a passionate admirer of Plato. Demos and Whitehead had met in London in 1919, for young Demos had impressed the Harvard Department, earned his Ph.D. quickly, and been enabled to study for a year in the English Cambridge.

---

*Imposed by the Fordney-McCumber Act of 1922.

Demos told me[16] that he could not recall that first conversation, but vividly remembered the one which occurred upon his being assigned to assist Whitehead. Whitehead took him by the arm, said "Let me explain my philosophy to you," and walked him up and down in front of Emerson Hall for more than an hour, expounding his world-view. Demos did not tell him that he did not understand it at all.[17]

Of course Whitehead felt some anxiety about lecturing for the first time on philosophy. Just how should he teach the ideas he wanted to expound, to students of whose capacities he knew nothing? And he was a bit worried about not having the general competence in his discipline which he had had when he taught mathematics, and which a professor in Harvard University should have. He was certainly competent in the philosophy of physics, but his main intention was to go beyond that, from the data of science and the concepts underlying spatio-temporal measurement to all sides of our experience of nature. He wanted to discuss idealism versus realism, and the basis of knowledge of the past and of the future, and to explore in a fresh way the ineluctable dualities of human existence—becoming and perishing, time and the timeless, actuality and possibility, individuality and continuity, fact and value. He had never been too shy to talk about these big subjects. Perhaps no one is. But conversation about them was one thing, lectures at Harvard another. So it was that in a letter, written the following April to North, who was taking on a new job, he said:

> I do so sympathize with you about having the wind up, over facing work above one's size and weight. Throughout my whole life, I have been facing a series of situations of that kind. I don't think I am at all modest as to the things which I know I can do. But somehow the actual tasks, which I have had to undertake, have always involved a lot of things for which I know that I am incompetent.* And as to my lectures here when the session opened—Oh my!

As Whitehead's course was listed as a middle-level one, he could assume that his students were familiar with Aristotelian logic, some of Plato's Dialogues, and the general positions of the chief modern phi-

---

*In his first teaching job (1884) Whitehead was an Assistant Lecturer in Mathematics at Trinity College, Cambridge; he was to give honors students, in small classes, the special preparation for the Mathematical Tripos which it was customary to get from a coach. Whitehead knew that he lacked the intimate knowledge of these examinations which the coaches had. The last task that Whitehead had to undertake in his mathematical career was to assume the chairmanship of the large Department of Mathematics at the Imperial College in London when Forsyth retired in 1923. It was not his forte.

losophers. The presentation of his own ideas would involve contrasting them with those doctrines in the European tradition which he accepted and those which he rejected, especially in the thought of Plato, Descartes, Newton, and Hume. He had begun to reflect on some of them decades earlier, and in recent publications had included some criticism of Aristotelian logic and of Hume.* He felt quite sure that he was right in the basic criticisms he would make of Descartes' position and Hume's. But he would not undertake an examination of their texts, or write lists of their premises on the blackboard. What he had to say would not be said as a scholar; his fresh approach would in fact be more valuable; but the selectiveness of his learning might be noticed. Well, he could handle that, by confessing it. In fact, he made a habit of exaggerating his ignorance.

v

The lectures began on Tuesday, September 23. The Harvard philosophers all came to Emerson Hall to hear the first one, along with almost all the graduate students and the college seniors who were concentrating in philosophy. Harvard had caught an original thinker, the most distinguished man who had recently written in English on the philosophy of science. What did he have to say to them?

James Wilkinson Miller, then a freshman graduate student—he would become one of Whitehead's junior colleagues, and finally professor of philosophy at McGill University—sent me his recollection:

> After the appropriate interval following the stroke of the bell, Whitehead came in, dressed in nineteenth-century style, looking like Mr. Pickwick, and beaming benevolently.[18]

The chairman of the Department, Professor Woods, came with him to the platform and gave a short speech of introduction. Whitehead began by saying what an honor it was to be at Harvard—the university of William James. He probably mentioned other famous names. Then he launched at once into his lecture, which he had specially prepared for this occasion.

There does not seem to be any transcript of what Whitehead said. What is certain is that he surprised and dumbfounded his audience. Demos was probably the only one who had a notion of what was

---

*See Chapter VI, Section vi.

coming. The others thought of Whitehead as an expert in the philosophy of natural science, of physics in particular. They expected that his
lectures would be from the point of view of the book they knew, his
Concept of Nature (1920), with perhaps occasional deviations into *Principia Mathematica*. Nothing of the sort came from Whitehead's mouth.
As Miller remembers it,

> the opening lecture plunged us into a morass of absolutely unin-
> telligible metaphysics. . . . His longest and most difficult sentences
> all ended . . . with the gleaming words, " . . . you know." We, of
> course, didn't know *anything*, so far as that lecture was concerned.
> When the hour ended we were completely baffled, and in despair
> about the course, but we were also all in love with Whitehead as a
> person for somehow the overwhelming magic of his being had
> shown through.[19]

Miller was a student of epistemology and logic, of Hume and Russell;
he had little sympathy with metaphysics. This orientation was strong at
Harvard; half of Whitehead's hearers were like Miller. The best-known
professional philosopher among them, Ralph Barton Perry, said afterward, "Those generalizations are too sweeping."[20] A younger man,
Henry Sheffer, was the one who taught symbolic logic and carried on
research in it. He was heard to mutter as he left the room, "Pure
Bergsonianism: Pure Bergsonianism!"[21] In this Department, that was
name-calling; one talked about facts and logical relations, not about
becoming or "process" and "reality"; profundity was out, cool analysis
was in. It might in some sense be true, as Whitehead said, that "we
experience the universe," but one did not dwell on this kind of fact.

Demos remembers Whitehead's first lecture as a kind of oration. He
told me that in his conclusion "the angels were singing."

The professor whose interests were broader than those of anyone
else, Woods, was probably pleased. So, I am sure, was Ernest Hocking;
he was the unashamed metaphysician among them. The others, and the
students, would simply have to learn what kind of thinker was here.

The title that Whitehead had supplied for his course was "Philosophical Presuppositions of Science." Miller and his friends would expect
presupposition to be treated as a logical relation between propositions.
Russell would have written on the blackboard some sentence expressing a proposition, like "Tuberculosis is caused by Koch's bacillus," and
explained that it presupposes that some diseases are caused by bacilli,
and that every disease has a cause.

But Whitehead wanted to talk about the dependence of a scientist's conscious activity of identifying and investigating a phenomenon on the general features of his experiencing the world, both features which as a scientist he sets aside—for example, the values of nature—and those which he uses, like the distinction between possibility and actuality. In Whitehead's practice, philosophy became the endeavor to describe the totality from which scientists abstract. This had first place in his mind. Just before he left England, he had written in a Preface for the second edition of his *Enquiry Concerning the Principles of Natural Knowledge,* "I hope in the immediate future to embody the standpoint of these volumes (that on *The Concept of Nature* and *The Principle of Relativity*) in a more complete metaphysical study." But this intention was not generally known: the second edition of the *Enquiry* would not be published until 1925.

The next year, and for three years thereafter, Whitehead gave his course a title that warned the unwary: "Philosophy of Science. General Metaphysical Problems." The students now enrolled would get a little less metaphysics and more philosophy of mathematics and of physics in the second semester than in this one; that was because Whitehead's lecture course and his seminar went with each other, in Whitehead's mind and for the graduate students; and Woods's suggestion, accepted by Whitehead, was that he offer a first-term seminar in metaphysics and a second-term seminar in logic. Consequently, this autumn, graduate students heard Whitehead's metaphysical ideas in lectures and discussed them with him in the seminar.

vi

How did Whitehead spend a lecturing day in his first term?* At nine o'clock he lectured at Radcliffe to nine or ten undergraduate and postgraduate women; only four of these were taking his course for credit. He then went to an office in Widener Library that Harvard had given him, to look over his notes. After refreshing himself with an orange and a little sandwich, he went to the Colonial Club for a short rest and a look at the English news in the New York papers. At the twelve o'clock lecture in Emerson Hall, his audience was about forty men, including some of the faculty. More than half were auditors who wanted to hear him expound his philosophy. "At the end of the lecture men come up

---

*I draw on the description contained in his letter to North, November 9, 1924. The full text of the letter will be found in Appendix B.

and ask questions. I usually make an appointment or two for a chat in my room at some other time." By about a quarter of two, he would be home for lunch and a rest. After tea, he read or wrote up lectures. "We dine at seven, and go to bed at any time between 9 and 11." Whitehead was an early riser.

He told North in a later letter, "I lecture on what I like, and examine the men on my own course."[22] To keep the credit students from worrying about their grades while they were trying to understand his ideas, he made a habit of not giving any grades lower than B minus.

Whitehead did not "deliver" his lectures. Seated in a chair behind a table on the platform, he spoke to the class, which did not interrupt him. Occasionally he consulted what he had written down for his guidance. He did not keep those notes. I have not found anyone who attended the lectures at Harvard in 1924–25, took detailed notes, and kept them. But Louise R. Heath kindly supplied me with her notes of Whitehead's lectures at Radcliffe that year. The ideas that he presented in the first weeks are of most interest, for he was expounding his own philosophy, the ideas that, as I said in Section i, had accumulated in his mind. On October 21 Professor Hocking began to attend the lectures. His notes from then to the end of the academic year may be found in Appendix 1 of Lewis S. Ford's *The Emergence of Whitehead's Metaphysics*.[23] Those notes are valuable, because Whitehead enlarged or changed his thought as he went on in the course. Sometimes he began a lecture by saying he had been muddled in the preceding one.

Dr. Heath's notes of the early lectures[24] show that Whitehead began by saying that each age has its dominant philosophy, which reveals some aspect of a rationalism in human life. He proposed to elucidate the nature of the scientific movement not by looking for the scientist's motives—that is a psychological business—but by asking what there is in the nature of things which requires that science should have the character it has. This is a metaphysical question. But metaphysics, Whitehead said, is more than an exploration of the presuppositions of science; its business is the critical appreciation of the whole intellectual background of man's life; it is as near to poetry as to science.

In the first lecture at Radcliffe, and repeatedly thereafter, Whitehead insisted on the essential *togetherness* of things. In the past, he said, this was obscured by Aristotelian classification and its success. He maintained the "complete relativity of reality," and was expressing it "from the point of view of a realist who finds Spinoza the most significant of modern philosophers." Early in the Radcliffe lectures Whitehead declared that reality was process, or becoming, in which a social entity is realized. "True reality is achievement of reactive significance." Of course, nothing becomes in an instant of time; but the continuity of the flux exhibits atomic structures as embedded in itself.

When Whitehead said that we must start from experience, he noted Hume's skeptical argument about knowledge of other occasions of experience. He then repeated the sharp criticism of it that he had expressed in his presidential address to the Aristotelian Society two years earlier, and concluded that Hume left scientific generalizations without any justification. (The title of that presidential address was "Uniformity and Contingency";* it is a neglected classic.)

Soon Whitehead took up the status of physical objects. He presented three theories: (i) the substance theory; he thought it "a linguistic cook-up" to reduce all relations to predicates of substance; (ii) Bertrand Russell's theory that the object is a class of sense-data; is that what a boy perceives when he catches a ball? (iii) Whitehead's own theory that the percipient somewhat vaguely but very insistently apprehends the conditioning of the sensory data; Whitehead only suggested this theory, which he did not affirm in print until *Symbolism: Its Meaning and Effect* was published in 1927.

After remarking that for scientists electromagnetic phenomena "on the whole give us the fundamental elements on which the universe is built up," Whitehead devoted several lectures to an exposition of Maxwell's Equations for the electromagnetic field. He was as untechnical as he could be. "Curl" and "divergence" did not appear, and instead of speaking of differentials, he spoke of a temporal rate of variation and a spatial rate of variation. He went on to the post-Maxwellian discoveries of electrons and protons, and to Planck's constant. His idea was to give, as background for discussion of the physicist's presuppositions, some idea of the world as the physicist saw it. I do not think that in later years he repeated his heroically untechnical exposition of Maxwell's Equations.

Still, I was surprised to see how much of the language and doctrine of *Science and the Modern World* Whitehead used in his first lectures at Radcliffe. The "fallacy of misplaced concreteness" is there. So is the claim that modern science was born of the union of methodical observation and a conviction of the rationality of God. And he spent a good deal of time on his theory (not expressed after that book) that both electrons and protons are built of ultimate corpuscles which he called

---

*See Chapter VI, Section vi.

primates. An ingredient of the lectures which is absent from *Science and the Modern World* and from Whitehead's later publications is frequent criticism of Russell's position on the issues discussed in the lectures.*

A few other points in Whitehead's early lectures at Radcliffe should be noted. He remarked that the process of becoming, which is reality, is open to consciousness, but an individual's consciousness is aware of only a small part of it. Process is essentially transition to otherness in which something is always retained. We should think of the existence, both of an atom and of a living thing, as rhythmic. (Whitehead called attention to the chapter on rhythms in his *Enquiry*.) Biology is the youngest of the sciences, and the study of physiological process has as good a chance as any other for the discovery of new *physical* facts. "No finite entity (Spinoza's modes)" is in itself independently real, but is "a mere abstraction." And of course he came down hard on using "configuration at an instant" as a basic concept in physical explanation.

From what Whitehead said in his first lectures, it appears that most of the key ideas of his mature philosophy were in his mind when he arrived from England; they needed precise verbalization, review, and further development into a system.† On November 23, writing to North about his lectures, he could say, "I am gradually feeling my way into a metaphysical position which I feel sure is the right way of looking at things."

vii

Whitehead met his seminar on metaphysics Friday evenings from 7:30 to 9:30. According to his own class book, fifteen students enrolled in it in the fall of 1924. A few faculty members also attended. A student read a paper on an assigned topic. Whitehead usually started the discussion, then broke in from time to time. He wrote to North on November 9:

> It is great fun. The men‡ really discuss very well, with great urbanity and desire to get at the truth. There is rather less assertiveness and aggressive running of set theories than there would be at Oxford or

---

*For example, Whitehead discussed Russell's Introduction to the English translation of A. V. Vasiliev's *Space-Time-Motion*, which Whitehead had recommended to his class.

†In "Whitehead as I Knew Him" Hocking wrote, "Any impression that he began his mature philosophical work in America is far from the fact."

‡This is Whitehead's slip. There were a few women in the seminar.

Cambridge. Also, of course, they are not so witty, or epigrammatic. Any epigrams, that there are about, are let loose by me. I cannot exaggerate to you how much the educated well-bred American dislikes bounce or assertiveness.

(Much has changed in American universities since 1924.)

At the beginning of the fall term several graduate students in philosophy went together to Whitehead and asked if he would give a course on *Principia Mathematica*.[25] He answered that he would consider making it the topic of his seminar on logic in the second half of the academic year. One of those graduate students, Charles A. Baylis, informed me that when the time came Whitehead held discussions of ★1–★5, "The Theory of Deduction," with which the system of the *Principia* began.[26] Those articles presented only the primitive ideas and propositions which were used in the logic of elementary propositions (propositions which make no reference to "all" or "some"), the definition of *implication,* and the immediate consequences of these. Whitehead explained that the controversial definition of "*p* implies *q*" as "either *p* is false or *q* is true"* was harmless; but he did not, so far as Baylis remembered, discuss C. I. Lewis's sharp criticism of it.† Sheffer and Eaton attended this seminar, but Lewis did not. He was working on his epistemology, and Sheffer always worked alone; there was little interchange between the three eminent mathematical logicians in the Harvard Philosophy Department at this time.

Another student in the seminar on logic was a very bright senior in Harvard College, J. Robert Oppenheimer. According to his memory, Whitehead

> gave a seminar on the Principia, and we worked through it at a pace, which was both breakneck and shambling. From time to time he would come to a theorem which puzzled him, and typically he would say, "Well that was one of Bertie's ideas." I learned a lot from him, perhaps more than I needed to know of mathematical logic and a little, for one never knows enough, of the greatness of the human spirit.[27]

It is not possible that the seminar "worked through" the three volumes of the *Principia,* at any pace, in one semester. But ★1–★5 occupy only 37

---

*This is known as Russellian or material implication.

†This, and Russell's answer to it (which might be summarized as "The definition is harmless"), were set forth in Volume I, page 267.

out of almost 2,000 pages. Surely Whitehead selected some later articles of the *Principia* for exposition and comment; this would account for the "breakneck and shambling pace" that Oppenheimer remembered.

viii

In Whitehead's 1924 correspondence with Lowell and Woods, work with individual graduate students was not mentioned. But when he wrote to Woods on February 24 to accept his suggestions about the lecture course and seminars, he added,

> I shall expect, and hope, that individual students, or groups of students, may find it profitable to come to me at other times for informal discussion.

On September 24, Susanne Langer wrote to Whitehead at Woods's suggestion.[28] She was a Radcliffe graduate student, and wanted Whitehead's guidance in the writing of her Ph.D. thesis. She was living in Worcester, Massachusetts, where her husband, the historian William L. Langer, was teaching at Clark University. She came in by train to attend Whitehead's Friday evening seminar, and for an individual conference about once a month.[29] Her thesis was in symbolic logic. His direct supervision of it was minimal: he read a few pages of an early draft, to see if she had a good idea. After he saw that she did, she submitted nothing more until the thesis was completed.[30] There was none of the chapter-by-chapter blue-penciling that became customary when America went in for the mass production of Ph.D.s after the Second World War. In Whitehead's time, the candidates were assumed to be grown up, and the professors were assumed to be engaged in research when not teaching.

Mrs. Langer's first published work was an article, "Confusion of Symbols and Confusion of Logical Types."[31] It disagreed with Russell's handling of that subject in the second edition (for which he alone was responsible) of *Principia Mathematica*. She took the manuscript to Whitehead, who said he could find nothing wrong with it. He then sent it to the editor of *Mind*, G. E. Moore, asking him to publish it and, if he had any doubts about that, to send it to Russell.[32]

Dissatisfied graduate students, if they were philosophizing along unusual lines, found a champion in Whitehead. Scott Buchanan was such a student. The Department was not inclined to accept his Ph.D. thesis, "Possibility," but Whitehead persuaded them to do so, and practically took charge of Buchanan's final oral examination in 1925.[33]

Whitehead's power in the Philosophy Department was always great.

During term, the Whiteheads were at home to students on Sunday evenings. Others were welcome too. Nothing was allowed to interfere with these at-homes, which became extremely popular; only the Frankfurters' rivaled the Whiteheads'. The refreshments were simply cookies and hot chocolate.

In 1920 Harvard got C. I. Lewis to join the Philosophy Department. He had earned a high reputation with his *Survey of Symbolic Logic*. When Whitehead came, Lewis had begun work on his theory of knowledge, which he called conceptualistic pragmatism. Whereas for Whitehead metaphysics was prior to epistemology, for which it must provide a niche, Lewis was quite Kantian. The year 1929 would see the publication of both Lewis's *Mind and the World Order*[34] and Whitehead's magnum opus, *Process and Reality*. In his copy of the latter, Lewis wrote this marginal comment on one passage: "Has got the metaphysical cart before the epistemological horse, as usual." Whereas Whitehead's philosophy was deliberately speculative, Lewis eschewed speculation, and viewed philosophy as an effort to analyze and make explicit what we already know. In short, these two men were philosophical opposites. But there was no one in the English-speaking world who was Whitehead's equal in speculative philosophy, and no one who was quite Lewis's equal in analytic philosophy. Since Woods, Perry, and Hocking were already at Harvard, and the junior men included H. M. Sheffer, H. A. Wolfson (who became an authority on Spinoza and on medieval philosophy), R. M. Eaton (who soon wrote a superb *General Logic*), and the psychologists L. T. Troland, E. G. Boring, and Gordon Allport, it is fair to say that in 1924, when Whitehead arrived and Lewis was given tenure, a second golden age in philosophy, at least the equal of the first, began.*

There was no Harvard "school" of philosophy; the men of the first golden age had established the tradition of not adding a new man who had the same mentality as someone already there. Another habit was that of general fidelity to an injunction which Charles W. Eliot, President of Harvard in the first golden age, had uttered in his inaugural address, back in 1869: "Philosophical subjects should never be taught with authority." Whitehead never wanted to do that. There was a third

---

*Woods died in 1934, Eaton in 1935. I should say that the second golden age ended in 1936–37. That was Whitehead's last year in the Department, and the first for W. V. Quine, with whom a new period began.

tradition which suited him perfectly. As Ralph Barton Perry said of the earlier age,

> There grew up in the Department as its most characteristic mark the idea that the study of philosophy meant the achievement and defense of some philosophical "system" of one's own. [35]

Before this, the teaching of philosophy had been almost entirely historical. Now Sheffer was busy with his "relational logic" (unfortunately never published by him), Perry with his general theory of value, Lewis with his theory of knowledge.

As the new notable professor, Whitehead was asked to make several speeches in his first year at Harvard: on October 19, at the annual reception for graduate students and faculty of the Department of Philosophy; on April 5, to the Harvard Overseers' Visiting Committee on Philosophy; on May 29, at Wellesley College's celebration of its fiftieth anniversary.

Special lectures which he gave in his first year will be noticed in the next chapter.

ix

The reader of the preceding volume of this biography will recall that I pictured Whitehead as a loner.* He had a great many good friends but no confidant, no friend with whom he was completely intimate. This was also the case throughout his years at Harvard. He was on excellent terms with all the members of the Philosophy Department, and with many others, such as L. J. Henderson, Felix Frankfurter, and Henry Osborn Taylor. But his wife was no loner at all. In the fall of 1924 she met a friend of the Hockings, Rosalind Greene; the two soon became devoted to each other. An American of Dutch descent,† Rosalind was the wife of Henry Copley Greene, a Harvard man who wrote plays, and translations from the French; both he and Rosalind had been in France many years; in the war he had been in charge of reconstruction and relief with the American Red Cross. Greene had studied philosophy, and from 1926 to 1928 would be Instructor in it at Harvard. Rosalind was in her late thirties. The Greenes had four beautiful daughters; the youngest, Ernesta, was the one who was in the most delicate health, but only

---

*See, for example, Volume I, page 127.

†See Whitehead's remark on this in his letter of March 15, 1925, to North (Appendix B).

one of the four outlived their mother. Evelyn Whitehead's letters to Rosalind Greene show that Evelyn's love and sorrow for Eric, and Rosalind's loving concern for her ailing daughters, formed quite a bond between them. Rosalind showered flowers and other tokens of warm friendship on the Whiteheads. For Alfred's sixty-fourth birthday there was a party, with little Ernesta doing the icing on the cake.[36] At the end of June 1925 the Whiteheads spent a week in the Greenes' country house near Newburyport, Massachusetts.

To be sure, the Whiteheads' feelings toward Rosalind Greene were charged with sentiment. Both Alfred and Evelyn were sentimental people. In speech and writing, he controlled his sentiments; she did not, she gushed. He was benevolent; she loved or hated. He was almost always reasonable; of her I would say what she truly said of Hocking's wife, Agnes: she's wonderful, but you mustn't expect her to be reasonable.*

It was Agnes Hocking who first brought Evelyn and Rosalind Green together. Agnes's father was the Boston poet Richard Boyle O'Reilly. Undoubtedly a genius, she was the creator of the Shady Hill School in Cambridge.

In November, at the Greenes' house, Ernest Hocking gave an exposition of Whitehead's new metaphysical ideas; the Whiteheads were present. On June 1, 1925, the Hockings drove the Whiteheads, along with Jim Woods and Winthrop Bell, to Newport, Rhode Island, to visit the place where Berkeley wrote *Alciphron*. Bell, a Canadian, was Instructor and Tutor in Harvard's Philosophy Department.

In both English and American academic circles, the fact that early in 1924 Whitehead had decided to migrate to Harvard soon became generally known. From the University of California at Berkeley he received an invitation to teach in its 1925 Summer Session. The offer came in a letter written by John P. Buwalda, Dean of the Summer Sessions, on July 15, 1924. He said that the normal teaching load was two courses of five lectures per week, but that a somewhat lighter schedule "can usually be arranged" for foreign scholars who were unaccustomed to such a load. The Session ran from June 22 to August 1; the honorarium would be $1,000. It was thought that he might like to give one course of lectures in mathematics and one in philosophy, but this could be decided later. Plainly, the purpose was to get the man Whitehead.

---

*See, in Appendix B, the second paragraph in Whitehead's letter to North on December 21, 1924.

On August 5, ten days before he left London, Whitehead accepted the invitation by letter. The normal teaching load was "decidedly more" than he could undertake; he could lecture for four hours a week. He proposed one lecture course "in Philosophy, namely the Philosophy of Science, including logical and metaphysical questions arising therein," and one course in Applied Mathematics, dealing with either Electromagnetism or Advanced Dynamics.

Whitehead would not have had to make special preparations for the summer teaching in Berkeley: he could boil down the philosophy lectures of his first year at Harvard, and some lectures he had given at the Imperial College. Nevertheless, he backed out of his acceptance of the California invitation. On December 10 he wrote in a letter to North's wife, Margot, "We have dropped our California project for next summer, with some relief on all counts—but it was impossible with Jessie arriving in July." Jessie herself gave me a different motive for the decision: fear that the altitude reached in going over the Continental Divide by train would be too much of a strain on her mother's heart.[37] No doubt this occurred to Whitehead; and in fact, in all his twenty-three years in America, he never went farther west than the University of Wisconsin at Madison. Evelyn wanted to be on hand when Jessie arrived. I think it likely that another motive played quite a part: Whitehead did not need the extra money, and he wanted to develop further the ideas he had expressed in his Harvard lectures rather than repeat them elsewhere.

Whitehead never again made a commitment to do summer teaching. Berkeley invited him for the 1926 Summer Session. On December 1, 1925, the President of the University of California, William Wallace Campbell, wrote Dean Buwalda that he had happened to see Professor Whitehead in Cambridge, and that Whitehead told him he could not come and hoped to come in 1927 but could not make a definite promise. The relations between the two philosophy departments were very friendly. Berkeley asked Whitehead again for the summer of 1929, without success. I suppose that some other universities tried and failed to get him for their summer sessions.

The famous Boston physician Richard C. Cabot and his wife, Ellen, were intimate friends of the Hockings. In July 1925 the Whiteheads spent weekends at the Cabots' cottage fifteen miles from Boston. For August and the first half of September, they lived in a cottage on the edge of Lake Seymour in Morgan Center, northern Vermont; it was owned by L. J. Henderson, who was away and had placed it at their disposal; it was always referred to as Professor Henderson's camp, and was ideal for living the simple life.

Jessie's arrival actually occurred on June 29. The ship docked in New York. Evelyn, always possessive toward her, went to New York by train to meet Jessie. Alfred pulled strings to get a job for Jessie in the Harvard College Library, Widener. As she knew some Arabic, she was reasonably qualified for the job, and held it until she reached retirement age.

In December 1924 Whitehead had two bouts with flu. The dramatic illness in this first American year was Evelyn's. As Whitehead wrote to North on August 16, "We picked a wonderfully decorative wildflower, like a gigantic wild mint. She crushed the leaves in her hands and put her face in it to smell." This was an Englishwoman's introduction to poison ivy.

August 16 marked the first anniversary of the Whiteheads' embarkation from Liverpool. A celebration was called for; he had written in May to Samuel Alexander, telling him how much he had enjoyed the switch from mathematics to philosophy. A bonfire was lit beside Lake Seymour. House guests were Raphael Demos and a wealthy young friend interested in philosophy, Roger Pierce. Those two, along with Jessie and the faithful servant, Mary, then went for a row on the lake by starlight.[38]

It had been an enjoyable and productive year. Although Whitehead spent the rest of his life in the American Cambridge, he never became a citizen of the United States, but remained a visitor from England. Writing to North about a motor trip across the Canadian border, he said, "We . . . thoroughly enjoyed seeing the Union Jack over the Canadian Customhouse."[39]

Whitehead, as I said earlier, was very much a family man. He achieved a great deal in philosophy at Harvard. But when he wrote to North on December 10, 1924, about North's children, he said, "Bringing up a family is the most anxious of all occupations but, on looking back on life, it is by far the achievement most worth while."*

---

*The entire paragraph should be read (see Appendix B).

CHAPTER VIII

A New Philosophy of Nature

i/The invitation to give a course of eight lectures at
the Lowell Institute. Character of this lectureship.
The change in Whitehead's title. Delivery of the first
lecture. The thesis to be illustrated in the course.
Writing the Lowell Lectures.

ii/Publication of the books Whitehead wrote in
America. Macmillan's donation of its Whitehead
correspondence. Macmillan's early information that
Whitehead would be a Lowell Lecturer.

iii/Advance from relatedness of extended events
(*Enquiry*) to activity of realizing a value.
Comparison with Spinoza. Wordsworth and
Shelley. Use of "Value."

iv/The infinite realm of "eternal objects." Introduction
of Whitehead's concept of God. "Prehension."
"Organism." The "simple location" of matter.
Mistaking scientific abstractions for the concrete
realities of nature.

v/Additions to the Lowell Lectures for manuscript of
Science and the Modern World. Its two subjects. Early
publication.

vi/Big sale. Cambridge's mistake. Invitation from the
Atlantic Monthly, and Whitehead's reply.

vii/Whitehead's feeling about science. Concern with
rival cosmologies. The preachers of scientific
method.

viii/"Requisites for Social Progress." The new
philosophy of nature as a pan-valuism. Need to
draw out habits of aesthetic apprehension. Need for
both change and conservation.

ix/The chapter on Einstein's Theory of Relativity.
Epochal character of time. Whitehead on the
quantum theory.

x/Epistemology in *Science and the Modern World.*
Whitehead's account of the genesis of his organic
philosophy.

xi/A logical blunder. Physics and Whitehead's "theory
of aspects." Looseness of style in *Science and the
Modern World.* Transitional character of this book.

xii/Samuel Alexander and his way of philosophizing.
Alexander's influence on Whitehead. Whitehead's
marginalia in *Space, Time, and Deity.* Alexander on
the quality of deity; Whitehead on God's primordial
nature.

xiii/Bergson's alleged influence on Whitehead.

xiv/Arrangements with the Macmillan Company to
publish *Science and the Modern World.* Whitehead's
attitude toward business. His wife's role.

With Whitehead's acceptance of the Harvard professorship in hand, President Lowell was able on March 18, 1924, to invite him to deliver a course of eight lectures for the Lowell Institute in Boston, on any subject he pleased. Whitehead accepted this invitation on April 1, choosing as his subject "Three Centuries of Natural Philosophy." He explained that he

> would sketch in broad outline the growth of modern science with especial reference to its influence on modern mentality, and to the influence of technology on the social structure, comparing it to the effect of the rise of literature in the first millennium B.C. as the result of the popularization of writing.

Whitehead added that, as Lowell knew the audience intimately, he would be "grateful for any suggestion or criticism as to the suitability of this line of thought." In his reply Lowell expressed delight that Whitehead could give the eight-lecture course, and commented:

> the subject of "Three Centuries of Natural Philosophy," with the outline you give of it, seems to be very good. Of course you cannot expect a large audience, but that is quite unimportant.[1]

No one else's opinion mattered at this point; A. Lawrence Lowell was the sole trustee of the Institute.* His own preference ran toward lecturers on history—political history. Providing several series of free public lectures was no longer, as it had been in the nineteenth century, the primary function of the Lowell Institute, but it was still a notable one; the invitation that came to Whitehead was an honor. The likelihood that the lecturer would present important new ideas was always

---

*Government not by a board but by a single trustee, preferably a kinsman, was specified in the founding document, the will of John Lowell, Jr. Since his death in 1836 only two trustees, both Lowells, had run the Institute prior to Lawrence Lowell's accession in 1900.

much in this trustee's mind, as it had been in his predecessors' minds. Often a Lowell Lecturer turned his lectures into a book. William James's *Pragmatism* and Bertrand Russell's *Our Knowledge of the External World* (which Russell read out under the title, "Scientific Method in Philosophy") were recent examples. As the fee was only $100 per lecture, the opportunity to formulate the ideas for his next book was generally an invited lecturer's main reason for accepting; so it was in Whitehead's case. He consulted his Bostonian friend Jim Woods on the propriety of composing his Lowell Lectures with the book more in mind than the audience, and was reassured.

Before Whitehead left London for the American Cambridge, he sent material for announcing his eight lectures to the Institute's curator, Professor William H. Lawrence, and with this material, a suggestion for changing the overall title. The new title would be "Science and the Modern World." This fitted the lectures that were delivered a little better than "Three Centuries of Natural Philosophy," but no short title could be adequate. At the University of London on January 24, 1923, Whitehead, one of eight scientists giving single lectures on "Some Aspects of Natural Philosophy," called his "The Quest of Science Today and as Exemplified in Its History." What a cumbersome title that was! Accurate, no doubt, but pure Whiteheadese. I don't think he felt any need to talk to Evelyn about a single scientific lecture at London University. He did talk to her quite fully about his American undertakings. Probably the title "Science and the Modern World" was Evelyn's idea.[2] She had a good sense for what would sell.

The lectures were scheduled for February 1925; they would be at 5:00 P.M. on Mondays and Thursdays (excepting February 23), and would conclude March 2. The place was Huntington Hall, in the Rogers Building (since razed), at 491 Boylston Street. The lectures were free and open to anyone, but tickets had to be obtained from the Lowell Institute.

At precisely five o'clock on Monday, February 2, the center door to the stage of the hall opened and a tall beadle stepped forward, followed by a small, short man with a manuscript. The lectern was too tall for him to see the audience over its top, so the beadle procured a card table and set it beside the lectern.[3] Professor Whitehead could see his audience by standing behind the card table to read his lecture. Who introduced him? Nobody. This course of lectures had been advertised in the *Boston Evening Transcript*. What the lecturer had to say would show how justified the trustee was in choosing him. There was no need for the platoon of vice-presidents, deans, department chairmen, and colleagues, which nowadays precedes invited speakers everywhere. Professor Henderson and Harvard administrators could have obliged, but "No introductions" had been one of the founder's stipulations for the Lowell Lectures. He was a smart man.

Huntington Hall could seat 900. The first lecture, entitled "Science and Modern Civilization," was entirely about the origins of modern science. It attracted a large audience, but Whitehead's high-pitched, bell-like voice did not carry beyond the first few rows. That was especially unfortunate, because he was making his debut as a philosopher before the educated public, and the lecture was profound. I shall not go over its argument, but I must call attention to his careful language in stating the thesis of the lecture course. After placing his audience in the sixteenth century and contrasting the quiet beginnings of science with the bloodshed of the Reformation, Whitehead said,

> The thesis which these lectures will illustrate is that this quiet growth of science has practically recoloured our mentality so that modes of thought which in former times were exceptional, are now broadly spread through the educated world.[4]

Most writers would not bother to avoid saying that they will *demonstrate* their thesis, but the logician Whitehead used that word sparingly. Then he went on to qualify his thesis:

> Perhaps my metaphor of a new colour is too strong. What I mean is just that slightest change of tone which yet makes all the difference.

To illustrate this he used William James's phrase "irreducible and stubborn facts," and asserted that the union of passionate interest in them "with equal devotion to abstract generalisation" is the novelty that science has brought to our mentality. The villain of the story, "scientific materialism," was introduced near the close of this lecture.

I have not found a transcript of the Lowell Lectures as delivered, and so have been quoting from the first edition of the book *Science and the Modern World,* relying on Whitehead's assertion in the Preface of that volume that the Lowell Lectures, "with some slight expansion, . . . are here printed as delivered," with the addition of a few chapters.

On December 21, 1924, Whitehead wrote a birthday letter to North.* After saying that Harvard's three-week first-term examina-

---

*North was born on December 31, 1891.

tion period in January would be "a complete holiday" for him,* he continued:

> I want the time to write up the eight Lowell Lectures which come off in February. I have now broken the back of the second lecture† and have thought out the whole course. But I want to have them nearly all finished before the course begins.

Fifteen years later he told Lucien Price, "I was never more than one week ahead."[5] These lectures formed his first public pronouncement in America, and so he spent much time perfecting them. Until all had been delivered, Whitehead gave up his usual letters to North. On March 15 he wrote him that the Lowell Lectures "amounted to writing a book in about two months," and "were a great strain on me."

ii

The publisher of the books that Whitehead wrote in America was the Macmillan Company of New York; Cambridge brought out English editions a few months later.‡

In 1966, when both Whitehead and his wife were dead, Macmillan donated its Whitehead file to the New York Public Library. Much of it went elsewhere or was lost; the Library received only items dated between mid-1924 and late 1927, and four dated 1938.[6]

The first item in the Library's collection is a memorandum dated June 27, 1924, from Macmillan's President, George P. Brett, to his Assistant, Curtice N. Hitchcock. It says that Whitehead has accepted a chair in philosophy at Harvard for the next five years, and will give Lowell Lectures next winter on "Three Centuries of Science." "We ought to get in touch with Professor Whitehead the moment he arrives or even before in order to secure this book for American publication." On July 1 Hitchcock wrote a businesslike letter to Whitehead, reminding him that for many years Macmillan, as the American representative of the Cambridge University Press (which had no New York office at

---

*Raphael Demos, as his assistant, would read the examination papers for Whitehead's lecture course.

†This, on the seventeenth century, was printed as Chapter III in *Science and the Modern World*.

‡However, the Princeton University Press published, as *The Function of Reason,* a set of three lectures which Whitehead delivered at Princeton in 1929, and the University of Chicago Press published two lectures (*Nature and Life*), given there in 1934; the English editions of these works were by Oxford and Cambridge, respectively.

this time), had sponsored his books in the United States. Whitehead never replied to this overture. In the New York Public Library collection there are only two letters from him, but there are many fascinating letters written to Hitchcock by Evelyn, acting as her husband's business manager; I shall discuss them later.*

Brett's memorandum to Hitchcock was accompanied by two pages from the Quotation section of the May 2, 1924, issue of *Science*. The journal reprinted an unsigned article from the English journal *Nature* which announced Whitehead's imminent move to Harvard for five years. This article gave a well-informed account of what he planned to do there, and criticized the British university system for the "inelasticity" that made it necessary for a man of such "eminence, charm of manner, and inspiring intercourse" to go elsewhere for "the opportunity of completing his research."

The author had to be some admirer of Whitehead who knew all about the Harvard appointment. He could have been Henry Osborn Taylor or L. J. Henderson, or a close English friend like T. P. Nunn. The forthcoming Lowell Lectures were not mentioned, being outside the intent of this article.

Taylor was probably the source of Brett's early information about the Lowell Lectures. Macmillan was his own publisher. Later, when *Science and the Modern World* came out and the Whiteheads did not want Macmillan to sell a specially low-priced edition to the *New Republic* for use as a gift to new subscribers, Taylor was the friend who suggested that Macmillan send Whitehead a suitable royalty agreement;[7] he was the intermediary.

iii

Other facts about the publication of *Science and the Modern World* will be noticed in later sections of this chapter. It is time now to consider the philosophy of nature that Whitehead expounded in this book. I shall continue to reserve the phrase "philosophy of natural science" for the three books written in his last years in England, which were discussed in Chapter VI.

Recall that in the first chapter of his *Enquiry* Whitehead asserted that the fundamental characteristic of nature is its passage, or creative advance. But in that book as published in 1919, this was treated as little

---

*See Section xiv of this chapter.

more than the temporal dimension of the extensive relatedness of events. In Note II to the second edition—its Preface was dated August, 1924—Whitehead said that the correct doctrine, that not extension but "process" is the fundamental idea, "was not in my mind with sufficient emphasis." In Note I, referring to the work he hoped "to undertake in the immediate future," he spoke of analyzing "the process of the realisation of social entities." The difference between the words *relatedness* and *realization* marks the difference between the standpoint of the earlier philosophy of natural science and that of the new philosophy of nature.

In the Lowell Lectures, the creative advance of nature is conceived as the outcome of an "underlying activity of realisation." Noting an analogy with Spinoza, Whitehead says,

> His one substance is for me the one underlying activity of realisation individualising itself in an interlocked plurality of modes.[8]

These modes are finite events. Is there something that they all have in common because it is the essence of realization in itself? Whitehead raises this question and gives his answer to it in the chapter "The Romantic Reaction," immediately after presenting the views of nature that he found in Wordsworth and Shelley. He calls the romantic reaction to the triumph of scientific materialism "a protest on behalf of value."[9] In his philosophy of natural science, Whitehead fenced nature in by deliberately excluding any reference to values, moral or aesthetic. As he put it in *The Concept of Nature,*

> The values of nature are perhaps the key to the metaphysical synthesis of existence. But such a synthesis is exactly what I am not attempting.[10]

In *Science and the Modern World,* when Whitehead brings up the question of what it is that emerges into actuality in every event, he notes that no one word can be adequate and nothing may be left out; still, he has a ready answer.

> Remembering the poetic rendering of our concrete experience, we see at once that the element of value, of being valuable, of having value, of being an end in itself, of being something which is for its own sake, must not be omitted in any account of an event as the most concrete actual something. "Value" is the word I use for the intrinsic reality of an event.[11]

iv

There is another basic concept which Whitehead introduced into his new philosophy of nature when he appealed to Wordsworth and Shelley: eternality. His notion was that of an infinite realm of "eternal objects." Examples of such objects are colors, shapes, forms, and *character* that an event may exhibit.[12] He analyzed this realm in the chapter "Abstraction," which he added to the Lowell Lectures. He shunned the name "universal" for an eternal object, as he wanted nothing but what he said about this category to be in the reader's mind. In an accompanying added chapter, "God," he presented his concept of God. God is a principle, the "Principle of Concretion" that is required if a particular concrete event is to issue from earlier events and the welter of eternal objects.[13] Whitehead's God is the supreme metaphysical ground of limitation.

A fundamental concept which appears in *Science and the Modern World* was introduced early in the Lowell Lectures. Whitehead gave it the name "prehension." He explained that this word was to mean apprehension which is not necessarily cognitive.[14] When one event, or "actual occasion" (as he came to call them), takes account of another in its environment, that is a prehension of the environmental occasion. In the prehending occasion, many concurrent prehensions are integrated. Whitehead calls the integrating occasion an organism.[15] By that word he generally means a temporally bounded process which organizes a variety of given elements into a new whole.

Whitehead's idea that nature consists of organisms is his alternative to the traditional idea that it consists of bits of matter, each of which has the property of simple location, that is,

> in expressing its spatio-temporal relations, it is adequate to state that it is where it is, in a definite finite region of space, and throughout a definite finite duration of time, apart from any essential reference of the relations of that bit of matter to other regions of space and to other durations of time.[16]

The meaning of simple location is independent of the adoption of an absolute or a relative theory of space and time.[17] In the account of our perception of nature that Whitehead inserted into his Lowell Lectures, he maintained that we never perceive simply located bits of matter. But it is possible to arrive at them by constructive abstraction from the prehensive unifications of which we are aware. The real error of the scientific scheme that was so victorious in the eighteenth century and prevailed through the nineteenth consisted in mistaking its powerful abstractions for the concrete realities of nature.[18]

v

Whitehead sent the manuscript of *Science and the Modern World* off to New York on July 9, 1925. In his covering letter, addressed to "The Manager, The Macmillan Company," he wrote, "If you can push through the printing, we can get the book on the market for this autumn." The Cambridge University Press, he said, did not find it necessary to send him galleys. He had gone carefully over this typescript, and would be able to return page proofs "within 24 hours of their receipt." Once Whitehead had finished with a piece of writing, he wanted pronto to move on. And he hoped that his philosophical ideas would attract a wide public. I expect that he was most eager to know what reception the non-historical parts of the book would get. The chapters entitled "Abstraction" and "God" were not at all about science and the modern world; they were the first-published parts of the general metaphysics he was adumbrating. He never wrote to please his readers, but he was anxious to see how the ideas that he had not had a chance to develop and express in England made out in the New World.

Macmillan published the book in October, 1925.

In his letter of July 9 Whitehead explained that besides the addition of these two new chapters to the Lowell Lectures, "slightly expanded, as mentioned in the contract,"* his manuscript included two lectures delivered elsewhere but not yet published. One, "Religion and Science," was, so far as I know, his first public post-war utterance on religion; he had given it on April 5 as a Phillips Brooks Lecture at Harvard.† The other, "Mathematics as an Element in the History of Thought," was a lecture he had given on April 14 to a special meeting of the Mathematics Club at Brown University.

In the Preface to *Science and the Modern World,* which Whitehead dated June 29, 1925, he said that the additions to the Lowell Lectures were meant "to complete the thought of the book on a scale which

---

*In the contract, dated June 24, 1925, and signed by Whitehead and President Brett of Macmillan, Whitehead gave the company the sole right to publish in volume form "the material of his Lowell Lectures 1924–25." No mention was made of slight expansions (or added chapters). Possibly Whitehead was misinformed; possibly slight expansion was mentioned in an earlier, outdated contract; anyhow, it was customarily allowed.

†It will be discussed in Section iii of Chapter IX.

could not be included within that lecture course." In his letter of July 9 he wrote:

> I have completed the book so as to carry out the full scheme of thought which was curtailed for these [Lowell] lectures, . . . The whole makes a continuous train of thought, and the previous history of the material does not mean that the scheme lacks unity—at least in my mind.

Thus Whitehead believed that the parts of the book hung together. His assertion of a continuous train of thought might be taken to imply the absence of any doctrinal additions or changes. I should not, however, be willing to go to the stake for taking his language so strictly. He may have intended little more than assurance to Macmillan that they were not getting a hodgepodge. Still, some weight must be given to Whitehead's belief in the unity of his book. It is hard to say how much; few authors are willing to admit that their manuscript lacks unity. It is pretty certain that during his first half dozen years in America Whitehead's thought was always on the move, and this movement generally expanded or made more explicit what had been vaguely in his mind.* There are different degrees of vagueness, and the degree got diminished by his effort to explain his ideas to his Harvard and Radcliffe classes in 1924–25.

Science and the Modern World had two subjects. First, the story of the rise and influence of modern physical science; second, Whitehead's new philosophy of nature, and, as an appendage to this, contributions to the new metaphysics that he believed his philosophy of nature required. Whitehead skillfully fitted the launching of his new ideas onto his history. Still, they were two subjects. Many readers who were entranced by his telling of the story despaired of understanding the new philosophy; but it began the big job that needed doing.

Since the material that Whitehead added to the Lowell Lectures made a substantial difference in bulk (about thirty percent) and subject matter, it may be said to be unfortunate that "Lowell Lectures, 1925" was on the title page. A bigger example of this was the publication of *Process and Reality* as "Gifford Lectures delivered in the University of Edinburgh during the session 1927–28": ten lectures, delivered in 1928, became twenty-five chapters. This sort of thing is bound to happen as long as we publish lectures given by men whose minds refuse to retire.

---

*That is how he put it when I asked him about his early entertainment of ideas that he wrote up later.

The announcement of the Lowell Lectures[19] said that they would include some comment on Tolstoy, Ibsen, and Bernard Shaw in the discussion of literature and science, but their names do not appear in *Science and the Modern World*. As the Preface noted additions to the Lowell Lectures but not omissions from them, I infer that Whitehead did not mention these writers. I think that he was too busy finding the best verbalization of his new philosophy to have time to compose incisive comment on Tolstoy, Ibsen, and Shaw. Besides Wordsworth and Shelley, he had used Pope and Tennyson to show the effects of Newtonian science on literature. Those effects were what he wanted to bring out; enough was enough.

vi

In the mid-1920s there was a fair expectation, most widespread in America, that the gulf between the science of matter in motion and our experience of value could be bridged by a philosophical scientist of sufficient genius. *Science and the Modern World* sold like hot-cakes.*

The Cambridge University Press was taken completely by surprise. The Secretary to its Syndics, S. C. Roberts, wrote:

> We ordered five hundred copies in sheets [from Macmillan] and soon realised that it was a ludicrous miscalculation. The work was hailed as the most important contribution to its subject since Descartes, and we hastened to set up our own edition, which was many times reprinted.[20]

From Roberts's successor, R. W. David, I learned in 1968 that over the years Cambridge had sold more copies of *Science and the Modern World* than of all of Whitehead's other books combined.[21]

A book in which a new philosophy is heralded is likely to be more ardently welcomed than the definitive statement of that philosophy. And *Science and the Modern World* was the right length: substantial, but not oppressively so. When *Process and Reality: An Essay in Cosmology* was published four years later, it was found to be too intricate and many-faceted for popularity.

Macmillan was not the only American publisher that wanted White-

---

*As my own case was not unusual, I mention it. *Science and the Modern World* was one of the two books that led me, a person who had received only an engineering education, to take up the study of philosophy. The other was Will Durant's popular *Story of Philosophy*. The Whiteheads were much amused when I told them this.

head's Lowell Lectures. The Harvard University Press tried to get them, and almost succeeded.* Sometime in the autumn of 1924 Ellery Sedgwick, editor of the *Atlantic Monthly* and top-drawer in Boston, invited Whitehead to publish the Lowell Lectures in the *Atlantic* before turning them into a book. On November 16 Whitehead sent a reply that began with honest encomiums, then raised the points that were important to him: "absolute freedom" to publish later as a book, and *no delay* of the book "until all the lectures have gone through the magazine." In the end, Sedgwick got none of the Lowell Lectures, only the Phillips Brooks Lecture "Religion and Science."

vii

The desire to reconcile opposed parties rather than to champion one of them has appeared in my account of Whitehead's life as an essential trait of his character. The same trait appears in his reaction to competition among world-views. In the Preface to *Science and the Modern World* he tells us that in the past three centuries the cosmology derived from science has asserted itself at the expense of those derived from ethics, aesthetics, and religion. The pursuit of science is praiseworthy, and indispensable to civilization, but Whitehead does not want it to run away with us. One of the important functions of philosophy, he says, is to criticize cosmologies,

> to harmonise, refashion, and justify divergent intuitions as to the nature of things. It has to insist on the scrutiny of the ultimate ideas, and on the retention of the whole of the evidence in shaping our cosmological scheme. Its business is to render explicit and—so far as may be—efficient, a process which otherwise is unconsciously performed without rational tests.[22]

The championing of science, notably in the last hundred years, has seldom been expressed in terms of cosmologies; it has most often taken the form of insistence that the scientific *method* is the right way, and the only right way, to deal with situations. As first developed in the natural sciences, its hallmarks are isolation of a problem, careful observation, framing and exploring hypotheses in the imagination, and testing by repeatable experiments. In everyday life and in the social sciences, the isolation of the problem is made urgent by a feeling of need to change a situation that is being experienced as not good. In *Science and the Modern*

---

*See page 179 below.

World Whitehead does not explicitly discuss the claim to sovereignty made on behalf of this method. The claim was most often advanced in America, where it seemed highly appropriate to the reign of technology. But Whitehead was an Englishman and a mathematician, and old-fashioned enough to ponder "the nature of things." It would be natural, but mistaken, to think that proponents of the scientific method are less dogmatic and more flexible in outlook than proponents or opponents of scientific materialism as a cosmology. Who is less open to persuasion than the man who says, "There are many cosmologies and anyone is free to frame another, but I show you how to think, the only way that leads to sound conclusions about anything"?*

viii

Whitehead entitled the last of his series of eight Lowell Lectures "Requisites for Social Progress."† In it his wisdom stands out. I shall call attention to only a few highlights.

No sooner has he reminded his audience that in the philosophy which he has sketched *organism* takes the place of *matter,* than he declares, "An organism is the realisation of a definite shape of value."23 Since he is convinced that everything in nature is such a realization, it would be correct to call his new philosophy of nature a "pan-valuism," however clumsy that label is.

In the nineteenth century scientific materialism and the manufacturing system became partners; when the assumption that matter in itself is devoid of value was taken seriously, much ugliness was produced.

Whitehead brings the idea of value into every topic he discusses in this lecture. An example is the need to balance specialist with general education. He had touched on this in more than one of his essays on education. Now he describes the *kind* of general education that is needed, needed most of all in a civilization that has been shaped by scientific materialism.

---

*The preachers of scientific method were riding high during the years that Whitehead taught philosophy at Harvard. Most of them were liberal social philosophers dedicated to reform. Only a few had an active interest in physical science, and none wanted to reduce cultural to material realities. The important point to all of them was: no recognition of any road to knowledge that is essentially different from the experimental road of the scientist. The philosopher they admired most, John Dewey, urged all philosophers to keep their thoughts inside problem-solving human situations and to stop theorizing about what he called "antecedent reality." Thus Whitehead's preoccupation with cosmology was ruled out. See John Dewey, *The Quest for Certainty* (New York: Minton, Balch & Co., 1929), passim.

†It was printed as the last chapter in *SMW*.

The type of generality, which above all is wanted, is the appreciation of variety of value. . . . What is wanted is an appreciation of the infinite variety of vivid values achieved by an organism in its proper environment.[24]

A simple illustration follows.

When you understand all about the sun and all about the atmosphere and all about the rotation of the earth, you may still miss the radiance of the sunset. . . . What we want is to draw out habits of aesthetic apprehension.

The last sentence conveys the requisite that Whitehead thought most imperative. If you wonder whether he was undervaluing the understanding he had learned and had taught in comparison with the apprehension that Evelyn possessed to a high degree, you may be relieved by noticing Whitehead's next illustration: the values involved in a factory.

Our attitude toward adventure and tradition is crucial. Whitehead wrote:

There are two principles inherent in the very nature of things, recurring in some particular embodiments whatever field we explore— the spirit of change, and the spirit of conservation. There can be nothing real without both.[25]

Whitehead had long been convinced of this necessary duality; he would dwell on it at length in *Adventures of Ideas*. Now he emphasizes the side that was most important to Evelyn. The human soul, he declares, cannot endure monotony; it needs to be "fertilised" by transient but vivid experiences; art meets this need.[26]

The late nineteenth century found out how to train men whose knowledge would be professional, that is, thorough and progressive within its limits, and supported by a lesser knowledge of neighboring subjects. Whitehead wrote:

This situation has its dangers. It produces minds in a groove. . . . Now to be mentally in a groove is to live in contemplating a given set of abstractions. The groove prevents straying across country, and the abstraction abstracts from something to which no further attention is paid. But there is no groove of abstractions which is adequate for the comprehension of human life.[27]

Because our life moves at a faster pace than formerly, professionalism has to be handled by greater wisdom.

Let us recall that when Whitehead wrote to his friend Mark Barr on January 13, 1924, about his interest in a possible offer from Harvard, he mentioned the opportunity to develop his ideas on education.* Now, in this last of the Lowell Lectures, he tells us what he most wants in education.

> Wisdom is the fruit of a balanced development. It is this balanced growth of individuality which it should be the aim of education to secure. The most useful discoveries for the immediate future would concern the furtherance of this aim without detriment to the necessary intellectual professionalism.[28]

The "without" clause reminds me that, though Whitehead was never content with things as they are, he kept an eye open for ongoing values.†

ix

Whitehead's new philosophy of nature had to be congenial to twentieth-century physics; so he devoted one chapter to the theory of relativity, and one to quantum theory. I do not see how in his first year at Harvard, what with his teaching, other academic duties, the Lowell Lectures, and social obligations, he could have any time for fresh scientific work. But in 1925, popular interest in the theory of relativity was strong. Whitehead could, and did, explain what Einstein had done, and the divergence from Einstein that he had presented in his *Enquiry*. He made no references to his formidable *Principle of Relativity,* and even said of the theory of extensive abstraction as it appeared in the *Enquiry* that it was "too technical for the present occasion."[29] There are no mathematical formulae in *Science and the Modern World*. For a Lowell Lecture audience, Whitehead thought it best to use words only. That increased the time it took to write the book, but much increased its appeal and its sale in bookstores.

The main difference that I find between the chapter on relativity and the treatment Whitehead gave the subject in his earlier books is the change, already remarked in Section iii above, from the mere relatedness of events in an extended continuum to the realization of an event as a prehensive unification of other things.

---

*See page 134 above.

†The exception is his blind eye toward the need for keeping uniform external examinations in the school system of a democratic state; see page 45 above.

A point that must be borne in mind is that whereas orthodox relativity theory deals with external relations between objects, Whitehead's theory concerns internal relations between events.

What Whitehead calls "the epochal theory of time" is announced in the chapter on relativity.[30] Nothing whatever can be realized in an instant; a duration is needed. So Whitehead conceives time not as a form of extensiveness but as a succession of durations. Each duration is the epoch, or arrest, required for a particular realization. This doctrine of the atomicity of time or—to express it in a way that avoids possible misunderstandings—atomicity of process, is hereafter a fixture in the cosmology Whitehead is developing.

In his unusually short chapter on the quantum theory—it and the relativity chapter were presented in one Lowell Lecture—Whitehead's main purpose is to show that the new discontinuities were wholly embarrassing to the old materialism but not to his new philosophy of nature, which provides a natural context for them.

None of Whitehead's writing is as dated as his treatment of quantum theory. The second half of the 1920s was a wonderful period of new developments by the physicists. *Science and the Modern World* was just a little too early to take it into account. Whitehead names no one, but his discussion fits the atom depicted in Bohr's early work.

I must doubt that he would have been much interested in responding to the newer developments; certainly not in any but very general terms like those he would use in *Process and Reality*. He had left the world of equations behind him and become a philosopher. At Harvard, Whitehead could leave mathematical physics to others, while he tried out his metaphysical ideas and dispensed wisdom.

X

In the Preface to *Science and the Modern World*, Whitehead tells the reader not to expect any discussion of epistemology, as that would have upset the balance of the work. In sketching his alternative to scientific materialism, he started from the perceptual field, and took it "for what it claims to be: the self-knowledge of our [total] bodily event."[31] Here an epistemological justification was desirable.* Whitehead simply con-

---

*Whitehead introduced what I have quoted with the statement, "I have started from our own psychological field, as it stands for our cognition" (*SMW*, p. 103). This way of putting the matter—he frequently uses "as it stands" or synonymous phrases—eases the reader into the assumption that the cognitions in question are trustworthy.

tinues to draw on well-known general facts of psychology and physiology.

When he has finished sketching his organic conception of the world, he says that it is "equally possible" to arrive at it if, instead of starting from psychology and physiology, we start from "the fundamental notions of modern physics," and that this was the path he actually followed.[32] However, he does not identify his starting point or narrate the steps of his reasoning. He says only that it was "by reason of my own studies in mathematics and mathematical physics" that he arrived at his convictions.[33] That tells us as little as possible. His next statement, "Mathematical physics presumes in the first place an electromagnetic field of activity pervading space and time," gets our hopes up, for we remember that Maxwell's *Electricity and Magnetism* was the subject of Whitehead's Trinity College fellowship dissertation.* But in the four pages which follow, on the abstractions that mathematical physics makes and on its analysis of an event in empty space, there is no reference to Whitehead's actual train (or trains) of thought.

That negative fact should not surprise us. In this biography we've often seen how little its subject was interested in himself. Most people talk too much about themselves. Whitehead seldom tells you just what *he did*. This type of reticence made him a better man, though a more difficult one to write about. It is fortunate that in England his work was in pure mathematics, not in experimental science. His role in America was that of a teacher who proposes systematic hypotheses to explain what's there for anyone to observe.

xi

In the four pages on mathematical physics which I referred to, Whitehead makes a logical blunder. After saying that physics ignores what anything is in itself, and considers only extrinsic realities, he asserts that physics presupposes "the organic theory of aspects."[34] "The organic theory" means Whitehead's, as making organisms basic instead of particles of matter. *Aspect* is the most overworked word in *Science and the Modern World*. Whitehead is always insisting that every event— indeed, every thing, of whatever type—enters into the being of other things. Thus an aspect of the object seen there is present here. Let it be

---

*See Volume I, pages 106–8.

granted that physics abstracts from the total character of its objects. You may then enclose physics in your own theory about intrinsic realities and their partnership with the extrinsic. This will not prove that physics presupposes your theory.

In the later *Process and Reality,* where the account of presence elsewhere is detailed, the vague word *aspect* is not used. Whitehead's addiction to it in *Science and the Modern World* tells us that his philosophy will develop beyond that book. His language was loose because his thoughts were not yet firmly organized. And he said, "It is obvious that so-and-so,"[35] when so-and-so is not obvious to us. Whitehead was expert in making general statements; many of the statements in the exposition of his new philosophy of nature are highly general because he hasn't got around to making the necessary distinctions. He writes vaguely of "a selective activity which is akin to purpose."[36] In later books he will specify the kind of teleology he wishes to defend.

xii

Whitehead's acknowledgments in the Preface to *Science and the Modern World* are sparse: he has found Lloyd Morgan's *Emergent Evolution* and Alexander's *Space, Time, and Deity* "very suggestive"; but then he says, "I am especially indebted to Alexander's great work."

Samuel Alexander, two years younger than Whitehead, was an Australian who came to Oxford at eighteen. Idealism was then the dominant philosophy there; its influence was evident in his first book, *Moral Order and Progress.*[37] But he soon became more interested in philosophy's dependence on the empirical sciences; he studied psychology for a year at Hugo Münsterburg's laboratory in Frieburg, Germany. Espousal of a realistic epistemology in a long series of articles was followed, when he was Gifford Lecturer at Glasgow in 1916–18, by a realistic metaphysics. These lectures, as published in two volumes with the title *Space, Time, and Deity* in 1920, were his major work. It was acclaimed in England and America, but is now even less popular than Whitehead's *Process and Reality.* In 1924, the year in which Whitehead went to Harvard, Alexander retired from the chair he had long held at Manchester. He died in 1938.

In Whitehead's old age he told me[38] that Samuel Alexander was the philosopher of his time from whom he got most. But he gave me no details, saying only that he and Alexander "conceived the problem of metaphysics in the same way," that is, as reconciliation of the unity of the universe (emphasized in Spinoza's metaphysics)* and the multitude of individuals (emphasized by Leibniz).

Whitehead also remarked to me that Alexander, almost alone among their British contemporaries, did not, implicitly at least, assume that our experience is basically an experience of sense-data. Perception, for Alexander, consisted in the "compresence" of an object and a subject who "enjoys" a "togetherness" with the contemplated object. This is not far from Whitehead's notion of prehension. Both men found activity and value pervading nature. If time allowed, I could single out and analyze several other similarities. This would not prove that Whitehead *derived* the doctrines in question from Alexander, but only suggest that he might have done so, had he himself no power of original thought and expression. I prefer to confine myself to what can safely be made out.

In a period when the endeavor to construct a general theory of existence was unfashionable, the production of Alexander's grand system could only encourage Whitehead to try his hand. He did not agree with the hypothesis of Alexander's Giffords—the "Space-Time is the stuff of which matter and all things are specifications."[39] But the checkmarks, scorings, and detailed comments in Whitehead's copy of *Space, Time, and Deity,* which he read in 1924, show that he liked many of the points Alexander made and the purport of most of the work, while the question marks that Whitehead scrawled in the margins show in what respects Alexander failed to convince him or was not definite enough.

Probably Whitehead read Alexander's major work before he left England, for many of his comments express points he would want to bear in mind when he was concerned with the second edition of his *Enquiry.* (The Preface to that edition is dated August 1924.)

Alexander's way of presenting his philosophy appealed to Whitehead. As John Passmore said of Alexander,

> he simply puts a hypothesis before us and then tells us to look and see how reasonable it all is, how admirably it squares with our experience. He does not exhort us, he does not argue with us, he merely bids us cast off our sophistication.[40]

---

*Alexander felt close to Spinoza. His lecture, "Spinoza and Time" (London, 1921), makes their relationship clear, while substituting Time for Thought in Spinoza's theory of Attributes.

Passmore also wrote,

> In his "Some Explanations" (*Mind*, 1921), Alexander goes so far as to assert that he *dislikes* arguments, a strange pronouncement from a philosopher.[41]

That would indeed have been a strange pronouncement from a run-of-the-mill philosopher, who does nothing but argue about the soundness of the arguments that fellow philosophers are using. But Alexander was not a run-of-the-mill philosopher. Like Whitehead, he was able to offer new initial premises.

In a passage that Whitehead marked in his copy of *Space, Time, and Deity*, the author, explaining that in his remarks on the interconnection of time and space he was not trying to prove the existence of space, wrote, "There is no room for 'must' in philosophy or in science, but only for facts and the implications of them."[42] How different this man was from Bertrand Russell! In place of Russell's hard, logical atomism there was a judicious chapter on "The One and the Many." Reading Alexander's philosophy instead of Bertie's must have been a great relief to A. N. W.

To Russell in this stage of his career, a very few epistemological principles (as well as all those of logic) were prior to metaphysics. But when Whitehead began his plunge into metaphysics in *Science and the Modern World,* he said that

> an account of the general character of what we know must enable us to frame an account of how knowledge is possible as an adjunct within things known.[43]

To Alexander also, theory of knowledge was not the foundation of metaphysics, as so many believed, but only a chapter of it.[44]

Early in his second volume, Alexander wrote that the relation of a conscious subject to the object which transcends it is not unique, but is "found wherever two finites are compresent with each other."[45] In his copy, Whitehead underscored this and wrote "Yes" in the margin. Neither man believed that consciousness was omnipresent; my suggestion is that Whitehead sympathized with Alexander's generalization of the subject-object relation. When Whitehead started to develop his metaphysical system, he would deal primarily with the transition from object to subject, and the concrescence of the subject. There is none of this in *Space, Time, and Deity.* But the idea of process—natural process and history, nothing Hegelian—is there, and is emphasized. Alexander speaks of a "nisus" in Space-Time.

Alexander was weakest in his treatment of point-instants as units of reality; Whitehead had done better with point-instants. Alexander had read his books on the philosophy of physics, and lamented his own lack of mathematical training. Further, he confessed to having a feeling of presumptuousness in writing about Space-Time without having the proper equipment.[46] There is quite a contrast between his treatment of Space-Time as "the empirical reality" and Whitehead's treatment of it as a continuum of abstract potentialities for the finite processes that are his empirical realities.

Space, Time, and Deity is divided into four Books; Deity is the subject of the last. In Whitehead's copy, the first three books are full of his marginalia, but there is not a single mark in Book IV.

Alexander's subject was not God, but the quality of deity. He identified it as, for us, "the next higher empirical level than mind." Samuel Alexander had a Victorian's fascination with the idea of evolution from one level of existence to the next higher level. Following Lloyd Morgan, he called the higher level "emergent," a term which implies novelty and contrasts with "resultant."*

Whitehead's thought was not restricted to the levels of existence on this little planet of ours. He liked Alexander's idea of a nisus in Space-Time, but did not limit the applications of what corresponded to it in his metaphysics. The God that he had introduced to his readers in *Science and the Modern World,* and later called God in his primordial nature, was, as he remarked in 1931, "Alexander's *nisus* conceived as actual."[47]

Alexander based his thought about the quality of deity on his conception of the religious sentiment in mankind. I think Whitehead's interpretation of the religious sentiment† was ampler.

xiii

With the notable exception of Whitehead himself, more students of his philosophy bestow the honor of first place among its progenitors upon Bergson than upon Alexander. In particular, the primacy that Whitehead gave to the idea of process is usually assumed to be due to Bergson's influence on him. But what is *the* idea of process? Only Whitehead's idea of process is in question. When we go afield, we

---

*"Emergent" was introduced by G. H. Lewes in the late 1870s.

†See pages 196–97 below.

might better—I shall not try to settle the question—consider the idea that Alexander expressed by "Motion"[48] to be closer to Whitehead's "process."

In his London years Whitehead enjoyed opportunities to be influenced by Bergson. He often chatted with his Aristotelian Society friend H. Wildon Carr, who had published a book on Bergson's philosophy in 1911.[49] And Jessie Whitehead told me that she remembered at least one occasion when Bergson was in her parents' house.[50]

Belief in a substantial Bergsonian influence mushroomed after a reviewer of the *Principles of Natural Knowledge,* Theodore de Laguna, wrote:

> Mr. Whitehead seems to have felt very keenly the force of Bergson's criticism of natural science as incapable of expressing the continuity of things. . . .
> . . . the ulterior aim of his whole work is to reform science so that it shall no longer be open to such criticism.[51]

The very long review in *Mind,* written by a friend of Whitehead's, C. D. Broad, did not assert an ulterior aim, nor mention Bergson. And the author, Whitehead himself? He put two references to Bergson into the book. In the Preface he named him as one of seven philosophers who "have initiated and sustained relevant discussions." This is not followed up. The other reference is in the concluding paragraph. Since it reveals Whitehead's feelings about life and death as well as his response to Bergson's philosophy, it deserves quotation:

> So far as direct observation is concerned all that we know of the essential relations of life in nature is stated in two short poetic phrases. The obvious aspect by Tennyson,
> Blow, bugle, blow, set the wild echoes flying,
> And answer, echoes, answer, dying, dying, dying.
> Namely, Bergson's élan vital and its relapse into matter. And Wordsworth with more depth,
> The music in my heart I bore,
> Long after it was heard no more.

Identification of Bergson's doctrine with the obvious does not suggest that Whitehead is accepting it. Quite the contrary; it suggests that Whitehead wants more insight than Bergson offered. When I asked him about de Laguna's interpretation of the *Principles of Natural Knowledge,* he replied that he had read Bergson but was not much worried by him.[52]

In *Science and the Modern World,* a note of sympathy is struck in

Whitehead's comment on Bergson's "so-called anti-intellectualism." He says that it should be construed as "a protest against taking the Newtonian conception of nature as being anything except a high abstraction."[53] That would make Bergson an ally in Whitehead's attack on scientific materialism. Now, Bertrand Russell had often tried to nullify Bergson's philosophy.[54] The criticisms were not distinguished; they relied on such obvious stratagems as fastening on Bergson's distrust of the intellect and turning it against him.

To me, Whitehead's comment was quite in character for him. It may be counted as an episode in the long story of his varied relations with Russell.* Russell's friends thought of him as the great Destroyer in arguments. To Whitehead, many roads led toward truth. Why not be hospitable to a new traveler? In philosophy, we are all groping, and no one owns the whole truth.

Back to the question of Bergson's influence on Whitehead. We saw earlier† that in February and March 1885, when Bergson had not yet published any of his philosophy, Whitehead as a young "Apostle" rejected what Bergson later called the "spatialization" of change.

Nobody should say that the Bergsonian influence on Whitehead can hardly be exaggerated. Of course it can be exaggerated. It is all too easy for the well-read Ph.D., on looking at a new philosophy, to say, "I know where he got this idea! and that one! and that one!" The gain is that he need not sweat long over a new idea if he misreads it as only a new version of one he knows.

Fortunately, it is hard to do this with the Bergson-Whitehead relation: the contrasts are too strong. In all of Whitehead's books from *Science and the Modern World* on, it is evident that his way of thinking, adventurous and systematic, defies Bergson's exhortation,

> Let us have done with great systems embracing all the possible, and sometimes even the impossible! Let us be content with the real, mind and matter.[55]

I once made a study, "The Influence of Bergson, James, and Alexander on Whitehead."[56] More than half of it was devoted to the alleged influence of Bergson. As influence is a causal connection, I explored the possibility that Whitehead derived from Bergson either his choice of problems to investigate or some essentials of his solutions to them. My

---

*Whether or not Russell used the term *anti-intellectualism* in describing Bergson's philosophy, that is the ism which Russell's readers attached to his victim.

†Volume I, pages 136–38.

conclusions (tentative, not final) were negative.[57] To that study I refer readers who believe that Whitehead's philosophy was influenced by these men.

xiv

The Macmillan Company of New York almost lost the right to publish Whitehead's Lowell Lectures of 1925. As Curtice Hitchcock of Macmillan tells the story, in the autumn of 1924 a man from the Harvard University Press "made some rather vague remark to Whitehead who didn't immediately connect it with Lowell Lectures."[58] Harold Murdock of the Harvard Press then made arrangements with Evelyn Whitehead to have Harvard publish those lectures.[59] But acting as her husband's business manager, Evelyn got the right to publish back into Macmillan's hands.

From Sydney Roberts, Secretary to the Syndics of the Cambridge University Press, Hitchcock learned that Cambridge never had a written contract with Whitehead for any of his books that they published. Roberts told him, "Whitehead always has his head above the clouds and is perfectly incapable of transacting business in a definite fashion."[60] And it was useless to write him, because he never answered letters.[61]

To Whitehead, preparing his lectures, performing other academic duties, and developing his mathematical or philosophical ideas always took priority over other kinds of activity. Social obligations outranked business, which came last.

Early in May 1925 the manager of Macmillan's New England branch, F. J. Flagg of Boston, was asked to discuss business with Whitehead. After many attempts he managed to see him. As Flagg wrote to Hitchcock, "This was entirely unsatisfactory. He apparently knows no more about business than a child. He finally referred me to Mrs. Whitehead."[62]

Evelyn was more than willing to talk business with Mr. Flagg. She told him that, frankly, she would prefer Cambridge in England and Macmillan in America to any other publisher of her husband's books. Their finances, she said, had been hit hard by the war; it was imperative that they realize as much as possible from the new manuscript. An American publisher had offered a royalty of 55–60 percent. Evelyn added that she was negotiating with the Cambridge University Press for a uniform edition of her husband's works; if Cambridge was willing to go ahead with this, she was disposed to give them the new manuscript despite the flattering offer of such a high royalty.[63] Evelyn did not identify the generous American publisher. Hitchcock immediately wrote Flagg that Mrs. Whitehead must mean 55 percent of the profits, not a 55 percent royalty on copies sold at retail; that was something no publisher could afford to offer.[64]

The final upshot concerning *Science and the Modern World* was that on June 25, 1925, Whitehead signed a contract; Macmillan was to give him a 15 percent royalty and, on receiving the manuscript, an advance of $250 against the royalties. These terms were not unusual; in fact, Macmillan and the Cambridge University Press had agreed on the 15 percent royalty the summer before. When Hitchcock wrote to Whitehead on July 1, 1924, expressing Macmillan's desire to publish Whitehead's Lowell Lectures, he also wrote to the Cambridge Press, saying that Macmillan wanted to be sure of having the American rights. Both Whitehead and Cambridge seem to have assumed that Cambridge would continue to be his publisher, in the old easygoing way, after his migration to America. Whitehead did not answer Hitchcock's letter, but Cambridge made an offer, which Macmillan accepted, for the American rights to publish these Lowell Lectures at a royalty of 15 percent of the American published price.[65] The book was to be manufactured in the United States, and Macmillan would put it on the market.

This practice was followed with Whitehead's later books.* Cambridge would produce the best editions. But in every case the author's financial agreements were with Macmillan.

---

*However, see the first sentence of Section ii of this chapter, and the footnote attached to it.

Alfred North Whitehead, undated portrait

Whitehead, ca. 1912

T. North Whitehead, 1915

Eric Whitehead, 1917

Jessie Whitehead, 1925

Whitehead with Eve Morgan, ca. 1935

Whitehead in front of Emerson Hall, Harvard, 1936

Whitehead with L. S. Henderson, H. O. Taylor, and
William M. Wheeler, date unknown

T. North Whitehead, undated portrait

Evelyn Wade Whitehead, ca. 1940

Whitehead leaving his last lecture at Harvard, 1939

CHAPTER IX

Religion

i/Invitation to give in February 1926 a course of four
Lowell Lectures on current topics in theology. Their
publication as *Religion in the Making* (*RM*).

ii/The Preface to *RM*. Unpopularity of *RM* in
comparison with *SMW*. Religion not primarily a
social fact. Solitariness. Religion not necessarily
good. Whitehead's general definitions of religion.

iii/The conflict between religion and science, as treated
in *SMW*, Chapter XII.

iv/Refusal to conceive of God as Almighty Power.
Refusal to conceive of religion as sanction of rules of
right conduct. The religious vision. Something that
will give meaning to the tragedy of World War I.
Reactions of Bertrand Russell and North and Jessie
Whitehead to the theistic turn.

v/Question of Whitehead's motives for abandoning
agnosticism. Whitehead's lack of interest in himself.

vi/The dedication of *SMW*; of *RM*.

vii/Whitehead's treatment of communal religion.

viii/Metaphysics defined as a science. Impossibility of
founding beliefs on historical investigations without
metaphysics.

ix/Meaning assigned to "the universe." Two ways of
analyzing the universe. Creativity as protean; as
ultimate.

x/Religious dogmas, necessary but alterable. Bishop
Henry Whitehead. A. N. W.'s acquaintance with
Buddhism.

xi/The problem of evil. God's goodness.

xii/The key to Whitehead's theory of religion. The
ultimate religious evidence.

xiii/Buddhism compared with Christianity. Preference
for St. John over St. Paul. Declines to give sermon
in Unitarian Church. Declines to christen Edsall's
child; Whitehead's unsureness of his religious
beliefs.

xiv/D. H. Lawrence's misreading of conclusion of RM.

xv/Ely's question of availability of Whitehead's God for
modern liberal religious feeling. All order aesthetic.
Whitehead's debt to his wife.

xvi/From God the enemy to God the companion.
Whitehead's metaphysical argument for God.
Metaphysical immortality. Distinction between
metaphysical notions founded on general experience
and those founded on religious experience.

B esides the free course of Lowell Lectures that was given in Huntington Hall, Boston, on a variety of subjects, the Lowell Institute in 1925–26 offered free public lectures on current topics in theology. These were given in King's Chapel, Boston, under the auspices of the Harvard Divinity School, the Episcopal Theological School at Cambridge, and the Andover Theological Seminary.[1] Whitehead was invited to give a course consisting of four such lectures. They were delivered in February 1926.

On July 19, 1925, Whitehead wrote to North:

> I am to deliver another course of Lowell Lectures in Boston next year on "Science and Religion," *i. e.,* on the scientific criticism of religion.

It is likely that when Whitehead wrote this letter he had not chosen all his topics for this new course of Lowell Lectures, but believed that he would have more to say about the conflict between science and religion than he had said in Chapter XII of *Science and the Modern World.** The general title he proposed and that the Lowell Institute announced for the new course, however, was, "Religion: Its Passing Forms and Eternal Truths."[2]

When the lectures that Whitehead delivered in February 1926 were published, without additions, as a book, the title given the book was *Religion in the Making.*

In the very short Preface to the book, which Whitehead dated March 13, 1926, he wrote:

> The aim of the lectures was to give a concise analysis of the various factors in human nature which go to form a religion, to exhibit the inevitable transformation of religion with the transformation of knowledge, and more especially to direct attention to the foundation of religion on our apprehension of those permanent elements by

---

*That chapter will be discussed on pages 186–87 below.

reason of which there is a stable order in the world, permanent elements apart from which there could be no changing world.

The last half of this description assures us that Whitehead will offer a metaphysical foundation for religion.

Religion in the Making was published in September 1926. Macmillan desired publication later in the fall, but Whitehead hurried the company, as he had done with *Science and the Modern World*.[3]

ii

Whitehead explained in the Preface that he was applying to religion "the train of thought" which he had applied to science in his earlier Lowell Lectures; the two books show "the same way of thought in different applications."

There was a great difference in the reception of the two books. The earlier one ran with the tides of the times; *Religion in the Making* ran against them. People were willing to believe that scientific materialism as a philosophy of nature needed to be bridled, but not that the prevailing philosophy of religion needed scrutiny.

The general subject of the first of the four lectures was the emergence of religion in history. Early in it, Whitehead set his face against the view that religion is primarily a social fact:

> Social facts are of great importance to religion, because there is no such thing as absolutely independent existence. You cannot abstract society from man; most psychology is herd psychology. But all collective emotions leave untouched the awful ultimate fact, which is the human being, consciously alone with itself, for its own sake. Religion is what the individual does with his own solitariness.[4]

The last statement has been repudiated almost as often as it has been quoted. Churchmen would have preferred something like "Religion is what the individual does with his gregariousness."* Whitehead supported his view dramatically by reminding us:

> The great religious conceptions which haunt the imaginations of civilized mankind are scenes of solitariness: Prometheus chained to his rock, Mahomet brooding in the desert, the meditations of the Buddha, the solitary Man on the Cross.[5]

---

*A philosopher, Donald A. Crosby, wrote a first-rate paper, "Religion and Solitariness," in which he analyzed Whitehead's meaning fully and sympathetically. In Section vii of this chapter I shall draw on part of Professor Crosby's paper.

I suppose that many churchmen felt sent to Coventry by what Whitehead said when he declared that if you are never solitary, you are never
religious:

> Collective enthusiasms, revivals, institutions, churches, rituals,
> bibles, codes of behaviour, are the trappings of religion, its passing
> forms. They may be useful, or harmful; they may be authoritatively
> ordained, or merely temporary expedients. But the end of religion is
> beyond all this.[6]

I resist the temptation to quote at greater length from the fine opening chapter of *Religion in the Making.* My temptation is natural, for I am
convinced by what Whitehead said there, and think that this book as a
whole is one of the best things he wrote as a philosopher. Science was
bound to go its own way, without attending to Whitehead, in responding to the new discoveries of the 1920s and 1930s; the men of religion
could have heeded him in their response to the turmoil of those decades,
and did not. They were weak in historical perspective and engrossed in
their social doctrine. In their role as public relations men, they could not
agree with Whitehead that religion is not necessarily good, still less
admit that the belief that it is good "is a dangerous delusion."[7] But
history was obviously with Whitehead. Recently, the savage character
of the appeals to religion that were made in the Middle East in the 1980s
corroborated his point.

The book received relatively more favorable reviews in the United
Kingdom than in America. The notable exception was a scathing review by the philosopher G. E. Moore.[8] Moore was preoccupied with
the question of the evidence for believing in religion.

In the opening section, "Religion Defined," of the first chapter, there
are many statements that begin, "Religion is . . ." There are two
which, I think, serve best as Whitehead's general definitions.

> Religion is the art and the theory of the internal life of man, so far as it
> depends on the man himself and on what is permanent in the nature
> of things.

On its doctrinal side, a religion is

> a system of general truths which have the effect of transforming
> character when they are sincerely held and vividly apprehended.

Whitehead had declared that the primary religious virtue is sincerity.[9]

These statements were too dispassionate to be welcomed either by
believers or by freethinkers.

iii

It turned out that in these Lowell Lectures on religion Whitehead was so occupied with religion in history, dogmas, and metaphysics that he had little time left for the conflict between religion and science. To get acquainted with his view of it, we must go back to Chapter XII of *Science and the Modern World*. Like so much that he wrote, this chapter was an address which he gave on a particular occasion. "Religion and Science" was presented Sunday afternoon, April 5, 1925. It was Whitehead's only contribution to the Phillips Brooks Lecture Series at Harvard in his first academic year there.

When writing to North a few hours before this lecture, Whitehead called his subject "the young lady of Riga problem." I did not understand this until North told me that the English pronounce *Riga* with a long *i,* not with a long *e* as Americans do. Then we have

There was a young lady of Riga,
Who smiled as she rode on a tiger.
They came back from the ride
With the lady inside,
And the smile on the face of the tiger.

Unlike Bertrand Russell and many other friends, Whitehead did not believe that science was devouring religion. He believed that both are "permanent elements of human nature."[10] In dealing with such matters, it had become his habit to look at them in a historical perspective. When we do so, we discover that there has always been a conflict between religion and science, and that each has undergone continual development.[11]

After observing that the different ways in which science and religion deal with such lives as those of John Wesley and St. Francis of Assisi make discrepancies inevitable, Whitehead said:

It would, however, be missing the point to think that we need not trouble ourselves about the conflict between science and religion. In an intellectual age there can be no active interest which puts aside all hope of a vision of the harmony of truth.[12]

Thus philosophy has a constructive job to do. Whitehead could not be content with an analysis of propositions that occur in science and of others drawn from religion.

The important question is, in what spirit we should face the conflict. He declared, "A clash of doctrines is not a disaster—it is an opportunity,"[13] and cited the discovery of argon as an illustration drawn from science.

Whitehead was much concerned about the fading of interest in religion. He insisted,

> Religion will not regain its old power until it can face change in the same spirit as does science.[14]

In the first half of this lecture his main points were

> that religion is the expression of one type of fundamental experiences of mankind: that religious thought develops into an increasing accuracy of expression, disengaged from adventitious imagery: that the interaction between religion and science is one great factor in promoting this development.[15]

So much for the conflict between science and religion. In the latter half of his Phillips Brooks Lecture Whitehead said little about science. He talked about what religion ought to be.

iv

After calling religion the reaction of human nature in its search for God, Whitehead asserted, "The presentation of God under the aspect of power awakens every modern instinct of critical reaction."[16]

I think that the embrace of this aspect of God is rooted in the instinct of fear and in our pre-scientific inability to cope with events. I have speculated* that when Whitehead, in his early thirties, was comparing the authority of Canterbury with that of Rome, a main reason why he rejected both and became an agnostic was his dislike of the doctrine of Almighty Power which they both maintained.

In the address which I have been considering, Whitehead noticed another factor that weakens the hold of religion: the presentation of it as providing a sanction of rules of right conduct. And the purpose of right conduct easily becomes "the formation of pleasing social relations," so that the religious life is in danger, alas, of becoming "a research after comfort."[17] The phrase was a bit of hyperbole, but Whitehead's point was sound.

He held that, in general,

> Conduct is a by-product of religion—an inevitable by-product, but not the main point. Every great religious teacher has revolted against the presentation of religion as a mere sanction of rules of conduct. Saint Paul denounced the Law, and Puritan divines spoke of the

---

*See Volume I, Chapter X, Section ii.

filthy rags of righteousness. The insistence upon rules of conduct marks the ebb of religious fervour.[18]

At any rate, what Whitehead sought from religion was something quite different. This appeared when, as he neared the end of his Phillips Brooks Lecture, he undertook to state, "in all diffidence," what he conceived to be "the essential character of the religious spirit."

> Religion is the vision of something which stands beyond, behind, and within, the passing flux of immediate things; something which is real, and yet waiting to be realised; something which is a remote possibility, and yet the greatest of present facts; something that gives meaning to all that passes, and yet eludes apprehension; something whose possession is the final good, and yet is beyond all reach; something which is the ultimate ideal, and the hopeless quest.[19]

I do not think that this remarkable passage would be composed by anyone who had a religious faith, as religious faith is customarily understood. The author was *looking for* something, something that will give meaning to what has happened; in Whitehead's case, to the carnage of the First World War, and Eric's death in it.

An agnostic will ask, what if the religious vision is a persistent illusion? Whitehead gave his answer at once. Apart from this religious vision, he said,

> human life is a flash of occasional enjoyments lighting up a mass of pain and misery, a bagatelle of transient experience.[20]

That is how human life looked to him during and after World War I. He could not have said this before that war decisively ended an age of secular progress and hope. Whether his harsh summary of human life is true or false, it appeared true to most of the people in the nations at war.

When I asked Bertrand Russell about his view of Whitehead's turn to religion, he gave it flatly and crudely: "Eric's death made him want to believe in immortality."[21] It would perhaps be more accurate, because less explicit, to say what Jessie immediately said when I brought up this subject: "Eric's death is behind it."[22] North expressed a similar view.[23] North's own convictions, like Russell's, were atheistic; he himself told me so. (But his was a quiet atheism.) Jessie seemed to me to be not so much atheistic as indifferent to the whole question of theism versus atheism. The children knew their father's mind well, and understood the war-engendered feelings in the family better than Russell did. Jessie added that the effect of Eric's death on her mother especially affected her father. Indeed it did.

V

Did Whitehead ever look into his motives for abandoning agnosticism? I think not, though I cannot demonstrate this. Remember, he never kept a diary. And he did not express his feelings about such things in letters, at least not in any that I have been able to discover. We have to fall back upon a feature of his unusual character: lack of interest in himself. In 1941 he began an attempt that had been urged on him (it would take his mind off the war), to extend his autobiography beyond the fourteen printed pages written for, and published in, the Whitehead volume of Schilpp's *Library of Living Philosophers*. He barely began an extension; then he lost interest. (Even his consent to participate in Schilpp's series had been given reluctantly.)[24] All his thought and action were outwardly directed. The kind of self-knowledge he thought it important for a thinker to seek was not awareness of his motives, but awareness of the limitations of the concepts he was using; and this, being a matter of stretching the outwardly directed imagination, is not self-knowledge at all. I think it unlikely that Whitehead ever took more than a passing glance at the motives behind his abandonment of agnosticism.

Would he have remained an agnostic but for the war? Probably not. The degree of this hypothetical probability cannot be estimated. I would say only that a thinking man who as a boy was brought up in a religion that did not repel him and who in his thirties becomes an unbeliever is likely, if he is at all religious by nature, to figure out his own theism eventually. That is what Whitehead the philosopher did. By contrast, a man with no tendency toward religion will either maintain a superficial piety all his life or, if he is as much exposed to agnosticism as Whitehead was from his Cambridge years on, will come to a simple atheism and stay with it.

vi

Whitehead had appropriately dedicated his first American book, *Science and the Modern World*, "to my colleagues, past and present, whose friendship is inspiration." In fact, he wrote his books only by getting away from his colleagues for a few hours each day. But he liked to raise people's spirits, almost to the point of flattering them.

He gave *Religion in the Making* a specific dedication: "to E. W." It was Evelyn who had been hardest hit by Eric's death, and who most wanted to know what religion meant to her husband. It was fitting that he dedicate the most personal of his philosophical books to her.

vii

Recall that in the Preface to this book Whitehead said that he would give a concise analysis of the factors in human nature which go to form a religion. In his first chapter he named four such factors: ritual, emotion, belief, and rationalization, by which he meant the revision of beliefs (including myths) so that they become agreeable to reason. He devoted most of this chapter to the contributions of communal religions to stable societies, and to the advance from such religions to those which arise in solitariness and express world-loyalty. For Whitehead, communal religion is not the real thing, it is only proto-religion.

An evolutionary orientation which tries to trace the development of religion from its earliest beginnings through distinct stages is no longer, I think, favored by cultural anthropologists. We do not know enough about prehistoric times to essay a probable account of the origins of the religious sentiment among mankind. And Whitehead's description of communal religion amounts to an outdated stereotype. His style in this book is oracular, but no more so than it was in his writings on education. The real defect in this part of *Religion in the Making* is the frequency of sweeping generalizations for which no data are cited. He relied too heavily on a few secondary sources. Indeed, he had done so in *Science and the Modern World*, without doing any serious damage to his account of the influence of the scientific mentality, to his rejection of scientific materialism, or to the sketch of his new philosophy of nature; these are not vitiated by the more accurate knowledge, which we now possess, of such things as Galileo's experiments. Whitehead's conception of religion as it ought to be, which is now his main concern, is not vitiated by defects in his account of the road that has so far been traveled toward it. But it *is* unfortunate that his book on religion was named *Religion in the Making*.[25]

viii

Whitehead began the third chapter of *Religion in the Making* with the assertion, "Religion requires a metaphysical backing; for its authority is endangered by the intensity of the emotions which it generates." In a footnote on the next page he defined metaphysics as a science, "the science which seeks to discover the general ideas which are indispensably relevant to the analysis of everything that happens." He does not define metaphysics as a science in any other philosophical book that he wrote. He did not need to do so here; he could have repeated the definition he gave in *Science and the Modern World*: "a dispassionate consideration of the nature of things, antecedently to any special investigation into their details."[26] ("The nature of things" is Whitehead's customary name for the most general characteristics of the totality of existence.) I think the fact that in February 1926 he defined metaphysics as a science reflects the continued presence of a mathematical scientist in this philosopher. In another year or two—when he begins to write *Process and Reality*—Whitehead will describe the task of metaphysics as the framing of a speculative philosophy. Thereafter, science more and more becomes to him something to be contrasted with philosophy and with religion.

The proper alternative to a metaphysical foundation for religion is the "curious delusion"

that the rock upon which our beliefs can be founded is an historical investigation. You can only interpret the past in terms of the present. The present is all that you have.[27]

If your present moment of experience does not show that it derives from your immediately prior experience, you lack the necessary basis for making any appeal to history. It is likewise true that if the present moment does not include any experience of deviation from your immediately prior experience, you lack a basis for believing in change. These two facts remind us of the ground that experience must provide for exploring the universe around us, so as to gain some conception of the nature of things.

ix

Whitehead embarked on metaphysical analysis in the third chapter of *Religion in the Making*. He named his subject "the universe, conceived as that which is comprehensive of all that there is."[28] He continued to use "universe" with this philosophical meaning throughout his later writings, but he also used it in its astrophysical sense whenever that was pertinent.

In Chapter V of his *Principles of Natural Knowledge* Whitehead had correlated different ways of analyzing nature. He now begins his essay into metaphysics by asserting that there are many ways of analyzing the universe. He then expounds two analyses. Both are needed; he does not suggest any others. The first analysis is into

(1) the actual world, passing in time; and (2) those elements which go to its formation.[29]

The formative elements had been introduced in *Science and the Modern World,* but not as succinctly as in the present description of them. They are:

1. The creativity whereby the actual world has its character of temporal passage to novelty.

2. The realm of ideal entities, or forms, which are in themselves not actual, but are such that they are exemplified in everything that is actual, according to some proportion of relevance.

3. The actual but non-temporal entity whereby the indetermination of mere creativity is transmuted into a determinate freedom. This non-temporal actual entity is what men call God—the supreme God of rationalized religion.[30]

In his second mode of analysis, Whitehead analyzes the temporal world

into a multiplicity of occasions of actualization. These are the primary actual units of which the temporal world is composed. Call each such occasion an "epochal occasion." Then the actual world is a community of epochal occasions.*

The nature of this community will be spelled out in detail in Whitehead's Gifford Lectures. Here he only justifies his use of "community" by saying,

Each unit has in its nature a reference to every other member of the community, so that each unit is a microcosm representing in itself the entire all-inclusive universe.[31]

Whitehead calls the units creatures of creativity, and explains the temporal character of the actual world by the fact that the creativity is not separable from its creatures.

Accordingly, the creativity for a creature becomes the creativity with the creature, and thereby passes into another phase of itself. It is now the creativity for a new creature. Thus there is a transition of the creative action, and this transition exhibits itself, in the physical world, in the guise of routes of temporal succession.[32]

Creativity, so perfectly protean, was Whitehead's metaphysically ultimate concept. It and the terms *many* and *one* will comprise the

---

*See Chapter VIII, Section ix.

Category of the Ultimate in *Process and Reality*. Remember what White-head said in *Science and the Modern World* when he compared his meta-physics with Spinoza's:

> His one substance is for me the one underlying activity of realisation individualising itself in an interlocked plurality of modes.[33]

Whitehead does not conceive of God as a *personal being*. This theism is a highly philosophical one. And the kind of immortality which he will describe in his Gifford Lectures will not be personal immortality.

When Whitehead discusses the way in which we know God, he agrees with the familiar view that our knowledge is not a direct intui-tion, but is reached inferentially.[34]

X

So much for the metaphysical foundation of religion, as Whitehead saw it early in 1926. I must now consider his treatment of religious dogmas. He began this in the second of his four Lowell Lectures on religion, and stated his conclusions in the last lecture. I have already covered some of this ground, for Whitehead held that there was, and always had been, but one fundamental religious dogma in debate: "What do you mean by 'God?'" All other dogmas were, and are, sub-sidiary.

Whitehead referred also to mathematical dogmas and dogmas of physical science. He did not, in these lectures, discuss the analogy he assumed to hold between those dogmas and religious dogmas, and my assessment of the analogy is best postponed to my last chapter.[35]

Churchmen tend to over-value their dogmas. Whitehead was cir-cumspect: "Religions commit suicide when they find their inspirations in their dogmas."[36] The inspirations are matters of history. Remember, in "The Aims of Education," Whitehead's protest against inert ideas, and his lively support for the doctrine that the purpose of education is to stimulate and guide the pupil's self-development. A similar attitude, with a similar feeling behind it, occurs when, ten years later, he writes of religious dogmas in these terms:

> The sources of religious belief are always growing, though some supreme expressions may lie in the past. Records of these sources are not formulae. They elicit in us intuitive response which pierces be-yond dogma.[37]

Of course dogmatic expression is necessary. Public concepts must be applied to what is experienced in solitariness.

But the dogmas, however true, are only bits of the truth, expressed in terms which in some ways are over-assertive and in other ways lose the essence of truth.[38]

Whitehead's conclusion about dogmas is about as uncompromising as he ever gets. Although dogmas have their measure of truth,

in their precise forms they are narrow, limitative, and alterable: in effect untrue, when carried over beyond the proper scope of their utility.

A system of dogmas may be the ark within which the Church floats safely down the flood-tide of history. But the Church will perish unless it opens its window and lets out the dove to search for an olive branch.[39]

Whitehead was referring to the Church of England, in which he had been reared.* His older brother Henry had retired in 1922 after almost thirty years as Bishop of Madras. Madras was the most important diocese in India, and needed the services of two men; against the strongest opposition, Henry Whitehead secured the appointment of an Indian, Samuel (later Bishop) Azariah. When Henry went to Madras in 1899, he was a strict Tractarian, but he swung over to an ecumenical point of view. A historian of the Church in South India has said of the change in his attitude,

Above all it was a steady growth in the understanding of the other man's point of view, and it was caused by a practical approach to the opportunities which South India seemed to offer.[40]

Henry and Alfred Whitehead did not look at all alike,† and they were as different as Oxford and Cambridge; but they shared many traits of character: energy, tolerance, breadth of view, common sense about problems; and *benign* was the adjective which each man's associates used. Henry's academic career was in the classics, and he did not have the mathematician's desire to seek, analyze, and relate general propositions. The philosopher Alfred thought in terms of ideas beyond the imaginations of other men, including his brother's. Very few letters between them are extant, and I dare not assert that either one substantially influenced the other. But, unless I have misunderstood *Religion in the Making,* the philosopher liked what his brother did in South India; in particular, it is probable that when A. N. W. compared a system of

---

*See Volume I, Chapters II and III.

†See the last of the family photographs in Volume I.

dogmas with Noah's Ark, his thought was that the Church will perish unless it adopts policies like Henry Whitehead's.

What Whitehead said about Buddhism in these lectures of 1926 owed something to past conversations with Henry, but much more to recent conversations with his closest friend in the Harvard Philosophy Department, James Woods, who had an expert's knowledge on Buddhism. Whitehead was not interested in the features on which experts differ; but, believing that Buddhism and Christianity were the major religions of the world, he voiced comparative remarks throughout these Lowell Lectures. Both, he thought, were in full decay.[41] And instead of trying to learn from each other, each had sheltered itself from the other.[42]

xi

When dealing with the chapter "God," in *Science and the Modern World,** I failed to call attention to the emphatic final paragraph of that chapter:

> Among medieval and modern philosophers, anxious to establish the religious significance of God, an unfortunate habit has prevailed of paying to Him metaphysical compliments. He has been conceived as the foundation of the metaphysical situation with its ultimate activity. If this situation be adhered to, there can be no alternative except to discern in Him the origin of all evil as well as of all good. He is then the supreme author of the play, and to Him† must therefore be ascribed its shortcomings as well as its success.

I do not see any escape from this simple argument. From St. Augustine to the present day, theologians have devoted their utmost skills to saving all of God's traditional attributes. Whitehead does not fall back on the private conception of evil or on any other conception that has been devised for this purpose. In his conception of God Whitehead gives up omnipotence, omniscience, and omni-infinitude (since a God that was infinite in all respects would be evil as well as good).[43] The divine attribute that Whitehead keeps and makes central is goodness. To him, "God" is the name for the force, or at least tendency, toward harmony in the universe.

---

*See page 163 above.

†Whitehead's publishers were not consistent in their use of initial capital letters in pronouns whose antecedents were *God*.

Whitehead's theory of the interaction between God and the temporal world is only suggested now; it will be laid out in *Process and Reality*. But we can observe now that it is a mistake to think that he has set up the creativity to be a kind of God beyond God. The mistake comes from a desire to ascribe to God everything that is metaphysically important. The universal creativity assures us only that every state of affairs will give birth to another. Whether the existents of the immediate future are better or worse than those of the present, is no business of the creativity.

xii

I think that the key to Whitehead's theory of religion is the general concept of "a rightness in things, partially conformed to and partially disregarded."[44] That there is such a rightness can only be known intuitively.

> This intuition is not the discernment of a form of words, but of a type of character. It is characteristic of the learned mind to exalt words. Yet mothers can ponder many things in their hearts which their lips cannot express. These many things, which are thus known, constitute the ultimate religious evidence, beyond which there is no appeal.[45]

It was characteristic of Whitehead throughout his years at Harvard to take cracks at the learned mind for exalting words. Here, it would be strange if he did not have Evelyn in mind as he wrote about mothers. Is he not exalting what he takes to be her feeling about Eric's death?* The last sentence reveals a good deal about the man who wrote it, but nothing about religious evidence. Pondering is not knowing, nor does it constitute evidence; at best it is a preliminary to knowing. Whitehead appears to be saying that Evelyn's feeling about Eric's death is conclusive.

xiii

One could not read *Religion in the Making* without concluding that, despite his balanced opinions and his occasional harsh judgments, Whitehead was definitely a friend of religion. He was not an uncommitted scientist to whom "religion" is only the name for a distinctive group of social phenomena.

---

*See page 188 above.

The central section of the last chapter of the book deals with the three traditions Buddhism, Christianity, and science. I have a strong impression that Whitehead had no emotional feeling for Buddhism, only a deep respect and a theoretical understanding. Here he contrasts the moral codes:

> To put it briefly, Buddhism, on the whole, discourages the sense of active personality, whereas Christianity encourages it.[46]

When Whitehead at Sherborne School was Captain of the Games, then Head Boy, he was helping his schoolmates to be active, physically disciplined persons. His successful competitive life as a student at Cambridge was as far from Buddhist practice as a young Englishman could get. His love for Evelyn was love of a vivid personality. He did not recoil from any of these experiences at any later time. The religion which he found appealing was Christianity. He prized its message for the modern world to rely not so much on force as on the slow persuasiveness of ideals. It endeavored to instill love.

Whitehead thought that St. Paul's teaching made fear dominant rather than love, and wanted us to seek God with the help of John instead of Paul.[47] When I wrote *Understanding Whitehead* I thought he was often unfair to Paul; now I simply do not know, and I lack the Pauline knowledge to justify an opinion.

The writings after *Religion in the Making* show a good deal of elaboration of the position he took there on religion, but no serious changes. He did not subscribe to a creed or join a church.

Almost twenty years later, he told Lucien Price that if he were to join a church, he would prefer the Unitarians; it was sad that they had so little influence.[48] But Whitehead had had a long time to join them, and in 1935 he turned down a splendid opportunity to speak in the Unitarian First Parish Church in Cambridge (where Emerson had given his Phi Beta Kappa address "The American Scholar"). A graduate of the Harvard Divinity School (Whitehead had occasionally lectured there), Leslie T. Pennington, was called to that church. Dr. Pennington wrote me that he thought Whitehead had been speaking more profoundly to the condition of our life than any other living philosopher; so he sent him the most persuasive invitation he could write to preach the sermon at his Installation Service.[49] Whitehead, in a gracious reply, declined to do so. He had talked it over with his wife, and agreed with her that acceptance would tend to identify him with Unitarianism and thereby impair the objectivity of his influence elsewhere.

Protection of his image was not a factor in the answer he gave to an invitation to officiate in a private religious ceremony. His young Harvard friends Dr. and Mrs. John T. Edsall were theists but not members of any church. They had read *Religion in the Making*. In 1930 they asked him, by letter, whether he would christen their firstborn, in words like these: "In the love of God I name this child Lawrence, and require of his parents that they bring him up in the ways of beauty and truth." There was to be a little ceremony, a "dedication" to God. Whitehead sent a reply in which he apologetically but firmly declined to do this. The Edsalls did not keep the letter, but Dr. Edsall told me[50] that Whitehead said in it that he did not feel entirely sure of his own opinions and would not wish to make any statement in connection with belief.

xiv

The conclusion of *Religion in the Making* received an unmerited accolade when D. H. Lawrence quoted and completely misunderstood it in *Lady Chatterley's Lover*.* Lady Chatterley returns from a tryst with Mellors to find that her husband has been reading "one of the latest scientific-religious books" (neither author nor title is named). He insists on reading out to her the final four sentences, which he especially relishes.

> The universe shows us two aspects: on one side it is physically wasting, on the other side it is spiritually ascending.
> It is thus passing with a slowness, inconceivable in our measures of time, to new creative conditions, amid which the physical world, as we at present know it, will be represented by a ripple barely to be distinguished from nonentity.
> The present type of order in the world has arisen from an unimaginable past, and it will find its grave in an unimaginable future. There remain the inexhaustible realm of abstract forms, and creativity, with its shifting character ever determined afresh by its own creatures, and God, upon whose wisdom all forms of order depend.

The adverbs in the first sentence gave Lawrence a golden opportunity to have Lady Chatterley respond to the passage with contempt. But it is a complete mistake to read Whitehead as a despiser of the body. For him, physical and mental are universal features of whatever is actual. And to Whitehead *qua* mathematician physicist, "physical" does not connote "carnal." The passage is about the world of physics, noth-

---

*Chapter XVI.

ing else. Of course Lawrence had no idea of what Whitehead meant by physical and mental, nor of his idea that the laws of physics which now prevail will be less dominant in the future.

xv

American academia is as far removed from D. H. Lawrence as you can get; so I should like next to notice a criticism of Whitehead's conception of God that was written by a professional philosopher. Stephen Lee Ely called his little book *The Religious Availability of Whitehead's God*.[51] Ely claimed that Whitehead's God is of no use to modern liberal religious feeling. He did not define modern liberal religious feeling, but assumed that it requires a God who wishes humanity well, whose values are fundamentally the same as human values, and with whom man can cooperate to eliminate what man himself finds evil. Since Whitehead did not explicitly endow his God with these qualities, his God should not be called good; he is in fact an aesthete of highly dubious moral character, not worthy of being called God.

Ely's desiderata were typical of Midwestern progressive political philosophy at the time (about 1940), and amounted to little more than that. But Whitehead *had* maintained that all order is basically aesthetic order derived from God's immanence in the world.[52] He conceived of aesthetic experience as feeling that arose from the realization of contrast under identity.

This was only a conception, one that came easily to a mathematician familiar with periodicities. Evelyn every day lived out and consciously looked for such aesthetic experiences. Whitehead's philosophical ideas owe a great deal to her in this way—as providing him with a model of what he considered most important. *Religion in the Making* is the first of his books which exhibit this relationship, and it is most evident there.

xvi

In this book Whitehead often summed up the enrichment of religion as it moves beyond the communal toward its ideal condition as the advance from God the enemy, whom you placate, to God the companion, whom you imitate.

He summarized the need for his metaphysical concept of God and its function in these words:

> The religious insight is the grasp of this truth: That the order of the world, the depth of reality of the world, the value of the world in its

whole and in its parts, the beauty of the world, the zest of life, the peace of life, and the mastery of evil, are all bound together—not accidentally, but by reason of this truth: that the universe exhibits a creativity with infinite freedom, and a realm of forms with infinite possibilities; but that this creativity and these forms are together impotent to achieve actuality apart from the completed ideal harmony, which is God.[53]

The motive for Whitehead's theistic turn is satisfied in his conclusion about Eric's death: what passes away "contributes its quality as an immortal fact to the order which informs the world."[54] Immortality is here ascribed not to a person but to a fact. We could say that Whitehead affirmed only a metaphysical immortality.

Finally, we must note that Whitehead draws a distinction between two kinds of metaphysical notions: those which are founded upon our general experience, and additional notions which are founded upon religious experience. The distinction is made in all the books in which he discusses religion. In *Religion in the Making* he observes that the attempt to make such additions is perfectly legitimate: but he adds,

we must be prepared to amplify, recast, generalize, and adapt, so as to absorb into one system all sources of experience.[55]

This was the policy Whitehead followed in all his philosophical creations, and recommended to every philosopher who seeks a broad understanding.

CHAPTER X

The Atypical English Philosopher

i/Whitehead at his first professional meeting of
American philosophers.

ii/The Sixth International Congress of Philosophy.
The paper "Time." Alexander's injunction to take
time seriously. Whitehead, Bradley, and Russell.
Replacement of change by supersession.
Transitional character of this paper.

iii/Philosophy as a short subject. North's book of
instruments.

iv/Lectures at University of Illinois. Their reception.

v/Invitation to give Barbour-Page Lectures at
University of Virginia. Choice of subject,
Symbolism. Attendance.

vi/Publication of *Symbolism: Its Meaning and Effect*. Its
Dedication. The reference to Locke in the Preface;
to Santayana.

vii/Definition of symbolism. Direct experience of an
external world. Two forms of such experience.
Perception of causal efficacy the more fundamental.
Answer to Hume's denial of it. Sensation of touch.

viii/Rehabilitation of idea of a cause. Appeal to naive
experience. Need for pragmatic check on
correctness of perception. What the pragmatists
failed to notice.

ix/ "Uses of Symbolism" (third lecture at Virginia).
Burke. Relative unimportance of presented sense-
data.

x/ Evelyn's contribution to *Symbolism*. The pathos
which haunts the world.

xi/ Answer to critics of *Symbolism*. Instinct in the
inorganic world.

xii/ Value of *Symbolism* among Whitehead's books. Its
conclusion.

I believe that the first professional meeting of philosophers that Whitehead attended in America was the annual meeting of the American Philosophical Association's Eastern Division,* held for three days in the last week of 1925. The host institution was Smith College, in Northampton, Massachusetts. Whitehead had been asked to present the initial paper in a symposium on Time, on December 30. He was now the outstanding newcomer among American philosophers, and this occasion was eagerly awaited. The other symposiasts were Professors W. P. Montague and W. H. Sheldon. Whitehead did not publish his paper; I must rely on a report of the symposium, written soon afterward by J. H. Randall, Jr.[1]

There was no real symposium, as the three papers were quite independent of each other, and none of the men seemed to have read the others' papers beforehand. What Whitehead had written for this session was too long for the allotted time; he had to curtail it. His paper, Randall said,

> consisted of a series of distinctions and definitions made with the mathematician's rigor to serve as the concepts for an understanding of physical events.[2]

These words will suggest to my reader how the majority of American professional philosophers reacted to this transplanted mathematician. Whitehead's audience made little immediate response to his novel ideas; they let themselves be floored by them. Few of his hearers were ready to start thinking in terms of actual occasions rather than changing substances, and few were ready to accept or to challenge the epochal theory of time, first presented in *Science and the Modern World* and now sketched again.

In the discussion which followed, Whitehead accused the other two speakers of considering the future as it will be when it is a dead past, instead of recognizing genuine novelty and becoming.[3] He had not

---

*This comprised rather more than half of the Association's membership.

much used those positive words in his English writings, but he had prepared the way for them in his doctrine of the passage of nature. Scientifically minded philosophers habitually ignore that side of nature, and think it a virtue to think tenselessly.

Science and the Modern World had been out for a little more than two months. Many of the philosophers at this Eastern Division meeting wanted to buttonhole Whitehead and ask him questions about passages in it. He tried to avoid this; he wanted to meet the younger men and to find out what lines of thought they were pursuing.

ii

Much more important was the Sixth International Congress of Philosophy, held at Harvard in September 1926.* For this congress Whitehead wrote a paper, "Time," subsequently published in its *Proceedings.*† Its extreme condensation makes it unusually difficult; only a few Whitehead scholars have given it the attention it deserves.

The paper starts out by noting Alexander's injunction to take time seriously. Then we should not try to think of the complete totality of all existence, nor of a plurality of existents, each of which is complete in itself without any essential transition to or dependence on the others. Neither the philosophers who want a monism like Bradley's nor those who embrace an atomistic pluralism like Russell's are taking time seriously. Whitehead does not name either man, but in his lectures at Harvard he often proscribed their doctrines.‡ I believe that these two were the philosophers of Whitehead's time who were his natural adversaries as he developed his own philosophy. You could almost say that he cut his metaphysical teeth on their works. You cannot really say it, because when he was a young man he had some metaphysical convictions and discussed metaphysical questions in meetings of the "Apostles."§

Whitehead always disagreed with most of Bradley's *Logic* and with his *Appearance and Reality,* and completely repudiated the idea that time is a self-contradictory feature of appearance. But he came to find valuable ideas in Bradley's later work. Not so in the case of Russell. Although Bertie was the greatest logician since Aristotle, in matters on-

---

*Whitehead wrote to Samuel Alexander, urging him to come, but he did not.
†Reprinted in *IS*.
‡Bradley and Russell were philosophical opponents, but they respected each other.
§See Volume I, pages 136–38.

tological he was, Whitehead thought—and would sometimes say to his Harvard students—completely mistaken.

Among earlier philosophers, Whitehead concentrated his attention on a very few. He had discussed Descartes and Locke in *Science and the Modern World,* but had not finished with them (as he had finished with Berkeley). In the opening section of "Time" he claims that Descartes on substances must be corrected, and he appeals to Locke for support. The correction is radical:

> If time be taken seriously, no concrete entity can change. It can only be superseded. . . .
>
> Thus in the place of Descartes's substance with "endurance" as one of its principal attributes, we must put the notion of an "occasion" with "supersession" as part of its real essence. By Locke, the phrase "perpetually perishing" is used in the same sense as "supersession" here.[4]

Time is a complex concept. For Whitehead, it arises from the application of three fundamental notions to occasions: supersession, prehension, and incompleteness.

Anyone who compares this paper with *Science and the Modern World* and *Process and Reality* will be struck by its transitional character. For example, in the later book the term *supersession* is not used, but the idea is fundamental and is often driven home with other words. The "events" of the 1925 Lowell Lectures are replaced by "(actual) occasions." The concept of prehension is plainly on its way to becoming one of the eight "categories of existence" in *Process and Reality*. The description of an occasion as "dipolar" (physical and mental) appears for the first time. So do the terms *objective immortality* and *presentational immediacy*.

iii

After the great success of *Science and the Modern World* and the mixed reception of his Lowell Lectures on Religion, Whitehead felt that his next book should be addressed purely to philosophers. He wrote about this in a letter to North on May 16, 1926. The passage will cause anyone who has looked at *Process and Reality* to gasp:

> I want to follow it [*SMW*] up with something purely addressed to philosophers—*short* and *clear*, if I can make it so! But I reckon that it will take me about two years to get that ready. My view is that a lot of modern philosophy is much too controversial—hunting rabbits

which bolt into the wrong burrows. There cannot be much in the subject. What there is to be said, ought to be put shortly—If one could only see how to do it. You see that I am rather echoing back to you, your own views as to the book on design. After all, philosophy is only the statement of the general design of things in general. It *must* be a short subject.

Father and son had been corresponding about the book North was planning. Its title, when it was finally published in 1934, was *Instruments and Accurate Mechanism: Underlying Principles*. He dedicated it to his father.

In mentioning to North the excessively controversial character of modern philosophy, Whitehead probably had their old friend Russell in mind. Bertie was always hunting rabbits which bolted into the wrong burrows.

I do not know, and I doubt whether anyone will ever *know*, whether Whitehead began a short statement of "the general design of things in general," and if he did, how far he carried it before he started work on his Gifford Lectures. The notion of the brevity of philosophy makes sense only if we bear in mind his original subject, mathematics, in every branch of which a properly axiomatized general theory spawns innumerable branchings and endless developments. Mathematics is not a short subject, because it includes both general theories and the endless developments from them. So too with philosophy. What Whitehead was saying was that philosophical discussion must be based on a general theory, and that this theory should be as short and clear as possible.

As in most of his private letters, Whitehead had the recipient much in his mind. In this instance he emphasized the importance of North's work by comparing it with what he himself was trying to do.

iv

Harvard's spring vacation in 1926 made it possible for Whitehead to accept invitations from McGill University, the University of Michigan, and the University of Illinois. At McGill he read a paper to the Philosophical Society. He did the same at Ann Arbor. Neither paper was ever published; they might have been one and the same paper.

The stay at Illinois lasted six days, in which Whitehead gave five lectures. These also were never published, but I can tell more about this visit, thanks to the late Sterling Lamprecht, who was then a member of the Philosophy Department there. The lectures were adumbrations of the ideas of *Process and Reality*. Few people understood them, but that did not cut down the attendance. On the contrary, as I have noted, larger rooms were needed for the second and third occasions. The notion that important new ideas would be broached by the author of *Science and the Modern World* had taken hold. Going to these lectures was the thing to do. Lamprecht later wrote to me:

> it was a *bon mot* in Urbana at the time that the philosophers did not understand the lectures but hoped that the mathematicians did, and that the mathematicians did not understand the lectures but hoped the philosophers did. People sometimes said frankly that they did not understand what ANW said but were charmed by his smile.[5]

He appears to have been the beneficiary of a quite naive conception of the frontiers of knowledge, entertained by both students and faculty at what was then a quite ordinary Midwestern university.

Whitehead was much more interested in talking to students than to the faculty. The Lamprechts and the Whiteheads were dined in a new fraternity house, and given a tour of it afterward. The only books in evidence were textbooks. Evelyn asked, "But where are the books you like to read?"[6] She saw that there can be no intellectual culture if the young read only what they are told they must read if they want the degrees to which all obedient students are entitled. A nation in which this happens is lucky if it escapes totalitarianism.

V

In April 1927 Whitehead delivered three lectures on the Barbour-Page Foundation (now called the Page-Barbour Foundation) at the University of Virginia. These lectures were given annually. He was pleased when the invitation reached him the preceding fall. It came from the Chairman of the University Committee on Public Occasions, Professor John J. Luck. But Evelyn had just suffered an attack of pleurisy and pneumonia; her worried husband mislaid Professor Luck's letter.[7] Belatedly he sent a very apologetic acceptance on December 10, 1926.[8] In it he proposed to lecture on "Symbolic Expression: Its Function for the Individual and for Society." Whitehead explained that he had not yet touched upon this subject in his publications, and hardly at all in his regular lectures at Harvard. Barbour-Page lecturers were required to choose subjects that were new to them. This requirement had an obvious reason; but it could result in the presentation of material that was too novel for a college audience. That was what happened in Whitehead's case (and, later, in T. S. Eliot's).[9] There was a large audience for the first lecture. On the night of the third one, Professor Luck was frantically calling faculty members to beg their attendance, but only about a dozen came.[10]

vi

The Macmillan Company published these lectures almost verbatim in November 1927, under the title *Symbolism: Its Meaning and Effect.*

Whitehead devoted over two hundred words to his Dedication, which was to the State of Virginia. It was written on his arrival in Virginia, "a great experience for an Englishman." In references to Sir Walter Raleigh, the dedication sought to evoke the spirit of romance. I think Whitehead was both saying what he supposed to be appropriate, and giving free rein to his usual feelings about his wife. This long dedication is one of the few passages from his pen that we could do without.

The Preface, slightly shorter, is consequential in two respects. In the first place, it tells the reader that some portions of Locke's *Essay Concerning Human Understanding* will help him to understand the lectures. North remembered that when he was young his father urged him to study the classic British philosophers; they were the most important philosophers. In the Preface to *Process and Reality* Whitehead will say that the main positions in his philosophy were anticipated in the later books of Locke's *Essay.* Secondly, the acknowledgment of the debt to Santayana's *Scepticism and Animal Faith* has great significance for Whitehead's assessment of Hume's theory of knowledge, both in these lectures and in the later Gifford Lectures. At Virginia he said that Santayana had shown "by every manner of beautiful illustration" that on Hume's premises there is no escape from what Santayana called "solipsism of the present moment."[11]

vii

Whitehead's definition of symbolism[12] is so broad that he can consider most of our perceptions symbolic. But his purpose in the first two lectures was to make an analysis of experience that would exhibit the elements in it which are not symbolic, but are directly recognized. In his first lecture he maintained that we enjoy direct experience of an external world.[13] He was not limiting "experience" to what we are conscious of, but including experience asleep or half-awake, drunk or sober; consciousness is a special feature which to some degree lights up some part of our experience.

He distinguished two quite different kinds of direct perception. Perception of contemporary things as displayed by sense-data, he called "presentational immediacy." It is what people usually mean by sense-perception. Its data can be clear, distinct, and vivid. The second kind of direct perception he called "perception of causal efficacy." In it we feel the action of the past (both within and outside ourselves) in shaping our present experience. Its data are vague and primitive. Mistakes in identification and all other errors in perception occur in symbolic reference from the one kind of perception to the other.*

Whitehead as a mathematician tends to consider the elements of a duality as on a par with each other; but here he views perception of causal efficacy as the more fundamental. There is no need to seek a reason for its relative neglect in his books on the philosophy of natural science; scientific observations are perceptions of sense-data. Those perceptions are of data that are strictly present. When we look at a nebula in the night sky, we are not looking backward through the time it took the light to reach us.[14] That is an astronomer's interpretation of what we see as *there now*.

Whitehead attacks Hume's denial that there is any perception of causal efficacy by simply asking for the meaning of "by" in his observation that if the idea of substance is perceived by the eyes it must be a color, if by the ears a sound, if by the palate a taste. Was Hume not assuming that what he called "impressions" are given by the causal efficacy of eyes, ears, and palate? And his argument must begin again over the perception of those sense-organs.[15]

The prime example of perception of causal efficacy is what Whitehead in later books called our sense of the withness of the body. This is an integral part of every human experience.

It would be a mistake to suppose that Whitehead's doctrine of causal perception is only a way of insisting that touch is more fundamental than any other kind of sensation. That was not his intention. He listed these examples of what is given in presentational immediacy: "colours, sounds, tastes, touches, and bodily feelings."[16]

---

*Perceptions of both kinds promote, and are promoted by, analysis of their data in terms of concepts.

viii

Whitehead rehabilitated the idea of a cause after Hume's destructive analysis of the causal relation between events, by looking afresh at what is given to us in any experience-event. We always feel that to some extent the experience came *from* some thing or things outside of and prior to itself.* His doctrines of the two modes of direct perception and symbolic reference do not express or rest on points of scientific evidence. They appeal to naive experience. And they show Whitehead's desire to be a Realist in his conception of empirical knowledge. He made a good case for two kinds of direct realism (which some have preferred to call naive realism); in holding that symbolic reference between them is ubiquitous, he gave representative perception its due.

Any instance of symbolic reference may be unfortunate, or downright mistaken; Whitehead was never in a hurry to state unqualified conclusions.

> In the case of perceived organisms external to the human body, the spatial discrimination involved in the human perception of their pure causal efficacy is so feeble, that practically there is no check on this symbolic transference apart from the indirect check of pragmatic consequences.[17]

As pragmatists (most notably Dewey and C. I. Lewis) insisted, the correctness of a sense-perception is to be tested by those further sense-perceptions which occur when we act upon the assumption that the perception is truthful. In Whitehead's terms, the effective distinction of perceptual truth from perceptual error requires the perceiver's thought to move from a given perception in the mode of presentational immediacy to future ones. The empirical character of the object perceived is filled out—as pragmatists seldom noticed—by the imaginable content of non-futural hypothetical sense-perceptions: by what the perceiver believes he, or someone like him, would observe from other places or would have observed at other times.

ix

One of the causes of the poor attendance at Whitehead's third Barbour-Page lecture was surely the outré character of the new theory of perception he had advanced. As a twentieth-century English phi-

---

*I call that "causation," and reserve "causality" for the grouping of objects or of events as causes and effects.

losopher, he was atypical. But when a student picks up *Symbolism* today, he is likely to stop after the second chapter because the epistemological analysis is over. He would then miss much that was essential to Whitehead. The arguments of the first two chapters are dependent on the third, "Uses of Symbolism," not for their validity but for their setting and import. The evidence from which the epistemology grew had a much wider base than inspection of given experience. Whitehead had reflected on human societies in a way that was like Edmund Burke on prejudice, or use and wont.[18]

Whitehead saw the character of human individuals, and the complex character of a part of society (say, Virginia in 1927), and the specific character of a home, or a tree, as the outcome of an inescapable inheritance transmitted from the past, and of sporadic or deliberate deviations from that inheritance. Such a view will be obvious to anyone who dispassionately considers the institutions, buildings, and customs in his environment. Whitehead described them beautifully in his 1926 article, "The Education of an Englishman." But anyone can see the truth in his point of view merely by observing the comparatively insignificant effect which the presented sense-data of the moment have in determining the various judgments, mental processes, and reactions of different men; the cumulative effect of personal and social history is what counts most.

X

On re-reading *Symbolism,* I am struck by the extent to which Whitehead's illustrations in his first two chapters could have come from conversation with Evelyn. The thought is his: the theorizing, the arguments, and especially the generalizations; the particulars could easily have come from her. I am not suggesting that anyone but Whitehead did the writing.

The writing is never bland. After the war of 1914–18, how could it be? The contrast he had exhibited between causal efficacy—"the hand of the settled past in the formation of the present"[19]—and the displays of presentational immediacy reaches its climax when he reminds us of

> the inscription on old sundials in "religious" houses: "The hours perish and are laid to account."[20]

Whitehead remarks that this contrast "is at the root of the pathos which haunts the world." A world without pathos would be unreal to sensitive human beings. The word *haunts* is one that he uses often, in later books as well as in *Symbolism*. It is very appropriate when the experience that he wants his constructive philosophy to satisfy is more a personal craving than an indubitable given that we all share.

xi

Some critics of *Symbolism* complained that Whitehead put out generalities instead of logical analyses like those that distinguished the books he wrote in England. They forgot that the subject matter is very different. Whitehead in the third Barbour-Page lecture is like, but better than, the older Whitehead of Lucien Price's *Dialogues*. A person who plans to read Whitehead's works in their chronological order does not have to wait for Part I of *Adventures of Ideas* to see his sociological side.

There is nothing wrong with general propositions as such. As an example of the originality of Whitehead's generalities, ponder this: after defining pure instinct as the response of an organism to the pure causal efficacy of its external world, without any functioning of presentational immediacy (and so without any symbolism), he says,

> The most successful examples of community life exist when pure instinct reigns supreme. These examples occur only in the inorganic world, among societies of active molecules forming rocks, planets, solar systems, star clusters.[21]

Who, except a philosopher who had been an applied mathematician instead of a learned scholar, would think of this?

xii

Whether or not you have read Whitehead's major philosophical books, *Symbolism* is worth study. What he says in his first two chapters is fundamental for his philosophy. To the criticism in *Science and the Modern World* of the assumption of "simple location" he adds an emphatic application to time: "There is nothing which 'simply happens.'"[22] The pure succession of time is an abstraction from the conformation of our present experience to our prior experience.

Whereas I have reservations about some parts of Whitehead's major philosophical books, I have none about the first two chapters of *Symbolism*. And all of that book shows Whitehead's many-sidedness. When what he says is something that others have said, you feel that he takes it seriously, so that it becomes a real part of his thought. One example is his remark that "the symbolic elements in life have a tendency to run wild, like the vegetation in a tropical forest."[23]

In his last chapter Whitehead wrote,

My main thesis is that a social system is kept together by the blind force of instinctive actions, and of instinctive emotions clustered around habits and prejudices.[24]

For him this was not a dogma, but a tentative generalization.

The last paragraph of the book begins:

It is the first step in sociological wisdom, to recognize that the major advances in civilization are processes which all but wreck the societies in which they occur;—like unto an arrow in the hand of a child.

Then this atypical philosopher shows us how English he is:

The art of free society consists first in the maintenance of the symbolic code; and secondly in fearlessness of revision, to secure that the code serves those purposes which satisfy an enlightened reason. Those societies which cannot combine reverence to their symbols with freedom of revision, must ultimately decay either from anarchy, or from the slow atrophy of a life stifled by useless shadows.

CHAPTER XI

Gifford Lecturer

x/Cable from "Whitchcad." New and better title,
Process and Reality. Surfeit of errors in text.
Corrected Edition, 1978.

xi/The Categoreal Scheme. Category of the Ultimate.
Eight Categories of Existence. A sample of the
Categories of Explanation. Santayana's complaint.
Being, becoming, and perishing.

xii/The "ontological principle." The eternal objects and
God's "primordial nature."

xiii/"Satisfaction" of an actual entity. A sample of the
Categoreal Obligations.

xiv/Duration of an actual occasion. What physicists
knew in 1928.

xv/"Societies" of actual occasions. Interpretation given
to ordinary objects in this process cosmology.
Physical and mental "poles."

xvi/A cell-theory of the universe. In genetic analysis,
simple physical feelings. Re-enaction. Analogy to
sympathy. Propositions as lures proposed for
feeling. Whitehead's thesis about consciousness.

xvii/Aim of an actual occasion. Secularization of concept
of God's functions. Organisms as self-determining;
moral responsibility. Whitehead's concepts of
growth and Bergson's philosophy. Contrast with
Hegel.

xviii/The continuum of potentialities for becoming. T. de
Laguna and the relation of extensive connection. His
work and Whitehead's definition of a projective
straight line without reference to measurement. The
chapter "Strains."

xix/Importance of the Preface to *PR*. Fusion of two
earlier cosmologies. Nine repudiated habits of
thought. Sensationalist doctrine of perception.
"Topsy-turvy" explanations of experience. Doctrine
of vacuous actuality. Perception and inference;
Russell. The "reformed subjectivist principle."

xx/"Anti-intellectualism" of Bergson, James, and
Dewey.

xxi/Bradley and Whitehead on becoming and perishing.
Whitehead's criticisms of Bradley. Realism and
absolute idealism.

xxii/Metaphysics and practice.

xxiii/Conclusion of Preface: replacement of piecemeal
philosophies by speculative schemes; folly of
dogmatic certainty.

xxiv/Eloquent beginning of Part V of *PR*. Flux versus
performance. "The most general formulation of the
religious problem." The ultimate evil in the
temporal world. The final opposites.

xxv/Whitehead's convictions, as expressed in a letter to
Mrs. Greene.

xxvi/Absence of proof. Message of Buddhistic religions.
God's "consequent nature." "Everlasting." The
double problem.

xxvii/Three traditional ways of conceiving of God.
Creativity, God, and the World. Conclusion of *PR*.

xxviii/Comment on Whitehead's theism. In 1931
symposium on *PR;* Whitehead's identification of its
key idea. Perishing and ordinary immortality.

xxix/The Whittakers, father and son. Plunge in
attendance at Whitehead's Gifford Lectures.

In a letter dated January 19, 1927, W. A. Fleming, Secretary to the University of Edinburgh, invited Whitehead to give the Gifford Lectures in Natural Theology at that university for the academic year 1927–28. This lectureship was founded at the four established Scottish universities in 1885 by Lord Adam Gifford. He had stipulated that "Natural Theology" be understood "in the widest sense of that term," and that the lecturers be subject to no religious test—they could be of any religion or of none; "so-called sceptics or agnostics or free-thinkers" were eligible if they were earnest seekers after truth.[1] (In 1929 the Gifford Lecturer at Edinburgh was John Dewey, who presented "The Quest for Certainty.") An invitation to be a Gifford Lecturer was now one of the highest honors in the English-speaking world; and the lectureship paid handsomely.

As so often happened in Whitehead's life, an extraneous circumstance played a part. In his founding document Lord Gifford desired that each lecturer be appointed for two years and give twenty lectures in all. It had become customary, however, for the appointee to give a series of ten lectures, and for a second series of ten to be arranged if desired. The Edinburgh Gifford Lecturer for 1926–27, Arthur Stanley Eddington, delivered a first series, on "The Nature of the Physical World," in 1926–27. He hoped to deliver a second series in 1927–28, but was not free to do so.[2] The academic Senate, which included Whitehead's friends and admirers E. T. Whittaker and A. E. Taylor, then unanimously resolved to invite Whitehead for 1927–28.[3] It turned out to be a happy decision for philosophy, if not for the Edinburgh public. (Lord Gifford had stipulated that the lectures be open to the public.)

If Edinburgh had not issued the invitation, one of the other three Scottish universities* would soon have succeeded in getting the author of *Science and the Modern World* to be a Gifford Lecturer.

The fact that the academic year in Britain usually ran about a month later than its counterpart in the United States introduced the possibility

---

*St. Andrews, Aberdeen, and Glasgow.

of Whitehead's being able to accept the invitation without having to ask
for a term's leave of absence from Harvard. On February 17 Evelyn
wrote to President Lowell on behalf of her husband, who was "laid up
with a sharp attack of lumbago," to ask whether he could leave Harvard
in time to reach Edinburgh by June 1. Lowell immediately replied that
there was no problem: the new arrangement of three-week reading
periods at the College, with no lecturing duties, provided professors
with time to travel. On February 27 Edinburgh received Whitehead's
cable of acceptance.

A letter from Norman Kemp Smith, Professor of Logic and Metaphysics, had accompanied the official invitation, but Whitehead did not
write a reply to it until April 6. Then he asked whether the first fortnight of June would be an acceptable time for delivering his Giffords.
Harvard had just made his appointment permanent, and although an
earlier visit to Edinburgh was not impossible, "anything earlier would
seem rather a tax on their goodwill."

Earlier in this letter Whitehead wrote:

The honour is one which I greatly appreciate, and it gives me an
opportunity to put out a systematic work on the metaphysical notions which are occupying my mind. Also, no small part of the
attraction is the prospect of having some conversations with you,
and A. E. Taylor, and Whittaker.

That was typical of Whitehead. He continued,

As to the subject and title—I am inclined to think that
            "The Concept of Organism"
expresses what I want to lecture about, and is a reasonable title. If any
objection to this title occurs to you or any improvement on it, will
you kindly let me know. Otherwise, I will let it stand at that. . . .I
propose to deliver ten or twelve lectures, and then expand them for
publication.

Publication was not a requirement, but it was customary.

Edinburgh's session ran through June. Whitehead's Giffords were
scheduled to begin Friday, June 1, and to continue on Mondays,
Wednesdays, and Fridays until the tenth and last one was delivered on
June 22.

                              ii
Work on "The Concept of Organism" began with the summer of
1927, which the Whiteheads spent in a cottage on the shore of Caspian

Lake, in Greensboro, Vermont. It was there that Whitehead's metaphysical system was created and his magnum opus, later named *Process
and Reality,* was shaped. On August 22 he described his progress in a
letter to his son:

Darling North

It seems years and years since I wrote to you. But I have
written nearly half a book on Metaphysics this summer and
have not wanted to break my thoughts in any way. Anyhow, I
have now got nearly 9½ chapters finished out of a projected
plan of 20 or 25 chapters. I am rather pleased with the result, so
far. Since August 15th I have been having a complete holiday
and at last have got rid of the metaphysics buzzing round and
round in my head.

We saw in Volume I that Whitehead's correspondence with Bertrand
Russell when they collaborated on *Principia Mathematica* was the one
great exception to his habit of not writing to friends about the progress
of his work. It is fortunate that some letters to his son North survive
from the years in America.* As Whitehead himself kept no records, I
shall not try to identify the 9½ finished chapters of *Process and Reality.*†
We know that he wrote very slowly and elided a good deal as he went
along.[4] I think that his first draft of a chapter was his last draft of that
chapter, apart from additions of one or more paragraphs which there
was occasion to make as he got his manuscript ready for publication.

iii

As a mathematician, Whitehead had been particularly concerned
with Grassmann's creations, Clerk Maxwell's, and, before these, the
great Newton's. In his *Enquiry* he had discussed the interpretation of
Newton's laws of motion; there, and in his other writings in England
after the war, he had attended carefully to the differences between his
own view of the foundations of physics and Newton's. As a philosopher, Whitehead felt something akin to piety toward Plato and toward a

---

*See Appendix B for the full text of these letters.

†Most of Lewis S. Ford's *The Emergence of Whitehead's Metaphysics, 1925–1929* (Albany: State University of New York Press, 1984) was a detailed history, based on the
published text of *Process and Reality,* of the composition of this long book. Whether the
method of higher criticism that biblical scholars applied successfully to the Pentateuch can
be applied with comparable hope to an essay in cosmology written by one old man in the
1920s must be doubted.

few of the great modern philosophers. He would begin the Preface to *Process and Reality* with these statements:

> These lectures are based upon a recurrence to that phase of philosophic thought which began with Descartes and ended with Hume. The philosophic scheme which they endeavour to explain is termed the "Philosophy of Organism." There is no doctrine put forward which cannot cite in its defence some explicit statement of one of this group of thinkers, or of one of the two founders of all Western thought, Plato and Aristotle. But the philosophy of organism is apt to emphasize just those elements in the writings of these masters which subsequent systematizers have put aside.

In the letter to North about his progress in the summer of 1927 he commented:

> I think that I have got my metaphysics into capital order now. I have managed, to my own satisfaction at least, to make quite plain where I agree and disagree with the big seventeenth century men, especially Descartes, Spinoza, John Locke, and (later) Hume.*

On Whitehead's sixty-fifth birthday Evelyn had given him the two-volume translation of Descartes' *Philosophical Works,* by Elizabeth S. Haldane and G. T. R. Ross.

> The upshot of my studies is to "boost up" John Locke, as the best of the lot of them—not the most consistent. But self-consistency is not the first requisite, though it is the final test. He denies fewer obvious facts than do other people, and gets them about as consistently together as you can hope to do. Of course, I think that I have improved on him: it would be no fun writing metaphysics unless one could do that. But I adopt his general view of the literature, practically *in toto.* He has one great merit: he knows a lot more than metaphysics.

iv

On November 13 Whitehead wrote to North, "My material for the lectures is accumulating excellently." His letter of March 7, 1928, is priceless. In it he said:

> I am pegging away at the Gifford lectures. I am rather pleased with the book. It will be stiff reading, and will not—as I expect—please

---

*According to the editors of the Corrected Edition of *Process and Reality,* the edition of Locke's *Essay* which Whitehead used was the thirtieth, printed in London in 1846. He had inherited his father's copy of it.

the philosophic world. But I have elaborated my ideas into a new approach to philosophy. It seems to me that this new way deals much less in abstractions than does the old way. Philosophers seem to me to be playing about with a "book" tradition, and not trying to express the facts directly observed.

I think Whitehead was dead right in his criticism of what philosophers were doing. His preoccupations with mathematics and education, his being only an amateur in philosophy, had saved him from "book" philosophical traditions in England, and he already had a mind of his own when he took part in discussions at the Aristotelian Society. In this letter to North, he next wrote an indispensable description of his purpose in the Gifford Lectures:

> I am trying to evolve one way of speaking which applies equally to physics, physiology, and to our aesthetic experiences. The ordinary philosophic abstractions won't do this. My private opinion is that in the last 150 years the chief ability of the world has not gone into philosophy—perhaps wisely. Modern philosophers are very analogous to English musicians—you can say lots of nice things about us, but after all we are *modern* philosophers, or *English* musicians, as the case may be.*

Of the five parts into which Whitehead divided *Process and Reality*, Part II, in which there is much discussion of Descartes, Newton, Locke, and Hume, is the least essential for my purpose. On the book as a whole, readers who want to see more of Whitehead's handling of its topics than I can provide here may wish to consult the Prospectus of his Gifford Lectures which he sent to Edinburgh University.†

V

Process and Reality is a good example of one of the usual characteristics of intellectual landmarks—that of being hard to read just because it is original. In 1948 I wrote that Whitehead's book was about as long as Kant's *Critique of Pure Reason*, and quite as backbreaking. So far as I know, this remark has not been challenged. But with passing generations, the book has come to appear less frightening. People still com-

---

*Ralph Vaughan Williams was Whitehead's friend, the same age as Bertrand Russell, and a Trinity College man at Cambridge, where he earned a B.Mus. in 1894.

†It is reprinted in my "Whitehead's Gifford Lectures," *Southern Journal of Philosophy* 7, No. 4 (1969–70): 335–38.

plain of its terminology, and some always will—those who assume that new ideas in any non-mathematical subject can always be adequately expressed in language acceptable to the editors of *Reader's Digest,* and that when this doesn't happen the author is at fault (he is obscure either deliberately or because he hasn't taken enough pains). The author of *Process and Reality* has been foolishly accused on both counts.

If you come to the book with an open mind and a little acquaintance with modern philosophy before Whitehead, you will see that the new terminology was a practical necessity, and you will find the terms peculiarly apt.

I doubt that *Process and Reality* was put together well; certainly it was badly proofread and poorly indexed. These faults are characteristic of Whitehead's philosophical books. He was absorbed in his ideas, not in ordering them nicely for the public; long before the Macmillan Company sent him galleys, his mind had moved on to some new undertaking.

vi

In his first Gifford Lecture, after saying that the lectures would be an essay in Speculative Philosophy, Whitehead defined speculative philosophy as

the endeavour to frame a coherent, logical, necessary system of ideas in terms of which every element of our experience can be interpreted. By this notion of "interpretation" I mean that everything of which we are conscious, as enjoyed, perceived, willed, or thought, shall have the character of a particular instance of the general scheme.

Here there is no beating around the bush, no effort to build up a solemn metaphysical mood in the reader. The straightforward style is like that which you would expect to find on the first page of a scientist's paper which investigates a new field or applies a new method to an old field.

Whitehead did not say or imply that *his* speculative philosophy was coherent, logical, and necessarily true. The word *speculative* itself suggests that a system with these properties is the *ultimate goal* of speculative philosophy. "Take it from here" was always his parting message.

vii

We saw in Chapter VIII that Whitehead's new philosophy of nature proposed a system of the world in which the basic fact is everywhere some process of self-realization which grew out of previous ones and itself added a new pulse of individuality and a new value to the world. The Gifford Lectures adopted and developed this conception. So far as familiar classifications are concerned, then, I should first of all classify Whitehead as a pluralist; he denied that ultimately only one individual (God, or the Absolute) exists. But he saw that Spinoza the monist had made as valuable a deposition as Leibniz the pluralist. Whitehead did not propose that their systems be reconciled (at some cost to each). He wanted their insights, along with those of Plato, Locke, and other giants, to be used in a new system. Whitehead's hospitality—"Philosophy," he wrote, "never reverts to its old position after the shock of a great philosopher"[5]—makes it tempting to consider him an eclectic. But, taken as a whole, his deposition cannot be subsumed under any philosophical movement of the twentieth century or accurately seen as the joint effect of other philosophers on its author. It has its own elements and its own structure, and must be understood in its own terms.

The members of Whitehead's pluralistic universe are interconnected. No monist ever insisted more strongly than he that nothing in the world exists in independence of other things. In fact, Whitehead criticizes traditional monisms for not carrying this principle far enough; they exempted eternal being from dependence on temporal beings. Independent existence is a myth, whether you ascribe it to God or to a particle of matter in Newtonian physics, to persons, to nations, to things, or to meanings. To understand is to see things together, and to see them as, in Whitehead's favorite phrase, "requiring each other." A system which enables us to do this is "coherent."

Whitehead's name for a unit of existence is "an actual entity." Each one achieves its individuality as a unique synthesis of earlier ones and its selection of eternal objects. When this synthesis is completed, it stays in the universe as one of the infinite number of settled facts from which the individuals of the future will arise: "The many become one, and are increased by one."[6] The universal creativity moves on.

The view that all actual entities are in the grip of creativity suggests a general principle which Whitehead thinks that every metaphysical scheme, so far as it is coherent, must follow. The principle is that ultimately there is but one kind of actuality.

There is no going behind actual entities to find anything more real. They differ among themselves: God is an actual entity, and so is the most trivial puff of existence in far-off empty space. But, though there are gradations of importance, and diversities of function, yet in the principles which actuality exemplifies all are on the same level.

The last statement represents an ideal which Whitehead, so far as his concept of God is concerned, does not fully achieve. Every actual entity except God is an "actual occasion."

viii

Our experience of the universe does not, at first glance, present any obvious prototype of actual entities. Selves, monads, material atoms, and Aristotelian substances have been tried out in the history of philosophy. Whitehead develops the theory of a different kind of entity— *an experience*. The doctrine that experience comes in drops or pulses, each of which is an indivisible unity, is to be found in the psychology of William James; but James never outlined a system of the world on this basis. The very idea seems odd; when we speak of an experience, we assume that it belongs to an animal body with a nervous system. Whitehead's chief meaning in calling an actual entity a pulse of *experience* is that the entity exists in and for itself. "Experience," he wrote, "is the self-enjoyment of being one among many, and of being one arising out of the composition of many."[7] Each appropriation of any one of the many is a prehension of that one, and the new actual entity is a concrescence of prehensions. Whitehead had introduced the term *concrescence* in his 1926 paper "Time."[8] It had become part of his lexicon.

In March 1927 Whitehead had told his seminar in logic that there was enormous difficulty in stating precisely the elements that go into an experience: everyone has to oversimplify. "Our own knowledge of what our experience is is always dim and fitful."[9] Every prior actual entity in the history of the universe must be prehended. But the nascent actual entity has also to deal with the infinite realm of eternal objects. It will prehend some, and exclude ("negatively prehend") others. Here Whitehead was taking seriously the fact that if a process is to have a definite outcome, some possibilities for it must be selected, others rejected.

Whitehead called positive prehensions "feelings," and explained:

> This word "feeling" is a mere technical term, but it has been chosen to suggest that functioning through which the concrescent actuality appropriates the datum so as to make it its own.[10]

So a "feeling" is not a state, nor a relation, but an act with a vector character. Whitehead's conception of this object-subject transaction is not at all modeled on the knower-known relation, which is a rare occurrence in the universe.

ix

Our experience usually discriminates not just a single actual entity but rather a whole nexus of them united by their prehensions. That is how you experience your body or your past personal history. Whitehead wrote,

> The ultimate facts of immediate actual experience are actual entities, prehensions, and nexus.* All else is, for our experience, derivative abstraction.

Most philosophers thought that Whitehead's doctrine of a self-creating drop of experience was unintelligible. It did not fit their habitual way of thinking: first an enduring subject, then experiences for it. But Whitehead looks upon process as not only the emergence of new patterns among things but also the becoming of new subjects.

> The ancient doctrine that no one crosses the same river twice is extended. No thinker thinks twice; and, to put the matter more generally, no subject experiences twice. This is what Locke ought to have meant by his doctrine of time as a "perpetual perishing."[11]

When an actual entity has become, it ceases to be a subject, and in that sense "perishes." As a "superject" of creativity, it is an object for all future subjects. In the Preface to *Process and Reality* Whitehead wrote that the relatedness of actualities

> is wholly concerned with the appropriation of the dead by the living—that is to say, with "objective immortality" whereby what is divested of its own living immediacy becomes a real component in other living immediacies of becoming.

This language makes us wonder if Whitehead was thinking of Eric's death. That was never far from his mind; but the words in this passage are meant to refer not only to persons but rather to every "puff of existence" in the universe. Every actual entity has subjective immediacy; to deny this would be to assert that some actualities are "vacuous," that is, are composed not of pulses of experience but only of matter, perhaps in a very subtle form. Whitehead's use of "living" in place of "subjective" to qualify "immediacy" I take to reflect his constant memory of Eric's death.

Did Whitehead generalize from human life and death to universal becoming and perishing? I think not. The character of nature which he

---

*Plural of nexus.

emphasized in his philosophy of natural science was its creative advance. In his 1926 paper "Time," he replaced the notion of change by that of supersession. What is superseded must have perished. This is as true of inorganic processes as of those in living creatures. The world is always becoming; as it becomes, it passes away and perishes.

X

On April 11, 1928, Kemp Smith received this cable from Whitehead:

TITLE GIFFORD LECTURES IS PROCESS AND REALITY   SYLLABUS
FOLLOWING SHORTLY BY MAIL
WHITCHCAD

There is nothing to be surprised at when some word even in a short message is misspelled in telegraphic transmission; but what happened to Whitehead's name was a bad omen of what would happen when Macmillan published *Process and Reality* in 1929. Over two hundred errors were listed in the corrigenda published in 1963.[12] The Cambridge University Press corrected ninety-nine of these in its edition, but it remained true to say that we possessed a better text of Plato's *Republic* than of Whitehead's magnum opus. Many of the errors were Whitehead's fault. The indispensable *Corrected Edition* (the work of David Ray Griffin and Donald W. Sherburne) was not published until 1978.[13] I shall use it in all quotations and references.

There is no extant information about what Whitehead had in mind when he changed the title of his Gifford Lectures. The change was plainly an improvement. His *Concept of Nature* was addressed to physicists, other natural scientists, and philosophers interested in the foundation of natural science. His Gifford Lectures were not being particularly addressed to biologists and philosophers interested in the foundations of biology. "The Concept of Organism" would have misled prospective hearers and (later) purchasers. A title that suggested metaphysics was needed, and "Process and Reality" was a perfect choice.[14] "Organism" was kept in the phrase "the philosophy of organism," which Whitehead used throughout the lectures as the name for the speculative philosophy he was expounding.

xi

Whitehead's second Gifford lecture was the hardest one to understand, for it presented his Categoreal Scheme: the categories, forty-five in all, that he would use in his cosmology.* His procedure was like that of the mathematician who states all his undefined terms and his axioms before applying any part of this apparatus to any topic.†

As Whitehead's list of categories appears in *Process and Reality*, there comes first the Category of the Ultimate, which is presupposed in all the other categories; it consists only of the terms *creativity*, *many*, and *one*.[15] But then come eight Categories of Existence, twenty-seven principles which he calls Categories of Explanation (every explanation in his cosmology should be an instance of one of them), and nine Categoreal Obligations, that is, conditions to which every actual entity is obliged to conform in its process of becoming.

I shall now present enough of the Categoreal Scheme to allow my reader to taste its flavor, before resuming the general discussion of Whitehead's metaphysics.

Among the Categories of Existence, we are already acquainted with the two that are most fundamental: actual entities and eternal objects. There are several intermediate categories, which express how all entities of these two types "are in community with each other, in the actual world": prehensions, propositions, nexus, subjective forms ("private matters of fact"), contrasts‡ ("modes of synthesis of entities in one prehension"), and multiplicities ("pure disjunctions of diverse entities"); Whitehead preferred the last term to *classes*, which could arouse irrelevant associations with Russell's problems about classes in *Principia Mathematica*.

The first Category of Explanation asserts

That the actual world is a process, and that the process is the becoming of actual entities.

---

*Whitehead had discussed with C. I. Lewis the question of the proper adjectival form of *category*. Lewis was writing *Mind and the World Order*, and needed it. They agreed that *categorical* was bad because of its established use in logic. But as they had only *talked* about this, Lewis wrote *categorial*, Whitehead *categoreal*, a word which Webster does not recognize. (I owe this information to Professor H. N. Lee.)

†But Whitehead was not writing mathematics; he was working out a strange new philosophy. He does not complete the application of his Categoreal Scheme to one topic, for example, to Space-Time, before moving on to a different topic. He discusses each topic again and again, each time bringing out more of its meaning in the philosophy of organism. *A Key to Whitehead's "Process and Reality,"* edited by Donald W. Sherburne (New York: Macmillan Co., 1966), is a topic-by-topic presentation of the essential passages in the book.

‡This category "includes an indefinite progression of categories, as we proceed from 'contrasts' to 'contrasts of contrasts,' and on indefinitely to higher grades of contrasts."

The second Category of Explanation reads:

> That in the becoming of an actual entity, the *potential* unity of many entities is disjunctive diversity*—actual and non-actual—acquires the *real* unity of the one actual entity, so that the actual entity is the real concrescence of many potentials.

The third Category of Explanation asserts

> That in the becoming of an actual entity, novel prehensions, nexus, subjective forms, propositions, multiplicities, and contrasts, also become; but there are no novel eternal objects.

Whitehead named his fourth Category of Explanation the "principle of relativity." It tells us that

> it belongs to the nature of "being" that it is a potential for every becoming.

The actual entities antecedent to a particular actual entity comprise its "actual world."[16] The sixth Category of Explanation reads:

> That each entity in the universe of a given concrescence *can,* so far as its own nature is concerned, be implicated in that concrescence in one or other of many modes; but *in fact* it is implicated only in *one* mode: that the particular mode of implication is only rendered fully determinate by that concrescence, though it is conditioned by the correlate universe. This indetermination, rendered determinate in the real concrescence, is the meaning of "potentiality." It is a *conditioned* indetermination, and is therefore called a "*real* potentiality."

You see that Whitehead's language was precise, and that its demands on the reader were substantial. When George Santayana read *Process and Reality* in 1929, he found the technical terms "pseudo-technical," and said that they were avoidable by the precise use of ordinary words.[17] In fact, there is nothing pseudo about them. Santayana was a purely literary philosopher; Whitehead came from mathematical logic. Remembering the meaning of Whitehead's term *perishing,* we can see the relationships between "being," "becoming," and "perishing" in the philosophy of organism. Becoming draws on being, or "process" on "reality"; and what becomes, perishes. The universe, at every moment, consists of becomings.

---

*In the Corrected Edition of *Process and Reality* the editors inserted the phrase "in disjunctive diversity" because Whitehead did so in his Macmillan copy of the book.

xii

The eighteenth Category of Explanation, and its name, require special attention.

That every condition to which the process of becoming conforms in any particular instance has its reason *either* in the character of some actual entity in the actual world of that concrescence, *or* in the character of the subject which is in process of concrescence. This category of explanation is termed the "ontological principle." It could also be termed the "principle of efficient, and final, causation." This ontological principle means that actual entities are the only *reasons*; so that to search for a *reason* is to search for one or more actual entities.

The effect of this fundamental doctrine is to put all thought into an ontological context. In the last analysis, there is no such thing as a disembodied reason; no principles of order—in logic, natural or social science, epistemology, ethics, or aesthetics—have any substance except what they derive from one or more actualities whose character they express.

An eternal actual entity must be responsible for the fact that the infinite multiplicity of eternal objects forms an ordered realm.

It is here termed "God"; because the contemplation of our natures, as enjoying real feelings derived from the timeless source of all order, acquires that "subjective form" of refreshment and companionship at which religions aim.

This God is not *before* all creation, but *with* all creation, by being immanent in every concrescence. God's ordering of the eternal objects bestows a certain character upon the creativity of the universe, in virtue of which pure chaos is not possible.

xiii

The twenty-fifth Category of Explanation cannot be omitted from our sample:

The final phase in the process of concrescence, constituting an actual entity, is one complex, fully determinate feeling. This final phase is termed the "satisfaction." It is fully determinate (a) as to its genesis, (b) as to its objective character for the transcendent creativity, and (c) as to its prehension—positive or negative—of every item in its universe.

That paragraph is a good specimen of Whitehead's use of his experience in mathematical logic when constructing a cosmology.

I shall proceed more rapidly, with less quotation, in sampling the nine Categoreal Obligations. The first one, the Category of Subjective Unity, postulates that the feelings in an incomplete phase of an actual entity's becoming are compatible for integration. The Category of Objective Identity demands that there be no duplication of any element in the objective datum* of the satisfaction of an actual entity. The Category of Objective Diversity demands that there be no coalescence of different elements in the objective datum. The Category of Conceptual Valuation procures the derivation of feelings of eternal objects from physical feelings. The Category of Conceptual Reversion asserts the secondary origination of conceptual feelings, in which the eternal objects felt are partly identical with and partly diverse from these. The Category of Transmutation provides for "transmuted" feelings, in which the datum is the contrast of a nexus as one with an eternal object; this gives a meaning for the notion of the quality of a physical substance. The Category of Freedom and Determination says that the concrescence of an individual actual entity is internally determined and externally free.

xiv

Whitehead does not say what the time-span of an actual occasion is. His cosmology offers a *general way* of thinking about the pluralistic process of the universe; it proposes basic concepts, but does not automatically apply them. The specious present of human experience and the quantum events of atomic physics seem to be the best samples of actual occasions that we can discern, but the Categoreal Scheme may be tried out on larger scales too.

When Whitehead applies the philosophy of organism to the sciences, he limits himself to the general ideas of physics and biology, and avoids all detail. He scarcely had time to keep up with the rapid advances that were made in the 1920s. But we must remember that in 1928 electrons and protons were the only particles known to physics, gravitation and electromagnetism the only forces.

xv

An eternal object, as a definite character, may be realized in one actual occasion after another, through each prehending that character in

---

*As opposed to the initial datum.

its immediate predecessor. A nexus composed of one, or simultaneously of many, such strands, Whitehead calls a "society of occasions," which has that eternal object as its defining characteristic. Such processes of inheritance occur in human societies, in the usual meaning of the word. But Whitehead gives the general idea a much wider application; through it, he can define personal identity, and a philosophy of process can have a place for *things,* for frogs and mountains, electrons and planets, which are certainly neither becomings nor eternal objects. Thus personal minds and material bodies have their places in the philosophy of organism, but as variable complexes rather than as metaphysical prototypes.

The differences between the various kinds of things in nature then go back to the different contrasts, repetitions, divisions, and modes of integration involved in the chains of prehensions by which actual occasions make up "societies" with different defining characteristics. Whitehead sketched some of the main principles involved.* He sees societies arising and decaying, societies within other societies which sustain them (consider the animal body), societies on all scales of magnitude. The structure of nature comes out well—in fact, beautifully—in the philosophy of the flux.

The mind-body dualism was more often accepted in the 1920s, especially among professional philosophers in America, than it is now. Whitehead not only rejected it; in *Process and Reality* he generalized the mind-body problem, and showed how two contrasting kinds of activity could be integrated within every actual occasion. An occasion is a throb of experience, so of course its "physical pole" cannot consist of matter, in the sense of a permanent, unfeeling substance, and consciousness is too slight and occasional to define the "mental pole." (Whitehead told me[18] he regretted using the "pole" language; some readers gave it a wider connotation than he had in mind.) The "physical" activity of an occasion is its absorption of the actual occasions of the past, its direct *rapport* with the environment from which it sprang; its "mental" side is its own creativeness, its desire to realize ideal forms by means of which it makes a novel, unified reaction to its inheritance. Whitehead names prehensions of eternal objects "conceptual feelings."[19] Each occasion integrates them with its physical feelings, thus effecting a fusion of the already actual and the ideal.

---

*It is not only readers interested in natural science who should find the chapters in *Process and Reality* on "The Order of Nature" and "Organisms and Environment" fascinating.

xvi

Whitehead called actual entities the cells of the universe.[20] As in biology, the cells are organic wholes which can be analyzed both genetically and morphologically. These two analyses, each five chapters long, make up the detailed theory of actual occasions in *Process and Reality*. He does remarkable things in each.

The first, "The Theory of Prehensions," offers an analysis of the self-creation of an experiencing subject. A "simple physical feeling" feels a single feeling in a prior actual occasion.[21] The later feeling is a reproduction or re-enaction of the earlier one; Whitehead said to me (in the late 1930s) that he ought to have introduced this idea explicitly in his Categoreal Scheme.

A simple physical feeling is a unit of causation, which may be called physical memory. It is also "the most primitive type of an act of perception, devoid of consciousness."[22]

Earlier in *Process and Reality* Whitehead had described the initial phase of an actual occasion as a physical feeling which, "in the language appropriate to the higher stages of experience,"[23] is an unconscious *sympathy;* in terms of his system, this consists in "feeling the feeling in another and feeling conformally *with* another."[24]

The initial phase is followed by a ferment of qualitative valuation effected by conceptual feelings; this or that possibility is felt to be important or trivial or irrelevant, or not wanted.

In every experience, conscious or unconscious, every proposition arises as a "lure for feeling."[25] Whitehead cites "there is beef for dinner today" as an example of "a quite ordinary proposition";[26] but he exhibits the many kinds of propositions, and relations between them, that logicians recognize, in terms of a variety of propositional feelings.[27] It would take a large diagram to display all of them. A proposition must be true or false. To Bertrand Russell, as to most logicians, that is the *only* business of a proposition. But if you are constructing a cosmology, the functions of propositions in nature cannot be neglected.

Whitehead advances the thesis that consciousness is the indefinable quality that emerges when a positive but unconscious feeling of a nexus as a given fact is integrated with a propositional feeling about the nexus originated by the "mental pole." Consciousness is how we feel this contrast between "in fact" and "might be."[28] It is well developed so far as the contrast is well defined and prominent; this is bound to be the case in negative perception, for example, in perceiving a stone as not gray, whereas perceiving the stone as gray can occur without conscious notice. The difference between these two cases supports Whitehead's idea about consciousness, and leads him to proclaim the negative perception the triumph of consciousness and the harbinger of a free imagination.[29]

Consciousness is not a basic factor in Whitehead's cosmology, because it is not even present in every human experience. The same remark applies—the tradition of modern philosophy to the contrary notwithstanding—to thought and to sense-perception. Kant was "led to balance the world upon thought—oblivious to the scanty supply of thinking."[30] In the last book Whitehead wrote, *Modes of Thought,* he observed that "we experience the universe, and we analyze in our consciousness a minute selection of its details."[31]

xvii

The initial data of an actual occasion's feelings include everything in its environment, awaiting unification in a fresh perspective. This will be guided by the occasion's aim. However, "according to the ontological principle there is nothing which floats into the world from nowhere."[32] The only possible source of the aim is God, as Whitehead conceives the primordial nature of God. He is secularizing the concept of God's functions in the world. On the derivation of an actual occasion's aim from God, this passage must not be forgotten:

> This function of God is analogous to the remorseless workings of things in Greek and in Buddhist thought. The initial aim is the best for that *impasse.* But if the best be bad, then the ruthlessness of God can be personified as *Atè,* the goddess of mischief. The chaff is burnt.[33]

But, as we have seen, it is up to the new concrescence to modify the aim and so determine its own final character. Whitehead wrote that

> the actual entity, in a state of process during which it is not fully definite, determines its own ultimate definiteness.[34]

That is essential to Whitehead's concept of organism. At the human level it is, he observes, "the whole point of moral responsibility."[35]

Whitehead sympathized with Bergson's protest against materialism, but in his genetic analysis of an actual occasion he showed how theoretical concepts *can* express the inner growth of things. His conception of growth has points of similarity with Hegel's, but differs in having no use for "contradiction," and in presenting a hierarchy of categories of feeling rather than a hierarchy of categories of thought.[36] The conditions of synthesis are not the dialectical antagonisms of opposites, but aesthetic contrasts among ideal forms, and between these forms and those in the occasion's immediate predecessor. The latter appears in the wave-vibration that is so pervasive in mathematical physics.

xviii

Although the process of becoming is atomic, potentialities for future becomings form a continuum which is divisible, both temporally and spatially. Whitehead does this in "The Theory of Extension," which is the subject of Part IV of *Process and Reality*.[37] Only the physical pole of an actual occasion is divisible; the mental pole is "incurably one."[38]

In the Theory of Extension Whitehead made an important improvement on his treatment of the subject in the *Principles of Natural Knowledge*. There he had taken the whole-part relation between events as undefined. But in 1922 Theodore de Laguna had shown that the whole-part relation could be defined in terms of the more general relation of extensive connection.[39] Whitehead learned of this in the summer of 1927, when the de Lagunas and Whiteheads were both in Greensboro, Vermont. In *Process and Reality* Whitehead took extensive connection between regions as primitive. He remarked that his earlier procedure had required him to introduce the theory of durations before defining what is meant by a point of timeless space; "what should have been a *property* of 'durations' became the definition of a point."[40]

De Laguna's own work was limited to spatial relations, Whitehead's was not. De Laguna used "solid" as his undefined relatum, and took as his point of departure the behavior of things toward one another as we manipulate them. Whitehead's approach to extensive relations was more general than this, which was quite foreign to him. He did not use it, but neither did he criticize it; he simply adopted the notion of extensive connection and credited de Laguna with making the *Process and Reality* treatment of extension possible.*

Near the close of the Theory of Extension you come to something no one would expect to find in a book of metaphysics: the definition of a straight line without reference to measurement. Whitehead attached great importance to this; primarily, I think, because the accepted procedure of defining a straight line as the shortest distance between two

---

*Later, Whitehead told his Harvard classes that it would be best to begin the theory of extension with the relation of betweenness among regions.

points took for granted the geometrical relations displayed to perception in the mode of presentational immediacy. He defined the *projective*
straight line, which, he believed, has the intuitive properties of the
straight line of naive experience.

Whitehead's proof of the uniqueness of the straight line was quite
complicated. He assumed the existence of a class of oval regions,
adopted de Laguna's undefined relation of extensive connection, and
then applied his method of extensive abstraction much as he had done in
the *Principles of Natural Knowledge*. He did not try to reduce the characteristics of extension that he enumerated to a minimum number from
which all others could be deduced. His main interests were no longer in
that kind of project.

The next chapter of *Process and Reality* was called "Strains." A strain
is "a feeling in which the forms exemplified in the datum concern
geometrical, straight, and flat loci."[41] This chapter began with a heart-
felt declaration that was soon followed by a reference to Maxwell's
Equations.

> There is nothing in the real world which is merely an inert fact.
> Every reality is there for feeling; it promotes feeling, and it is felt.
> Also there is nothing which belongs merely to the privacy of feeling
> of one individual actuality. All origination is private. But what has
> been thus originated, publicly pervades the world. Thus the geo-
> metrical facts concerning straight and flat loci are public facts charac-
> terizing the feelings of actual entities. It so happens that in this epoch
> of the universe the feelings involving them are of dominating impor-
> tance. . . . Fundamental equations in mathematical physics, such as
> Maxwell's electromagnetic equations, are expressions of the order-
> ing of strains throughout the physical universe.[42]

xix

In the Preface to *Process and Reality* Whitehead wrote, "In these lectures I have endeavoured to compress the material derived from years
of meditation." That Preface, only four pages long,* must be *studied* by
everyone who is interested in Whitehead's philosophy. Earlier in this
chapter I noticed some of the points he made in it. I want now to call
attention to the most important ones that remain.

---

*As the pages are quarto, my reader would get little information from endnote refer-
ences to them by number; so I shall omit such references in my discussion of the Preface.

In attempting a new cosmology, Whitehead says, it is perhaps wise to fuse the two cosmologies

> which at different times have dominated European thought, Plato's *Timaeus* and the cosmology of the seventeenth century, whose chief authors were Galileo, Descartes, Newton, Locke, . . . with modifications demanded by self-consistency and the advance of knowledge. The cosmology explained in these lectures has been framed in accordance with this reliance on a positive value of the philosophical tradition.[43]

The Preface lists nine "prevalent habits of thought, which are repudiated, in so far as concerns their influence on philosophy." The one which the authors of *Principia Mathematica* had rejected is trust in "the subject-predicate form of expression." "The trust in language as an adequate expression of propositions" was always characteristic of Russell; I do not find it in any of Whitehead's works. Russell thought ill of Kant, while Whitehead took him seriously; but Whitehead would not accept "the Kantian doctrine of the objective world as a theoretical construct from purely subjective experience." Of course a man with a background in mathematical logic would take care to reject "arbitrary deduction in *ex absurdo* arguments." Whitehead was being critical of Bradley and many other nineteenth-century philosophers when he objected to the "belief that logical inconsistencies can indicate anything else than some antecedent errors."

Two of the nine mistaken habits of thought now demand special notice. "The sensationalist doctrine of perception" is the doctrine of *mere* sensation. Whitehead will call it a "law" that "the late derivative elements [in experience] are more clearly illuminated by consciousness than the primitive elements."[44] Neglect of this law, he will assert, produces "most of the difficulties of philosophy."[45]

> Experience has been explained in a thoroughly topsy-turvy fashion, the wrong end first. In particular, emotional and purposive experience has been made to follow upon Hume's impressions of sensation.

Another repudiated doctrine is "the doctrine of vacuous actuality," that is, of actuality devoid of experience. Whitehead accepted the subjectivist's bias that entered modern philosophy with Descartes: the subject's conscious experience is the primary datum for philosophy. But he rejected what he called "the subjectivist principle"—that this datum consists only of universals, for example, of the roundness and grayness from which we infer that we are in the presence of a round gray stone. Russell had taken this position in *The Problems of Philosophy*, and Whitehead had criticized it in his 1911 letter about the manuscript.* Whitehead insisted that the stone itself was a datum. He was always suspicious when philosophers interpreted as inferred what the plain man supposed he had perceived. Whitehead had explained the occurrence of perceptual errors in the first two of his lectures at the University of Virginia.† Cambridge's publication of these lectures in the spring of 1928 relieved him of the need to deal with the subject in his Giffords, but it is fully discussed in the chapter "Symbolic Reference," and elsewhere, in *Process and Reality*.

Whitehead adopts what he calls "the reformed subjectivist principle," that "the whole universe consists of elements disclosed in the experiences of subjects." You cannot be more emphatic than this:

> apart from the experiences of subjects there is nothing, nothing, nothing, bare nothingness.

XX

As he so often did, Whitehead in the Preface to *Process and Reality* exaggerates his indebtedness to other thinkers. After saying that he is "greatly indebted to Bergson, William James, and John Dewey," he tells us that

> One of my preoccupations has been to rescue their type of thought from the charge of anti-intellectualism, which rightly or wrongly has been associated with it.

Bertrand Russell had treated all three of these men as guilty of anti-intellectualism. Whitehead's phrase "rightly or wrongly" was meant, I think, to leave open the possibility that Bertie was partly right. It is not obvious what Bergson's type of thought has in common with Dewey's. I said enough about Whitehead's relation to Bergson in Chapter VIII, and will discuss his relation to Dewey in the next chapter.

Whitehead seldom goes into detail on his indebtedness. He would rather make a general statement and let that blessed word *obvious* cover the situation. So he says, "Among the contemporary schools of thought, my obligations to the English and American Realists are obvious."‡

---

*See the discussion in Chapter I, Section v.

†See pages 208–10 above.

‡But his next sentence singles out T. P. Nunn, whose "anticipations, in the *Proceedings of the Aristotelian Society*, of some of the doctrines of recent Realism, do not appear to be

xxi

Whitehead's few remarks about his relation to the English philosopher of the Absolute, F. H. Bradley, have provided subjects for countless dissertations. It is clear that he likes Bradley's insistence on "feeling," and considers him an ally in the battle against "vacuous actuality," a battle in which Whitehead and Russell were on opposite sides. Bradley's polemical writing, however, shows a mind that is more like Russell's highly verbalized one* than like Whitehead's.

Whitehead begins a sentence in the Preface to *Process and Reality* by saying that "throughout the main body of the work" he is "in sharp disagreement with Bradley," and ends it with "the final outcome is after all not so greatly different."

Those disagreements were metaphysically central. Bradley maintained that only the eternal Absolute† is truly real; in Whitehead's cosmology only purely abstract entities are eternal. Bradley wrote, "If time is not unreal, I admit that our Absolute is a delusion." Whitehead's ultimate, creativity, is absent from Bradley; worse, Bradley ridiculed all such notions.

Neither of the authors of *Principia Mathematica* had taken any stock in Bradley's argument that relations necessarily involve contradiction. That is the most notorious instance of his high-and-mighty way with "appearance." (His Absolute is supra-relational.) In terms of the Categories of Existence in *Process and Reality,* a relation is a genus of contrasts. Whitehead observes that Bradley was

distressed—or would have been distressed if he had not been consoled by the notion of "mereness" as in "mere appearance"—to find that a relation will not do the work of a contrast. It fails to contrast. [46]

I remember Whitehead's comment, in a classroom lecture at Harvard, on one of Bradley's illustrations, Wolf-eating-Lamb as a qualification of the Absolute:

---

sufficiently well known." Nunn was Professor of Education in the University of London, and quite a polymath. He and Whitehead were good friends. Nunn had independently advocated a view of the rhythm of education similar to Whitehead's. An exponent of scientific method, he could also maintain that the prime contribution of the heroes of science to the world's cultural wealth is not the scientific method but the scientific life, a life devoted to investigations.

*See Volume I, page 225.

†We must try to think of Bradley's Absolute as not only infinite and eternal, but as a differentiated harmony of experience. It is not a self and is not God; Bradley was not a theist.

Hang it all! The wolf was enjoying himself and the lamb was in torture.

In another lecture[47] he said that Bradley ought to have welcomed Poincaré's notion of convention, for any finite thing is as good as any other, as a qualification of the Absolute.

I think that Whitehead saw nothing self-contradictory or unintelligible in the data of sense, and that this disagreement with Bradley went back at least to Whitehead's first philosophical writings. When he turned to metaphysics, he saw finite individuals as perfectly real, and really immanent in each other.

In an Explanatory Note on temporal and spatial appearance Bradley wrote, in the second edition (1897) of *Appearance and Reality*:

> Well, all this birth and death, arising and perishing of individuals, is it ultimately true and real or is it not? For myself, I reply that it is not so. I reply that these successive individuals are an appearance, necessary to the Absolute, but still an appearance.[48]

Thus, becoming and perishing were equally unreal to Bradley. It is not too much to say that he quietly denigrated the plain man's belief in them. They were equally real to Whitehead.

When Whitehead, in his Preface, looks forward to the last part of *Process and Reality*, he writes:

> It answers the question, What does it all come to? In this part, the approximation to Bradley is evident. Indeed, if this cosmology be deemed successful, it becomes natural at this point to ask whether the type of thought involved be not a transformation of some main doctrines of Absolute Idealism onto a realistic basis.

We must wish he had made a statement instead of raising a question, and had not left us to guess *which* doctrines he had in mind. Was he wholly uncertain?*

I shall leave it to the reader to reach his own view of the "approximation to Bradley" after I have dealt with the final part of *Process and Reality*.

---

*Whitehead's vagueness is a minor sin in comparison with the explicitness of John Passmore in his widely read *A Hundred Years of Philosophy* (London: Gerald Duckworth & Co., 1957). Passmore has Whitehead say that this transformation was his "object" (p. 343).

xxii

The plain man's belief in becoming and perishing is shown by the provisions he makes in his life insurance, by his last will and testament, and by a thousand other practices. Whitehead's attitude toward practice separates him from all philosophers who say that their conclusions need not be accepted "in practice." Bertrand Russell was one such. Hume admitted that no one could live by his philosophy. But to Whitehead, our practices have an essential place among the data of metaphysics. He went so far as to say, in the first chapter of *Process and Reality*, "Speculative Philosophy," what deserved a place in his Preface:

> Metaphysics is nothing but the description of the generalities which apply to all the details of practice.[49]

Our practice of expecting a future that will continue some features of the present and deviate from others is a good illustration: Whitehead's metaphysics is in agreement with that practice. But Russell was not happy unless he was denouncing common practices.

The explanation of a practice, I note, is the responsibility not of metaphysics alone but of it in conjunction with the philosophy of man, the biological and cultural sciences of man, and knowledge of specific circumstances. If some constant feature of human practice contradicts, or stands in no relation to, this conjunct, some member of the conjunct is defective. It may be hard to say which one this is.

xxiii

Whitehead begins the conclusion of the Preface by saying that piecemeal philosophizing has had its day, and asserting that all constructive thought on scientific topics is dominated by a general scheme of ideas, "unacknowledged, but no less influential in guiding the imagination." "The importance of philosophy lies in its sustained effort to make such schemes explicit, and thereby capable of criticism and improvement."

> There remains the final reflection, how shallow, puny, and imperfect are efforts to sound the depths in the nature of things. In philosophical discussion, the merest hint of dogmatic certainty as to finality of statement is an exhibition of folly.

Unfortunately, one result of the professionalization of philosophy which occurred in America and Britain at the beginning of the twentieth century was encouragement of the spirit of debate, not least on ontological questions.

xxiv

The fifth (last) part of *Process and Reality,* "Final Interpretation," is beautiful, provocative, and maddeningly short. It presents the theory of the relations between God and the temporal world which Whitehead has worked out; but when he announces the topic of this part in the first section, he does not mention God, and says only that the topic is "ultimate ideals."

That section begins, "The chief danger to philosophy is narrowness in the selection of evidence," mentions ideals that have held sway and been rebelled against in Western civilization, attributes greatness to both upholders and rebels, then concludes:

> Philosophy may not neglect the multifariousness of the world—the fairies dance, and Christ is nailed to the cross.*

This chapter of the book is entitled "The Ideal Opposites." Whitehead first reminds us of the inescapability of both permanence and flux. It is expressed in the lines

> Abide with Me,
> Fast Falls the Eventide.

He next brings up order as the condition of excellence, and the impulse toward something new. This pair, so essential in the theory of education and much emphasized in Whitehead's writings on that subject, must be borne in mind if we would understand ideals.

Whitehead wants *both* sides of each member of the pair. As he prepares the reader for his plunge into theology, he expresses his dramatic view of the historic role of organizations:

> The history of the Mediterranean lands, and of western Europe, is the history of the blessing and the curse of political organizations, of religious organizations, of schemes of thought, of social agencies for large purposes. The moment of dominance, prayed for, worked for, sacrificed for, by generations of the noblest spirits, marks the turning point where the blessing passes into the curse.† Some new principle of refreshment is required.[50]

---

*This sentence is not in William James's style, but that earlier Gifford lecturer at Edinburgh (*The Varieties of Religious Experience*) would have placed a heavy checkmark opposite it in the margin.

†Evelyn, with her keen sense of drama, must have agreed wholeheartedly with this passage. It is hopeless to try to estimate her degree of responsibility for the underlying idea.

Whitehead adds that the same situation is illustrated by "the tedium arising from the unrelieved dominance of a fashion in art."

He insists that the two elements must not really be separated.

> It belongs to the goodness of the world, that its settled order should deal tenderly with the faint discordant light of the dawn of another age.[51]

What justification did Whitehead have for this statement? Only what God's relation to the world—the topic he is coming to—provides. He frequently said to his Harvard classes, "The universe is fundamentally decent."

Whitehead anticipates the conclusion of his cosmology when he writes,

> the culminating fact of conscious, rational life refuses to conceive itself as a transient enjoyment, transiently useful. In the order of the physical world its rôle is defined by its introduction of novelty. But, just as physical feelings are haunted by the vague insistence of causality, so the higher intellectual feelings are haunted by the vague insistence of another order, where there is no unrest, no travel, no shipwreck: "There shall be no more sea."
>
>   This is the problem which gradually shapes itself as religion reaches its higher phases in civilized communities. The most general formulation of the religious problem is the question whether the process of the temporal world passes into the formation of other actualities, bound together in an order in which novelty does not mean loss.
>
>   The ultimate evil in the temporal world is deeper than any specific evil. It lies in the fact that the past fades, that time is a "perpetual perishing."[52]

The problem Whitehead faces is not just a problem for intellectuals. The problem of defining a straight line without reference to measurement may be such a problem. Here Whitehead is speaking to the human condition. We all feel anguish when we are struck by the fact that we crave novelty, and yet are "haunted by terror at the loss of the past, with its familiarities and its loved ones." He calls this a paradox. Whatever name we give it, it is a hard fact.

The chapter on "The Ideal Opposites" concludes with the observation that we are left

> with the final opposites, joy and sorrow, good and evil, disjunction and conjunction—that is to say, the many in one—flux and perma-

nence, greatness and triviality, freedom and necessity, God and the World. In this list, the pairs of opposites are in experience with a certain ultimate directness of intuition, except in the case of the last pair. God and the World introduce the note of interpretation.

XXV

On Easter Sunday, April 8, 1928 (a little more than a month before he was to sail for Britain), Whitehead wrote a letter to his dear friend Rosalind Greene, who was Evelyn's most intimate friend. In it he said:

I am working at my Giffords. The problem of problems which bothers me, is the real transitoriness of things—and yet!!—I am equally convinced that the great side of things is weaving something ageless and immortal: something in which personalities retain the wonder of their radiance—and the fluff sinks into its utter triviality. But I cannot express it at all. No system of words seems up to the job.

He found a system of words that did the job well enough to be published as the last chapter of *Process and Reality*, "God and the World." Although the chapter is not long, it presents much more than he said (to judge from the Prospectus) in his tenth Gifford lecture.

In "God and the World" Whitehead tells us, "There is nothing here in the nature of proof."[53] There are only "suggestions." They follow his attempt to show the ways in which the concept of God should be transformed if his philosophic system, which he admits is imperfect, be accepted. He remarks that he is only trying to add another speaker to Hume's great *Dialogues Concerning Natural Religion*.[54]

xxvi

Here is how he began the chapter:

So long as the temporal world is conceived as a self-sufficient completion of the creative act, explicable by its derivation from an ultimate principle which is at once eminently real and the unmoved mover, from this conclusion there is no escape: the best that we can say of the turmoil* is, "For so he giveth his beloved—sleep." This is

---

*This word was a favorite one with Whitehead.

the message of religions of the Buddhistic type, and in some sense it is true.

I do not know what Whitehead meant by the last clause, if he meant to convey more than a feeling that maybe this message is true.

But his metaphysics suggests a different, positive idea. We have thus far dealt only with that side of God which he called God's primordial nature. Each actual occasion, we remember, synthesizes all the occasions of its actual world. Why not apply this conception to God? What Whitehead calls God in his "consequent nature" is that side of God which is consequent upon the creative advance of the world.*

Whitehead argues that "by reason of the relativity of all things," every creature—that is, every completed actual occasion—must react on God, must be felt by Him.[55] Thus the primordial nature is only one side of God. In his consequent nature the temporal occasions are united with each other in a harmony of feeling which grows as new occasions arise. This is a creative advance without any "perishing." That is how Whitehead deals with what he had called the ultimate evil in the temporal world.

In that world some actual occasions, or nexus of actual occasions, become in unison; another name for that is "unison of immediacy." Whitehead does not merely want immortality in God for his son Eric. He wants Eric and his mother to enjoy unison of immediacy in God's consequent nature. In place of *immortal* he introduces the word *everlasting,* which he defines as "the property of combining creative advance with the retention of mutual immediacy."[56] This is his chief departure from the words he used in the letter to Rosalind Greene from which I quoted at the beginning of this section. I do not think the difference is substantial.

Is there *nothing* that Whitehead's God cannot do? Not quite. God as judge of the world loses "nothing that can be saved." This implies that some things in the temporal world are beyond being completely saved. Still, Whitehead says:

> The revolts of destructive evil, purely self-regarding, are dismissed into their triviality of merely individual facts, and yet the good they did achieve in individual joy, in individual sorrow, in the introduction of needed contrast, is yet saved by its relation to the completed whole. The image—and it is but an image—the image under which

---

*Possibly this idea was advanced in *Religion in the Making.* I think that it was only suggested there.

this operative growth of God's nature is best conceived, is that of a tender care that nothing be lost.[57]

Whitehead is right in wanting to think of God as "the chief ex-emplification" of metaphysical principles, not something "invoked to save their collapse."[58] An actual entity in the world begins with a "physical" reception of prior actualities, and completes itself by valuing them through the operations of its "mental pole." Dipolarity must also be characteristic of God. But the order is reversed. God's primordial nature is mental, in that it is an all-inclusive *conceptual* feeling of poten-tials for the world, whereas the consequent nature is an all-inclusive feeling of *actualities*.

In finite actual entities, we remember, consciousness arises only when a direct experience of actuality is integrated with a sense of the possible. So consciousness is absent from God's primordial nature, but not from the consequent nature.

Whitehead also tries to make us see how God, as he conceives of God himself—I should say, itself—is incomplete without the consequent nature. Since he thinks, and always thinks, that God and the World jointly make up the universe, his explanation is that the problem is not merely to see how the individuals of the world become immortal; that is only half of a double problem; the other half is to see how what is permanent (God in his primordial nature, which had been an essential factor in Whitehead's cosmology since *Science and the Modern World*) requires fluency as its completion. Whitehead claims that "civilized intuition has always, although obscurely, grasped the problem as dou-ble and not as single."[59] I can be sure of two points only—that his system requires solution of the double problem, and that what his heart most needs is a reason for belief in immortality.[60]

xxvii

Whitehead thought ill of the three main ways of thinking about God that have held sway in Western civilization "amid many variations in detail": God in the image of an imperial ruler, God as a personification of moral energy, God as an ultimate philosophical principle. "Hume's *Dialogues* criticize unanswerably these modes of explaining the system of the world."[61] To explain the system of the world was Whitehead's ultimate purpose, and to do *that* he needed his concept of God.

The structure of Whitehead's system requires him to hold that nei-ther God nor the World reaches a static condition. Both are in the grip of his metaphysical ultimate, creativity. Each is the instrument of novelty for the other.

But the principle of universal relativity does not stop at the consequent nature of God. That itself passes into the temporal world, as God's love for the world:

> For the kingdom of heaven is with us today. . . . In this sense, God is the great companion—the fellow-sufferer who understands.[62]

How, except by naming names, could Whitehead have made it plainer that he is being moved by his wife's anguish over their son's death? He continues:

> We find here the final application of the doctrine of objective immortality. Throughout the perishing occasions in the life of each temporal Creature,* the inward source of distaste or of refreshment, the judge arising out of the very nature of things, redeemer or goddess of mischief, is the transformation of Itself, everlasting in the Being of God. In this way the insistent craving is justified—the insistent craving that zest for existence be refreshed by the ever-present, unfading importance of our immediate actions, which perish and yet live for evermore.

That is the end of *Process and Reality*.

xxviii

What shall we make of this conclusion? Notice first how far Whitehead is from the popular view that God makes everything right. The phrase "redeemer or goddess of mischief" is indispensable. Next, we should observe that although the whole book is an essay in speculative philosophy, Part V is more speculative than the four preceding parts, in which the philosophy of organism is primarily applied to mundane experience—I should say, with considerable success. The addition of Part V does not spoil that success; it fits on so well that the coherence of the whole becomes a reason for accepting the conclusion.

Whitehead's theism is a highly philosophical one. He once said to me[63] that his concept of God's consequent nature was very like Spinoza's concept of God.

---

*The capitalizations in this sentence were first supplied by Whitehead in a typescript of Part V which he gave to Rosalind Greene. (She had recently suffered a tragic death in her family.)

God is not one of the Categories of Existence. He is not even the subject of any principle in the Categoreal Scheme. These facts should not mislead us. Something about God is said on almost every page of *Process and Reality*. The chapter "Some Derivative Notions," which immediately follows "The Categoreal Scheme," begins by introducing the primordial nature of God as "the primordial created fact." I think that Whitehead had his complex concept of God roughly in his mind when he first started writing his Gifford Lectures.

An informative example of Whitehead's use of his concept of God occurs in his discussion of living creatures in the chapter "The Order of Nature." God's purpose, he says, is to evoke intensities of feeling.[64] And God's aim for an actual occasion is "depth of satisfaction as an intermediate step towards the fulfilment of his own being."[65]

In 1931 Whitehead said in his response to the speakers at a large symposium on *Process and Reality*:

> Almost all of *Process and Reality* can be read as an attempt to analyze perishing on the same level as Aristotle's analysis of becoming. The notion of the prehension of the past means that the past is an element which perishes and thereby remains an element in the state beyond, and thus is objectified. That is the whole notion. If you get a general notion of what is meant by perishing, you will have accomplished an apprehension of what you mean by memory and causality, what you mean when you feel that what we are is of infinite importance, because as we perish we are immortal. *That is the one key thought around which the whole development of Process and Reality is woven.*[66]

Notice that in this identification of the one key thought Whitehead did not use the term *everlasting*. None of the symposiasts referred to Part V of *Process and Reality;* they may have lacked time to finish the book. However that may be, Whitehead did not suggest Part V to them. His remarks were about what, in his system, might be called ordinary immortality, in which a perished actual occasion becomes a component in later occasions.

xxix

The first of Whitehead's Gifford Lectures was chaired, in the absence of Edinburgh's Principal, Sir Arthur Ewing, by its distinguished Professor of Mathematics, E. T. Whittaker. He had been Whitehead's pupil and then his colleague at Trinity College, Cambridge. His son, Dr.

J. M. Whittaker (also a mathematician), wrote me[67] that the 1927 Gifford Lecturer, Eddington,

> was a marvellous popular lecturer who had enthralled an audience of 600 for his entire course. The same audience turned up to White-head's first lecture but it was completely unintelligible, not merely to the world at large but to the elect. My father remarked to me after-wards that if he had not known Whitehead well he would have suspected that it was an imposter making it up as he went along (this had actually happened in a lecture in Psychology at Oxford shortly before). The audience at subsequent lectures was only about half a dozen in all, so I am told, for I fear that I myself was one of the backsliders.

One of Whitehead's Harvard students, Mason Gross, was told that at the end the audience shrank to two, Kemp Smith and A. E. Taylor. "This was probably an exaggeration," Gross wrote to me.[68] It is clear from the account of Whitehead's Giffords in this chapter, as well as from the Prospectus he submitted, that as public lectures they were bound to be a fiasco.

Evelyn was visibly disappointed by the plunge in attendance. I doubt that her husband showed his feelings. He had done his work; its recep-tion was in the lap of the gods. The contrast with his audiences at Urbana, though sad, was just a sociological fact. The Urbana audiences had not heard a condensed technical statement of a big new metaphysi-cal system; that would have been a great tax on any audience. There was also this difference: the Edinburgh people *knew* they did not understand what they heard.

XXX

Whitehead wrote to Rosalind Greene and her husband about the city of Edinburgh:

> We had never before stayed there for any length of time. The longer we were there, the more beautiful we thought it. But as to its weather,—Oh dear!![69]

As one who has endured summer days of nothing but cold, driving rain in that beautiful city, I sympathize.

A few days after the last lecture, the Whiteheads visited North and his family; they lived in Teddington, near London. In 1921 North had had a son, whom he named Eric Alfred North. Whitehead delighted in the boy; but Eric told me that he felt his grandfather did not have a real relationship with him until he was an adolescent.[70] Much in Whitehead's mature life reflects the experience of highly responsible personal relationships which had been his as Head Boy at Sherborne School.*

In London Whitehead went to Athenaeum, and there enjoyed an afternoon of philosophical talk with Wildon Carr and Maurice Amos. It was like Aristotelian Society meetings at their best. When Evelyn came to fetch him they triumphantly brought her into the hall, where no woman was allowed, and continued their talk for a quarter of an hour.[71]

In or near Cambridge, Whitehead saw his oldest brother, Charlie, who, as he told the Greenes, was "lingering out the last few months of his life," and his sister Shirley, "more herself than ever in every way," "a huge featherbed, driven irresistibly forward," "an unrelenting steamroller."[72] She was witty, but her wit, like Bertie Russell's, was critical, even destructive. She was *so* unlike Evelyn.

The Whiteheads did not look up Bertie.[73]

After a short visit to Cambridge, where Evelyn gave a big dinner party for old friends, the Whiteheads found places to stay in Dorset for the rest of the summer. He was fond of Sherborne and its environs. The difference from Edinburgh weather was not lost on them. But I doubt that Whitehead ever developed the habit of devoting himself to a vacation. He left that to Bertie.

On August 15 Whitehead wrote to Rosalind Greene, "We have become greedy, and want America as well as England." But not Scotland. He had written to her on June 28, "Scotland is *not* our spiritual home. The Scotch are full of inhibitions, canny, and suspicious." Whitehead was canny, and did not lack inhibitions; perhaps one cause of his love of Evelyn was her relative freedom from them.

They sailed for New York on the *American Merchant* September 7. Whitehead, as usual, was a bad sailor. On the twelfth he wrote to North that he was all for a static world. "Damn the flux of things with its rockiness." But the fifteenth was "the most lovely day that I have ever seen on the Atlantic." It was followed by a little gale. The ship docked on the seventeenth, and they took the night train to Boston.

xxxi

On December 23 Whitehead wrote to North:

This last term has been the greatest tax on my imagination that I have ever had—*not* the most tiring physically. But I have been making the

---

*See Volume I, Chapter IV, Sections iv and vi.

final draft of my Giffords—and having to keep the whole scheme of thought in my head, so as to get all the points written up in order.

When we consider the size and complexity of his system, and the fact that he was no longer young, we ought not to find the number of lapses in the book surprising. No one could help him much. His Harvard students suggested critical difficulties which he tried to meet. Evelyn, as usual, suggested deleting some of the *also*s with which he began too many sentences, and making other stylistic improvements. Whitehead sent the last package of proofs to Macmillan on August 13, 1929.

Then, on November 4, he wrote to North about the book:

I do not expect a good reception from professional philosophers. It deserts the ordinary ways of putting things at the present moment. Also it is more speculative than philosophy in the recent past. In my opinion philosophers have been running into funkholes and so the subject has lost all interest.

Professional philosophers received the book with respect but did not take it up. What was called "doing philosophy" was coming to consist mainly of piecemeal discussions.

Fame

A t its commencement exercises in June 1926, Harvard bestowed an honorary doctorate of science on White-head. President Lowell's apt description of him on this occasion was, "A philosopher, generous and kind, whose thought pierces deeper than others look."

Then on June 21 Whitehead was in Madison, Wisconsin, to receive an honorary D.Sc. degree from Glenn Frank, President of the University of Wisconsin. *Science and the Modern World* had made its author popular in the Midwest. So far as I know, he received no such invitation from any southern university. He and Evelyn made no visits south of Virginia. And in those days very few proper Bostonians spent a bit of the winter in Florida.

A year later, Yale gave Whitehead an honorary doctorate.

I think he enjoyed his visits to receive honors. I also believe that a reason for traveling to receive them was that he knew they would give Evelyn a lift. I doubt that he ever completely set his work aside for a trip. As he had done when they traveled in Europe, he always had paper handy, on which he would jot down ideas for his current work as they occurred to him.

ii

In February 1926, meetings of a special Harvard committee, always known as the Committee of Four, began in Professor L. J. Henderson's Cambridge house. The Committee's members, besides Henderson and Whitehead, were the scholar in English literature, John Livingston Lowes (author of *The Road to Xanadu*),* and Charles P. Curtis, a scholarly lawyer and a member of the Corporation at Harvard. Their purpose grew out of conversation between Henderson and Whitehead on a train as they came home from a weekend at Henry Osborn Taylor's home in Cobalt, Connecticut, in the fall of 1925. They had talked about

---

*Henderson thought no better representative of the humanities could be found.

the success of the system of Prize Fellowships at Trinity College, Cambridge. Whitehead had begun his mathematical work as a Prize Fellow there.* Henderson reported this conversation to President Lowell. The result was a long evening of discussion at Lowell's house, with the addition of the astronomer Harlow Shapley and the Dean of Arts and Sciences, Kenneth Murdock. Lowell presented a plan he had formulated for what came to be called the Society of Fellows. There was much agreement, and plans were drawn up to make further contact with Trinity College. Lowes was in England, and would visit it; Whitehead cabled to ask for a hospitable reception for him. The Committee of Four wanted Harvard to establish a small society of students between twenty and thirty years of age who, instead of following the routine of Ph.D. work followed by a faculty job, would devote three years to the research that most interested them, with the prospect of renewal for another three. Their idea was that the best way to spawn genius in a university is to catch students young, provide them with subsistence and intellectual fellowship, and assure freedom from academic regulations and anxieties. The success of the idea was amply shown in the records of "Junior Fellows" compiled by Crane Brinton in *The Society of Fellows*.[1]

Applications were not solicited from prospective Junior Fellows. The Committee of Four, augmented by a few ex officio men, comprised the Senior Fellows; they administered the Society. They chose four to eight Junior Fellows per year. An interview was important; at Whitehead's suggestion, sponsors of Junior Fellows also were interviewed.

The Society got off to a flying start. The first batch of Junior Fellows included the philosophy graduate student W. V. Quine, who was working on logical theory, the new champion of behavioral psychology, B. F. Skinner,† the mathematician Garrett Birkhoff, the historian John C. Miller, the political scientist Frederick M. Watkins, and the chemist E. Bright Wilson, Jr.

Quine's selection raised a problem for which no provision had been made; he was married. I think that Whitehead persuaded his colleagues to provide a sum of money as a sort of marriage commutation.

The Society of Fellows met for dinners on Monday nights, and the

---

*On Whitehead's election to that fellowship, see Volume I, Chapter VI, Section iv. Let me correct an error on page 108 of that volume: "Playfair's" should be "Poynting's."

†His study, *Verbal Behavior,* was undertaken to meet a challenge raised by Whitehead in talk at a meeting of the Society.

Juniors without the Seniors lunched together twice weekly. All meetings were in Eliot House. The House system at Harvard had just been provided for by Edward Harkness's gift. President Lowell tried to get foundation funds for the Society of Fellows, but was unsuccessful; he had to use his own money, which was enough, but with almost nothing to spare. I think that the Society of Fellows deserves to be called the best achievement of his Harvard presidency. And he was the chief author—with some help, I think, from Whitehead—of the statement to which Junior Fellows subscribe.* Lowell called it the Hippocratic oath of the scholar. It read:

> You have been selected as a member of this Society for your personal prospect of serious achievement in your chosen field, and your promise of notable contribution to knowledge and thought. This promise you must redeem with your whole intellectual and moral force.
>
> You will practice the virtues, and avoid the snares, of the scholar. You will be courteous to your elders who have explored to the point from which you may advance; and helpful to your juniors who will progress farther by reason of your labors. Your aim will be knowledge and wisdom, not the reflected glamour of fame. You will not accept credit that is due to another, or harbor jealousy of an explorer who is more fortunate.
>
> You will seek not a near, but a distant, objective, and you will not be satisfied with what you may have done. All that you may achieve or discover you will regard as a fragment of a larger pattern, which from his separate approach every true scholar is striving to descry.
>
> To these things, in joining the Society of Fellows, you dedicate yourself.

To this first batch of Junior Fellows, the Society meant primarily Henderson, Whitehead, and Lowell. Whitehead himself provided a good example of the ideals to which the Junior Fellows subscribed. He never looked for fights. He did not try to defend his philosophy of organism, or even to explain its chief theses.

iii

Professor Donald C. Williams, who later joined the Harvard Philosophy Department, audited Whitehead's lectures. He told me that it was customary for undergraduates to ruffle their papers and shuffle

---

*Brinton wrote that you could not call this an oath.

their feet when a lecturer began to run overtime. Whitehead often forgot the time, but they didn't do that to him. "Once he talked overtime for half an hour, and nobody batted an eyelash." When he realized what he had done, Whitehead was quite overcome, and very grateful to the students.

After Whitehead died, Williams said to me, "I never knew what humility meant until I knew Whitehead." He was referring to humility as a personal attribute of a philosopher.[2]

One day early in 1930 I was looking over the philosophy books in the Harvard Square store of the Harvard Cooperative Society when Whitehead came in, walked to the same department, picked up Macmillan's printing of *Process and Reality,* and made just one remark to himself, "So that's out." This store sold many more copies of the book than were ever sold in the United Kingdom.

I came to Harvard as a freshman graduate student in the fall of 1929, lured by the presence there of the authors of *Science and the Modern World* and *Mind and the World Order.* It is still my opinion that no twentieth-century philosopher has done better than Whitehead in speculative philosophy or C. I. Lewis in analytic philosophy.

In my first term I heard Whitehead's lectures on the philosophy of science. I am sure that most of them were beyond me and many other students. Three years earlier Whitehead had expressed doubt that there could be any such subject; affirming it is too much like affirming that there is Protestant truth and Catholic truth. Beware of qualifications of that word. There are truths about many subjects, and philosophy can exclude no subject.

iv

Whitehead in his lectures was always looking ahead, not looking back. One of his students, Paul Weiss, thought that one would not learn from them that Whitehead was one of the authors of *Principia Mathematica.* He would bring up Russell's philosophical opinions when they were relevant to what he was saying, but he did not devote lectures to them.

In the 1920s and early thirties Bertie made lecture tours across the United States. Thus on a Sunday morning in 1929 he spoke in Symphony Hall, Boston, on the faith of an unbeliever. He gave a very different sort of lecture to a quite different audience under the auspices of the Harvard Department of Philosophy on October 26, 1931, with Whitehead in the chair. It was entitled "The Relation of Logic to Psychology." It filled Harvard's New Lecture Hall.

In his introduction Whitehead announced that we were about to hear a missing Platonic dialogue, "the Bertrand Russell." Some of Russell's discussion was hinged to examples that were familiar to anybody who knew of the collaboration between him and Whitehead. But Bertie was off on a new major tack; he dwelt on the role of conditioned reflexes in producing meaningful utterances. When the lecture was over, Whitehead closed the meeting by saying what he thought Socrates would have said in conclusion as he drew his cloak about him:

> I understand now, my dear Bertrand, the meaning of the good. It is, that my mouth is watering.

Russell had arrived in Boston the previous day. He stayed that night with Henry Sheffer, a brilliant young mathematical logician at Harvard. In the Introduction to the second edition of *Principia,* Russell had singled out Sheffer's replacement of several primitive ideas by one, incompatibility, as the most definite improvement made possible since the first edition was published. He had also called attention to "a new and very powerful method in mathematical logic" invented by Sheffer, who named it "notational relativity." Russell recommended to him the task of re-writing *Principia,* which the new improvement would demand. Whitehead had a high opinion of Sheffer. I'd say that he shared this with Russell, quite as much as he firmly refused to share the taking up of Wittgenstein.

Bertie spent the night after his lecture with the Whiteheads, and returned to New York the following day.*

James Wilkinson Miller was one of Whitehead's junior colleagues at this time. He has told me of a conversation which occurred in the midst of traffic while they were crossing Brattle Square. "You know, Bertie was born in the wrong century." "What century should he have been born in, Professor Whitehead?" Miller expected that the answer would be the seventeenth or the twenty-first or even the fifth century B.C. But the reply was "Oh, the thirteenth of course. He is pure Duns Scotus."

V

Something must now be said about the large symposium I mentioned late in the last chapter to present the key idea around which

---

*The Bertrand Russell Archives contain no correspondence with either of the Whiteheads about this visit.

Process and Reality was written. James Woods arranged the symposium as a celebration of Whitehead's seventieth birthday. It was held at the Harvard Club of Boston on February 14, 1931. The almost forty guests, besides his friends, included the polymath Morris R. Cohen, who spoke on Whitehead's contribution to mathematics, and the best-known philosophers in the eastern seaboard of the United States. Although the first addresses were simple misunderstandings of the method of extensive extraction, later speakers voiced serious questions about *Process and Reality,* and Whitehead's replies were informative about himself as well as the book.

William P. Montague confessed that he now felt like an old fogey. And he wondered what it is that passes from one actual entity to its successors, if not substance. W. H. Sheldon, of Yale, was "very anxious to know whether the philosophy of organism is objective idealism. Does he ascribe mind to the universe as a whole? Perhaps I ought to know this, but I am not sure." Sheldon described Whitehead's philosophy as "a rope tightly woven of three strands: Hegel, Bergson, and Avenarius. That is a strange company." He credited Avenarius with starting the protest against Cartesian dualism in modern times.

The longest, and most learned, address was by Arthur O. Lovejoy, of Johns Hopkins. He had been re-reading "another famous philosopher of the English Cambridge, the learned and pious Dr. Henry More of Christ's College." A quotation from one of More's poems defended the use of new words or of old words with new meanings. After confessing that his own attitude toward comprehensive systems was skeptical, Lovejoy concluded that "there is no book of our time which is a more faithful picture of the real world." My personal knowledge of Lovejoy and Whitehead leads me to believe that A. N. W. was most highly delighted by the following judgment of his big book:

> Most of all one gets from it a rebirth of philosophic wonder. It is a rejuvenating experience to read *Process and Reality.*

Whitehead's response to the guests at this celebration of his seventieth birthday was not only appropriate, it was beautiful. I can touch on only a little of what he said.

He explained that his reason for not discussing Hegel was that he had read only a single page of him. But his friendships with McTaggart and Lord Haldane had effected a Hegelian influence. As Whitehead had devoted so much of his life to mathematics and the elaboration of symbolic logic, the philosophy he had not read, he confessed, "passes all telling." He did not now say anything about Sheldon's finding that Avenarius was among those who should be credited with a strand of the rope Whitehead wove.

Several of the speakers had brought up Bergson, and Whitehead brought up Bradley. But to prepare for his identification of the key idea of *Process and Reality,* he said,

> I speak from very thin knowledge, but I rather suspect that I am a little more Aristotelian than either Bergson or Bradley.[3]

This was a valuable bit of self-knowledge.

Upon thanking Lovejoy for bringing Henry More to his support, Whitehead observed, "I think Bradley gets into a great muddle because he accepts the language which is developed from another point of view." And not only Bradley!

Whitehead said that he agreed very much with Sheldon on the necessity of order.

> But there is just the slightest twist of his phraseology which makes all the difference, and with that one twist of phrase I decisively disagree. Professor Sheldon talked of *the* order of the universe, *the* scheme of order. In this notion of the sole, unique order for the world (which perhaps is not what Sheldon meant) there hides the inadequate concept that the foundations of being contain in their nature no necessity for process. . . . The notion of the one perfection of order . . . must go the way of the one possible geometry.

Montague had brought up the question of entropy. Whitehead replied that the universe we live in now was indeed running down, its order giving way to a new type of order.

When Whitehead spoke of other orders of the universe, he contrasted our familiarity with "this absurdly limited number of three dimensions of space." It was typical of the mathematician to allow for an infinite number of possibilities.

Scotland did not come out well on this occasion. In thanking Morris Cohen for recalling the great past of mathematics, Whitehead named not only Grassmann but Sir William Hamilton, "not the Scotchman who was a bad metaphysician but the Irishman who wrote good mathematics."

Whitehead's final appreciation of the symposium was superb.

> I have been extraordinarily fortunate in that I have always had colleagues whom I could honour and whom I could love, at Trinity in Cambridge, and in London. Now finally in America my fortune has

culminated in what I consider to be an intellectual society as great as any which has existed.

He then quoted a statement from the *Republic* which was printed on his valentine only:

The philosopher who lives with divine and orderly people himself becomes divine and orderly, as far as it is in his power to do so.

---

vi

Victor Lowe had gotten this far in drafting the present chapter when he died. He had planned further chapters on Whitehead's years of retirement and on his death. Among Lowe's papers there are some very rough notes, a collection of obituaries, and brief letters of reminiscence from a few people who knew Whitehead, all of which were meant to serve as material for these chapters. There are, however, no drafts using the material.

Nothing can replace the narrative Lowe would have written of Whitehead's life from the time of the publication of *Process and Reality* to his death. No attempt will be made here to fill the gap, but a few events and dates can be given.

The Whiteheads continued to live the kind of life they had lived since coming to the United States. In 1931 T. North Whitehead and his family moved permanently to the United States, settling in Cambridge. Alfred and Evelyn traveled a little, visiting friends during the summers at various vacation spots in New England, and in 1930 going to Oxford for the Seventh International Congress of Philosophy. Whitehead continued to teach until 1936. His last lecture, on May 8 of that year, was attended by a large number of former students and admirers from outside the university.

During these years Whitehead continued to write. *The Function of Reason*—delivered as the Vanuxem Lectures at Princeton—was published in 1929, *Adventures of Ideas* in 1933, *Nature and Life* in 1934, and *Modes of Thought* in 1938. He gave a number of lectures and addresses, including the Presidential Address, "Objects and Subjects," to the Eastern Division of the American Philosophical Association in 1931.

Whitehead received many honors during his late years. Harvard,

Yale, and McGill were among the universities that gave him honorary degrees. He received the Butler Medal from Columbia University in 1930. In 1931 he was elected Fellow of the British Academy. As early as 1903 he had been made a Fellow of the Royal Society. C. D. Broad, in an obituary notice,[4] pointed out the singularity of membership in both societies: only Sir J. G. Frazier, to his memory, had previously received this double recognition. In 1945 Whitehead was awarded the Order of Merit, the highest honor the Crown can give for outstanding personal achievement.

On the occasion of Whitehead's eightieth birthday, his Harvard colleagues organized a party for him. More than fifty people attended, among them personal friends as well as Harvard colleagues. Whitehead was presented with greetings signed by numerous students and friends, and made a few brief remarks in reply.[5] He took the tribute to be for Evelyn as well as for himself. She supplies, he said, "those vivid insights and immediate activities which count for so much in our joint life." The two of them, Whitehead went on, had suffered "unforgettable intimate tragedy" during the previous world war. "The only way to meet tragedy is to interweave it with loving activity. Evelyn and I are grateful to Harvard beyond words, because we can love it."

In the rest of his remarks Whitehead turned away from personal matters and spoke of philosophy. Good work in philosophy, he said, can best be done in a democracy. Agreement should not be the aim of philosophers, though they may hope for "a certain mutuality of vision," not expecting much by way of confirmation of their views. Narrowness is to be guarded against:

> The whole stretch of life should be vividly present. Every philosophy lecture room should have two exhibits—at one end of the room a baby in its cradle, at the other an emeritus professor—the future and the past. And in between, the surging present, the confused thoughts of the lecturer and his class. It has for its function to exhibit the unrealized possibilities which the past suggests, while living in the turmoil of the present.

During Whitehead's last year, so his son reported to Victor Lowe, Whitehead felt that his mind was failing. He died on December 30, 1947, of a cerebral hemorrhage. He was cremated and his ashes were scattered in the graveyard of Harvard's Memorial Church, where a service was held for him on January 6, 1948.

CHAPTER XIII

Whitehead's Philosophy as I See It

There are a few respects in which I could criticize White-head's philosophy, but I shall not do so in this essay. I shall present my overall view of it. This is positive, even enthusiastic. I flatter myself that my favorable view does not issue from any desire to find the philosophy indispensable in the service of religion, or of morals, or of anything other than philosophy as Whitehead conceived it. I began to study him early, and in a condition that approached innocence. My undergraduate work was not in college, but in an engineering school, and I had not read any philosophy until, in 1928, I was introduced to the subject by two books: Will Durant's popular *Story of Philosophy* and Whitehead's *Science and the Modern World*. Durant's expositions of the great philosophers were superficial, but so invariably warm that he did not tilt me toward accepting any one in particular, which is what usually happens in college philosophy courses. I felt a strong allegiance to the science I was most familiar with, mathematical physics; Whitehead was a mathematician who had written a philosophy of physics and was beginning to integrate physical science with value-experience. Since there were signs of genius in his book, I went to Harvard to study under him and the other men in what was truly Harvard's second golden age in philosophy.

The way in which Whitehead went about the integration of science and values struck me, and still strikes me, as the only right way, the only way that is broad enough. Although he had that integrative problem in mind, he did not aim simply at its solution, but expected this to be one result of work on a larger task. That task was the construction of a general theory of everything that we experience, a scheme of ideas such that "everything of which we are conscious, as enjoyed, perceived, willed, or thought, shall have the character of a particular instance of the general scheme." Every reader of Whitehead is familiar

Originally published in *Process and Context*, ed. Ernest Wolf-Gazo (Bern: Peter Lang, 1988). Reprinted by permission of the publisher.

with this statement of his goal in *Process and Reality*, but it cannot be too often insisted upon that correct understanding of the statement is the best key to understanding his work. Most philosophers today do not take it seriously; they say that they have got beyond grandiose ideas. But Whitehead's idea was simply that of a *general theory*, conceived as it ought to be conceived in the twentieth century. Give up the preoccupation with the statements that Whitehead and other philosophers have made about experience, the world, or the sciences; give up the intent to discover just what the philosopher meant by a particular statement, and the grounds on which it can be judged *true* or *false*. For Whitehead's goal, it is not statements but general *theories* that are to be judged, and they are not to be divided into the true and the false, but valued in proportion to their power to accommodate the multi-form facts of experience. (Whitehead upheld the possibility of finite truths, but that is another matter.) A new theory that aims at much greater power than familiar theories requires a new terminology—something which people accept in science but, alas, resist in philosophy, and resisted in Whitehead's case.

If the new terminology is accepted, anything that cannot be accommodated by a new general theory calls for some revision of the theory or of what is used in applying it. The process is unending. Near the end of his life Whitehead wrote to a friend:

> there is no suggestion in my mind—nor (I hope) in my works—of a clear-cut adequate philosophic system. All we can do is to gaze dimly at the infinitude of things, which lies beyond our finite apprehension. Words are inadequate for experience, and experience is inadequate to grasp the infinitude of the universe. Of course, this is a commonplace; but it cannot be repeated too often.

A philosophic system is "adequate" if *nothing* can ever be found in human experience that is uninterpretable in its terms. Whitehead knew that his system was inadequate, and declared that complete adequacy was unattainable by human beings, although the history of philosophy shows improvements in adequacy.

Of course he did not construct his system by gazing dimly at the infinitude of things. He generalized from human experience, which insists upon the formulation of certain *kinds* of ideas, such as ideas of identity and diversity, possibility, compulsion, value, and purpose. When he set out to construct his system, philosophy for Whitehead was the search for premises that would apply to experience in the broadest sense, the sense in which, as he later said, "we experience the universe,

and we analyze in our consciousness a minute selection of its details."
Hence the outcome was a System of the World.

He was always aware that proof is hypothetical: so far as the premises are true, deductions from them are true. I am discouraged when I
hear an admirer of Whitehead say he *proved* that the universe is a living
organism. The admirer has his own motives for wanting to think so;
Whitehead did not suppose that he had proved this, or any categorical
proposition.

William James said, "Systems must be closed." Whitehead's position
was that a system must be open to revision. It should be constructed as a
speculative theory, not as a set of truths calling for vital commitment.
Commitment should come later, as a result of comparing available
philosophies.

James also spoke of philosophy as giving us a sense of alternatives to
what we believe. Whitehead saw that what suggests alternatives is a
more general idea.

The breadth of his system naturally, but unfortunately, has tempted
some to label it a synthesis of the sciences. No; he did not try to unite
either the principles or the conclusions of the sciences. These are among
the data which his "Categoreal Scheme" must accommodate. The
Scheme is obliged to provide a niche for every known science, including deductive and inductive logic. In *Process and Reality* he provided a
niche for logic as it existed in 1928 and for the physics of that time, and
indicated niches for a few other sciences, including epistemology. I
doubt that any science then existing fell outside his philosophy of organism. As with any set of axioms, Whitehead's Scheme had to provide
a niche for every notion he used later, and for every proposition he
would have a right to propose. I think he was fairly successful in meeting this requirement.

Unless a philosopher, like C. I. Lewis, deliberately limits himself to
reflective analysis of concepts in current use and refuses to speculate, the
method Whitehead recommended and practiced seems to me the only
right one for metaphysics. It is not for everyone. If you have not his
degree of genius, you had better stick to the history of philosophy, to
studying Whitehead's deposition and exploring its possible applications, or to comparisons with others. In trying to understand Whitehead, it won't do to pick out a word or a principle and try to analyze its
meaning; for example, to ask whether he means "perishing" in an
absolute or relative sense. For every sense which you propose for an
isolated word, there is a passage in which Whitehead seems to use it in

an opposite sense. *Process and Reality* is a long book; there is no escape from steeping yourself in it.

A full view of Whitehead's method must note his rationalistic faith. This was faith that experience will reveal no elements which are, in his words, "intrinsically incapable of exhibition as examples of general theory." This faith, he said, "forms the motive for the pursuit of all sciences alike, including metaphysics." Preservation of that faith despite disappointments "must depend on an ultimate moral intuition into the nature of intellectual action—that it should embody the adventure of hope." In all his work Whitehead held fast to this moral intuition, while doing what no one else would attempt: a treatise on *Universal Algebra,* the long collaboration with Russell on *Principia Mathematica,* his fine memoir "On Mathematical Concepts of the Material World," his non-Einsteinian theory of relativity, and finally his speculative metaphysics.

ii

My work on Whitehead's biography, extending over almost two decades, has convinced me that without his forty years in mathematics he could not have tried to write *Process and Reality.* He was an unusual mathematician; he did not write stacks of paper on subjects that others were pursuing, but attended, more than most, to framing sets of axioms. Look at his two tracts, *The Axioms of Projective Geometry* (1906) and *The Axioms of Descriptive Geometry* (1907). No claim for the self-evidence of the axioms is made. Nor was such a claim made in *Principia Mathematica;* general success in application to existing mathematics was the test. Even so, general success in application to experience is put forward as the test of Whitehead's metaphysical system. The main difference between the two is that no presumption of clarity can be made for the axioms of the latter.

Whitehead's work in mathematics gave him an ideal preparation for constructing a really new philosophy. He was saved from being ensnared, as professional philosophers are, by current philosophical language.

If a geometer like Whitehead were convinced, as he was when he wrote *An Enquiry Concerning the Principles of Natural Knowledge,* that "the fundamental characteristic" of nature is its passage, its "creative advance," how would he deal with philosophy's traditional problem of the many and the one?—By conceiving that at every event-particle in nature there occurs an integration of many event-particles elsewhere into one new event-particle here-now, an addition to the accumulated process of the universe. That is "the ultimate metaphysical principle" of *Process and Reality,* with event-particles replaced by actual occasions. For Whitehead had moved beyond experience as providing the sensory data of natural science, to experience in its entirety, as providing the data of metaphysics.

The fundamental characteristic of nature, creative advance, was replaced by the fundamental characteristic of actual occasions, that they are creatures of Creativity. Whitehead first used this word in *Religion in the Making* (1926). A year earlier, in *Science and the Modern World,* he used the phrase "substantial activity." However named, the idea is the inmost core of his philosophy. In his Categoreal Scheme Whitehead set down the three notions "Creativity," "many," and "one" as comprising the Category of the Ultimate. This, he said, "replaces Aristotle's category of 'primary substance.'"

The ultimacy of Creativity has not been well received by professional philosophers. Whitehead denied that it was an entity, so why is it needed in addition to his explicit Categories of Explanation and Categoreal Obligations? (He said that they presuppose the Category of the Ultimate.) I answer: if there is no universal characteristic that the entities of a system share, you have not got a system of those entities. In the axiomatic treatment of a pure mathematical science the elements are merely abstract until an interpretation is specified. The elements, as *any* entities that satisfy the axioms, become entities of a certain kind. Whitehead's Scheme was not about abstract entities, but about the final concrete entities comprising the actual world. He called every concrete entity an individualization of the universal creative force. That is simply how Whitehead *saw* the world. I think he saw it truly.

Most of his readers are needlessly bothered by the question, How can I recognize an actual occasion? My answer is that anything in human experience may be treated as an actual occasion so far as it approximates to the design of an actual occasion set out in the philosophy of organism. Whitehead himself so treated a "drop of experience," which lasts as long as a "specious present." What about other events? When I asked him whether the emission of a single quantum of energy was an actual occasion, he replied, "Probably a whole shower of actual occasions." It seems to me that an event which has a duration of years, such as the determination and execution of a specific national policy, might also be considered an approximation to an actual occasion. The philosophy of organism offers only a *general way* of thinking about the pluralistic process of the universe. Whitehead left its applications to us. Not nearly enough of that has been attempted.

Until recently I balked at Whitehead's doctrine of the realm of eternal objects. Then I saw that I had been wrongly assuming the self-consistency of this realm. In his set of comments on *Process and Reality* (published in *Essays in Science and Philosophy*) Whitehead explained that it includes "all possibilities of order, possibilities at once incompatible and unlimited with a fecundity beyond imagination." He continued: "Finite transience stages this welter of incompatibles in their ordered relevance to the flux of epochs. . . . The notion of the one perfection of order. . . must go the way of the one possible geometry."

Whitehead saw clearly that every achievement, even the unity achieved by a trivial actual occasion, requires the exclusion of possibilities that might have been realized. Hence his concept of "negative prehension." I used to be bothered by the distribution of negative prehensions: the actual occasions in an insect negatively prehend so many more eternal objects than I do. But Whitehead's system requires only the truth of the hypothetical proposition that if the insect, on any occasion of its existence, had one of my potentialities, it would have the option of either actualizing it or refusing to actualize it. The idea of comparing quantities of negative prehensions is illegitimate.

This example illustrates the fact that Whitehead started from the highest kind of existence we know of, and construed lower kinds in its terms. The natural alternative in cosmology is a process materialism with emergent evolution.

Whitehead was not so foolish as to identify progress in human life with novelty. Strife among partisans of new directions, and between them and upholders of tradition, must be expected. Peaceful progress requires the finding of ways to convert destructive conflicts into contrasts between opposites which can then live together, while destructive possibilities are negatively prehended. (This view of progress reflects Whitehead's personal outlook on human life, and his habits: he was a reconciler, seldom a militant.) The turning of potential conflict into contrast is also important in art. We have here one of the ways in which Whitehead's system shows that it is not an idle intellectual exercise, but immediately relevant to human life.

Even before he constructed his system, in *Symbolism* he did one of the most valuable, and most needed, things in modern philosophy. He rehabilitated the idea of a direct experience of the external world, as an experience of causation. The immanence of the past in the present then became a cardinal doctrine in his system of the world.

Every philosopher uses some general conception of Experience. Whitehead worked out his own, and boldly generalized from it to a world-view which might be called a new pan-psychism. (He was not happy with that label; "pan-valuism" would be better.) The concept of Experience is a great contribution to philosophy. As I lack space to discuss it, I will only call attention to his sound description of the experience of causation as in its primitive form emotional, and to his original analysis of the self-creating and purposive side of an experience. It is a pity that he was too much a Victorian to discuss the aspects of experience on which Freud built his theory.

From what I have said so far about Whitehead's philosophy of organism, you will see why I think it is a usable philosophy. And it will repay attention as long as there is real interest in constructive philosophy. For example, his system was a monadology, but much superior to Leibniz's.

iii

World War I was the most important influence on Whitehead's philosophy. He had always taken a personal interest in his pupils; many of them were on the casualty lists. In 1918 his younger son, Eric, was killed. He himself, with great self-discipline, thought out the *Principles of Natural Knowledge;* he dedicated it to Eric. The last words in the book were Wordsworth's:

The music in my heart I bore,
Long after it was heard no more.

In 1916 Whitehead had delivered a famous presidential address to the Mathematical Association, "The Aims of Education." It dealt with education for a creative life. But the fact that every life and every creation perishes was forever in his mind. When Harvard gave him the opportunity to philosophize, he tackled the notion of perishing. He first did so in his 1926 paper "Time." In the set of comments on *Process and Reality* to which I referred earlier, he spoke of Aristotle's "suggestions on the analysis of becoming and process," and continued: "I feel that there is a gap in his thought, that just as becoming wants analyzing so does perishing. Philosophers have taken too easily the notion of perishing. . . . The world is always becoming, and as it becomes it passes away and perishes." The two are linked by his doctrine that in perishing an occasion of experience acquires immortality as an *object.* Thus, as he said in the book's Preface, the relatedness of actualities "is wholly concerned with the appropriation of the dead by the living . . . whereby what is divested of its own living immediacy becomes a real component in other living immediacies of becoming." Nothing that happens is a mere matter of fact.

But is perishing the last word? The war weakened the agnosticism that Whitehead had embraced circa 1897. Apart from religion, human life seemed to be "a flash of occasional enjoyments lighting up a mass of pain and misery." He did not try to find a church with dogmas acceptable to him, but worked out his own philosophical theism.

He dealt first with God as primordial. The realm of eternal objects cannot be conceived as floating in the air, since those which are unrealized in the actual world would then have no effective relevance to the future. There must be an actual entity in which all the eternal objects—not only the mathematical Platonic forms, but all qualities as potentials for realization at some juncture in the world's history—are held eternally together in their eternal relations to one another. Whitehead called this actual entity God. His primordial nature is unchanging; its effect is to bestow a universal character on the otherwise purely protean Creativity, so that the actualizations of eternal objects in the temporal world cannot be purely chaotic. Such is the immanence of God's primordial nature in the world.

The pages of the last part of *Process and Reality* occupy but one-twentieth of the book. The subject is God's "consequent nature," which Whitehead thinks of as endlessly in process with the world. As actual occasions become and perish, God receives them into his experience, in which they are purified. Whitehead's words glow, but his tone is tentative. If he were reasonably sure of this doctrine, he would have done well to include his concept of God in his Categoreal Scheme.

Whitehead's doctrine of immortality in God gives permanent meaning to the tragedy of his son's death. In all probability this was part of his motive for writing it, but that does not warrant our dismissing it. The doctrine, in Whitehead's hands, is perfectly beautiful. My personal opinion, as a skeptic about religion, is that if God exists, He is the sort of being Whitehead imagined, and conceived of as always *with* the world. In all his writings on religion, he denounced as barbaric the idea of an a priori omnipotent Creator.

The Second Edition of *Principia Mathematica*

Preparing a new edition of the three-volume *Principia* that the Cambridge University Press had published in 1910–13 was an interesting job for Russell, but only a headache for Whitehead.

Early in 1920 Russell asked the Press about its stock, and whether the Press "would contemplate reprinting the first volume at any time." On February 11 A. R. Waller, Secretary to the Syndics of the Cambridge Press, answered that they had in stock no copies of Volume I, only one of Volume II, and four of Volume III.* Nothing was done to get *Principia Mathematica* back into print until three years later. None of the parties involved wanted a new edition pronto. The work could not bring the Cambridge Press much profit, but the special symbols would require much labor and expense.†

Whitehead was overloaded with academic duties at the University of London, and the center of his interest had shifted to the philosophy of natural science. Russell had maintained his mastery of the foundations of mathematics, but he wanted to, and did, spend most of 1920 and much of the two following years abroad.

The crux of the matter was the unavailability of the first volume.‡ In his letter to Russell, Waller said that the Syndics could not afford to reprint Volume I, and that the earnings of Volumes I, II, and III were being reserved to pay for the printer's composition of Volume IV. That volume, on Geometry, was to be written by Whitehead alone. He did a good deal of work on it in England, and intended to finish it at Harvard, but was too busy constructing his new philosophy there.§

---

*He added that the Press's agents abroad had a few copies of each volume, but they were probably too soiled to be of use.

†Russell's biographer, Ronald W. Clark, wrote: "The type was still standing." Dr. Kenneth Blackwell, the Archivist at the Bertrand Russell Archives, McMaster University, discovered a few years ago that Clark was mistaken.

‡This was not relieved by the presence of forty-four copies of Volume III at the binders.

§As late as 1930, Whitehead still hoped to complete Volume IV of the *Principia*.

The Cambridge Press considered itself bound to publish Volume IV by the reference to it in the Preface to Volume III.

In November 1922 Russell's publisher, Stanley Unwin, proposed to make an arrangement with Cambridge to reprint all three published volumes by a special semi-photographic process. Nothing came of this.

When Russell, early in 1920, made his inquiry of the Cambridge Press about its stock of the *Principia,* he was full of the ideas of Wittgenstein's *Tractatus Logico-Philosophicus.* He had spent a week, ending just before Christmas 1919, at The Hague with his brilliant former pupil, discussing the manuscript of this little book. It was in Wittgenstein's rucksack when he, an officer in the Austrian army, was captured by the Italians in 1918. Its author believed that it solved all the problems of philosophical logic, and that a fresh start along its lines was needed; *Principia Mathematica* was now a futile exercise.

I doubt that any philosopher ever had a greater influence on the impressionable Russell than Wittgenstein did at this time. But Russell also knew that the work to which he and Whitehead had devoted ten years was not a complete loss. He encouraged Wittgenstein, and promised that he would write an introduction to the *Tractatus* (he did); but he would also do what was needed to make the *Principia* available again.

By March 1923 Russell and the Cambridge Press were considering a reprint of Volumes I–III. On the twentieth he wrote to the Press that he had consulted Whitehead, and that they were agreed in wanting the text reprinted without changes other than those already noted in the *Errata;* but they thought it would be desirable to notice work done in mathematical logic since the publication of the *Principia* that was relevant to their treatment of the subject. Russell added that the new matter could be made to fill just one page of print, and he suggested that it be placed "at the beginning of Vol. I in Roman pageing as Preface to the Second Edition."

When Russell next wrote the Press, on September 6, 1923, this short Preface, after two summer months of work on it, had become a long, unfinished Introduction. He asked for more time—in fact, a whole year—as he was engaged for an American lecture tour in the spring. Sydney Roberts, the new Secretary to the Syndics, granted him the year. Finally, in September 1924 Russell submitted the new material, consisting of the Introduction and three appendices. All four embodied Russell's logical atomism* and his understanding of the ideas in Witt-

---

*This cherished doctrine was the subject of eight lectures that he had given in London in 1918.

genstein's *Tractatus*. The second edition of *Principia Mathematica*, by Whitehead and Russell, was published in 1925. It contained no indication that only Russell was responsible for the new matter in it. On the contrary, Russell used the plural throughout.

Whitehead was left to state the facts. He sent a Note to the Editor of *Mind*, saying that Russell alone was responsible for the new matter and concluding, "I had been under the impression that a general statement to this effect was to appear in the first volume of the second edition."

It was not until almost ten years later that Whitehead had the interest and time to write out his seasoned judgment on the *Principia*, including his alternative to what Russell had composed and published in their joint names.*

In his *Life of Bertrand Russell* (published in 1975), Ronald W. Clark wrote as follows about Whitehead, Russell, and the preparation of the new edition:

> The friendship had not been restored to its pre-war strength and it appears that Russell now decided to go it alone. . . . Whitehead had little sympathy either with logical atomism or with Wittgenstein, and it appears that he let Russell get on with the task, without comment but without collaboration.

This passage was in agreement with the general opinion among historians of mathematical logic.

In 1986, however, a letter from Whitehead to Russell, dated May 24, 1923, was found in the papers of Dora Russell, his wife at that time.† I shall quote most of the letter, as it shows that in the spring of 1923 Whitehead tried to collaborate. His tone and his wit are pretty much the same as they had been during the pre-war collaboration. Only the old habit of always encouraging Bertie is not there; Whitehead knew of Russell's enthusiasm for Wittgenstein, and probably wondered whether he himself would be able to approve of what Bertie would now write.

Dear Bertie
. . . .
Yes, I thoroughly agree that we cannot undertake a reorganisation of the text. But I will send you my ideas for appen-

---

*See Alfred North Whitehead, "Indications, Classes, Numbers, Validation," *Mind* 43 (1934): 281–97.

†This letter was discovered by the Russell archivist, Dr. Kenneth Blackwell. I am indebted to him and to Russell's daughter, Katherine Tait, for giving me access to it.

dices to the various "Parts" of the book,* mostly in the form of Press corrections to the proofs, e.g., on the first two sheets you will find a series on the various meanings of "function", entirely due to the infernal niggling criticism of Johnson.† I think a short note on the various meanings citing some of the occasions of their use might be useful. *A priori,* I should have thought that the text is plain enough. . . .

I don't think that "Types" are quite right.‡ They ("Types") "tending towards the truth", as the Hindoo said of his fifth lie on the same subject. But for heaven's sake, don't alter them in the text.

I will send you sheets 3 and 4 at the end of this week, to arrive on Monday. . . .

Yours affecty,

Alfred Whitehead

Presumably Russell received this letter shortly before he began his two summer months of work on the Introduction to the new edition. If Whitehead kept Russell's response, it did not survive the general destruction of Whitehead's papers and correspondence in 1948, just after his death.

In one respect, at least, Russell welcomed Whitehead's participation. On October 21, 1923, he wrote to Roberts of the Cambridge Press, "While I am in America (Jan.–April [1924]) it will be necessary to get Dr Whitehead to attend to the proofs."

Russell's letter continued, "He (i.e., Whitehead) also has certain ideas about the prefatory material, but I think he and I can arrange about that without troubling you." This was rash, because Russell should have known that Whitehead could not honestly accept his endorsement of Wittgenstein's ideas.

Renewed collaboration between the authors of *Principia Mathematica* became practically impossible early in 1924, when Whitehead accepted Harvard's offer of a chair in philosophy. Before he sailed, he was overwhelmed with final duties at the Imperial College and in the University of London. When Russell finished the Introduction to the new edition,

---

*The three volumes of *Principia* were divided into six parts.

†W. E. Johnson of Cambridge, author of a three-volume treatise on logic.

‡I think the reference here is to ★12, "The Hierarchy of Types and the Axiom of Reducibility," in Volume I of the *Principia;* "The Theory of Logical Types," Chapter II of the Introduction to the first edition—Russell was primarily responsible for that chapter—also is in point.

Whitehead was already in the American Cambridge. Russell sent a copy to him, and got no reply (Whitehead seldom replied to the mail he received); after a decent interval, Russell submitted his new material for *Principia* to the Cambridge Press. In fact, he had discussed the entire manuscript, not with Whitehead, but with the brilliant Cantabridgian F. P. Ramsey. The former collaborators had separately gone their own ways.

It is barely possible that Russell took Whitehead's spring 1923 letter as a sign of collaboration that would justify his use of the plural throughout the new matter he was about to write. That was not at all justified, to be sure; but Bertie was absorbed in what he wanted to do. Back in 1911, when Whitehead sent him several basic criticisms of the typescript of *The Problems of Philosophy*, he did not acknowledge them in any printing of the book. They assailed the convictions that he then held most dear.

Russell's Introduction to the new *Principia*, as published, begins with unexceptionable notices of the improvements demonstrated by H. M. Sheffer and Jean Nicod. Sheffer showed that the pair of undefined ideas, negation and disjunction, could be replaced by one, incompatibility between propositions, symbolized by a stroke and written $p|q$. (The idea goes back to Charles Peirce.) Russell uses the stroke in the Introduction and all the appendices. Nicod showed that the five initial unproved propositions could be replaced by one.

On the second page Russell takes up that blemish on the structure of *Principia*, the axiom of reducibility,* and recommends the way of dealing with it proposed by Wittgenstein in the *Tractatus*, namely,

> to assume that functions of propositions are always truth-functions, and that a function can only occur in a proposition through its values. . . .
> We [sic] are not prepared to assert that this theory is certainly right, but it has seemed worth while to work out its consequences in the following pages.

Russell devoted one of his appendices to the difficulties of this view. He was characteristically scrupulous in his discussion of them.

I shall skip over other respects in which the new matter of the second edition reflects Wittgenstein's influence.

Whitehead did not think well of Wittgenstein or of his ideas, and seems never to have been influenced by him. There was opportunity.

---

*See Volume I, page 274.

Before the war, when Wittgenstein was Russell's student at Cambridge, Russell took him to meet Whitehead. And in August 1913 Wittgenstein was a visitor at the Whitehead country house in Lockeridge, Wittshire. There was never any meeting of minds. Three things about Wittgenstein annoyed Whitehead intensely. (1) He was passionately certain of the correctness of his opinions. (2) He kept insisting that you *must not* ask this, that, or the other philosophical question. (3) Instead of trying to bring science and philosophy closer together, he drove them farther apart, by making philosophy a very special kind of linguistic activity.

It is hard to imagine any greater contrast between philosophers than that between the author of *Science and the Modern World* and the author of the *Tractatus*. If Russell did not sense this, it was because Wittgenstein was the object of his current enthusiasm, while Whitehead, Russell thought, had gone in for bad metaphysics.*

----

*Russell wrote a quite critical review of *Science and the Modern World* in *Nation and Athenaeum* 39 (May 29, 1926): 206–7.

Letters from
Alfred North Whitehead

August 20, 1924–August 12, 1929

Although Whitehead wished to have his papers and letters destroyed, some material escaped. Most important, T. North Whitehead kept a series of letters that his father wrote to him and his wife, Margot, and he loaned these to Victor Lowe for use in the biography of Whitehead. On May 21, 1965, North Whitehead and his sister, Jessie, wrote jointly to Lowe, encouraging him to write about Whitehead and giving him permission to use whatever material he could find, including letters written by or pertaining to their father and mother. The letters, they wrote, were "to be printed at your discretion, with no further appeal to us."

The originals of the letters are currently on loan to the Special Collections Division of the Milton S. Eisenhower Library, Johns Hopkins University. The transcriptions were made by Victor Lowe and checked by Nancy Thompson. In presenting them I have not tried to give a diplomatic edition. Whitehead's emphasis has been kept only where it affects the sense of his words; otherwise, as when he underlines the place or date of composition, it has been dropped. I have not annotated the letters, since most of the references Whitehead makes are sufficiently clear as they stand.

S.S.Devonian
August 20th/24

Darling North

All well—and thank goodness at last an absolutely calm day: result, general happiness. For the first three days there has been a nasty
head wind, strong with a rough sea. The boat is steady and hardly
rolled, but it pitched a good deal. Luckily our cabin is right in the
centre. Mummy was not absolutely ill, but very unhappy, and
stayed in her bunk most of the time. Poor Mary succumbed entirely,
but has proved herself a good traveller.

It has been horribly cold; but we are going to the south of west,
and so today it is warmer but still with a chill wind. We get to the
latitude of the Azores and then come up again to Boston.

The people in the boat are mostly New England Yankees going
home. A nice quiet set—inoffensive, if not exciting. There is one
man and his wife whom we like a lot—by name Lord. I think he is
also in University work. He is that sort of man. He knows people of
that sort and has been staying at Oxford. Mary is in a cabin with a
wife of an American Missionary in India, coming home after six
years—with more children than converts—nice people, rather pathe-
tic.

We managed the journey to Liverpool and getting onto the ship
with great success. The Leyland agent [went] with [us] on the Liverpool platform, and took charge of our luggage—and has put it on
the boat—at least I hope so.

Intellectual operations have hitherto been reduced to the basic
principle of not being seasick. We had a lovely evening view of the
Irish coast and saw the Fastnet light. We passed along the coast for
hours; and I did not see a house let alone a village or small town. But
after that, the weather got colder and rougher, and I ceased to make
acute observation on the various phenomena.

Darling, thanks for your letter: I loved it.

I will continue this letter in a day or two, and post it on board. So
that it will be my last English letter. Though I am sitting on deck
surrounded by the Yankee language—

August 24/24   Sunday Mid-day

Since I wrote we have had fine days, smooth and very warm. The
sudden change to hot weather in the Gulf Stream has been trying,
but very pleasant. We shall probably get into Boston on Tuesday afternoon.

The boat is getting to know itself and become a social unit. On the whole a nice cultivated set of people—some of them remarkably interesting.

You will be interested to hear that Mummy and I went to service this morning in the saloon—attracted by the prospect of a sermon from a man who has struck us immensely by his strength of character and outlook. The best New England type is immensely interesting—but rather overwhelmed by its conscience.

We are now sitting out on the upper deck—Mummy discussing the price of petrol with a Yankee woman who sits next to us—among other topics. I have not been able to do any writing on board—either too jumpy (at the beginning), or too much desultory conversation since the fine weather.

Today being Sunday, no shuffleboard is allowed, but only poker in the smoking room.

The boat is doing about 13½ knots at its best, and 12 when there is a headwind. We find the life tiring and rather wearing. I don't understand why people go for a sea-voyage to rest; it doesn't act that way with us—though yesterday and today are much better.

Monday. Aug.25.

Another perfectly calm day, but rather colder. Apart from fog, we shall certainly land tomorrow afternoon. The voyage has been a success. It is boring and in a way tiring. But Mummy's neuritis is better. On the whole we have been lucky in the weather: three bad days at first, but nothing very serious—and since then, calm. The passengers excellent—some of them we have liked extremely and hope to see again—only a very small set of impossibles who are anyhow quiet and not bother.

I will close up this letter, and start another when we are in Cambridge. Dearest love to you all. Tell Margot that I have worn her waistcoat and that is has been just what I wanted on deck after dinner.

Your loving Daddy

I have written an analogous rambling letter to Jessie.

Tuesday. August 27*
Off Boston   S.S.Devonian.   2·30 P.M.
3·30 Summer Time

Darling North

Such a disappointment—just when we were off Boston harbour, about to pick up the pilot in half-an-hour, a sudden storm struck us and is still keeping it up. They say that it has come up from the Gulf of Mexico—anyhow it is a very healthy production. It was quite smooth before lunch—our luggage piled in the passages ready for landing, everybody tipped, goodbyes said and cards exchanged— when suddenly the wind began to howl, etc.—just like the stage storm in Wagner's Der Fliegende Holländer introducing the hero— the imitation on Nature's part is quite perfect. The Custom house shuts at six, so there is no hope of getting in tonight—the ship has been put about and we are going slowly in the wrong direction. The ship is behaving perfectly, as you may understand from the fact that I am writing this letter and not lying on my bunk. There is extraordinarily little motion considering the nature of the provocation.

One silly woman came up to apologise to us for the inclement nature of the American weather which was greeting us. We assured her that we blamed the Creator far more than the Yankees. She seemed quite relieved at our taking that view of it. People are dotted about the saloon, playing cards and soothing babies—all with the general air of having left the general direction of affairs to Providence.

Love to Margot—Goodbye darling.

Daddy

Thursday Aug.28/24
403 Radnor Hall
Charles River Road
Cambridge   Mass

Darling North

Here we are, safe and well. Mummy is decidedly rested—her neuritis has gone—and the warmth and brightness agree with her. She is full of energy though tired after a busy morning. We are at present in

---

*The date should be August 26.

a lovely flat, overlooking the Charles River—about the breadth of
the Thames at Kew—everything most convenient. We landed yesterday morning, and found the Osborn Taylors, Prof.Woods, and
Marjorie Tuppan on the quay waiting for us—the poor things had
been there since 8.A.M. and we got off the boat about 11·30. But
what surprised me most was that all our packages were there also.
During the hurricane the day before all our cabin luggage had been
tumbled in wild confusion in the passages and saloons. For it had all
been taken out of the cabins for immediate landing. We had an-
chored at the Quarantine station on the previous night, after the
storm—passengers had to be on deck dressed at 6 A.M.—but nothing
happened till 7:30 when an American doctor counted us by way of
inspection—then breakfast—then about 9:30 another American doctor turned up, and told Mary that she had a goitre by way of de-
pressing her spirits. Then the really serious business of the
immigration officer commenced—our great difficulty was to get to
him—and as we didn't want to stand for an hour in a long queue, we
sat down and waited till near the end. Once there, he merely glanced
at the Consul-General's personal card of introduction and signed up
for all three of us at once. We had no bother at the Customs—the
law requires that every package should be unlocked and
unstrapped—and 25 packages (big and little) took some doing—but
the Customs man took no interest as to what was inside. I can give
high marks to the Boston Port Authorities. A "Transfer Company"
sent our heavy trunks straight to Brattle St. The Osborn Taylors had
provided two automobiles which took the whole party and our travelling luggage to this abode. They then went to their hotel, while
Mummy and Miss Tuppan and Mary had lunch there and I lunched
with Woods at the Colonial Club and went over the College and saw
my lecture room and private room in College. We had tea, and then
the Taylors motored us to their hotel for a second tea, and then back
to the Club for dinner with Woods. Finally we got back, and a nice
young couple—man and wife—turned up with an invitation from an
old gentleman of 82 to go and see him at the earliest opportunity.

   Cambridge is a very intimate place, all in relation to the College—
with great charm of greenness and shrubs and foliage, with the touch
of a southern summer on it—a network of roads of small detached
houses, with a comparatively small centre for shops.

   Of course there is a manufacturing working-class quarter, out of
sight, towards Boston, down the river.

   The house in Brattle St—No 116—is very attractive—but we [are]
not certain how it will work. We only have it for nine months, and
may try for one of these apartments at Radnor Hall. Anyhow there is
plenty of time in which to make up our minds. We hope to get into

it in a few days, with a little luck. This morning we explored the shops—interviewed the Bank Manager—or rather, the Vice-President of the Bank—and generally settled down. Anglo-Saxondom seems rampant here—they warm up when they find one is English, not because they are pro-English, but because presumably the[y] have got hold of an instance of the genuine article.

After dinner. My letter was interrupted by the appearance of Woods for tea. He is a great pet—rather nervous in manner—I expect that we shall become great friends. Then Miss Kahnweiler turned up—"that awful woman" as Osborn Taylor called her. She is a friend of the McDougall's who had the keys of the flat. She has been very kind in a Germanic severe and imperative way, with a good deal of inquisitiveness and desire to boss. Mummy has dealt with her firmly but politely—we have overwhelmed her with thanks and kept her at a distance. But she really is kind under her peremptoriness. We are going to supper with her on Sunday.

The day has been hot. It is quite believable that we are on the latitude of Rome.

You have never seen so many private cars of sorts as there are here—especially at the rush hours. An American citizen on his own legs will soon be a curiosity—or will be arrested, as we arrest tramps who sleep under hedges.

We have heard with barely concealed pride that yesterday's storm nearly sank a liner which was following us. Frankly, where we were at the mouth of the bay it was not nearly bad enough for that sort of thing. Mummy and I could stand on the sheltered side of the deck and look at it. If it had gone on much longer, a new situation would have arisen so far as my internal arrangements were concerned—but as it was, it passed off in time for the enjoyment of a good dinner.

Would you send this letter to Jessie, as I have written in too great detail for repetition—Dearest love to you all

Daddy

Whitehead
8 Elmfield Avenue
Teddington
Middlesex
England

Arrived well great kindness met Osbon [*sic*] Taylors Woods Marjorie
Tuppan very comfortable most satisfactory

Love Mummy Daddy

Sept 14/24
at 403 Radnor Hall
Cambridge, Mass

Darling Margot

North tells me that you are very occupied in your mind over the
withdrawal of Roy from the Bedales Prep, and would like to know
exactly what I think about it. School is so important that I very
much sympathise with you, if you feel it is a great worry and responsibility to adjust your mind. I will tell you now exactly what I
think and why I think it, and will not fear about being long and
prosy.

In education on the intellectual side, we have to think (i) of the
definite precise knowledge and technique to be acquired, (ii) of the
types of interest, embodied in a pleasurable imaginative life, to be
fostered and developed, and (iii) of the rebound on character created
by success or failure under the headings (i) and (ii).

I will drop (iii) for the present, though of course the final character
evolved is the main thing. But we cannot discuss it, till we are clear
about (i) and (ii).

(i) and (ii) are of course interconnected, the precise knowledge
should give intellectual backbone and efficiency to the general interest, and the general interest should give reality and meaning to the
precise knowledge. The choice of subjects must depend partly on the
child—his aptitudes, etc.—and partly on his opportunities in life,
e.g. University requirements and future profession.

But the real difficulty in education comes from the balance between pushing on in precise acquirement and between fostering individual effort and initiative so as to develop creative interest. Both

take time, and the key to all educational difficulties is that there is not enough time.

In truth the balance of time requires adjustment for each individual child. But in practice there are two large types. *A*   There are children who are very quick and facile at picking up the details of what they are taught. These children get on quickly, and usually are easily interested just because they keep things in their heads and compare them.

Among these children are a large proportion of the ablest, and also a lot of intermediates who will develop ably if they can be got to think deeply.

But also a certain proportion damp off somewhere between 17 and 25, because they won't think things out—superficial with nothing in them.

B   These are children who are slow at details and who are apt to get behindhand in their acquirement of knowledge and technique. Most of these are intellectually rather slow and some never acquire any great grasp. But in quite a flexible proportion, the slowness comes from the unconscious trick of overdeep thinking, of getting at some point which is not supposed to be in their horizon and which cannot really be explained without a wholly different mental atmosphere. What I mean is that slowness very often arises from isolated unrelated bits of deep thought which confuse the child. Obviously some of the potentially best intellects will be in this group.

The danger of this group is discouragement: they never get a small series of triumphs. They feel stupid and give up trying.

The *Type A* children are often (though not always) literary or mathematical (pure mathematics), the *Type B* children are often scientific, though they may be poetical. Most children would be either literary or scientific according to direction of interests. Nearly all children want an admixture of both sides in their education.

Now children of Type A want *pushing on*. If they are not pushed on they get into the lazy habit of winning a lot of easy successes in memorizing and showing facility in the elementary stages. They don't want so much encouragement in this preliminary initiative, because they are always finding their tasks easy. They want to be pushed on over their precise technique so as to get to problems which really will make them think. They enjoy the sense of progress, and they are thereby kept in view of the real depth and difficulty of things. This is the sort of boy whom latin prose—as written by scholars—brings out and interests.

Children of Type B want *encouragement in coordinating their ideas,* and in gaining interesting glimpses of things, without the *preliminary burden of too much technique.* Their technique will come later, but meanwhile they must be given the chance of seeing the meaning and connection of things on the level of native insight. They will gain interest and grasp and coordination; and gradually the technique as a simplified orderly way of managing the subject will acquire sense and meaning for them.

Now the older type of education—originating without much attention to psychology—concentrated in pushing the children on in precise technique. It was also too narrow in its basis of things studied.

But in the hands of able teachers, it suited boys of type A very well. In the last 12 years the curriculum of every public school of the older type has been remodelled. The balance of subjects is now quite broad enough. But they still retain the emphasis on pushing on in precise knowledge.

I think that the better schools of this class suit boys of A type very well.

The newer types of education have been elaborated largely by experiments on children of type B. The successful experiments—such as Bedales—suit this sort of child well. They keep up freshness and interest, and learn to work without discouragement. Altogether, at least half, if not two-thirds, of the children ought to be educated in this way.

Finally, I do not think that the Bedales methods suit children of the A-type. They drop off into a weak discursiveness, with a superficial glibness. It is not what their nature wants.

Now as to the effect on character: I strongly believe that the proper intellectual development according to the natural wants of the individual child is a large element in character-formation. The whole inner imaginative life receives its tone from the intellectual formation: furthermore the habit of receiving the proper impress either of discipline or creative encouragement is an essential element in morals.

If the intellectual development is mishandled, there are the gravest risks to character unless the other elements in the environment are unexpectedly favourable. To stunt intellectual development warps outlook and reacts on character.

For these reasons, long before I heard a whisper of Roy's removal from Bedales' I told Mummy that I doubted whether Bedales was the best place for him. But I have not—nor has Mummy—stated or hinted, directly or indirectly, my doubts. The boy was happy and so far doing well, so I kept quiet.

When I heard that for reasons of finance he might have to be removed, I did not say anything (except to Mummy) but I did not think it a disaster from any point of view—except that a new school is naturally an anxiety. I think that if he could gain ultimately a Winchester Scholarship it would be probably the best thing for him.

You know—don't you, dearest—that if we had it we would give anything for the future of any of the children. But really—except to please you—I should hesitate very much before making an effort to keep Roy at Bedales. I think that there is a risk of it spoiling his character by implanting in him shoddy intellectual habits, and

P.T.O.

also that it endangers his very real chance of becoming one of the considerable forces of his generation.

That is exactly what I think. Mummy has read to me her letter, and she has put in half the words what I have been trying to say.

I do not feel that I can diverge now into a chatty letter. It does not seem to go with this little treatise.

People are just beginning to come back, so our little holiday is ending. We are both very well, and enjoying ourselves.

Dearest love to you and North.

Daddy

I have only got a large envelope here

Saturday. Oct 4/24
504 Radnor Hall
Charles River Road
Cambridge Mass.

Darling North

Your letters and Margot's are a great joy to us. We think of you "smarting up" the house, and of Eric's conversational powers. But see that Margot is careful, so long as her headaches trouble her. It is so difficult not to do too much—it is a problem whose solution has always beaten Mummy.

At this physical instant Mummy and Mary and the two McDougall boys (aged 17 and 15 ½, both absolute pets) and the American Express men and an American Customs' agent (in the morning) are busy unpacking the furniture and getting a semblance of order into the new flat. We shall sleep there tonight, but of course it will be mere camping. I am writing in my room in the Widener

Library (the University Library) having delivered two lectures today, one at Radcliffe College (Women) and one at Emerson Hall which houses the Harvard philosophical department. Last night (Friday night) I had a seminary from 7:30 P.M. to 9:30 P.M. So on Saturday afternoon—it is now about 5:30. I am rather tired.

When we get into it, the flat will [be] absolutely perfect—with a divine view, and planned exactly rightly and of the proper size. It will almost run itself as we look at it.

We have got rid of our house in Brattle St. It was taken at 9.A.M. on the day it was turned over to us, and today the lease has been signed—so that is off our mind. People are rather astonished that Mummy managed to acquire simultaneously one of the most desirable small houses and one of the most desirable flats in Cambridge, things that people wait years for.

We shall be glad when we are really settled. Our camping in other people's houses has been a great strain.

The other day I had a long talk, nearly two hours, with President Lowell—the head of the University—whom I sat next to at a small public dinner. I liked him. He is rather heavy at first—but absolutely without any pomposity or pretension, straightforward, and interested in ideas, especially history.

Goodbye, Darling. Dearest love.

Daddy

504 Radnor Hall
Charles River Rd
Cambridge, Mass.
Sunday   Oct 19/24

Darling North

All well here—Mummy has just retired for an hour-and-a-half's rest (2·15 P.M), and then we shall pay a call. She is tired but triumphant. With the help of Angus McDougall she has unpacked the last two book-cases, and put the books on the shelves, and has finally finished the dining room. So now only Jessie's room remains to be put in order. We have brought the right amount of books. There is a little room on the shelves, but not much—just the amount for some growth. All the books are in the dining room, a very few in this room—my study—with my cardboard boxes. Altogether, if we had know[n] the flat beforehand, we should have brought about the same furniture as we have actually got over here. So we are lucky to be so well out of that gamble. Furthermore we find that it has given satisfaction that during our stay here we are making it a real home. Certainly for us, it is everything. Thank Margot ever so much for the fresh batch of Eric's pictures. They are delightful. I wish she could have seen the pleasure that they have given.

Yesterday, we were taken [on] a motor-drive through some typical New England Country and saw some show spots and show houses—Lexington, where the first shot in the American Revolutionary War was fired, and so on. The Autumn charm of the country, the lovely old wooden houses, the fin[e] country simplicity of the people, were touching in the extreme. This was in the afternoon. On the whole it was a busy day. In the morning I delivered two lectures, in the afternoon from 2–6 drive as above, dining out from 7–8, then a large reception of the Philosophy Department (including Psychology, and some lawyers, with students, and wives, about 80 in no) to whom I made a long speech of about an hour's length. The[n] home very tired. Each session there is a reception of that sort with someone to give the address, followed by larger plates of ice-cream than I should have thought possible on this restricted planet. Both items were somewhat wasted on me, as the address was mine, and at the previous dinner the ice-cream had already been ample and satisfying.

I am enjoying my lecturing: I have managed to "place" my style, and general way of doing things, in a fairly satisfactory way, at least to my own satisfaction. The two hours' seminary—7 to 9 PM on Fridays—is very amusing. About twenty come. To a large extent it consists of discussion—the men cross-question me as to points arising in my lectures—also I get them to write short papers on such points. They sustain their parts very well—politely, but keeping their ends up.

There is a three-party general election here running concurrently with ours at home. It is on Nov 4th. So the English election news gets rather crowded out. But I see that the London correspondents of the New York papers prophecy a Labour gain of about 20 to 30 seats. I cling to my old estimate of 80 to 100, which I thought probable in the summer before we sailed. The sympathy of the sort of Americans whom I see is with Ramsay Macdonald, on account of his foreign policy.

Over here everybody is accusing everyone else of being a crook—the standard method of expressing political disagreement. Except that the third-party people, never having held office, can only be accused of being cranks. Then there is the Ku-Klux-Klan, which is also a live issue. It is Protestant, Anglo-Saxon, 100% American, Anti-negro, and predominantly Republican (=G.O.P.=Grand Old Party). The problem before the G.O.P. leaders is to handle this topic so as to retain the K.K.K votes, and yet not to offend either the Roman Catholics, or the non-Anglo-Saxons, or the Negroes. It takes some doing; but there is plenty of ability over there.

Then there are the middle Western farmers, who are secure of the home-market and grow wheat for export. They have got to be persuaded that a tariff which raises the price of everything else is just what they want to set them on their legs. The G.O.P. has tackled this job also. A wet autumn (for the wheat harvest) would have dished them; but luckily it was fine, and the tarif[f] has been vindicated. Altogether the betting seems heavily on Coolidge, unless there is a complicated muddle which will result in Congress (*not* the formal electors) having to choose between Coolidge, or Davis, or Bryan. Nobody wants Bryan who is not the third-party man. But in this case, he will get elected, unless Coolidge's men vote for Davis. The details are too abstruse for a letter.

We continue to admire the extraordinary personal kindness of the New Englanders. They are really delightful, not only to us, but to each other. This does not exclude unbending competition in business and professions. But then there are so many openings for a native-born American of character, ability, and education that, if a man cannot make good, he is felt to be a little deficient somewhere. Anyhow they are steeped in the full individualism of the Manchester school. But personally, they are very cultivated, very modest, and very kind—not a bad combination.

Goodbye, Darling. My dearest love.

Daddy

504 Radnor Hall
Charles River Road
Cambridge, Mass.
Nov 1st, 1924

Darling North,

What a crash!—In the General Election, I mean. I suppose that we are now in for five years of Conservative Government, with a slight bias towards the Die-Hards. Anyhow, so long as Curzon is not at the Foreign Office, and they do not starve Education, the Nation will be there after five years, all right and ready to go ahead. But, badly managed foreign affairs and a badly equipped nation will spell disaster. I do hope that the various Progressist [sic] sections will end their insane quarrels, mostly personal, and fix on a policy which will achieve something substantial and yet have a chance of getting carried in the next Parliament.

I loved your letter about your experiments on accuracy. It gave me a sense of chatting to you in the vividest way. So far I have not had time to digest it on its purely scientific side—I shall certainly do so; and if any ideas occur to me, will push them across the pond to you. But I do not think that it is likely that I shall have anything to say on that point.

Mummy is well. We are both very flourishing, and simply loving this place and its people—so immensely kind, with such sensitiveness of feeling. And the weather!! We are told that it is one such Autumn in a decade, or even more rarely. But I have never known such a succession of lovely days—brilliant sunshine, fresh air of about the right temperature, and the vivid autumn colours, browns and yellows and scarlets beyond belief. When the colour does go on a dull day, it collapses much worse than in England. Also this climate never gets the elusive haunting charm of the English haze, quivering even on the finest day. Here the landscape stares at you in the sunshine—but such a stare!

Yesterday (Saturday) was lovely, and we were taken for a motor drive in the afternoon. We went to Andover, about 20 miles off, by some small lakes on the way—a beautiful drive, ending in one of the quiet charming little New England Townlets. The road all the way along was rather like the Portsmouth Road on a Bank holiday—hundreds of cars, and about two people on foot,—perhaps there were five, but not more.

We have got a busy day before us after lunch. From 4–7 P.M. we meet the staff of the combined philosophical and psychological department at tea—with their wives. Mummy and I will be standing, shaking hands and saying appropriate things to above 50 people as they file past us. It is the American way of expressing pleasure at our arrival. Then in the evening, as usual we are at home to my pupils. Probably about eight or ten will come. They are mostly postgraduates—rather shy, but chatty and very confiding. A good many come from remote places in the Middle West, or from some isolated town on the Pacific Coast. Also they make terrific sacrifices to come to College, some working as waiters or domestic servants during their spare hours. Altogether, I find them very appealing. It seems such a responsibility to secure that so much earnestness and effort are not wasted. They argue very well. My seminary class—on

Fridays, 7:30–9:30 P.M.—is a discussion class. Some one reads a paper on a topic which I want elucidated, and then we discuss. They are candid, sincere, and invariably polite. This greatly helps one in endeavours to put before them the exact point of difficulty. They are less witty, and less irreverently epigrammatic, than analogous Cambridge Undergraduates; but they greatly enjoy anything in that way which is put before them. The one thing which the cultivated American hates and loathes—especially the cultivated New Englander—is anything approaching to bounce, or self-assertion, or boasting, or boosting. Their own *Babitts* (*vide* Sinclair Lewis) are heavily on their nerves. It has become almost an obsession with them. A typical Harvard professor shudders at the very thought of grandiosity. He calls the College Grounds the "Yard", and deprecates the pretentious exterior of the new library.

But of course the men suffer from not having lived all their lives in an atmosphere of long realised and still realising achievement—intellectual, literary and artistic. So much which is obvious, and full-blooded, and alive in Europe, has here to be seen through opera-glasses or by the help of illustrations. But there is a definite determination here to pull the nation together; and (as a preliminary precaution) to stop emigration, [*sic*] so as not to be overwhelmed by alien tradition. They mean to civilise their Babitts and to impress their American version of Anglo-Saxon tradition on their mixed population.

Also there is a very definite cleavage between New York and New England, expressed on either side by a certain contempt, but this is rather a side issue.

In fact U.S.A. is in the midst of a very definite struggle between those who mean to carry on the Old World culture via English traditions with modifications, partly because this is their one chance of a united nation with high civilisation and partly because they like the brand, and between those who *either* don't want any Old World culture, *or* who means to keep their peculiar European brand regardless of the claims of "100% Americanism".

Accordingly England is rather a battle-flag. Of course, like other flags, it is liable to get lost in the scuffle. But at present, it excites reactions which are really quite surprising.

We loved the photos. Thank Margot ever so much—
Our dearest love to you all—

Daddy

504 Radnor Hall
Charles River Road
Cambridge, Mass.
Nov.9th/24

Darling North,

All well here. Osborn Taylor is staying at the Colonial Club here, and enjoying himself like a boy, and rather an injudicious boy at that. Kenneth McDougall—the youngest boy, aged 16—broke his arm on Friday, running and falling on the school playground. Mummy was sitting with him yesterday afternoon, playing endless games of "coon can". In you[r] last letter you asked how our day went—so I will give you a skeleton diary of my own day, and leave Mummy to give hers.

I usually wake about 6 A.M. (±), as I have now done for some years. Between 6:30 and 6:45, I get up and am dressed about 7·40 to 7:45. Then Mary wheels in one of those three-tiered dumb waiters with our breakfast on it, Mummy being in bed. Tuesdays, Thursdays, Saturdays are my lecture mornings, viz 9–10 at Radcliffe (repetition of Harvard course) and 12–1 at Harvard in Emerson Hall. The lectures begin about 7 to 10 minutes after the hour, so they are 50 minute affairs. I leave home about 10 minutes to 9. Radcliffe is a *short* quarter mile away. Our back windows look straight at it. I take with me a small attaché case with my material for the morning. By the bye, Mummy and I usually end breakfast with a glass of cold water each. The dryness of the climate makes it necessary.

My class at Radcliffe has 9 or 10 members—4 undergraduates, or postgraduates, taking it for "credit" as the phrase is, and the others "auditors" in the technical language used here. They are an intelligent set of young people.

I then go to my room in the Widener Library—the University Library—and look over my notes for the 12 o'clock lecture and enlarge them, and at 11:30 have an orange and a small nut sandwich. One wants some sort of liquid in this climate if one is not to get done up. I then go to the Colonial Club—which is practically the Staff Club and the old Cambridge Club, just across the road from Emerson Hall—and have a quarter of an hour's rest and wash up, and read the English News in the New York papers. There is not very much of it. At my twelve o'clock lecture the audience is just 40—mostly postgraduate and including about 10 members of the staff. I think that they are interested. Anyhow the majority need not come unless they like, and the audience has rather increased lately.

At the end of the lecture men come up and ask questions. I usually make an appointment or two for a chat in my room at some other time. Anyhow I do not get away till about 1:20 or 1:30.

Radcliffe is about the same distance from Harvard (rather less) as from us—the path goes along the edge of a common with a monument to the Civil War (1864–6) in the middle of it. This is the rough map [See Whitehead's sketch, page 296.]

In this map the area of the College yard etc. has got into a small dot. It is really bigger than the Cambridge Common. The Colonial Club is the small dot just outside it at the end of the arrow.

I get back to lunch at about 1:45. In the afternoon I rest at first. We have tea at abt 4 to 4:30 in my study. (Callers don't want it). After tea I read or write up lectures. We dine at seven, and go to bed at any time between 9 and 11—but usually rather early.

On the other days, I work at home in the morning, and often go to College in the afternoon (late) to see some men. On Fridays there is the Seminary 7·30–9·30 in the evening. About 17 or 20 men, including some of the staff. I arrange for a student to read a paper, and we discuss it. I usually start the discussion, and intervene at irregular intervals. It is great fun. The men really discuss very well, with great urbanity and desire to get at the truth. There is rather less assertiveness and less aggressive running of set* theories than there would be at Oxford or Cambridge. Also, of course, they are not so witty, or epigrammatic. Any epigrams, that there are about, are let loose by me. I cannot exaggerate to you how much the educated well-bred American dislikes bounce or assertiveness. It is really too much on his nerves, so that even a strong maintenance of opinion is felt to be getting towards self-advertisement. Of course there is an ocean of Americans who are not well-bred and educated—as is in other countries. But New England is certainly dominated socially by the better class.

Baldwin's Cabinet is much better than I had dared to hope for. He really is going to try and govern on moderate lines. If his majority will let him do so, things won't be so bad. But I have my doubts. The only paper here which is worth looking at is the Christian Science Monitor. The others are astonishingly bad. In the mere technical get up, they are so inferior. The proof-reading and the printing are atrocious—hardly a column without a misprint, and the illustrations are simply not to be compared with those of the Times or Manchester Guardian. There are a lot of them (i.e. illustrations) but nearly useless. The Boston papers are down on the New York papers; and the Sunday papers are down below anything you can imag-

---

*In the original, the words "running" and "set" are very hard to read.

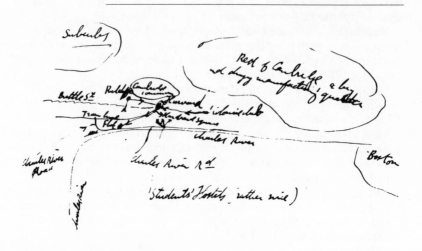

ine in futility, and larger than you could have thought possible. One paper makes a pile—but futility itself—nothing wrong, except that an excess of futility is the blackest evil. I am sure that in hell the Devil manages his torments of [*sic*] being eminently respectable and by talking incessantly like an American Sunday newspaper.

The leaves are mostly off now—not quite, but nearly so. This has been the driest finest autumn on record here—perfectly glorious weather. There have been a lot of forest fires and the smoke makes a sort of foggy haze even here, at a hundred miles distance. But it is getting colder, and the weather is dull today. It looks as though it were breaking up. But there is no actual rain yet.

In the elections here, the local interest was greater than the Federal interest. The Democratic candidate for the State Governorship had been in prison for personation at a civil service examination. He got a majority of Boston votes, but the solid New England farmers were unanimously against him. The feeling was very strong. He was defeated by a good majority, but he was not so absolutely out of the running as one might have hoped in a more perfect world. I have got a suspicion that in American politics the high-brow honest people are hopelessly off the pitch in their social ideas and that the corrupt demagogues are often advocating the right thing.

Anyhow Coolidge's triumph puts 100% Anglo-Saxon Americans firmly in the saddle for the next four years. I don't believe that they have got a ghost of a social policy. It seems to me that they are wasting an enormous opportunity over here, of getting things straight

before they are overcrowded. But it is the sort of opportunity which
always is wasted.

Dearest love to Margot and you—Your loving

Daddy

504 Radnor Hall
Charles River Rd.
Cambridge, Mass
Nov 23/24

Darling North

All well here. At last the long spell of dry weather has ended. It
first became piercingly cold, and then yesterday became warm again,
and began to rain in the afternoon, and has continued so doing on
and on during the whole night. It is a great relief. Mummy had
found the cold snap on the top of the excessive dryness rather trying,
and had to lie up for one day. But the nice warm moisture is refreshing. Yesterday was the excitement of the Yale-Harvard football
match, played at Newhaven—where Yale is. Harvard was licked.
There is some depression here over the football team; every University, Protestant, Catholic, or Non-Sectarian, large or small, State-
controlled or Independently managed, has licked it.

The games here are the focus of a vast and complicated
ceremonial, leading up to the sacrifice of the victims in the arena.
The victims do not enjoy it, but are compensated by the honour.
The object of the whole affair is the production of a certain type of
herd-emotion, which is considered desirable and is apparently also
delightful. It is as though all the rowing at Cambridge were abolished except such as directly bears upon the Oxford-Cambridge race,
and then the undergraduates were trained to ritual exercises on the
banks of the Thames; in order to work up mass-emotion. There is
too much nervous excitement about the American youth for them to
have the same sort of enjoyment in a mild game of a rather ineffi-
cient type, as we get from that sort of thing. They would prefer to
chop wood and feel themselves "frontier's-men". The fact is that this
climate does not go with that type of keyed-down enjoyment. There
is a perpetual urge in it to go "one better": also there is the consciousness of great opportunities. This latter consciousness is probably mistaken so far as the coming generation is concerned—at least
in comparison with the past. But the young have it. Of course my

postgraduate students are of an exceptional type. They are essentially quiet men with a taste for thinking, who are going into the rather poorly paid profession of teaching.

I am gradually feeling my way into a metaphysical position which I feel sure is the right way of looking at things. I am endeavouring to get it across to my men in lectures. It seems to interest them. Anyhow they like to see philosophy divorced from the mere procedure of commenting upon what other people have said. The numbers attending are slightly increasing.

We went to a delightful dinner-party last night. As usual the hours were early, 7–10. Indeed we were later than we expected and had ordered our cab at 9:30.

By the bye, who got in to Parliament for the University of London? If you have already sent information which will include this, do not bother about the question. Thank Margot immensely for the papers she has sent. It has been dear of her. Eric's photo is too delicious. By the time you get this, I suppose Sheila's mumps will be well over. Give Roy and her my dearest love.

There is a delightful simplicity about the young Americans from remote places. A married postgraduate student is going to bring his wife this evening, to our home. But having no one to look after the small girl, aged 2 ½, to my consternation he at once proposed to bring her along too. Of course I accepted the suggestion, and we are wondering how we shall get along with it. But the absence of the usual provisions for domestic help, makes things pan out into simplicity.

In Cambridge here, there are a lot of people who are comfortably off, but no one very wealthy—and some poor. It is rather like Cambridge or Oxford in that way.

This afternoon we are going to tea at the William James's. He is a son of the philosopher, and she is from Chicago. Both of them very taking young people. We are to meet Mrs. Walter Page, the widow of the American ambassador in London during the war.

Goodbye, darling. All my love to you both

Daddy

504 Radnor Hall
Charles River Road
Cambridge, Mass.
Dec 10/24

Darling Margot

Just a line to give my dearest love to you and Roy and Sheila and Eric. Tell them that we shall be thinking of them on Xmas day. Thank you ever so much for your letters and the papers you have sent me—they have been just what I wanted and I have blessed you, dearest.

Mummy is finding the climate suits her, so far as I can observe. She gets very tired, but she does a lot and is very energetic and on the spot. The general warmth of the houses, passages and bedrooms, is good for her. The sudden changes in temperature—rises and falls of 30°—are trying, but much less so than I feared. We are so glad to hear from North of the way in which you are picking up strength. You really seem to have turned the corner. Of course this letter will reach you just when you are tired out with running Xmas for the children, and will be most ill-timed. Certainly life here is very strenuous for the women. It is really impossible to get casual help. Poor Mummy has worked like a slave at getting the house ready. Finally it is all arranged. But, adding to all this the streams of visitors, it has been no joke for her.

In fact settling in to new work, in a new social environment, in a new apartment, in a new country is certainly full time work for two people—at least so we have found it. But we are pleased with ourselves. The adventure of coming here has, so far, been a success. We have dropped our California project for next summer, with some relief on all counts—but it was impossible with Jessie arriving in July. I must stop now; my Xmas letters have been all delayed by Influenza.

Dearest love

Daddy

504 Radnor Hall
Charles River Road
Cambridge, Mass
Dec 10/24

Darling North

My dearest love and good wishes to you for Xmas. On Xmas day we shall be thinking of you and Margot and the children—and we shall know that you are thinking of us. Owing to the difference of time you will have done some of your thinking before we are awake, and we shall keep it up a bit longer—but it will be the same day and we shall be together.

We are delighted with the news you have been sending us as to Margot's health and the children generally. I can so well imagine their various stages of growth. Bringing up a family is the most anxious of all occupations but, on looking back on life, it is by far the achievement most worth while. I don't mean solely the production of individuals one loves devotedly—of course that is immense. But in the recollection of it, when life holds so much that is recollection, there is a colour and meaning in the retrospect even of the most anxious moments which relieves life of that sense of barrenness which I have often noticed damping elderly people who have never had such intimate jobs.

I must write a short letter because I have only just shaken off an attack of influenza. It hung about me for about a fortnight in a general seediness and culminated in four days in bed, very sorry for myself—no high temperature, so no real anxiety. In fact I was glad that the seediness did confess itself to be influenza.

I gave my first lectures today, driving there and back. I celebrated the occasion by a general lecture to my class on Evolution and how it fitted into my metaphysical standpoint. I think it interested the men, from the way in which it stood some ordinary ideas on their heads.

I expect that little Eric will rather dominate Xmas day with his conversational talents and his general capacity for dealing with toys. At three years old one is at the maximum efficiency for that occasion. The graph slowly drops for some years and then rapidly declines. When you are 63, it has fallen well below the zero axis.

My dearest dearest love to you all, Margot, Roy, Sheila, Eric and to you.

Your loving Daddy

504 Radnor Hall
Charles River Road
Cambridge, Mass
Dec 21/24

Darling North

Many happy returns of your birthday and all my love and good
wishes. Thirty-three years old, Is not it? Mummy is sending you our
little present. Expend it on books, or on something personal which
you want and is rather an extra. It is for pleasure and not necessity.
My Xmas letter writing has been greatly cramped by some mild influenza which has been hanging about me for some time. I have been
doing my work for the last ten days, but it came on again in another
milder form. I did not have to stay in, but cancelled social engagements. Yesterday I gave my last lectures and now have a ten days recess. Then after a fortnight's lecturing, there are three weeks mid-
term senior examns which are for me a complete holiday. So altogether I don't do badly. I want the time to write up the eight Lowell
lectures which come off in February. I have now broken the back of
the second lecture and have thought out the whole course. But I
want to have them nearly all finished before the course begins.

Mummy has been rather overdone by my seediness, and had a
slight heart attack yesterday and the day before. No cause for alarm,
and this morning she is practically well. Also she can rest all day. On
Thursday, she was disturbed just as she was in a deep sleep in the
middle of the afternoon by an absurd blunder of Agnes Hocking—an
impulsive, kind woman, who rushes to arrange everyone's life on
the kindest principles. She told Richard Cabot—an overconscien-
tious New Englander who has an important engagement for every
half-hour of the day—to call for Mummy at 3:15 and take her to a
school entertainment about a mile off. Accordingly Cabot turned up.
But unfortunately Mrs Hocking had forgotten to mention the arrangement to Mummy, and also it was the wrong day. Anyhow
Mummy feeling that some awful mistake had been made by her in
the way of forgetting, jumped up, dressed, was driven off in a great
hurry by Cabot who ought to have been somewhere else, and was
dropped at the school, merely to find that she had to telephone for a
cab to bring her back. This little incident prevented her resting just
when she wanted to, and was the cause of yesterday's collapse. But
she has had a thoroughly good night now, and is up and about. I
have told the incident at length because it is very illustrative—that
Mrs Hocking should have thought it possible to tell an immensely
busy man of some importance to fetch Mummy in his car, and that
he should of course have complied at great inconvenience, is just like

them. Of course no one, not a millionaire, keeps a chauffeur. Cabot is a millionaire, via his wife, but is much too conscientious to spend money in that way. The idea of the New Englanders flaunting wealth is quite wrong. They are much more likely to be living on half their incomes, and either investing the rest or giving it away—about equal chances which.

It is [a] bright, but bitterly cold day. The thermometer is at 10°, and it is nearly 12 o'clock. We have had practically no snow as yet. Anyhow you can imagine, that the smallest crack of open window, almost a mere loosening of the fastening, i[s] quite sufficient to air the room. One does not feel the cold indoors, because the steam heating warms the whole building, through and through.

I have been very interested over your calculating machine: I am sorry that its errors would accumulate. Though I am not surprised: calculating machines must be the very devil. Let me know what has happened.

Yesterday, as frequently is the case, a stranger was brought in to my lecture and introduced to me afterwards. He was a very nice Frenchman, about 38 yrs old. He turned out to be the consulting engineer in the employ of the big New York financial firm which is nibbling at Mark Barr's machine. He has been to London to inspect it. He thinks very well of it, and wants his firm to take it up. But they are still hesitating. He told me that Americans don't like to touch things which cannot be sold by the millions. Anyhow he has great hopes. Mummy and I have been in despair about the Barrs: this has given us some hope. The Frenchman is coming again in about three weeks, so we shall see him and hear the news.

What a fool the India-Office made of itself over Mr A.! The American papers of course had every detail about him printed at once. I was rather shocked to find that it seems quite accepted that the Midland Bank was justified in paying 3000£ to a man of Newton's antecedents, to induce him to give evidence of a certain kind. On that ground I sympathised with the jury: because, whatever one thinks of the Robinsons, there was really no trustworthy evidence that they were in the conspiracy. The one man who must be pleased with the result is Lord Halsbury.

There is rather an interesting idea to be tried in New York—of a sky-scraper church. Namely the church on the ground floor, and a model parish in the form of apartments running up to 22 storeys above it. Altogether they mean to house 1000 people—Methodists. The amusing point about this country is that they are always ready to try a new idea, and there is endless loose cash about to shoulder the expense.

Dearest love to Margot and you, and a happy New Year
Your loving

Daddy

504 Radnor Hall
Charles River Road
Cambridge, Mass.
March 15/25

Darling North

It is a long time since I last wrote. The Lowell Lectures—eight of
them—amounted to writing a book in about two months. And as
they form my first public pronouncement here, the book had to be
something better than mere popular reflections. Anyhow I tried to
make the lectures so—with tolerable success, I think, so far as the
immediate audience was concerned. They have still to survive the
test of print. Anyhow, they were a great strain on me; and I am only
just feeling sufficient rebound to be able to think of anything else.

You probably will not get a letter from Mummy by this mail. She
is in bed with a feverish attack, and general aching. It may be influenza (mild), or it may be the result of fatigue. She has had a lot to do
in the house, and also fell down, and bruised herself. We have been
inoculated against influenza, so an attack ought not to develop. She is
now (11.A.M. Sunday morning) in bed in a deep sleep,—Mary and I
are in hopes that when she wakes she will have thrown off the fever-
ishness. We have an excellent young doctor—Dr Taylor—who came
last night and prescribed bed, and some mild medicine. There is no
reason for any alarm. It is a feverish attack which has been properly
looked after from the first—and may be practically over tomorrow,
or even this evening. Probably it means a couple of days in bed.

Since I last wrote— weeks ago—we have had an earthquake—
quite as large a one as I want. Luckily Mummy was at a flappers'
dance in a wooden school-room with only the ground floor. But in
the flat—on the fifth floor—we had front seats for observation. I had
the feeling that our buildings were swaying just as much as they
could without something giving way. The factor of safety seemed to
be about 1 : 5—certainly not more. The last earthquake of the same
sort in this neighbourhood was in 1760; so no immediate action
seems to be necessary, if the periodicity is unaltered.

Spring has come now—bright days and a warmer sun—also temperature well above freezing pt, with occasional lapses. But the winds are cold. Tell Margot that her waistcoat is now coming into full use. It is just what I want. During the winter—when (in the picturesque language of the weather-reports over here) "the thermometer was hobnobbing with zero all over New England"—the houses are very warm and out-of-doors one wants heavy overcoats and scarves; so the waistcoat was not much in use. But now it is ideal, and I bless her daily for it.

The spring here is not nearly as beautiful as in England. The grass has been burnt brown by the frost, and altogether it lacks the general tenderness and charm.

2.P.M.   Mummy woke up, and I went and got her some ice-cream for lunch. Ice-cream is the favorite diet for invalids here. It is not so rich as in England. The climate makes it very refreshing. I do not think that she will [be] rid of her attack for two or three days. I will send you a week-end cable which you will get just before this letter. She ought to be well by that time.

I enjoy your letters immensely. It is nice to know what you are thinking about. Just at present, I am in an easy patch of my College lectures. I have got to my own ideas as to space and time. So I am simply amplifying and making reflections upon my "Concept of Nature". I must say that the Americans are an appreciative set of people. I find the students and my colleagues very easy to work with. I lecture on what I like, and examine the men on my own course. It certainly enables one to be more interesting.

They are more international than we are in Europe—in some respects. They are generally interested in what different people have thought at all sorts of places and times—for example, in the philosophy department here, there is Woods, who has lived in India for some years studying Brahmanism, and who is also a Chinese scholar; Perry and Hocking who do the modern and American Philosophy; also two men who are specialists on Symbolic Logic (in addition to myself), a Jew who is an expert on Spinoza and the medieval Jewish and Arabian philosophers, a Roman Catholic Belgian for scholastics, myself, and some younger men who do the classical Philosophy and what is wanted *passim*. I am inclined to think that Woods is the best of the lot—in addition to being a fine orientalist, he is a good classical scholar, and versed in classical philosophy. He is however not well known, nor is he adequately appreciated here. Among the younger men, there is Eaton, a Californian with a charming young wife from Alabama whom Mummy is very fond of. Also there is Bell who is a Canadian, very obviously English as distinct from Yankee: he did a lot of work as a Foreign Office Agent in Germany after the War. During the war, the German(s) had him in prison at

Ruheleben. He was at Emmanuel for three years and took the Moral Science Tripos. Bell is a delightful man—rather older than the other men of his standing on the staff. He was put back by the war and his work at the Foreign Office. He has a great admiration and fondness for America—with a touch of criticism where they fail to be English, which (at its best) is his ultimate standard.

We are very worried just now at the illness of little Ernesta Greene (aged nine years)—a brilliant little girl who has just had a dangerous, and only partially successful, operation. She is the youngest child of Rosalind Copley Greene, who is the person here whom Mummy has taken to, beyond the others. She is a most delightful woman, about 38 years old—very good looking and cultivated in every way—also devoted to her children, four girls 17–9 in ages. She is of Dutch ancestry. By the bye, the order of precedence is this:—if you are of Dutch, or English, or French ancestry, you let people know it. Otherwise you let it be understood that your antecedents are of an excellence practically indistinguishable from one of these three.

But for all this, there really is a passion for democracy here. It is a great mistake to think that all the leading people are engrossed in money, or social climbing. Certainly it is not the case in New England. Of course in Virginia, it is quite different. Yesterday I read a testimonial on the merits of a Virginian, who is applying for a postgraduate student. Its main point was about the man's pedigree and his social charm. There are other states where it is a social lapse to ask what a man was doing five years earlier. Altogether under a veneer of uniformity, there are immense sectional differences. This comes out in their politics. Each State has its two parties many concerned in questions of great interest—an arbitrary selection of these parties federate into the Republican Party, and the other lot make up the Democratic Party. The result is that in the Senate party discipline is very slack. Just at present the Senate, with a Republican majority, is engaged in a deadly quarrell with Coolidge the Republican President. According to precedent, Coolidge cannot be reelected for a third term, so he is a little indifferent as to whom he quarrells with. He has got four years before him and is more popular than the Senate.

We are looking forward to Jessie at the end of June. She must get her visa in the best way you can manage it—probably for one year, and we must get it extended. But perhaps the Ambassador in England will be stirred up to make an exception for her. Dearest love,

Daddy

504 Radnor Hall
Charles River Roads
Cambridge. Mass.   April 5/25

Darling North

I am afraid we have been worrying you with contradictory tele-
grams as to Jessie. We have been worried ourselves, not knowing
what to do for the best. Anyhow, we are now agreed with advice
which have been given us, that she had better come over, and risk
the question of future residence.

I gather now that Jessie comes by the *Baltic, White Star Line, arriving at New York on June 20.* Is this correct? We are making our plans
on that supposition—so let us know at once, *if* there should happen
to be any misunderstanding.

Old Jessie, except the telegram which told us this fact, vouchsafes
no information as to her actual arrangements and types of difficulty
in making them, or what the possibilities of getting over are—this
has been one of our difficulties in making up our minds. It is rather
like dealing with a baby in arms. Anyhow we take the plans as now
settled. But do not disdain to jot down in your letters any scrap of
additional information as to Jessie's movements, or arrangements,
which you happen to know.

Mummy had a nasty illness, following on her fall. It is now over
and she is in her usual health—sometimes tired, and sometimes
doing a lot. The spring-weather has come. Today is brilliant sun-
light, and the further stretch of the Charles River, which I can see as
I am writing, is sparkling with a most lovely blue [See Whitehead's
sketch, page 307.]

It has been the mildest winter, and the earliest spring on record.
But, even a record spring here is very inferior to an average English
spring—the greenness, the flowers, the wonderful sense of life in
damp warmth, are absent. Their autumns are more brilliant, much—
and the gaiety of their sun-shine is better. But our spring, and general tenderness of country scenery is unapproached by anything over
here.

We have been having some charming evenings. The other day we
dined in Boston, with one of the leading bankers and his wife—
elderly people, living in a typically old Boston house—1800 or
1810—with it odd fan-lights and interior arrangements generally.
We were a party of eight—the other three couples being all typical
old Boston people, of the sort written about by W.D. Howells.
Strong liberals of the Gladstonian type. The two couples who live in
Boston both take in the "*Manchester Guardian*". Tell Margot this. It
will make her think well of our New England friends. These sort of

people give one the impression of more wealth, with less show, than anything you can imagine. The *Corporation* of *Fellows* (about six or eight of them) who are the ultimate authority which runs Harvard, entirely consists of men like this.

They are all interconnected. They either have each others' surnames as their own second Christian names, or live in streets named after each other, or have towns in New England named after them. They are very disgruntled because they have lost control of the city-government, which is in the hands of Irish Roman Catholics. As a result, they are now apt to brood over their English ancestry—a new phase, I suspect. I also suspect that the Irish Roman Catholics have a good deal to say for themselves in taking the City-Government out of their hands. My belief is that, though they did not embezzle (as the Irish politicians do), they entirely disregarded the interests of the immigrant Irish.

Also, they do not have many children, so the differential birthrate and the laws of arithmetic are against them, so far as the future is concerned.

Stevie Barr is with us—staying for about ten days. He has developed into such a nice boy—very nice manners, well-informed, and interesting—also with a power of being silent and quiet on the proper occasions. We are very pleased with him. The Barrs (i.e. Mark and Mabel) are now near Cleveland, at Elyria (named after people named Ely, and not a mis-spelling of Illyria). A wealthy manufacturer is having one of Barr's machines made, as an example—he is doing it as well as it can be done. But I do not think that anyone has, as yet, taken up the commercial manufacture. But obviously, this is a long way. Stephen and his parents are somewhat at cross purposes as to his future.

Yesterday afternoon (Saturday) we were driven out to Concord—about 25 miles—and Mummy got a puppy at some kennels there, a

Cocker Spaniel, about 12 weeks old, for little Ernesta Greene, aged 10 years, who is just recovering from a bad operation with a lot of pain afterwards. The present has already been an enormous success, and—we gather from telephone messages—the Greene household now revolves round the puppy.

The telephone is here a mode of social intercourse—at least among women. When any urgent idea occurs to anyone, which they think will interest Mummy, they ring her up to tell her.

It is just lunch time—and I have got to speak this afternoon to a large audience, Sunday lectures—my subject being Science and Religion—(i.e. "the young lady of Riga" problem). So I shall not have any more time to write later, being booked afterwards for tea, then someone to supper, then our Sunday "at home"—so have no more free time till about 11·30 P.M. Goodbye, darling. Love to all of you—Margot, and Eric—and send it to the family at school. Give me news of Roy's school career.

> Your loving Daddy

> 504 Radnor Hall
> Charles River Road
> Cambridge, Mass
> April 12th/25 Easter Sunday

Darling North,

Your letter telling of your transference to the Electrical side, and of Jessie's *departure* on June 20th (not *arrival,* as we gathered from the cable, and as I stated in my last week's letter) came last night. It was so jolly to get it. The weekly letters are a joy. We like to hear all your little and big details, just as they come into your mind.

I do so sympathise with you about having the wind up, over facing work above one's size and weight. Throughout my whole life, I have been facing a series of situations of that kind. I don't think I am at all modest as to the things which I know I can do. But somehow the actual tasks, which I have had to undertake, have always involved a lot of things for which I know that I am incompetent. And as to my lectures here when the sessions opened—Oh my!—So I quite understand your feelings. But here is a secret of which I am beginning to suspect the existence—viz.—there is a lot of incompetence about—the real worry is, that occasionally it is found out and one feels oneself eminently fitted for the provision of such an occasion. So on the whole, the knowledge of the secret does not help much.

Mummy is well again, though often tired. Today we have a lot facing us. We lunch out, to meet John Dewey, the leading American Philosopher, at Columbia Univt, New York. Then at 3 30, we go to hear Ernest Hocking (our colleague here, a dear man) lecture on the Religion of the Future from 4–5—then we walk back to tea here with the Hoaglands (young married couple) and her father and mother, (Profr and Mrs Bush)—he is another Philosophy man at Columbia—he combines this avocation with the other very agreeable one of being a millionaire. Then from 8–11 our usual "at home". Luckily I have specially invited very few people. Dewey is the leading pragmatist, who continues the William James tradition. He has been in China for two years, just before Bertie went there. The Americans are devoting a lot of attention to China, and (very sensibly) are making great efforts to attract their learned class. Our Government makes a great mistake in ignoring such things. You hear more about China here and find more Chinamen here being treated as sensible and important human beings, in the course of six months, than you will meet in England during twenty years. I think that the Chinese would prefer England, but England is entirely indifferent. In England, there is always the dominant feeling that anything outside the traditional English modes of thought must be worthless. Over here, they have the cheerful feeling that anyone who is sufficiently civilised to wear clothes may have hit on a good notion. This openness to new ideas often finds very silly expression—but it has its merits.

You are quite right to go over to electricity. With your double experience you will be a valuable man, in or out of a Government Department. It is important not to be a narrow specialist in a very restricted groove. But it will mean a lot of worry at first. I was glad to hear that Roy has been getting on all right at his school. That is one anxiety terminated in the right way. I am sure that he is the sort of boy who wants pushing on. The great danger is dilettanteism. I have known so many clever and facile men have their careers wrecked in this way.

Last night I had to make an afterdinner speech. The Visiting Committee of our Department gave a dinner to the Departmental staff. We were about thirty in all. I was between Henry James (son of William James), in the chair, and a New York lawyer—the leading man in the New York bar—a charming man. I had not had any time to prepare, but it seemed to go off all right.

We gather that America is steadily swinging round to the League of Nations. Anyhow that is the prevalent opinion among the sort of people whom we meet here. Some of them have been stumping the country on the question, and they say that the Middle West is coming around. The Middle West—the *West,* as they call it here, California is just California, or "The Pacific Coast"—is the really determining factor. It looks upon New England as effete—though it sends its best men here to be educated—, and has barely heard of Europe. Anyhow it does not worry about it. So it is a long business to convert it. But opinion there now seems to be changing.

On Tuesday, we motor down to Providence, about fifty miles to the south, on the coast, in Rhode Island—not an island but a State with a small island attached. There is a small University there, Brown University. I am giving a lecture on "Mathematics as an Element in the History of Thought". It will go in with the Lowell Lectures, and be published in a volume entitled "Science and the Modern World". We stay the night there with the Chancellor, have lunch on Wednesday with the Lords (Mr Lord is a Unitarian clergyman whom, with his wife, we came over with from Liverpool) and get back in the afternoon. We are looking forward to it.

Our spring—when we get it—beats anything that they can do here in that way, so far as beauty is concerned. The New England country doesn't put up flowers, or spring trimmings of any sort. Nature here comes out because it is ordered to do so, and not because it wants to.

Dearest love to you all. Goodbye darling

Your loving Daddy

At the Greenes' Country Cottage
Nor Newburyport, Mass.
Whitsunday. /25. May 31st

Darling North

We are staying with the Greene's for this weekend, about 35 miles north of Boston, and about 5 miles inland. It is a lovely morning (9:30.A.M.) following a wretchedly cold wet day yesterday. Spring here is just as chancey as in England—rather colder, when it is cold, and hotter, when it is hot. I am sitting on a sort of Cornish granitey hillock,—very typical of New England—, surrounded by bracken, and dwarf juniper bushes, and New England cedars (also juniper, really) in shape like Irish yews, and small silver birches. In the meadow just at the foot, there is a little tidal river about the size of the Cam, which floods the meadows a[t] high tide. The weak point in the whole situation is (or are) the mosquitoes. I am describing this because it is a very typical bit of New England scenery. I forgot the State Road in the middle distance, about 300 yards of it in sight, with a constant stream of motors on it—this is the most typical sight of the lot.

Mummy has been rather out of sorts. I do not think the New England diet quite suited her—at least, not in the proportions which we had adopted. But the doctor prescribed a regime which has been completely successful. But on the whole, her life here is suiting her extremely well, and she is in excellent spirits over it. There are several people with whom we have been really intimate—and luckily they are the people whom we most naturally have to do with. The point to remember is that among the old New Englanders, everyone is everyone else's cousin. The epigram that "Boston is not so much a city as a state of mind" is profoundly true.

Tomorrow we are going for a long motor expedition into Rhode Island, to Newport, about eighty miles south of Boston (we leave this afternoon) with the Hockings (in their car) and Woods and Bell—the men, Hocking, Woods, and Bell, are my philosophical colleagues. It is a pilgrimage, and picnic, to the place where Berkeley wrote one of his dialogues—the Alciphron, I think. Incidentally, we are also going to have tea with Admiral Sims.

Our hosts here are great charmers—Mrs Greene—i.e. Rosalind Greene—is American Dutch, and her husband is New England—, also there are four daughters, the eldest eighteen and the youngest ten. The eldest had her first two cigarettes last night under the critical survey of her younger sisters. The female part of the family from the Mother to Ernesta, the baby, form rather a galaxy of beauty,—in this way reminiscent of the Shuckburghs—, very gay, with the terrific New England conscience in the background producing unexpected touches of primness. Ernesta, I see, is just climbing the rock behind me with a puppy, firmly grasped by the scruff of the neck, swinging in her right hand. She is just about to grow out of the stage which Eric is just about to grow into.

I told Rosalind Greene that I was about to write to you, and she sent her love with an invitation to come and stay next year.

My first session of lectures is now over. It has been rather an effort, and therefore a strain. But I have enjoyed it immensely. I have had t[he] same feeling as you have in an examination—the joy of defeating the examiners. On the whole, I think that I have done it. It might have been done much better, but it was done. My class, which largely consisted of postgraduates who come for their own pleasure, increased in the latter part of the session. So I am in good spirits, though I now know what I ought to have said as distinct from what I did say.

On Thursday and Friday I was at the celebration of the 50th year
of Wellesley College—a big Women's College about 20 miles from
Boston, in magnificent grounds, 400 acres of woodland, with a lake.
There were about 1000 guests—a pageant (very well done, with a
producer and experts on stage lighting from New York) on Thursday evening, and a terrific [. . .]* of speeches and services and a
luncheon on Friday, starting at 10 A.M. After Lunch, I had to address
a very exhausted audience at 2:30 P.M. It was not an occasion (by that
time) for subtle disquisition. But, as usual in America, there was a
row of reporters to take down in cold print every word one said. At
the end of four hours all occasions should become strictly private.

We are looking forward to Jessie's arrival, either on June 28th, or
29th, or 30th. She is to come straight to Boston. I have sent her a letter, but in case it goes wrong I repeat some of the instructions:—

Her station in New York is the *Grand Central,* her railway line is
the
New York, Newhaven, Hartford, and Boston Line.

She must take a *taxi* to the station from the docks. If she has too
much luggage for the taxi (they don't take very much) she must send
her luggage by the express forwarding company, which the Custom
house man will show her at the docks. She can direct it straight
through to our home address. (I forgot to tell her about the forwarding express company in my letter, so please pass on this information.
The boxes must [be] properly labelled with *stick* and *tie* labels). At
the Railway Station she must check through to Boston (South Station, the terminus) all the luggage she can. There are very few por-
ters, and not much room in the carriage—so *hand* luggage in the
carriage is a nuisance. But hand luggage which she can manage herself is all right.

The first train is about 11:25 A.M, (daylight time) i.e. 10:25 A.M
standard time. (Ordinary clocks in the Town, daylight, and *Station*
clocks *standard*.) (Trains about *hourly* during the day.) The night train
starts at about midnight, but you can get on the train about two
hours earlier and *go to bed.* The journey takes about 6 hours. Tell her
to *look around* on landing in case some one meets her. But remind her
that in New York and elsewhere, you have got to be *much more careful* than in England. If you do not know the ropes, and begin to be
adventurous, you easily get into real danger. We shall meet her at the
South Station, Boston, if she will wire the train.

The heat has driven me indoors. Mummy is chatting with the
Greene family in the verandah opening out of this room. All veran-
dahs and windows are netted with mosquito wire. It really doesn't

---

*Original is illegible.

spoil the outlook. The light here is so vivid, that its slight diminution doesn't matter. There is a slight suggestion that one is looking at tapestry which has become real.

The U.S.A. is going to join in the World Court and ultimately with the League of Nations—so all the best observers tell us. But the New England sentiment is so overwhelmingly in favour of that course that one has to take their estimates with a grain of salt. The real importance of New England is that it sets the tone in education for all America. A lot of westerners and southerners come here. Collectively, the New England Colleges and Universities are the Oxford and Cambridge of U.S.A., with more influence, if there is any difference. Politically, New England is rather a back number. The West does not know very accurately on which side of the Atlantic it lies, and what its relation is to Old England. But anyhow it is the sort of place to which you send young people to finish their education. For example, on Friday I was driven to Wellesley Station by a girl who comes from Kansas City—a nice friendly young creature, with her own car, as all the older students have at that place. It is a College for wealthy girls, about 1600 of them.

Here in Massachussetts, the English v. Irish feud is at its height—worse than in Great Britain. The Irish control Boston, and the English control the State. So the State Legislature is protestant, and the Mayor is Catholic.

Apropos of Kansas City, I was told that in 1916—towards the end—in the main daily paper the war news was not of front page importance.

But the oddest story was told me this morning by Rosalind Greene. Her brother lives in Virginia and commanded a regiment of men from the mountains in the South West of Virginia, where there is an English stock completely isolated since the seventeenth century. The men (i) did not know whom they were fighting—French, or German, or on which side of the ocean, (ii) had a horror of their officers who were all northerners (it took eight months to produce fraternisation, (iii) here is a story of one of the privates:—The man limped and Colonel Huydekopper (Mrs Greene's brother) enquired—"Oh, I was shot in my knee—Why and how?—I had a little dispute with a friend—But hadn't you your own gun?—Oh yes, my friend died."

The great mistake is to look on America as one country. For example, here in the North Mr Bryan and his anti-evolution campaign are looked on as an immense joke. The State of Tennessee is to have a big trial of a school master for teaching evolution. It is to take place in a small town of about 2,000 inhabitants. They are talking of building a temporary stadium to hold 20000 for the final trial, by way of exploiting the interest and attracting visitors. But the New York and

Boston papers are so occupied in dishing up humorous accounts, that I will not vouch for the truth of the rumor. The free shooting in Chicago is still vigorous—but the Chicago people one meets are singularly offensive.

We have been thinking of you and Margot and Eric at Portsmouth. But I have kept this letter to American news, as more interesting to you.

Dearest love from Mummy and me.

Daddy

504 Radnor Hall
Charles River Road
Cambridge, Mass.
Monday, June 29./25

Darling Margot

We—Mary and I—are waiting for a telegram from New York to say when Mummy and Jessie will come to Boston. Mummy went to New York on Saturday by an express. It is a five hours journey— but she went in a Pullman and it was a cool day. She is staying at Mrs Osborn Taylor's Club, and is to be met and looked after by a young man whom we know slightly. Jessie's boat is reported as due to berth in N.Y. at 9 A.M. today. With luck Jessie will be through the Customs by noon, and I hope that they will be here by dinner this evening. Meanwhile I have been getting some flowers to smarten up the flat.

We have been up at Rowley—nr. Newburyport—at the top of Mass., with our friends the Greenes. We are very intimate with them now. Both of them have spent years in France. We were there for a week and came back to meet Jessie. While we were there, the temperature had fallen from about 90° in the shade to about 50° to 55°— so we sat over fires. At first Mummy had a touch of sciatica— painful and liable to be prolonged. But luckily it went in a day or two. Cambridge is empty now—almost everyone is on the "North Shore", i.e. north of Boston up to Maine. This is the beautiful shore, after you pass some dismal swampy marsh which extends for about 10 miles from the town.

Thank North for the telegram as to J's examination. I do not know how important a failure in one subject may be. Probably she can take it by itself at a later period, if necessary. Anyhow I shall not bother her with it immediately on arrival. Exams are beastly things.

If she can scrape up a little *Arabic,* they will welcome her at the Widener Library. They have Arabic books and want somebody on the staff who can tackle them. Anyhow she will have to get back to England to be finally fixed up—unless we can manage a wangle.

Thank you so much for your letters to Mummy about the children and yourselves. I cannot tell you how much we have enjoyed them, You really have made all the difference to our life here.

I have been tremendously interested about Roy. There seems to be every chance of his developing according to his early promise. I am glad that his schoolmaster seems to understand him. He wants careful grounding, so that he can push on according to his general sharpness of intellect. Let me know all your impressions about him as he gets on. It is great luck that he is happy at school: it aids a nice growth of character, besides being a good thing in itself. The photos of the three children are immensely admired here: they are continually being fetched out.

I do so long for you to see our flat: it is so nice—really lovely, with a delightful view. Nobody here has ever seen a black mirror before, and it produces a most striking effect in the room.

We are in the neighbourhood of Cambridge all July with a cottage about 15 miles off with a big estate attached to it. But probably we shall only go there for weekends—anyhow our plans are fluid till we have got Jessie here and can look about us. In August we go up to the woods in Vermont—all America leads the simple life for about eight to ten weeks in the summer. The only alternative is to go to Europe. On July 4th they have their Independence Day: it seems to be chiefly marked by eating salmon and green peas. Since they have adopted the settled habit of saying nice things about England, the oratory on such occasions lacks some of its fire and degenerates into a work of art. The general tone on Lexington Day—first shot in a revolutionary War fired—was to insist on what a wonderful country England is, and how still more wonderful it is to be separated from it. Such a topic wants a little managing. Of course the Irish here could treat the occasion in the good old way. But that is just what the Yankees do not want. The President is staying on the North Shore and is to speak in Cambridge on that day.

All the American politicians are fully aware of the two oceans—Atlantic and Pacific—and of the countries on their further shores. But their difficulty is that the majority of their constituents, in the Middle West, have barely heard of them, and anyhow have no interest in such remote facts.

At present the great excitement is the trial of Mr Scope [*sic*], to start on July 10. He is a schoolteacher in Tennessee who is being prosecuted for teaching *Evolution,* which is illegal in that State. The result is that the "South" is in a wild state of excitement over Evolution, and publishers cannot issue scientific handbooks quickly enough. I have come to the end of my paper. Goodbye—and dearest love to you and North and the family.

Your loving Daddy

504 Radnor Hall
Charles River Road
Cambridge. Mass
July 19/25

Darling North

At this moment—11·30 A.M, Sunday—we are not at home. We are spending the week-end at the Richard Cabots' cottage about 15 miles from Cambridge. It is the simple life: just we three—Mummy, Jessie and I—looking after ourselves in the country. Luckily, water and electricity are laid on. But, as usual with the simple life, one or other of us was fully occupied from 6 A.M. to 10.A.M. this morning in carrying it on. Since then we are sitting out in the woodland—junipers (small trees, here called New England cedars), and dappled shade: a lovely day, fresh, warm, and sunshiny. We are going back tonight by motor at 10 P.M: Jessie's work on Monday begins at 9.A.M. We shall come back here on Friday for about 10 days. In August we go up to Vermont.

5 P.M.   Two little girls, aged 7 and 9, turned up as I was writing this morning, and—seeing that I was a stranger—engaged me in conversation for about an hour. They live in a house about a quarter of a mile away. Next Saturday they have engaged to bring, for my inspection two white kittens and a selection of dolls. Then the "simple life" intervened, and a rest after it—so here I am, still finishing your letter. It has been a perfectly lovely day, and we are enjoying ourselves immensely in the shade and the clear air.

It is the holiday time now, even for the business people. For example, in Boston from the beginning of July to the middle of September all shops shut on Saturdays, and [are] done at 5 P.M. daily.

I was sorry to hear about Sheila. Give her my love. At her age, all such weaknesses can be corrected. But it is hard on her anyhow. Your descriptions of your six weeks on the channel were most satisfactory. You have ended your optical life—at least, your *exclusively* optical life—in a blaze. The more that I think about it, the more certain I am that eminence as a designer of fine instruments depends on the *double* experience of optical and electrical design. There is no other source of accuracy known to science—in addition, of course, to a sound working knowledge of the physical properties of materials. You are extremely wise to check your immediate optical career in order to get hold of the other side. I suspect that you will find that it takes at least a year till you can get hold of things. But I gather that they are prepared to give you time.

Of course, you will have noticed that the English Government is forming a Council of Scientific Research on the same lines as the Council of Imperial Defence. This means a leading Cabinet minister as chairman. They obviously expect a continuous expansion in the scientific services. You have gone into that line at a very fortunate moment. It is *the* profession with a future.

The papers here are full of the Scopes Evolution Trial in Tennessee (I am very doubtful as to the spelling of this state's name). The remote simplicity of these distant states is extraordinary. Also you have always to remember this point about American democracy:— There is here as large a class of highly cultivated people as in England: this is certainly true of the East and of Chicago. But almost every form of political and other public life takes its orders from below. The almost direct influence of English University opinion on Parliament and County Councils—especially County Councils—is absent here. I do not mean merely Oxford and Cambridge. My experience on the Senate of the University of London was one of almost continual influence on the policy of Governmental bodies. But here such bodies take their orders from below, or secretly from purely business men. I am greatly struck by the excellence of the English *local* government as compared with the American opposite numbers. Analogously their method of appointing clergy by the direct choice of the congregations after trial of a number of men for successive periods, degrades the clergy from all independence. Altogether, there is just as much culture and genius here; but it has much less influence than in England.

Apropos of this, I am to deliver another course of Lowell Lectures in Boston next year on "Science and Religion" i.e. on the scientific criticism of religion. I think that the Harvard people rather want to get a hearing for an independent foreigner who is more likely to be listened to than one of their own men. But this is a guess, so do not pass it on.

Goodbye, darling—dearest love—It is time for supper—so goodbye—

Your loving Daddy

P.T.O
P.S. Cambridge. Monday Morning
Mummy cannot write this week: she has had a nasty little accident:
slight in its ultimate effects, but very painful. Last night when we had
returned home to Cambridge, she slipped in her bath, and hit her rib
on the *right* side, just under her breast. It is badly bruised—perhaps
just cracked—but *not* broken. The doctor gives her from three days
to a week of some pain when in a false position. But she can get
about now that she is properly bandaged.

Mummy wanted to write. She is so sorry about Sheila. She wants
to sen[d] Margot all her love and sympathy—and her love to Sheila.

Also very anxious about Florence.

at Profr Henderson's Camp
Morgan Center
Vermont
Sunday, August 16th/25

Darling North

It is exactly a year today since we embarked at Liverpool. We are
going to celebrate it with a bonfire this evening, on the shore of the
lake. It is a glorious day, and we are sunning ourselves in the verandah, enjoying a slight breeze, with the water lapping on the granite
rocks at our feet. In a few minutes Roger Pierce will motor Mummy
over to Newport, about 14 miles away. They will meet Jessie at 4:30
P.M. She comes today from Boston, starting at 9 A.M. It is the
Boston-Montreal express, and Newport is the last stop before the
Canadian border. Our fortnight here has been an unmixed success.
The camp is a wooden cottage with one *large* room, + kitchen and
small bedroom, and exactly suited for its purpose. The days are not
too hot—some decidedly cold—the village people delightful—and
the scenery perfect. Mummy has enjoyed herself immensely—
though she has had ill-luck. We picked a wonderfully decorative
wildflower, like a gigantic wild mint. She crushed the leaves in her
hands and put her face in it to smell. It turned out to be a poisonous
plant, like stinging-nettle, so she has suffered very badly for three
days. It is practically over now, and today she is feeling particularly
well.

On Friday we motored to "Derby-Line", a town on the border,
named after the line between Canada and U.S.A, which was—I
suppose—settled by some deceased Lord Derby. The town on the
Canadian side is called Rock-Island and Strickland—and just beyond

is a bigger town, "Sherbrooke". We are about 5 miles from Derby-Line in the straight and about 10 miles by road. We went a little way into Canada, and had tea; and th[o]roughly enjoyed seeing the Union Jack over the Canadian Customhouse. We got the impression—perhaps due to our imaginations—that the populations on both sides of the border are making a nefarious living by bootlegging. Anyhow our village friends tell us that the bootleggers take their stuff along the country-road which runs along the lake just above our woods.

Jessie has been staying with the Greenes about 30 miles north of Boston. We hope that we shall all have another month up here. It is doing us a lot of good. J. could not get away from her library work before. She could get into Cambridge daily from the Greenes.

I have just seen Mummy and Roger Pierce off. It is about 200 to 300 hundred yards through the woods up to the road. From the road, you can hardly see that there is a path into the woods down to the lake.

We have been very sorry to hear that Sheila has to lie up so strictly. It is hard times on her—give her our dearest love. We are thinking of you all at Swanage. At this moment, I suppose that you are half way through your stay there. We have just got your letter written before starting.

Mummy and I have been reading a course of Phillips Oppenheim. Henderson's library is very strong on this classic author. It is impossible to think of anything more serious, after accomplishing the simple-life's task of making the beds, washing, and generally keeping oneself clean—a morning's work, combined with reading our letters and the Boston Herald. I gather from this paper that we have fixed up a satisfactory agreement with France. I hope that this is true.

I am sending you three picture postcards of the lake. The photos manage to dwarf the banks. Also, as most of the country is forest, they naturally photo the bare patches which seem to be natural curiosities to the inhabitants. I have written on the backs of the cards.

Our neighbours in a camp in the woods about 200 yds nearer to Morgan Centre are very friendly agreeable people. We get vegetables from them, sent from their garden near New York. The village here is not strong on vegetables. Mummy is trying to get some ice-cream in Newport for their two small boys. You get that sort of thing at a drug-store here—and fortunately they are open on Sundays.

Dearest love to you all—

Your loving Daddy

Monday.Morning.   Jessie and Demos turned up safely. We had a jolly evening and sat round a bonfire by the lake. The four young, including Mary, then went for a row on the lake by starlight.

504 Radnor Hall
Charles River Road
Cambridge. Mass

Darling North

I have found that a long letter of mine, written to you weeks ago, was not finished or posted. It is out of date now—but I am sorry.

We are getting on excellently. Mummy is really very much better: her rib is now confining itself to an occasional stab in a false position. It does not seem to check her activities. Also the ivy-poisoning is at last worn out: there is an occasional mild threat, but it seems now to be really gone. Against these troubles, you must remember that her neuritis has quite disappeared: this was really a serious threat in England, and the cure has made a great difference to her.

We both find that we have to lie down during the day for a siesta, after lunch. Mummy sleeps for about a hour, usually. Almost everyone has to do that here: the quick changes of temperature, and the dryness are exhausting. Of course, they call Boston damp and foggy, but I am speaking according to our standards.

Jessie is getting on capitally. When she came, she was worn out and jumpy, and things were not easy. But now nothing could run more smoothly than her general life. She has won great commendations for her work in the Library. The Head of her department thanked Woods for recommending her, and also telephoned to Mummy to tell her how much he appreciated her services. Also she has been promoted to more responsible and pleasant work among 16th century books.

We are in hopes that she will be able to get her permanent quota number by spending a night in Montreal. President Lowell has been awfully good about it, writing to headquarters in Washington. But nothing is quite certain yet.

Her ball takes place next Saturday, Nov 14. Mummy is going as "A Spanish Lady at the Court of Naples"—*my suggestion* after I had seen the sort of costume she was rigging up, somewhat Spanish and somewhat Italian. Jessie is going in Empire dress. I have a judge's wig and shall put on my black doctor's gown. It is to be Jessie's night, so the ball is to open with a general presentation to her,—she sitting on a raised dais at one end of the room. It is awfully kind of Agnes Hocking and Rosalind Greene to have taken all this trouble. On the night of the dance the two Miss Thorpes'—grand-daughters of Longfellow—are giving a young dinner party for her: they are about Jessie's age and are singularly charming.

All the nicer girls of the old families do something here: for example, Anne Thorpe teaches in a school, and Erica Thorpe does some rather stren[u]ous job in Boston—looking after police-court cases of women, I think. Cambridge is really a very simple place—somewhat of a garden of Eden, with some very bad breakdowns.

New England is a back number so far as the business and productive sides of the United States are concerned, and also is merely a summer playground for the smart set. But it is a big intellectual centre—tempered with "hold-ups".

The Americans seem quite unable to deal with their crime-wave. On the face of it, there seems an astounding inefficiency somewhere. In the last few months, in Cambridge alone, more than 90,000$ have been extracted in this way, in broad daylight, and the robbers have always got away. When a firm takes out money from a bank to pay its employees, it sends an armoured car with guards holding revolvers in their hands. These hold-ups are almost always when there is known to be something worth getting—though of course there are exceptions, occasionally. All the post-offices in Boston—about 80 of them—had armed guards for a few weeks in October. On the other hand, people omit to lock their front doors at night—we don't, but many do. The main way in which a criminal gets punished is when the police shoot him at sight. But the difference to ordinary life, if you are reasonably careful as to what you do, is negligible. Only the ordinary cinema-film is much more realistic in its picture of American life than one would imagine in England. But it does not affect ordinary people to any noticeable extent.

I hope that you got the solution of the problem all right and could understand it. I am trying to get a simple way of proof. I have got it all but one point which I want to think over. I could explain it verbally, but doubt if I could write it out.

We were very pleased to hear that you have had some more congratulations from F.E. Smith. I was expecting that since your transfer to the Electricity Section you would not be doing much for about 18 months.

When you are over here, I think that I can get you some good introductions to see things. There is a big naval Station at Newport, and Ernest Hocking knows some of the Admirals. The Americans are immensely kind; and there seems always to be someone who will go to any trouble, if one wants anything. We are beginning to pay back some of the hospitality with little Tuesday dinners. We can only dine eight. Next Tuesday we are having De Wulf (a Belgian scholastic philosopher), James Woods, Miss Longfellow, the Greenes, and Osborn Taylor. Jessie will come in afterwards: Osborn Taylor turned up unexpectedly.

Old Miss Longfellow is about 80, or over—she is a great card, with a very decided habit of mind.

Goodbye darling. It is nearly eight o'clock on Sunday evening, and some of my men will be coming in a few minutes. Dearest love to you all

Your loving

Daddy

504 Radnor Hall
Charles River Road
Cambridge. Mass. Nov 21st
1925

Darling North

All well here. Mummy has been tired for the last fortnight, and has had to lie up a good deal. But she has really had a lot of engagements which she has managed to keep. So that her inability to get really rested is explained. But she is being careful, and will soon get back to her normal state. For instance, last night we had planned for a quiet evening and for her to go to bed at 9 o'clock. But—it being Sunday night—about ten people came in, knowing that we are at home usually. The result was an animated evening till about 11 P.M.

Geoffrey Young and his wife are over here and lunched with us yesterday. He has some job about students trips, for Europeans to come to U.S.A. I am giving him a luncheon party today at the Colonial Club, that he may meet men who can give him advice and information. They go back early in December. They now live at Cambridge. They are going to ask you and Margot down to see them, so as to tell you all about us. You remember he lost his leg in the war. His wife is perfectly and absolutely charming—very simple and kind in every way.

I am sending you a summary of the problem, rather clearly written out—merely results. But I have added to it the additional case when Kv is *small*. I think you will be able to direct the calculations rather easily from these formulae. Things look so much easier when the proper abbreviations—e.g. s for sin Kv and s for sinh Kv—have been hit upon. It is useless for me to try the numerical calculations. If there is any other *critical* case, please let me know.

Dearest love to all

Your loving Daddy

504 Radnor Hall
Charles River Road
Cambridge. Mass. Dec.9th/25

Darling North

This letter should get to you about Christmas time. My dearest
love and Christmas wishes to you all—Margot, Roy, Sheila, Eric,
and yourself. We are well here, indeed very flourishing. Mummy
gets tired, but I do not think more so than in London. She does a lot
when she is up, but is learning to rest between whiles. Apart from
the ill-luck of her broken rib and ivy-poisoning—and it is a large
exception—I think that this climate suits her, mainly because her
rheumatism and neuritis are so much better.

Jessie is *very* flourishing. She has made a good start both in the Library at her work, and also generally among people. When she came
over, she was in every way out of sorts: the change in country, with
its newness, has been in every way good for her. She has been given
an extension of permit of residence for another six months. Meanwhile the American Consul at Montreal has put her name on his list
of applicants. Accordingly we hope for a permanent permit with
merely a journey to Montreal to pick it up—a two-days job in all.
But it may be some time before the Consul there clears off his previous applicants on his list. Her new permit expires on July 1st—or
thereabouts—so she may have to get another one.

This arrangement is due to the vigorous action of Lowell—the
president of the College. I like him immensely: he is not effusive, but
he is kindness itself. He is the exact reproduction of an advanced liberal member of Parliament of the year 1880, or thereabouts—"civil
and religious liberty", "freedom of thought", and "sensible progress"
are evidently written all over him. They are not bad marks to have
on one.

I am telling the University Press to send you a copy of my new
book—Science and The Modern World—; it consists of my Lowell
Lectures with some additions. There have been no reviews of it yet;
it has only been published for a few weeks. The Cambridge Press is
doing it in England.

We are rather worried by the illness of our friend Rosalind
Greene—some internal disorder. Mummy sees more of her than of
anyone else. Rosalind and James Woods—the chairman of the Department of Philosophy—are our main supports, so far as intimacy is
concerned. But poor Rosalind is really very seedy: she is not in bed
yet, but hardly gets out. She is to be x-rayed soon. You will remember she organised the fancy-dress dance at which Jessie was introduced to Cambridge society—at least to its old Yankee section.

I have been delighted at the accounts you and Margot have sent of your work at the Laboratory. It seems to me that if an occupation in life had been specially created for you, it would have been not unlike your present position. Also F.E. Smith and Drysdale are additional mercies. It is not often that there are two men, quite so nice, for one's immediate chiefs.

I have been worrying in my odd moments over the arithmetic which I sent you. In an earlier MS I made a certain coefficient $1/5$, and in a later one $1/10$—I think that I drew attention to the discrepancy. I now enclose an MS doing it all over again, keeping the actual numbers till the end. Unless I have somehow repeated an old slip, it seems that the earlier M.S. was right, and that the coefficient *is* one-fifth.

A happy Xmas to you all, darlings. Do not worry about us here: our general health is keeping quite satisfactory: Mary is looking after us like a Trojan: and the people around us are as kind as they can be. By the bye—fired by your example—Mummy has had a radio, without a loud speaker, installed in Mary's room. She (Mary) is overjoyed. In Mummy's first attempts at listening she first got hold of a man expounding to state of the New York Stock Exchange, and then switched off onto a sermon of a Jewish Rabbi. So she came away with a lot of curious information which she passed on to me. But there is now more expertness in getting on to the concerts.

Goodby darling

Your loving Daddy

504 Radnor Hall
Charles River Rd
Cambridge, Mass. May 16th/26

Darling North

At last the session is nearly over. Lectures end about May 30th. The work has been enjoyable—but has been very exacting, because I have been trying to put across to the classes a somewhat novel point of view all the time, and was reducing it to a verbal expression as I went along.

Mummy's health is *much* better now. The winter was trying to her—not alarming, but she could not do much—and there was the danger that the spring w[ould] not pull her round again. The ivy-poisoning and the broken rib had made the preceding summer a drawback instead of a help. She was seeing people all the winter, and driving out to parties, etc., but was unable to walk, or undergo any exertion.

But now she really is entirely vigorous again—able to walk, and has practically lost all the pain from her rib. A good summer in Vermont will be excellent, and in the autumn you ought to find her in better health than when she left England.

The Coal Strike has been followed here with intense interest. On the whole, sympathy is evenly balanced. The "low-wages theory" of the masters is looked on as a sign of their lack of imagination in regard to modern industrial organization. But the issue of the strike and the orderliness has caused an outbreak of unbounded admiration at the political good sense of England.

Over here the telephone is the mode by which feelings are expressed—so Mummy has been having a succession of telephone messages expressive of admiration of England. Also my colleagues have been saying nice things about England, all the time.

Our jaunt to the Middle West, and Montreal was a flaming success. The people adored Mummy. We liked the University type of Middle Westerners. The Illinois undergraduates from the farming districts are delightful young people, and are mostly of English descent. The country is as flat as a pancake, with the black earth of our fen districts.

Yesterday we saw Rosalind Greene off. She is taking her three younger daughters—ages 16 to 10—to France and Switzerland for the summer and autumn. Harry Greene and the eldest daughter—Francesca aged 18—start in a month after Francesca has done her university exams for this session.

We are rather bereft at Rosalind's departure—for they are the people we are really intimate with. She went in a R.M.S.P boat, The Ohio, which touched at Boston. Last night she sent Mummy a wireless from the boat "Proud to be sailing under your flag". You can always trust an American for a graceful touch. She belongs to the same *genus* as Lena Mirrlees—but a widely contrasted species. She has a definite and scholarly knowledge of literature *e.q.* Medieval French—in fact a certain Yankee seriousness as to definite fact.

We have to hang about here till June 24 apropos of the winding up of University business and a couple of honorary degrees—one of them will mean going to the Middle West beyond Chicago. It is rather a nuisance as we do not want another long journey. But the Middle West is a little oblivious to the existence of Europe, and it does not do for an Englishman to damp down its interests in that direction, however slight and indirect. But we travel in great comfort, and take a drawingroom. The expence is not overmuch and it makes all the difference in a 24 hours journey.

We are counting the days till you and Margot come over. We try not to get over-excited about it. But it is really the one thing we can really think of. Tell me if there are any definite works which you want to see. Here there is the famous Mass. College of Technology—a very enlarged "Imperial College of Science and Technology". There is also "Alvan Clark", the optical works, in the neighbourhood. Perhaps they would show you over. I know nothing about them. But I could certainly get you an introduction.

I gather from you that the Naval people at Newport, R.I., are no go—being too awkward as to official secrets. But let me know as to what is in your mind. I *do* want to have a chat with you—I mean *chats* and *chats*. There is no one little thing that I want to say—but hosts of general ideas and details and points of view that I want to get at.

My book—Science and the Modern World—is going swimmingly—already reprinted—As to its permanent value, one cannot tell. I want to follow it up with something purely addressed to philosophers—*short* and *clear,* if I can make it so! But I reckon that it will take me about two years to get that ready. My view is that a lot of modern philosophy is much too controversial—hunting rabbits which bolt into the wrong burrows. There cannot be much in the subject. What there is to be said, ought to be put shortly—if one could only see how to do it.

You see that I am rather echoing back to you, your own views as to the book on design. After all, philosophy is only the statement of the general design of things in general. It *must* be a short subject.

I have found an unposted letter of months' ago. It has some information—so I push it over to you.

Dearest love—goodbye darling

Daddy

603 Radnor Hall
984 Memorial Drive
Cambridge. Mass
Sunday March 25th/27

Darling North

The household has been afflicted with the colds—or very mild influenza—which are going the round of Cambridge—first Jessie, then Mary, and now Mummy. We are taking every care of Mummy—she has been in bed for the last three days, and Taylor comes daily. But there is *nothing on her chest,* and with due care she should be perfectly well in two or three days. I will send a week-end telegram next Sunday, which will arrive before this letter—so you will have the end before the beginning, and this letter need give you no anxiety.

We have been very disappointed: for Saturday was Francesca's birthday—her 19th—and she had done us the honour to include us in the young dinner party which celebrated the occasion. We could neither of us go—but were very complimented at this attention from the young.

For this half-session the Perrys are away—on the "Western exchange"—this refers to a system whereby Harvard sends yearly a professor who perambulates through a group of western Colleges, of the smaller sort. Next session 1927-/28, we shall be very bereft: James Woods is in France for the whole year, Ernest Hocking for the 2nd half of it, and Raphael Demos for the whole year. The Eatons will be back, which will be a comfort—we are very fond of them, and there is always something doing when they are about. In that way, they are a younger edition of the Mirrlees parents. I do hope that you see them this year before they come back.

I have just been into Mummy to ask about a message to you, and she tells me that yesterday she sent off a cable—so you know all about the cold. She sends her dearest love and will probably write. Our visit to Virginia has been extended by four days, at Lowell's request, to enable us to be present at some celebration in Philadelphia. So we shall have a full fortnight in the south, exclusive of travelling—April 17 to April 30, *inclusive.* This ought to set Mummy up for the summer.

I am getting on famously. Yesterday, besides walking about in the course of my lectures, I walked home—and I think that it did me good. I am very anxious not to bring back any inflammation, and there is no antecedent test of what I can do—so I go slow. There is now no pain, and my apparatus for bracing me up is very comfortable.

Profr Conway of Manchester (England) is coming to lunch with James Woods: the latter lunches here every Sunday. Mummy has just finished "Lord Raingo" by Arnold Bennett and liked it a lot. It is all about Lloyd George's administration.

The chief excitement here is about Sacco and Vanzetti two Italians who *six* years ago were convicted of murder, for robbery. Ever since then the State of Massachusetts has been trying to make up its mind as to whether or no they should be executed. There seems very little doubt but that they were entirely innocent, and were convicted because of the hysteria as to Bolsheviks which was then raging—they are extreme "reds". Frankfurter has just written a very powerful exposé of the whole case. It is a Dreyfus case over again, with all the typical symptoms of such cases—especially in the fact that every possible irrelevance has crept in, namely as to who acted well or ill under circumstances which have no bearing on the guilt of the two men.

Criminal Law Courts are not the strongest point of this great country.

Goodbye, Darling

Your loving Daddy

Monday August 22nd/1927
Plympton Camp
Caspian Lake—Greensboro'
Vermont

Darling North

It seems years and years since I wrote to you. But I have written nearly half a book on Metaphysics this summer—and have not wanted to break my thoughts in any way. Anyhow I have now got nearly 9 ½ chapters finished out of a projected plan of 20 or 25 chapters. I am rather pleased with the result, so far.

Since August 15th I have been taking a complete holiday and at last have got rid of the metaphysics buzzing round and round in my head.

We have had a lovely time here: first, from June 25th to August 1st Mummy and myself quite alone, seeing the Mitchells about every other day: then Francesca and Joy Greene and Jeffries Wyman— young physiologist, age 26: and from August 15th Rosalind, Harry, Francesca, and Katrine, and Jeffries. The scheme has worked to perfection. I do wish you could see this place in its glory. Unfortunately it is capable of putting up a succession (two to four) of rainy cold days—these are the price to be paid for the wonderful air and vegetation, of the other days. Mummy has had two nasty little set backs—not serious, but wanting care. First a few days of lumbago. How caught, we don't know. It gave way before diet, warmth, and the local doctor—a nice young man, whom we were glad to get to know and trust (within limits). Then a wretched girl came to dine with a bad influenzic cold which Mummy caught from her. This has also gone, and for three days she has been clear of it. Last night (Sunday) we spent the evening at the Woodwards, and had supper there—all except Katrine who went to bed early, after a long walk. We go back next Monday night, Aug. 29th, and, after changing luggage at the flat, go on to the Greenes' at the River House . . . for a week.

Term begins on Sept. 26th so we shall have nearly 3 weeks to settle back in Radnor Hall. Then you come: Hurrah! We are counting the days. Jessie's trip to California has been a flaming success. The second part of it—namely, staying at Berkeley for a month—is equally successful with the climbing month. All the Sierra Club people are entertaining her and taking her about. She arrives back on Sept 8th. We have been delighted at your cablegram about the success of the caravan. The family Whitehead has done well over its holidays this year.

I am longing for a chat with you—about everything, philosophy, science, and persons. We have heard from Phil Johnson: he enjoyed his stay with you beyond measure—so much, that the rest of the trip seems to be a slight letdown. He gave a flaming account of you all *i.e.* Margot, Eric, You. We are very stirred over James Woods marriage: next session, without him, will be rather desolate for us. We have always consulted him about things, as they turned up.

I think that I have got my metaphysics into capital order now: I have managed, to my own satisfaction at least, to make quite plain where I agree and disagree with the big seventeenth century men, especially Descartes, Spinoza, John Locke, and (later) Hume. The upshot of my studies is to "boost up" John Locke, as the best of the lot of them—not the most consistent. But self-consistency is not the first requisite, though it is the final test. He denies fewer obvious facts than do other people, and gets them about as consistently together as you can hope to do. Of course, I think that I have improved on him: it would be no fun writing metaphysics unless one could do that. But I adopt his general view of the situation, practically *in toto*. He has one great merit: he knows a lot more than metaphysics.

The Greene children have been great dears—Katrine is suddenly starting into great beauty, of a rather stately character. But, as she is only fourteen, the stateliness is more in promise than actuality. Including Jeffries they are the most charmingly well-bred, gay, young things to have about. On Friday, we—*i.e. excepting* Rosalind and Mummy—drove up to Lake Seymour, to lunch with the Hendersons in our old camp—a most successful expedition, in all about 110 miles: magnificent views, and a very lively argumentative discussion with the Hendersons.

Goodbye and love to you all. Oct 2nd will soon come.

Your loving Daddy

603 Radnor Hall. Memorial Drive
Cambridge. Mass.
Nov.13. 1927

Darling North

We have enjoyed your letters—your visit has been a perfect success and has made all the difference. It is difficult to believe that a week could "weigh in" so effectively. Mummy is now really *much better*. She went on improving slowly, but very slowly, and on a low level of strength. Then suddenly one day, she woke up feeling really vigorous—about a week ago. It is as though something—a clot, or something in the lungs—has cleared up. She says that she seems to have gone back to her old state of health about a year before her illness. Usually the colder weather has at first depressed her in strength, but she seems to have been slightly stimulated by it. The result is that we can look forward to the winter with less anxiety: Mummy is really reacting in the way of gaining strength and resisting power. The turn came as quickly as it did on that night at the height of her illness. One reason—curiously enough—which led to Mummy's recovery was a rather painful scene with Mark Barr. My private opinion is that Mark is going to pieces—or rather, that for years he has gone to pieces. I am very doubtful whether he will keep his post at the Business School here. His habit of exploiting his friendships, chiefly by way of borrowing but also in other ways, is getting him into difficulties. Anyhow, he will have another chance. But his vanity, and his habit of gaseously showing off in conversation, make him a bad colleague so far as I can judge from what I hear. He was born to live in the smoking rooms of intellectual clubs in London or New York.

I suppose that Margot is in Germany now. It is just what she wanted. How are you managing about Eric for this month? Of course, he is at school most of the time. Have you any domestic capable of filling the bill when he comes home? Or is he sufficiently grown up to look after himself for a few weeks? Mummy has had delightful letters from the children—Roy and Sheila. We are just longing to get to England, and see you all at home.

My material for the lectures is accumulating excellently. I really think that I shall get hold of a proper detailed exposition of what I mean. Things are opening out. My classes are going well. The seminary on Friday nights has been the best that I have had in any year over here. Three or four young doctors—neurologists and psychologists—are coming, as well as the ordinary graduate students: also the wives of two of them. One of the latter is about the ablest of the whole seminary, and wrote a capital paper the other day. After the formal seminary, the doctors and wives and the readers of the papers stop and have chocolate and talk with us. Last Friday they did not go till nearly twelve, after a vigorous discussion.

We are anxious about Phil Johnson. He is getting nervous, and jumpy, and depressed. I do not think that it is primarily over his work, though both Ralph Eaton and I had to tell him—independently and without any concerted arrangement—that he was not tackling it in the right way. But I do not think that *that* was the root of the matter. Anyhow he has gone home to Cleveland, Ohio, for this week end.

The Greenes are on the whole flourishing. Francesca is doing her work excellently. She is a clever girl and works hard. Though how she does it amid her other avocations is beyond my comprehension. Anyhow she is in excellent spirits. We are looking forward to having her in England with us. She is a sensible, well-bred, and decorative young thing. Rosalind is in a better way, all round. She seems to have got the better of her internal ailments, which are now, for the time being, again latent. Also she is in good spirits—the only sign of worry is that we are not so sure that Ernesta is quite as physically well as she ought to be. Last Saturday—yesterday week—we dined there, and stayed to watch a small dance that they gave. I see Francesca every other day at my Radcliffe class.

Jessie is flourishing. She is joining the Apalachian club. This club is a walking club which makes week-end expeditions among the Massachusetts' hills. The Apallachian hills—I do not know how to spell their name—are the most swagger set in the neighbourhood: hence the name of the club. She wrote a paper for a Library Association which is to be printed.

Our Sunday evenings are going off in great style. Last Sunday's was one of the best that we have had.

I must stop now, as I want to write to James Woods and—if I have any strength left—to Shirley.

Your loving Daddy

603 Radnor Hall
Memorial Drive
Cambridge, Mass.
March 7/28

Darling North

Mummy has not written this mail because she is in bed with a nasty cold. It is running a perfectly normal course, and she is taking great care of it. Also Taylor is looking after her. So there is no reason to fear that it will play any tricks on her lungs. It is just a heavy cold. Naturally it is disappointing because we wanted to get her through the winter without one. I will send a wire when it is better. She sends her dearest love to you all.

We were awfully pleased to get Margot's letter, and to hear of the brilliant success of the house. I am sure that the move is wise. Your views on Adult Education at the working men's College seem excellent. I do not feel that I know enough to criticize. You are obviously right in your general ideas. The real difficulty is to get the proper balance of things in practice—having regard to the particular sort of students, the sort of staff, and the various particular circumstances. Nothing but commonsense, and a continual readiness to readjust can tell you anything there. In reforming, one is rather apt to "lean over backwards", as they say here. I am glad that you are doing this job. It is thoroughly interesting and very important. I have never seen any scheme for the improvement of the general state of life, that does not presuppose a population more educated than mass of people actually are.

The Greenes are in trouble over illness: Rosalind has been in bed for about a week or more—temperature, from some internal infection or other. Also Francesca for nearly a month with a pain in her chest. I think that she overtired herself last term and at Xmas time; and things are functioning badly through exhaustion and an attack of grippe. They have been in the country in Mrs Lyman's house—well looked after, in every luxury. They came back on Tuesday. But Rosalind is still in bed. Francesca much better.

As to my own work, I am pegging away at the Gifford lectures. I am rather pleased with the book. It will be stiff reading, and will not—as I expect—please the philosophic world. But I have elaborated my ideas into a new approach to philosophy.

It seems to me that this new way deals much less in abstractions than does the old way. Philosophers seem to me to be playing about with a "book" tradition, and not trying to express the fact directly observed. I am trying to evolve one way of speaking which applies equally to physics, physiology, psychology, and to our aesthetic experiences. The ordinary philosophic abstractions won't do this. My private opinion is that in the last 150 years the chief ability of the world has not gone into philosophy—perhaps wisely. Modern philosophers are very analogous to English musicians: you can say lots of nice things about us, but after all we are *modern* philosophers, or *English* musicians, as the case may be.

Anyhow, all this is taking a lot of time, and really I am not thinking about anything else. We are just counting the days till we embark on May 17. We can hardly bear to think of it. I reckon that we shall have about three days with you before going up to Edinburgh. I start lecturing there on June 1st and give ten lectures, every other day.

The session here has been going well. My classes have been the largest I have had, and uncommonly nice men among them. Young Americans are perfectly delightful pupils.

Dearest love to you all

Your loving Daddy

AMERICAN MERCHANT LINES
S.S. American Merchant
Wednesday. Sept 12. 1928

Darling North

Five days on a moderately rough sea have reduced me to a state of complete idiocy. I suppose that it is the state ironically termed a "rest-cure". Neither of us actually succumbed: but from Saturday afternoon up to yesterday, inclusive, we were both profoundly unhappy. Mummy managed to appear at all the meals—breakfast excepted. But I secluded myself in the cabin. Yesterday we were better, and today practically well. But *bored* with the ocean. It is chill, choppy weather, with gusts of rain occasionally. On the whole the wind has dropped—but is freshening again. We are excellently looked after. Our cabin-steward is a pet. He brings us our breakfast at 7, or 7:15—and our hot water about 8:30. Also we like the deck-steward. Mummy is really taking the voyage excellently—weather permitting. There are a very quiet set of passengers. Our deck-chairs are next to a nice American woman, who for some weeks was staying with English friends just outside *Wimborne* leaving on the Saturday before the Queen came.

When you left the boat, we had dinner almost immediately. Then we watched the boat being towed out of the dock. We did not seriously start down the Thames till nearly midnight—when we were in bed. But the lights in the docks were really beautiful. I see that our speed is about 13.86 knots on a good day. You and Margot gave us a beautiful time this summer. The children were more than all that we had hoped for—pets. We have been thinking of you bobbing about in the Champion. But I doubt if the sea is bad enough for your purposes, though it is too violent for ours. By the bye, after the Albert Docks, the only land I saw was Start Point in Devonshire. The weather was misty, and we have had a lot of fog-horn going.

This letter discloses the utter blankness of my mind. I am, as at present advised, all for a static world. Damn the flux of things with its rockiness. I will finish the letter when we are near New York.

Saturday. Sept. 15 11:00 A.M.

We are both well—with good sea-legs—no "swell" on the ocean to speak of—a mild following wind—warmish. We are to arrive at New York at 3 P.M (standard time) on Monday, according to the official notice. By these summary notes, you will infer that things have considerably cleared up since Wednesday. But not all at once. For my fears of the wind freshening were completely verified, and by midnight on Wednesday there was a mild gale. We were not seasick—but tired and headachy throughout Thursday—the sea and wind remaining very unpleasant. The whole boat was very unhappy. But yesterday things mended—also the Captain, after hesitating between New York on Tuesday morning with reduced speed and Monday afternoon with increased speed, elected for the latter, as I prophesied he would, having regard to the many advantages of punctuality.

The passengers going West are a much more depressed set than those going East. The latter had their holiday in front and were in high spirits—this lot are tired out, and going back to work. But they are a pleasant set of people.

We shall take the night train to Boston. There is no train between 4:00 P.M (standard time) and 11 P.M. We cannot catch the former, except by a miracle touching the hearts of the American customhouse officers. We shall get to Boston at 5:50 A.M (Standard) *i.e.* 6:50 (Daylight)—and have breakfast at home. I shall try to get a thermos flask at the Grand Central Station, so that we can have some hot coffee before getting up in the train. We can board the train in New York at 9 P.M (Standard). We shall do this and try to get some rest. If possible, we shall get a compartment and do the journey in comfort.

I will add a final note on Sunday evening. Goodbye and love for the present.

Sunday. Sept 16. 8:45 P.M.

We have just seen the Nantucket lightship. So at last we are across the ocean.

Today has been the most lovely day that I have ever seen on the Atlantic. We might have been on the Mediterranean. The ship has cheered up wonderfully. We shall probably reach New York ahead of our time, and may catch an afternoon train to Boston.

Dearest love to Margot, the children and you

       Your loving Daddy

603 Radnor Hall
984 Memorial Drive
Cambridge. Mass
Dec. 23. 1928

Darling North

My dearest, dearest love to you for your birthday—and for the New Year—and to Margot and the children. Today is the first day of the Christmas recess. This last term has been the greatest tax on my imagination that I have ever had—*not* the most tiring physically. But I have been making the final draft of my Giffords—and having to keep the whole scheme of thought in my head, so as to get all the points written up in order. The title will be "Process and Reality: An Essay in Cosmology". It is an attempt to revive speculative philosophy. This effort and the lectures have driven every other form of composition—even letters—out of my head. But now that lecturing is over, some sense of freedom has come. So much to explain my silence.

We have been anxious about Margot, and your letter telling us that the X-rays showed no ulcers was a great relief. Give her my dearest love and sympathy and "happy new-years". Also thank Roy for his letter to me. I liked it so much.

Mummy has got through the term really very well. She has to rest a great deal: but she *does* rest, and yet also accomplishes a very active life. So though in a sense she is weaker for her illness of two years ago, on the whole she seems better than at any time since we landed here—indeed since the stress of the war.

For example, yesterday in the morning she was busy preparing for Xmas. At 11:30 she drove over to Brookline for Jeff. Wyman's marriage to Ann Cabot, (where I joined her at 1:20 after my lectures). At 2:15 we were back home and Mummy rested: at 4:30 the Master of Balliol came in for an hour's chat or an hour and a half: we had dinner quietly together—Jessie away for the weekend with the Forbes family—: at 8 PM. Dr Edsall came in and stayed till 11 P.M.

It was an active day because Lindsay and Edsall both were talking seriously. Of course *physically* she was sitting quietly after 2:30. But the morning's work and the wedding were a good deal. So on the whole, I am very pleased with the way in which she is getting through the winter. But she wants care.

We are all in great anxiety over Francesca's illness—horribly frightened. Poor Rosalind and Francesca cooped up in that remote corner of France, away from everyone: It will not bear thinking about. Also the poor child seems in a good deal of pain for the last month. But we are assured that everything is going well: so we must hope for the best. It seems to me to have been a sad error of judgement on the part of poor Harry Greene, to have taken them over. The most perfect arrangements could have been made here, without all this separation. But of course—not being a doctor—my opinion is not grounded on any real knowledge.

I congratulate you on the success of the year. It was rather a critical occasion. It is no use telling people about the importance of scientific technology unless the goods are produced. But it is so easy to have an initial run of ill-luck. No one can foresee exactly how well a apparatus will work. Our Governing set—higher civil servants and statesmen—are such appalling dunderheads about science. My belief is that all the American disorder in governmental affairs + a technologist like Hoover at the top is probably a much better and safer form of Government than our men with literary training + complete

indifference/ignorance* as to the scientific possibilities in the future.
I incline to believe that in education we are barking up the wrong
tree—and are producing charming people, who are in truth incapable
of coping with modern conditions—museum specimens of interesting antiquities, in fact.

What a gale you had—Lindsay tells us that half the best elms in the
Christchurch meadows at Oxford have been blown down.

My class of graduate students for this year have been a nice lot—
we are having an assembly of eighteen for Christmas Eve—after half
of them from the Pacific Coast. Goodbye darling

Your loving Daddy

Lake Caspian
Greensboro'
Vermont
August 12th/29

Darling North

At last I have got through with my Gifford Lectures—final proofs
corrected, Index printed, and the last corrections put in. It is the big-
gest piece of imaginative work which I have attempted, and has been
a great strain, especially for the last year. Whether it will be a success
I cannot have any idea. It is rather an ambitious book, of the sort
which may be a dead failure. We post the last package tomorrow.

Mummy has been a lot rested here—enjoying it immensely.
Though the occasional thundery weather upsets her at times. We are
very quiet here at the moment—George Morgan being away for ten
days. He comes back tomorrow. He is a nice young man, aged
twenty three—working very hard at his thesis for his Ph.D. He is
with us for the whole summer.

We think of you all caravaning in Cornwall. I cannot tell you how
pleased we are at the good news you have been sending us about the
family, including Margot and yourself. Do not overdo yourselves.
Remember that—as Mummy has told you—we want Miss Whyte to
stay with you over next year, including next summer. We can quite
well afford it, and there must be no hesitation about it. Then next

---

*[In the original letter, Whitehead interlineated "indifference" above "ignorance."—
Ed.]

year we will have a wonderful time in England with you somewhere in the country, and the burden of the children as to details will be taken off Margot.

Mummy has had a good many worries. First, with regard to the Greenes. It is horrible to think of Rosalind and the children exiled in that small hospital in the Pyrennees. (I never can spell that word). Also Ralph Eaton and Hortense have separated, and both of them poured out their troubles to her for many months, with finally a grand climax in June. My sympathies are all with Ralph, but I am afraid that his life has demoralized him and that he will not settle down again to teaching philosophy.

But our great consolation and joy is the bungalow which we are building at the foot of the Blue Hills. I do not think that you have seen the country on that side of Boston—south of the Town. This is easily the best scenery in the neighbourhood. The Hills are a public "Reservation", which extends for miles. Our bungalow is on a big private estate just at the foot of the Blue Hills. The whole district is held by a few wealthy Boston families—so we shall not be troubled by building developments.

It will make all the difference to Mummy's health. Vermont is too cold for us, and rather far. We want a place where we can go in the Easter Vacation, and in June and September. Probably we shall only come up here in August. We shall not own the Bungalow. The landlord, Mrs Barthol, is building it according to Mummy's design and charging us the rent based on the cost. It is exactly 14 miles from Radnor Hall. We shall have two bedrooms maid's bedroom, large living room, a porch, and a study, + kitchen and bathrooms. I have been rather anxious about Vermont, and wondering where we ought to go. This completely solves the difficulty.

On the whole Mummy has now quite got rid of the effects of her illness two years ago, when you and Margot were here. Her chest seems to me to be quite normal again, and her heart to be about as usual—easily deranged, but recovering quickly. She rests more than she used to, but gets through a surprising number of things during the week.

Jessie is having an orgy of climbing this summer—first with the Sierra Club in northern California, and then with a Boston club in the Canadian Rockies. They are going to climb Mount Robson, which is the crack peak of the Rockies. She is making a reputation as a mountaineer.

We have been very intrigued over your Russian Engineer. I hope that his designs are worth the trouble to you. He seems an equal mixture of genius, fool, and charlatan.

I wonder how your new First Lord of the Admiralty is getting on.

I see that he has been a working engineer—so he probably know[s] something of his job. So far I feel very pleased with the new Government. They have certainly made a good impression over here.

I am calling my new book *Process and Reality*. Also a little book of three lectures given at Princeton is coming out at the same time, *The Function of Reason*. I will tell the publishers to send you copies.

Did Mummy tell you that Roger Pierce's father died, and left all his money (about 35,000$ a year) to the Philosophy Department at Harvard. I am sorry for Roger. About half of the income left to Roger would have done more good in way of happiness. Anyhow the poor boy is very depressed.

I shall start writing letters again now that I have got this book off my chest. By the bye, Shirley will be here on Sept 23 or 24—for three weeks. I am looking forward to seeing her. There is an air of preposterousness in the thought of her impact on Boston.

Goodbye dearest, and love to you all

Your loving Daddy

603 Radnor Hall
984 Memorial Drive
Cambridge Mass. Nov 4/29

Darling North

Everything is reasonably well here. Mummy's health is *most satisfactory*. She can now undertake occasional fatigues and rest herself in a very short time. For example, last week on Wednesday morning we went to New York [9:00 A.M. to 2:50 P.M].* I had to be British Delegate at some ceremony of Columbia University—rather a dud affair, but that is "another tale". We stayed in our hotel mostly, for the days were cold and wet. But, even then, Mummy dined with the Wesley Mitchells' [the political economist and family, whom we are next to in Vermont]† at 6:30, back about 10:30. I had to be at a public dinner. Next morning we were tired out. But at 12:50, after lunch, we drove to the University for a big function, and returned at 5:30 P.M. We got into our sleeping car at 10:15 P.M at the Grand Central Terminus, started at 12:30 AM and had breakfast at home at

---

*Whitehead's brackets.
†Whitehead's brackets.

7:15 A.M on Friday. Now there was nothing very tiring in all this, for we took things very quietly. But it is the sort of thing to collapse anyone who has any serious weakness. But Mummy was quite fit on Friday. She drove out (14 miles) to our new Bungalow to superintend the building details in the afternoon, paid a visit to an intimate in Boston, and from 9:30–10:30 P.M. chatted to my pupils after their Seminary sitting here. Again there is nothing very fatiguing in all this, because no physical exertion involved. But it is the sort of thing which is impossible to anyone suffering from sheer exhausting weakness. Mummy also feels much better in herself. So altogether I am very relieved at her state of health. I am telling you all this in detail, because it is the only way of letting you know the exact situation out here. It is difficult sometimes to know how Mummy is, because she can run for a time on strength of will and nervous energy. But the absence of bad relapses and a fairly high level—of course with rests—show a real gain. She has really thrown off her illness.

The new bungalow is shaping for a great success. It is exactly what we want. Vermont is too cold for us and too far. Most country farmhouses—deserted and made over for visitors—are too isolated and with casual neighbours with whom we have nothing in common. This bungalow is on a large estate of woodlands and meadow, running up to a large "reserved" forest, forming a State Park kept for its beauty. There are three houses quite near, one of them the big house of the estate, and all of them inhabited by quiet nice Boston people. There are plenty of respectable men working on the estate. Yet in our meadow, we merely look out on meadows and woodland. Altogether it is ideal. The owner is ideal. She has simply told Mummy to build any sort of house she likes, and we to pay rent at 8% of the cost. Also we have the whole of the little meadow and its surrounding copses and trees for our use—about 2 ½ acres I should say. It is practically useless as grazing land, a hard layer of sandstone with some sour earth on the top. But it has a very pretty growth of long straggling grass and wild flowers. We face west and enter from the east. On the north we are bounded by a little stream which runs dry in the summer: and on the south by a hedge, with silver birch trees along it. [See Whitehead's sketches, pages 342–43.] Also parallel to the hedge, and *just* south of the house, there is a sudden rise of about 3 feet in the meadow, forming a nice quarterdeck running along the hedge on its north side. I enclose a diagram of the neighbourhood and of the ground plan of the house. All our neighbours are cousins of each other, *viz.* Philip Cabot who arranged the whole scheme, Dr and Mrs Barthol (our landlords), and the Eustaces' on the next estate. The whole district for some miles is owned—as a summer and autumn playground—by a group of Boston families.

We are therefore secure from the building of a speculative character. We have a great scheme for Margot and you and the three children coming over one summer, *e.g.* 1931, and we can all put up in the bungalow by the aid of the Porch, and the Dining room, turned into bedrooms. We can house a motor in Philip Cabot's barn.

You ought to have got a copy of my book by this time—Process and Reality. It represents what *I* can make of the world in general. But I do not expect a good reception from professional philosophers. It deserts the ordinary ways of putting things at the present moment. Also it is more speculative than philosophy in the recent past. In my opinion philosophers have been running into funkholes and so the subject has lost all interest.

I was very sorry to see that F.E. Smith has resigned from the Admiralty. Is it not rather a blow to the progress of your department? The new arrangement has a little puzzled me. Perhaps it only represents a short transition period.

I don't feel much trust in your Russian friend. It seems as though he might be concealing a good deal of trickery under the mask of buffoonery. That is my solution of the "Edgar Wallace" aspect of the incident.

We are already thinking of our passages for next summer. We shall arrive about July 1st and leave about Sept 12th. The Oxford Philosophical Conference is from Sept 1st to Sept 6th.

Dearest love to you all—Margot, and Eric, and the children at School. We are always thinking of you all.

Your loving Daddy

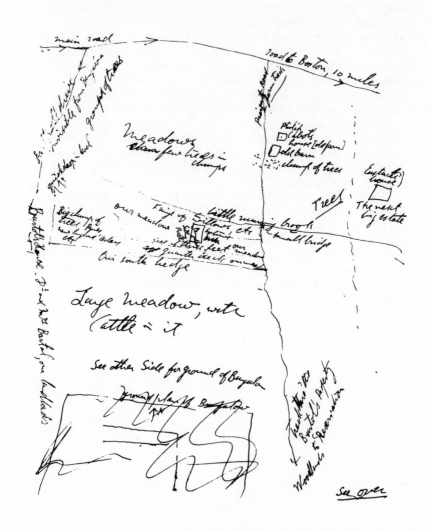

Philip Cabot.

Eustace's →

mostly porch

Bath room / mostly / Bed room | Kitchen | Dining room | 12'

W ←
Our meadow

Bath room & cupboard | 18 ft | main room | Fire place | entrance door | window | our meadow

18 ft

open

Bartols ←

our bed room | little pass | cupboard | Bath room | Bedroom

cupboard

rise in ground

↓ South

our meadow

Hedge with birch-tree
Bartol's meadow

over

with excellent cellar with ... storage places
&c.

Letter to Charles Hartshorne

The following letter was published in part in George L. Kline, ed., *Alfred North Whitehead: Essays on His Philosophy* (1963; Lanham, Md.: University Press of America, 1989). Through Professor Kline's courtesy it is now published in full, with the permission of Charles Hartshorne.

504 Radnor Drive
784 Memorial Drive
Cambridge, Mass.
Jan. 2nd, 1936

Dear Hartshorne

First, I want to tell you how touched and pleased Evelyn and I have been by the presentation of the volume of Philosophical Essays, in anticipation of my 75th Birthday. It was a wonderful experience.

Of course I have glanced through the contents, and now I am slowly studying the individual essays, before expressing myself to the contributors. I have just finished a second careful perusal of your essay.

My general impression of the whole book, together with my knowledge of the individual contributors, confirms my longstanding belief that in the oncoming generation America will be the centre of worthwhile philosophy. European philosophy has gone dry, and cannot make any worthwhile use of the results of nineteenth century scholarship. It is in chains to the sanctified presuppositions derived from later Greek thought. It is in much the same position as mediaeval scholasticism in the year 1400 A.D.

My belief is that the effective founders of the American Renaissance are Charles Peirce and William James. Of these men, W.J. is the analogue to Plato, and C.P. to Aristotle, though the time–order does not correspond, and the analogy must not be pressed too far. Have you read Ralph Perry's book (2 vols.) on James? It is a wonderful disclosure of the living repercussions of late 19th century thought

on a sensitive genius. It is reminiscent of the Platonic Dialogues.
W.J.'s pragmatic descendants have been doing their best to trivialize
his meanings in the notions of *Radical* Empiricism, Pragmatism, Rationalization. But I admit W.J. was weak on Rationalization. Also,
he expressed himself by the dangerous method of over-statement.

Now as to your recent work. Very naturally I have been immensely interested in it. Your article in the Philosophical Review
(July, 1935) gets to the heart of what I have been endeavouring to
say, in the most masterly manner. Of course a short article omits
whole topics which require elaboration. But you do get hold of the
principles of approach, apart from which all my recent writings since
1924 are a mere mass of confusion. Of course, I fully realize that in
the development of these principles there is room for grave divergence and much discussion.

Your essay in "Philosophical Essays" on "The Compound Individual" is most important, both in its explanation of relationships to the
Philosophical Tradition and in its development of the new approach
as it has gradually emerged in the last 50 years.

Finally there is your book "The Philosophy and Psychology of
Sensation". It entranced me by its development of the result of a
novelty of approach to questions buried under the faulty presuppositions of traditional thought.

I do hope that you have more work on hand.

There is one point as to which you—and everyone—misconstrues
me—obviously my usual faults of exposition are to blame. I mean
my doctrine of *eternal objects*. It is a first endeavour to get beyond the
absurd simple-mindedness of the traditional treatment of Universals.

As to the *loci* where I have treated the doctrine, of the chapter on
"*Abstraction*" in Science and the Modern World, and in "Process and
Reality", indexed under the headings "*Eternal Object*", "*Form*", "*Sen-
sum*", "*Pattern*".

The points to notice are

(i) that "Et. Obj." are the carriers of potentiality into realization;
and

(ii) that they thereby carry mentality into matter of fact; and

(iii) that no eternal object in any finite realization can exhibit the
full potentialities of its nature. It has an individual essence—whereby
it is the same eternal object on diverse occasions, and it has a relational essence whereby it has an infinitude of modes of entry into realization. But realization introduces finitude (in Spinoza's sense),
with the extension of the infinitude of incompatibles in the relational
essence.

(iv) The relational essence of each "Etern. Obj." involves its (potential) interconnections with all other eternal objects. The traditional

doctrine of the absolute isolation of universals is as great a (tacit) error, as the isolation of primary substances. The realization of the "compound individual" involves a finite realization of a complete pattern of eternal objects. The *absolute* abstraction of eternal objects from each other is an analogous error to their abstraction from some mode of realization, and to the abstraction of *res verae* from each other.

(v) The simple-minded way in which traditional philosophy—e.g. Hume, Bradley, etc.—has treated universals is the root of all evils. This is the great merit of the "*Gestalt*" people.

I am afraid I have bored you—But this letter is a measure of my interest in your work.

Sincerely yrs

Alfred North Whitehead

Notes

In these notes and the footnotes, the full-reference/shortened-reference system of citation has generally been used. Frequently cited works by Whitehead have been abbreviated as noted in the Bibliography. The frequently cited works of others have been abbreviated as follows:

Price, *Dialogues*   Lucien Price, ed., *Dialogues of Alfred North White-head* (New York: New American Library, Mentor, 1956).

Russell, *MPD*   Bertrand Russell, *My Philosophical Development* (New York: Simon & Shuster, 1959).

Russell, *Portraits*   Bertrand Russell, *Portraits from Memory and Other Essays* (New York: Simon & Shuster, 1963).

Russell, *Abiog.*   *The Autobiography of Bertrand Russell*, Vol. I, *1872–1914* (London: George Allen & Unwin, 1967).

Schilpp, *LLP-W*   Paul A. Schilpp, ed., *Library of Living Philosophers*, Vol. IV, *The Philosophy of Alfred North Whitehead* (Evanston, Ill.: Northwestern University Press, 1941).

I. Whitehead's First Years in London

1. For a full account of the move to London that I have just summarized, see Volume I, Chapter XV, Section v.

2. See Abiog. Notes, p. 11 in *ESP* or Schilpp, *LLP-W*.

3. In the United States the Home University Library was published, beginning in 1911, by Henry Holt & Co., New York. In quotations from Whitehead's *IM,* I use the American edition.

4. *IM,* pp. 52–57, 126.

5. Bertrand Russell to Lady Ottoline Morrell, June 21, 1911.

6. George Sarton, *The Study of the History of Mathematics* (1936; reprint, New York: Dover Publications, 1957), p. 54.

7. *IM,* p. 61.

8. Ibid., pp. 38–40.

9. Ibid., pp. 40–41.

10. Ibid., pp. 32–35.

11. Ibid., pp. 32–33.

12. See Volume I, Chapter VIII, Section i.

13. See Volume I, Chapter XII, Section iv, page 269. Relation-Arithmetic was primarily Russell's brainchild.

14. It is discussed in Volume I, Chapter XV, Section i.

15. Julia Bell to Victor Lowe, June 30, 1967.

16. Abiog. Notes, p. 10 in *ESP* or Schilpp, *LLP-W*.

17. See note †, page 9, above.

18. Chapter XIV of Volume I gives a full account of this memoir.

19. *Revue de Métaphysique et de Morale* 23 (May 1916): 423–54.

20. Patrick J. Hurley, "Whitehead's Relational Theory of Space: Text, Translation, and Commentary," No. 1259 in *Philosophy Research Archives* 4 (1978). My quotations will be from Hurley's translation, hereafter cited as RTS. Whitehead divided his paper into seven sections; my references will be by section number. Dr. Janet Fitzgerald translated slightly less than half of "La Théorie Relationniste de l'Espace" in an appendix to her *Alfred North Whitehead's Early Philosophy of Space and Time* (Washington, D.C.: University Press of America, 1979).

21. See Volume I, Chapter XIV, Sections i and ii, and note 6.

22. RTS, Sec. iii.

23. Ibid., Sec. ii.

24. Ibid., Sec. iii.

25. See Volume I, Chapter X, Section i, page 184.

26. Russell's relations with Mrs. Whitehead were discussed in Volume I, Chapter XI, Sections v and vi.

27. Gilbert Murray to Bertrand Russell, September 19, 1910.

28. The collaboration was the subject of Chapters XII and XIII in Volume I.

29. See Volume I, Chapter XI, Section v.

30. Kindly made available to me by her granddaughter Lona (niece of Mary and Alan Beeton), later Mrs. Peter Ward.

II. 1914–1918

1. On Forsyth, see Volume I, Chapter VIII, Section ii, pages 150–51.

2. See Chapter I, Section ii.

3. Third paragraph of Whitehead's essay, "The Aims of Education," *Mathematical Gazette* 8 (1916): 191–203; reprinted in *OT* and *AE*.

4. Hope Mirrlees, interview with author, August 8, 1965.

5. Gertrude Stein, *The Autobiography of Alice B. Toklas* (New York: Random House, 1933; New York: Vintage Books, 1961), p. 5.

6. Ibid., p. 148.

7. Published in *Proceedings of the Royal Society of London*, Ser. A, 94 (1918): 301–7.

8. The 1889 papers are described in Volume I, Chapter VIII, Section iv, pages 157–59.

9. T. North Whitehead, "Now I Am an American: Habit and Change" (copyright 1966), last paragraph of Chap. VIII.

10. Jessie Whitehead, reporting the words of another pilot on this patrol, in a letter to her uncle Charles Whitehead, March 16, 1918.

11. Quoted in the London *Times*, April 23, 1918.

12. *ESP*, p. 115.

13. Russell, *Abiog.*, Vol. II, p. 16.

14. This pamphlet has now been reprinted, with an introduction by Paul

Delaney and Kenneth Blackwell, in *Russell: The Journal of the Bertrand Russell Archives*, New Ser., Vol. 6, No. 1 (Summer 1986): 62–70. It is preceded in the same issue, pp. 39–61, by Paul Delaney, "Russell's Dismissal from Trinity: A Study in High Table Politics," which gives an interpretation of the whole episode.

15. Russell, *Abiog.*, Vol. II, p. 34; but see also Gilbert Murray's letter of April 9, 1918, to Russell, and the last paragraph of Russell's letter of May 6, 1918, to his brother Frank (both in the Bertrand Russell Archives, McMaster University, Hamilton, Ontario).

III. Whitehead on Education

1. Abiog. Notes, in Schilpp, *LLP-W*, p. 3.
2. *ESP*, p. 180.
3. *OT*, p. 3.
4. H. A. L. Fisher, review of *AE*, *The Nation & Athenaeum* 45 (June 22, 1929): 401.
5. Preface, *AE*, p. v.
6. Alfred North Whitehead, "Discussion upon Fundamental Principles in Education," *Report of the Eighty-seventh Meeting of the British Association for the Advancement of Science* (Bournemouth, 1919), p. 361.
7. *AE*, p. 51.
8. Sir John Adams, ed., *The New Teaching* (London: Hodder & Stoughton, 1918), p. 11.
9. *AE*, p. 6.
10. Ibid., pp. 1–2.
11. Ibid., p. 1.
12. Ibid., pp. 18–20.
13. Ibid., p. 3.
14. Ibid., pp. 8–9.
15. Ibid., p. 8.
16. Ibid.
17. Ibid., p. 16.
18. Ibid., p. 10.
19. Ibid., pp. 3–4.
20. See H. L. Mencken, review of *The Aims of Education*, *American Mercury* 17, No. 41 (June 1929): 251.
21. *AE*, p. 22.
22. Reprinted in Part III of *ESP* (1947), pp. 175–89.
23. Ibid., p. 175.
24. Ibid., p. 181.
25. *AE*, p. 12. Graphs were introduced into school mathematical teaching about 1898, and served as the entering wedge in breaking up the traditional presentation of algebra as, in effect, gibberish.
26. *ESP*, p. 185.
27. Ibid., p. 178.
28. *OT*, pp. 101–2.
29. Ibid., p. 102.
30. Ibid., p. 98.

31. Ibid., p. 95.
32. Ibid., p. 103.
33. *AE*, p. 123.
34. Ibid., pp. 124–25.
35. Ibid., p. 131.
36. Ibid., p. 128.
37. Ibid., p. 135.
38. Ibid., p. 122.
39. Bertrand Russell, *Our Knowledge of the External World as a Field for Scientific Method in Philosophy* (London: George Allen & Unwin, 1914; Chicago and London: Open Court Publishing Co., 1914).
40. See the entry in the Bibliography for "Technical Education and Its Relation to Science and Literature." The 1929 reprinting in *AE* omits only five lines from the scarce 1917 printing in *OT*, and so is used in these notes.
41. *AE*, p. 85.
42. Ibid., p. 83.
43. Ibid., p. 69.
44. Ibid., pp. 77–78.
45. Ibid., p. 74.
46. Ibid., pp. 88–89.
47. Ibid., p. 92.
48. Ibid., p. 90.
49. Ibid., pp. 67–69, 91–92.
50. *AE*, p. 82–83.
51. See Volume I, Chapter X, Section ii.
52. *ESP*, pp. 173–74.
53. Ibid., pp. 171–73. The address at the Stanley School was published, with the title "Education and Self-Education," only in Whitehead's *ESP*.
54. *OT*, p. 60.
55. *ESP*, pp. 190–91.
56. Ibid., p. 193.
57. Ibid., p. 189.
58. Ibid., p. 193.
59. Ibid., pp. 193–94.
60. Ibid., p. 194.
61. Ibid., p. 195.
62. The record of what Whitehead said is entirely on p. 361 of the *Report* of this meeting of the BAAS. See note 6 of this chapter. The brevity (about six hundred words) of the "Discussion upon Fundamental Principles in Education" led me, in the bibliographical entry for it in Volume I (p. 337), to misdescribe it as an abridgment of an address by Whitehead; the language is plainly Whitehead's, but he delivered no address.
63. *ESP*, pp. 196–97.
64. *AE*, p. 24.
65. Ibid., p. 30.
66. T. Percy Nunn, *Education: Its Data and First Principles*, 3d ed. (London: Edw. Arnold, 1945), p. 271.
67. *AE*, p. 56.
68. Ibid., p. 35.

69. Ibid., p. 58.

70. Ibid., p. 57.

71. Ibid., p. 52.

72. Ibid., p. 55.

73. Ibid., p. 46.

74. Except for the passing affirmation that I mentioned in Section v of this chapter, which was uttered in January of the same year.

75. *AE*, pp. 63–64.

76. Herbert Dingle, *Relativity for All,* 2d ed. (London: Methuen and Co., 1922).

77. L. C. Martin to Victor Lowe, September 26, 1972.

78. Sir Kelvin Spencer to Victor Lowe, September 11, 1975.

79. Education Supplement to the *Times* (London), November 30, 1916.

80. See Sir Richard Livingstone, *On Education* (Cambridge: Cambridge University Press, 1954), p. 207.

81. Reported in Keith Evans, *The Development and Structure of the English School System* (London: Hodder & Stoughton, 1985), p. 86.

82. Edward Youmans, interview with author, March 14, 1967; Joseph Segar, interview with author, March 15, 1967.

83. *AE,* p. 145.

84. Ibid., p. 147.

85. Ibid., p. 150.

86. Ibid., pp. 138–39.

IV. Last Years in England

1. University of London, Senate Minute 1789, March 19, 1919.

2. University of London *Gazette,* July 9, 1919, reporting Whitehead's appointment to the Council for the academic year 1919–20.

3. University of London, Senate Minutes 2021 and 2022, March 4, 1919.

4. University College, London, *Annual Report* (1923), p. 56.

5. University College, London, *Calendar* (1969–70).

6. Ernest Graham-Little, Letter to the London *Times,* January 2, 1948.

7. University of London, Senate Minutes 2849–2852, May 18, 1920.

8. University of London, Academic Council, "Report of Inspectors of Research, Teaching, and Equipment," October 20, 1920.

9. A. N. Whitehead to Registrar of Imperial College, March 6, 1924.

10. Ibid. (Whitehead's italics).

11. Imperial College, Board of Studies, Minute 425, May 4, 1915.

12. It was dedicated on June 23, 1970, by North's son, Eric A. N. Whitehead. See Sir Ross Chesterman, Warden of Goldsmiths' College, Letter to the Editor of the London *Times Educational Supplement,* July 19, 1970.

13. A. E. Dean, "Fifty Years of Growth," in *The Forge: The History of Goldsmiths' College,* ed. Dorothy Dymond (London: Methuen, 1955), p. 3.

14. Ibid., pp. 4–7.

15. Sir Ross Chesterman, interview with author, August 7, 1968.

16. Ibid.

17. Sir Ross Chesterman, memorandum on Whitehead sent to author with letter of February 2, 1968.

18. Ibid.

19. W. R. Matthews, *Memories and Meanings* (London: Hodder & Stoughton, 1969), p. 298.

20. Chesterman, memorandum of February 2, 1968.

21. Minutes of the Governing Body of the South Western Polytechnic Institute.

22. Ibid.

23. University of London, Faculty of Science, Minute Book for 1918–19, p. 217.

24. H.M. Stationery Office, 1921.

25. Alfred North Whitehead, "The Place of Classics in Education," *Hibbert Journal* 21 (1923): 248–61. Reprinted as Chapter V of *AE* (1929).

26. *AE*, p. 94.

27. Ibid., p. 98.

28. Ibid., p. 114.

29. Dame Dorothy Brock, interview with author, June 21, 1968.

30. Ibid.

31. Murray's printed memorandum is in the Russell Archives at McMaster University.

32. T. North Whitehead, "Now I Am an American" (unpublished autobiography, 1966), p. 89.

33. Sir Kelvin Spencer to Victor Lowe, September 11, 1975.

34. Mrs. Norah Nicholls, interview with the author, July 7, 1967.

35. H. Bradley to Victor Lowe, June 21, 1972.

36. Ibid.

37. L. N. G. Filon and A. N. Whitehead, "Memorandum on the Imperial College Question," May 27, 1924.

38. T. G. Henderson, "For a Biographer of Whitehead," *Revue Internationale de Philosophie* 81 (1967): 358–71.

39. Ibid., 359.

40. Geoffrey C. Lowry, unpublished typescript entitled "Pearls before Swine," seen by the author in June, 1965.

41. Governing Body of the Imperial College of Science and Technology, Minutes, March 26, 1920.

V. First Philosophical Publications

1. Abiog. Notes, in Schilpp, *LLP-W*, p. 13.

2. See *IS*.

3. L. A. Reid to Victor Lowe, August 14, 1965.

4. L. J. Russell to Victor Lowe, June 21, 1967.

5. Whitehead in conversation with Victor Lowe, May 14, 1941.

6. Ibid.

7. Alfred North Whitehead to Bertrand Russell, April 27, 29, and 30, 1905; September 22, 1910; and October 1, 1913 (Bertrand Russell Archives, McMaster University, Hamilton, Ontario); and January 10, 1914 (Lady Ottoline Morrell Papers, Harry Ranson Humanities Research Center, University of Texas at Austin).

8. Cf. Bertrand Russell's "Whitehead and *Principia Mathematica*," *Mind* 57 (1948): 138.

9. *CN*, pp. vii–viii.

10. Bertrand Russell, "My Mental Development" in *The Philosophy of Bertrand Russell*, ed. P. S. Schilpp (Evanston: Northwestern University Press, 1944), p. 12; see also Russell, "The Study of Mathematics" (1907), in his *Philosophical Essays* (London and New York: Longmans, Green and Co., 1910). His "A Free Man's Worship" (first published in 1903), also in that volume, embodies an emotional expression of this escapism.

11. In his essays on mathematical education; and in the philosophy he wrote after 1924, even though partly Platonic.

12. Russell, *MPD*, p. 99.

13. *AE*, p. 191.

14. Ibid., pp. 157–58.

15. Russell, *Portraits*, pp. 39–40.

16. Russell, *MPD*, p. 62.

17. Ibid., pp. 12–13.

18. *AE*, pp. 245–46.

19. Ibid., p. 207.

20. Ibid., p. 247.

21. Ibid., p. 206.

22. This occurs in "Commentary added on reading the Paper before the Aristotelian Society," *OT*, p. 215, reprinted with one omission in "Supplementary Notes on the Above Paper," *IS*, p. 99.

23. *AE*, p. 157.

24. Ibid., p. 161.

25. Ibid., p. 201.

26. Ibid., p. 182.

27. Ibid., p. 237.

28. Ibid., p. 181.

29. Ibid., p. 161.

30. Ibid., p. 181.

31. Ibid., p. 246.

32. Ibid., p. 245.

33. Ibid., pp. 158–59.

34. Bertrand Russell, "Logical Atomism," *Contemporary British Philosophy*, ed. by J. H. Muirhead (London: George Allen & Unwin, 1924), p. 363. See also *AE*, p. 218.

35. *AE*, p. 243.

36. Ibid., p. 231.

37. Ibid., p. 158.

38. Ibid., p. 230.

39. Ibid., p. 190.

40. Ibid., pp. 189–90.

41. Ibid., p. 246.

42. Ibid., p. 247.

VI. "Pan-Physics": Whitehead's Philosophy of Natural Science, 1918–1922

1. See, for example, John Passmore, *A Hundred Years of Philosophy* (London: Gerald Duckworth, 1957), pp. 337–40.
2. H. J. Easterling to Leemon McHenry, April 23, 1987.
3. These were the circumstances as of 1987. Ibid.
4. *R*, p. 4.
5. *CN*, p. 2.
6. Alfred North Whitehead, "Symposium: Time, Space, and Material," *Proceedings of the Aristotelian Society*, Suppl. 2 (1919): 44–57; reprinted in *IS*.
7. *IS*, pp. 56–57; see also *CN*, pp. 16–22.
8. *CN*, p. 16.
9. *IS*, p. 57.
10. Ibid.; cf. *PNK*, ★1.4.
11. *CN*, p. 15.
12. *IS*, p. 58; and *PNK*, ★2.4.
13. *PNK*, ★2.4.
14. *CN*, p. 4.
15. Ibid., p. 29.
16. *PNK*, p. vii.
17. *CN*, pp. 3–4.
18. *IS*, pp. 155–56.
19. *CN*, p. 4.
20. Ibid., p. 30.
21. Ibid., p. 44.
22. Ibid., p. 28.
23. *PNK*, p. v.
24. *CN*, p. 49.
25. Ibid., p. 52.
26. Ibid., p. 166.
27. Ibid., p. 34.
28. Ibid., p. 69.
29. Ibid., p. 110.
30. *IS*, p. 62.
31. Ibid., p. 245.
32. *CN*, p. 158.
33. Ibid., p. 29.
34. Ibid., p. 49; *R*, pp. 18–19. See also *PNK*, ★3.3–★3.8, ★16.1–★16.5, and ★20–★21.3.
35. Cf. *AE*, pp. 160, 176–77 (*IS*, pp. 24, 35); and see *AE*, pp. 218–20.
36. *CN*, pp. 197–98.
37. *R*, p. 13.
38. *R*, pp. 18–19.
39. See *PNK*, ★27, for the exact formulation.
40. *CN*, p. 84.
41. Ibid., pp. 80–82.
42. Ibid., p. 81.
43. *PNK*, ★18.3.

44. *R*, p. 88.

45. Reprinted in *IS*, pp. 125–35.

46. *PNK* ★34; see also *CN*, pp. 190–91.

47. *CN*, p. 192.

48. *R*, pp. v–vi.

49. *IS*, p. 134; see also *R*, p. 83.

50. Sir Arthur S. Eddington, "Physics and Philosophy," *Philosophy* 8 (1933): 31.

51. Lecture Series 5, Institute for Fluid Dynamics and Applied Mathematics, University of Maryland, 1951.

52. J. L. Synge to Victor Lowe, November 16, 1961.

53. Ibid.

54. Alfred North Whitehead, "Uniformity and Contingency," *Proceedings of the Aristotelian Society*, N.S., 23 (1922–23): 1–18; reprinted in *ESP* and *IS*.

55. Whitehead, "Uniformity and Contingency," pp. 1–2, citing Hume's *Philosophical Essays concerning Human Understanding*, III, "The Association of Ideas," in David Hume, *Enquiry concerning Human Understanding*. The Green and Grose edition of Hume's *Essays*, Vol. II (London, 1882), gives this passage only in a textual footnote to Section III of the *Enquiry concerning Human Understanding*, noting its occurrence in editions from 1748 through 1770. The passage is not included in the Selby-Bigge edition of the *Enquiry*.

56. Whitehead, "Uniformity and Contingency," p. 3.

57. Ibid., p. 9.

58. Ibid., p. 6.

59. Ibid., p. 14.

60. Ibid., p. 12.

61. Ibid., p. 13.

62. Ibid., p. 13. Bertrand Russell's comment is from *The Analysis of Mind* (London: George Allen & Unwin, 1921), Lecture V, "Causal Laws," p. 96.

63. The following letter is transcribed from a typed copy in Victor Lowe's possession:

Dec 27/07

Dear Bertie

Thanks for your MSS. I have not had time to examine them yet.

I am looking over Keynes' Dissertation. He runs a theory of Probability as a fundamental idea, with "certainty" as an extreme case, and "inference" as distinct from "implication" and from "formal implication." He thinks himself a devout follower of you, but as far as I can judge if his point of view is admitted Symbolic Logic becomes a piece of idle word play, and the other set of fundamental ideas are the really important things. I feel convinced that the frequency theory of proby is in the main true. Would you kindly criticize the following sketch and let me have your remarks soon if not too inconvenient.

Yrs affect

Alfred Whitehead

P.S. We ought to have a chapter on the point.

VII. Migration to Harvard

1. President Lowell to James H. Woods, March 11, 1920.
2. E. B. Wilson to W. E. Hocking, January 18, 1961.
3. Ibid.
4. Ibid.
5. *ESP,* p. 114.
6. W. E. Hocking, "Whitehead as I Knew Him," *Journal of Philosophy* 58, No. 19 (1961): 508; reprinted in George L. Kline, ed., *Alfred North Whitehead: Essays on His Philosophy* (Englewood Cliffs, N.J.: Prentice-Hall, 1963), pp. 7–17.
7. Whitehead to A. Lawrence Lowell, February 24, 1924.
8. Hocking, "Whitehead as I Knew Him," p. 508.
9. Quoted by Hocking, ibid.
10. Price, *Dialogues,* pp. 7–8. Price could have got this description at first hand only from Evelyn.
11. Hocking, "Whitehead as I Knew Him," p. 508.
12. Whitehead to North Whitehead, August 28, 1924.
13. Ibid.
14. Whitehead to North Whitehead, March 15, 1925.
15. Whitehead to North Whitehead, August 28, 1924.
16. Raphael Demos, interview with author, February 10, 1967.
17. Ibid.
18. J. W. Miller to Victor Lowe, May 15, 1970.
19. Ibid.
20. Raphael Demos, interview with author, February 10, 1967.
21. J. W. Miller to Victor Lowe, May 15, 1970.
22. Whitehead to North Whitehead, May 15, 1925.
23. Lewis S. Ford, *The Emergence of Whitehead's Metaphysics* (Albany: State University of New York Press, 1984). Ford published brief summaries of Hocking's notes through the lecture of March 28, 1925, and the notes in full thereafter.
24. Louise R. Heath, Notes of Whitehead's lectures in the autumn of 1924. Unless otherwise specified, her Notes are the source of information about Whitehead's lectures in the remainder of this section.
25. Charles A. Baylis to Victor Lowe, December 28, 1967.
26. Ibid.
27. J. Robert Oppenheimer to Victor Lowe, January 30, 1967.
28. Susanne K. Langer, interview with author, April 1966.
29. Ibid.
30. Susanne K. Langer, interview with author, May 12, 1969. My experience with Whitehead when I wrote my Ph.D. thesis in 1934–35 was similar.
31. Susanne K. Langer, "Confusion of Symbols and Confusion of Logical Types," *Mind,* N.S., 35 (1926): 222–29.
32. Susanne K. Langer, interview with author, April 1966. It was typical of Whitehead to tell Mrs. Langer, "The chief function of us old ones is to help you young ones get a start."
33. Scott Buchanan to Victor Lowe, January 14, 1967.

34. C. I. Lewis, *Mind and the World Order* (New York: Charles Scribner's Sons, 1929).

35. See Samuel Eliot Morison, ed., *The Development of Harvard University since the Inauguration of President Eliot (1869–1929)* (Cambridge, Mass.: Harvard University Press, 1929), p. 27.

36. Alfred North Whitehead to Ernesta Greene, February 16, 1925.

37. Jessie Whitehead, interview with author, June 20, 1966.

38. Whitehead to North Whitehead, August 16, 1925, postscript.

39. Whitehead to North Whitehead, August 16, 1925.

VIII. A New Philosophy of Nature

1. President A. Lawrence Lowell to Whitehead, April 16, 1924; quoted by permission of the President and Fellows of Harvard College.

2. In a March 16, 1926, letter to Whitehead's American publisher, Curtice Hitchcock of the Macmillan Company, Evelyn called herself Whitehead's "business manager."

3. Professor Harold N. Lee (who was present), in conversation with Victor Lowe, March 6, 1976.

4. *SMW*, p. 3.

5. Price, *Dialogues*, XIX (November 2, 1940).

6. Visit to Manuscripts Division, the New York Public Library, January 31, 1969; letter from Ms. Melanie Yolles, Manuscripts Specialist, to Victor Lowe, February 26, 1986.

7. Curtice Hitchcock to Whitehead, December 4, 1925.

8. *SMW*, p. 99. In the paper "Time" (1926) Whitehead gives this activity its permanent name in his philosophy: creativity.

9. *SMW*, p. 133.

10. *CN*, p. 5.

11. *SMW*, p. 131.

12. Ibid., p. 121.

13. Ibid., pp. 243–50.

14. Ibid., p. 97.

15. Ibid., p. 146.

16. Ibid., p. 81.

17. Ibid.

18. Ibid., pp. 81–82.

19. The Lowell Institute, 1924.

20. Sir S. C. Roberts, *Adventures with Authors* (Cambridge: Cambridge University Press, 1966), p. 102.

21. R. W. David, tabulation sent to Victor Lowe, August 26, 1968.

22. *SMW*, pp. ix–x.

23. Ibid., p. 271. See the emphatic passage about "value" which I quoted at the end of Section iii of this chapter.

24. Ibid., p. 279.

25. Ibid., p. 281.

26. Ibid., p. 283.

27. Ibid., pp. 275–76.

28. Ibid., p. 277.

29. Ibid., p. 172.

30. Ibid., p. 179.

31. Ibid., p. 103.

32. Ibid., pp. 212–13.

33. Ibid., p. 213.

34. Ibid., pp. 213–14.

35. See, for example, ibid., p. 216.

36. Ibid., p. 152.

37. Samuel Alexander, *Moral Order and Progress* (London: Trübner & Co., 1889).

38. Alfred North Whitehead, conversation with author in August 1942.

39. Samuel Alexander, Preface (dated October 1927) to 2d imp. of *Space, Time, and Deity* (London: Macmillan & Co., 1927), Vol. I, p. vi.

40. John Passmore, *A Hundred Years of Philosophy*, rev. ed. (New York: Gerald Duckworth & Co., 1957), p. 267.

41. Ibid.

42. Alexander, *Space, Time, and Deity* (London: Macmillan & Co., 1920), Vol. I, p. 47 (hereafter cited as Alexander, *STD*).

43. *SMW*, p. 220.

44. Alexander, Preface to 2d imp. of *STD*, Vol. I, p. xiii.

45. Alexander, *STD*, Vol. II, pp. 15–16.

46. Alexander, Preface to 2d imp., *STD*, pp. vi–vii.

47. Whitehead, in *Symposium in Honor of the Seventieth Birthday of Alfred North Whitehead* (privately printed by the Harvard University Press, 1932), p. 27; in *ESP*, p. 118.

48. See Alexander, *STD*, Vol. I, p. 61.

49. H. Wildon Carr, *The Philosophy of Change: A Study of the Fundamental Principles of the Philosophy of Bergson* (London: Macmillan & Co., 1914).

50. Jessie Whitehead to Victor Lowe, October 23, 1970.

51. Theodore de Laguna, Review of *An Enquiry Concerning the Principles of Natural Knowledge*, by Alfred North Whitehead, in *Philosophical Review* 29 (1920): 269.

52. Alfred North Whitehead, conversation with author in 1937.

53. *SMW*, p. 206.

54. For example, in "Mysticism and Logic," "The Philosophy of Bergson," and "Philosophy in the Twentieth Century." "Mysticism and Logic," first printed in the *Hibbert Journal* for July 1914, may be found in Russell's *Mysticism and Logic and Other Essays* (New York: Longmans, Green & Co., 1918; New York: W. W. Norton & Co., 1929; London: George Allen & Unwin, 1929). For "The Philosophy of Bergson," see *The Philosophy of Bergson* (London: Macmillan & Co., 1914). "Philosophy in the Twentieth Century," first printed in *Dial* in October 1924, may be found in Russell's *Sceptical Essays* (New York: W. W. Norton & Co., 1928; London: George Allen & Unwin, 1928).

55. Henri Bergson, *The Creative Mind: An Introduction to Metaphysics,* trans. Maybelle L. Andison (New York: Philosophical Library, 1946), p. 66.

56. Victor Lowe, "The Influence of Bergson, James, and Alexander on Whitehead," *Journal of the History of Ideas* 10 (1949): 267–96.

57. In *Understanding Whitehead* (1962) I wrote that as several persons who knew Whitehead when he was writing the *Principles of Natural Knowledge* or

shortly afterward attributed an important influence to Bergson, and none that I knew of denied this, I was no longer so skeptical about it. The persons were Sir Edmund Whittaker (in his *Dictionary of National Biography* article on Whitehead), Bertrand Russell, and F. S. C. Northrop (Filmer S. C. Northrop, "Whitehead's Philosophy of Science," in Schilpp, *LLP-W*, pp. 165–207). I have looked again at what they said. Northrop, after mentioning the fact that Whitehead often talked with Carr about Bergson, ignored the possibility that ideas which were like Bergson's were independently reached by Whitehead. Russell's strong dislike of both men's philosophies bracketed them in his mind. Whittaker, in his article in the *Dictionary of National Biography, 1941–1950*, p. 953, asserted only that in his *Principles of Natural Knowledge* and *Concept of Nature* Whitehead "gave his adhesion definitely to the general standpoint of the process philosophies associated with the names of Bergson, Samuel Alexander, and C. L. Morgan."

58. Curtice Hitchcock to George P. Brett, May 24, 1925.
59. S. C. Roberts to Curtice Hitchcock, May 11, 1925.
60. Ibid.
61. Ibid.
62. F. J. Flagg to Curtice Hitchcock, May 14, 1925.
63. Ibid.
64. Curtice Hitchcock to F. J. Flagg, May 15, 1925.
65. Curtice Hitchcock to Mr. Lathem of the Macmillan Co., August 18, 1924.

IX. Religion

1. A. Lawrence Lowell, *Eighty-sixth Annual Report of the Lowell Institute* (1926).
2. *Harvard University Gazette,* January 25, 1926.
3. Whitehead, in a note enclosed with Evelyn Whitehead's letter of March 16, 1926, to Curtice Hitchcock of the Macmillan Company.
4. *RM,* p. 16.
5. Ibid., pp. 19–20.
6. Ibid., p. 17.
7. Ibid., p. 18.
8. See *The Nation & Athenaeum* 40 (February 12, 1927): 664.
9. *RM,* p. 15.
10. *SMW,* p. 253.
11. Ibid.
12. Ibid., p. 258.
13. Ibid., p. 259.
14. Ibid., p. 263.
15. Ibid., p. 266.
16. Ibid., pp. 266–67.
17. Ibid., p. 267.
18. Ibid.
19. Ibid., pp. 267–68.
20. Ibid., p. 268.
21. Bertrand Russell, conversation with author, June 11, 1965.

22. Jessie Whitehead, conversation with author, June 1972.

23. North Whitehead, conversation with author, early autumn 1967.

24. Paul A. Schilpp to North Whitehead, May 20, 1938; A. N. Whitehead to Professor Schilpp, May 25, 1938, and September 12, 1939; Schilpp to Whitehead, October 14, 1939; John Dewey to Schilpp, January 23, 1941; Whitehead to Schilpp, January 29, 1941.

25. In the footnote to Section ii of this chapter, on page 000 above, Lowe says that in this section he draws on an article by Donald A. Crosby, "Religion and Solitariness" (1972). The article has been reprinted in Lewis S. Ford and George L. Kline, eds., *Explorations in Whitehead's Philosophy* (New York: Fordham University Press, 1983), pp. 149–69.

26. *SMW*, pp. 219–20.

27. *RM*, p. 84.

28. Ibid., p. 89.

29. Ibid.

30. Ibid., p. 90. Whitehead isn't always faithful to his conception of God as an actual entity with a special function. He sometimes identifies the function itself with God. For example, the final section, "Conclusion," of *Religion in the Making* begins, "God is that function in the world by reason of which our purposes are directed to ends which in our own consciousness are impartial as to our own interests," not "God's function in the world is to direct our purposes to ends . . ." But in reading statements like "The purpose of God is the attainment of value in the temporal world," we must think of God as an actual entity, not as a mere function, and not as a character of wisdom or of rightness which pervades the universe. The definitive exposition of Whitehead's concept of God comes later, in his Gifford Lectures.

31. Ibid., p. 91.

32. Ibid., p. 92.

33. *SMW*, p. 99.

34. *RM*, pp. 62–66.

35. This refers to a final chapter which Victor Lowe did not live to write.

36. *RM*, p. 144.

37. Ibid.

38. Ibid., p. 145.

39. Ibid., pp. 145–46.

40. Bengt Sundkler, *Church of South India: The Movement Towards Union* (London: Lutterworth Press, 1954), p. 52.

41. *RM*, p. 44.

42. Ibid., p. 146.

43. Ibid., p. 153.

44. Ibid., p. 66.

45. Ibid., p. 67.

46. Ibid., p. 140.

47. Ibid., p. 76.

48. Price, *Dialogues*, XXXVI (January 19, 1945).

49. Leslie Pennington to Victor Lowe, May 26, 1967.

50. John Edsall to Victor Lowe, July 23, 1966.

51. Stephen Lee Ely, *The Religious Availability of Whitehead's God: A Critical Analysis* (Madison: University of Wisconsin Press, 1942); reprinted in the Ford

and Kline volume referred to in note 25 above, pp. 170–211. The fact that most of Ely's citations are to *Process and Reality* is immaterial.

52. *RM,* p. 105.

53. Ibid., pp. 119–20.

54. Ibid., p. 80. The detailed theory of this contribution will not appear until Whitehead delivers the final part of his Gifford Lectures.

55. Ibid., p. 149.

X. The Atypical English Philosopher

1. John Herman Randall, Jr., "The Twenty-fifth Annual Meeting of the Eastern Division of the American Philosophical Association," *Journal of Philosophy* 23, No. 2 (1926): 36–46; see especially pp. 45–46.

2. Ibid., p. 45.

3. Ibid., p. 46.

4. Alfred North Whitehead, "Time," *Proceedings of the Sixth International Congress of Philosophy* (New York: Longmans, Green & Co., 1927), p. 59; or see *IS,* p. 240.

5. Sterling Lamprecht to Victor Lowe, September 18, 1965.

6. Ibid.

7. Alfred North Whitehead to John J. Luck, December 19, 1926.

8. Ibid.

9. Kendon Stubbs, Reference Librarian, Alderman Library, University of Virginia, to Victor Lowe, August 30, 1966.

10. Ibid.

11. *S,* p. 33.

12. "The human mind is functioning symbolically when some components of its experience elicit consciousness, beliefs, emotions, and usages, respecting other components of its experience" (ibid., pp. 7–8).

13. Ibid., p. 28.

14. *PR,* p. 324.

15. *S,* pp. 50–51.

16. Ibid., p. 25.

17. Ibid., p. 80.

18. Whitehead brought up Burke and expressed his opinions of him in "Uses of Symbolism" (ibid., pp. 70–73).

19. Ibid., p. 50.

20. Ibid., p. 47.

21. Ibid., p. 82.

22. Ibid., p. 38.

23. Ibid., p. 61.

24. Ibid., pp. 68–69.

XI. Gifford Lecturer

1. Extracts from the Trust Disposition and Settlement of the late Adam Gifford, from Miss C. E. Giles, Secretary to the Gifford Committee, University of Edinburgh, in July 1965.

2. Miss C. E. Giles to Victor Lowe, July 30, 1965.

3. W. A. Fleming to Alfred North Whitehead, January 19, 1927.

4. Price, *Dialogues*, XIX (November 2, 1940).

5. *PR*, p. 11. [As Lowe notes on page 000, all citations from *PR* are from the edition corrected by David Ray Griffin and Donald W. Sherburne, and not from the older, Macmillan/Cambridge edition.—Ed.].

6. Ibid., p. 21 (Category of the Ultimate).

7. Ibid., p. 145.

8. Alfred North Whitehead, "Time," *Proceedings of the Sixth International Congress of Philosophy*, (New York: Longmans, Green & Co., 1927), p. 64; or *IS*, p. 246.

9. Lecture notes taken by Paul Weiss.

10. *PR*, p. 164.

11. Ibid., p. 29.

12. George L. Kline, ed., *Alfred North Whitehead: Essays on His Philosophy* (Englewood Cliffs, N.J.: Prentice-Hall, 1963), pp. 200–207.

13. New York, Free Press.

14. Its contrast with F. H. Bradley's famous *Appearance and Reality* was a merit; Whitehead considered the latter Bradley's feeblest work. Henry Veatch (a pupil of Whitehead's) to Victor Lowe, November 28, 1967.

15. *PR*, Pt. I, Chap. II, Sec. ii.

16. Ibid.

17. George Santayana to J. Middleton Murry, December 11, 1929, in *The Letters of George Santayana*, ed. Daniel Cory (New York: Charles Scribner's Sons, 1955), p. 248.

18. Alfred North Whitehead, conversation with author, December 2, 1936.

19. *PR*, p. 23 (Category of Explanation, xi).

20. Ibid., Pt. III, Chap. I, Sec. i.

21. Ibid., Pt. III, Chap. II, Sec. i.

22. Ibid.

23. Ibid., p. 162.

24. Ibid.

25. Ibid., p. 25 (Category of Explanation, xviii).

26. Ibid., p. 11.

27. Ibid., Pt. III, Chap. IV.

28. Ibid., pp. 266–67.

29. Ibid., Pt. II, Chap. VII, Sec. ii.

30. Ibid., p. 151.

31. *MT*, p. 121.

32. *PR*, p. 244.

33. Ibid.

34. Ibid., p. 255.

35. Ibid.

36. Ibid., Pt. II, Chap. VII, Sec. iv.

37. He is known to have said that if he were to do the book over he would make Part IV precede Part III (Sydney Rome to Victor Lowe, March 24, 1968).

38. *PR*, p. 285.

39. Theodore de Laguna, "Point, Line, and Surface, as Sets of Solids," *Journal of Philosophy* 19 (1922): 449–61.

40. *PR*, p. 287.

41. Ibid., p. 310.

42. Ibid., pp. 310–11.

43. Ibid., Preface, p. xiv. Later in *Process and Reality* Whitehead wrote, "The safest general characterization of the European philosophical tradition is that it consists of a series of footnotes to Plato" (ibid., p. 39). This has often been misquoted as the foolish remark that European philosophy is a series of footnotes to Plato.

44. Ibid., p. 162.

45. Ibid.

46. Ibid., p. 229.

47. Classroom lecture by Whitehead, March 18, 1937.

48. F. H. Bradley, *Appearance and Reality,* 2d ed. (London: Swan Sonnenschein & Co., 1897), p. 613.

49. *PR,* p. 130.

50. Ibid., p. 339.

51. Ibid.

52. Ibid., p. 340.

53. Ibid., p. 343.

54. Ibid.

55. Ibid., p. 345.

56. Ibid., p. 346.

57. Ibid.

58. Ibid., p. 343.

59. Ibid., p. 347.

60. Whitehead considered unworthy of comment the construing of immortality "in terms of a final pair of opposites, happiness for some, torture for others" (ibid., Pt. V, Chap. II, Sec. v).

61. Ibid., p. 343.

62. Ibid., p. 351.

63. Alfred North Whitehead, conversation with author, April 2, 1940.

64. *PR,* Pt. II, Chap. IV, Sec. x.

65. Ibid.

66. *ESP,* p. 117 (emphasis added). Whitehead continued, "And in many ways I find that I am in complete agreement with Bradley." This implies that there were some ways in which he found that his agreement with Bradley was not complete. On this occasion he touched on several of them.

67. Dr. J. M. Whitaker to Victor Lowe, July 20, 1965.

68. Mason Gross to Victor Lowe, April 4, 1973.

69. Alfred North Whitehead to Rosalind Greene, June 28, 1928 (Radcliffe College, Schlesinger Library, Radcliffe Archives).

70. Eric Alfred North Whitehead, conversation with author, May 21, 1967.

71. Alfred North Whitehead to Rosalind Greene, June 28, 1928.

72. Ibid.

73. Kenneth Blackwell, Russell Archivist, MacMaster University, to Victor Lowe, September 16, 1987.

XII. Fame

1. Crane Brinton, *The Society of Fellows* (Cambridge, Mass.: Harvard University Press, 1959).

2. One of the most revealing accounts of Whitehead's personal manner in his Harvard lectures is the paper written after his death by F. H. Page, "A. N. Whitehead: A Pupil's Tribute," *Dalhousie Review* 28 (1948): 71–80.

3. *ESP,* pp. 88–89.

4. *Mind* 57, No. 226 (1948): 141.

5. What follows comes from notes of Whitehead's remarks taken by W. E. Hocking.

Bibliography

This bibliography is believed to include everything written by Whitehead and published in his lifetime.* It is arranged chronologically. No translations of his books are listed. Post-1947 printings of Whitehead's books are mentioned only if they are cited in the notes to this volume.

"A Celebrity at Home: The Clerk of the Weather." *Cambridge Review*, February 10, 1886, pp. 202–3.

"Davy Jones." *Cambridge Review*, May 12, 1886, pp. 311–12.

"A Visitation." *Cambridge Fortnightly*, March 6, 1888, pp. 81–83.

"On the Motion of Viscous Incompressible Fluids: A Method of Approximation." *Quarterly Journal of Pure and Applied Mathematics* 23 (1889): 78–93.

"Second Approximations to Viscous Fluid Motion: A Sphere Moving Steadily in a Straight Line." *Quarterly Journal of Pure and Applied Mathematics* 23 (1889): 143–52.

"On Ideals: With Reference to the Controversy Concerning the Admission of Women to Degrees in the University." *Cambridge Review*, May 14, 1896, pp. 310–11.

"The Geodesic Geometry of Surfaces in non-Euclidean Space." *Proceedings of the London Mathematical Society* 29 (1897–98): 275–324.

UA   *A Treatise on Universal Algebra, with Applications*, Vol. I (no others published). Cambridge: Cambridge University Press, 1898.

"Sets of Operations in Relation to Groups of Finite Order." Abstract. *Proceedings of the Royal Society of London* 64 (1898–99): 319–20.

"Memoir on the Algebra of Symbolic Logic." *American Journal of Mathematics* 23 (1901): 139–65, 297–316.

"On Cardinal Numbers." *American Journal of Mathematics* 24 (1902): 367–94.

"The Logic of Relations, Logical Substitution Groups, and Cardinal Numbers." *American Journal of Mathematics* 25 (1903): 157–78.

"Theorems on Cardinal Numbers." *American Journal of Mathematics* 26 (1904): 31–32.

---

*This is a corrected and amplified version of the Bibliography published in Volume I.

APG   *The Axioms of Projective Geometry*. Cambridge Tracts in Mathematics and Mathematical Physics, No. 4. Cambridge: Cambridge University Press, 1906; New York: Hafner Publishing Co., 1971.

          Liberty and the Enfranchisement of Women. Cambridge: Cambridge Women's Suffrage Association, 1906.

MC   "On Mathematical Concepts of the Material World." *Philosophical Transactions of Royal Society of London,* Ser. A, 205 (1906): 465–525.

ADG   *The Axioms of Descriptive Geometry*. Cambridge Tracts in Mathematics and Mathematical Physics, No. 5. Cambridge: Cambridge University Press, 1907; New York: Hafner Publishing Co., 1971.

          "The Philosophy of Mathematics." *Science Progress in the Twentieth Century* 5 (October 1910): 234–39.

          "Axioms of Geometry." Div. VII of "Geometry." *Encyclopaedia Britannica,* 11th ed. (1910–11).

          "Mathematics." *Encyclopaedia Britannica,* 11th ed. (1910–11).

          "Non-Euclidean Geometry." With Bertrand Russell. Div. VI of "Geometry." *Encyclopaedia Britannica,* 11th ed. (1910–11).

PM   *Principia Mathematica*. With Bertrand Russell. Vols. I–III. Cambridge: Cambridge University Press, 1910–13; 2d ed., 1925–27.

IM   *An Introduction to Mathematics*. Home University Library of Modern Knowledge, No. 15. London: Williams & Norgate; New York: Henry Holt & Co., 1911.

          "The Place of Mathematics in a Liberal Education." *Journal of the Association of Teachers of Mathematics for the Southeastern Part of England* I (1911). Reprinted in Pt. III of *ESP* (1947).

          "The Principles of Mathematics in Relation to Elementary Teaching." *Proceedings of the Fifth International Congress of Mathematicians* (Cambridge, England, August 22–28, 1912), 2:449–54. Reprinted as Chap. V of *OT* (1917).

          "Presidential Address to the London Branch of the Mathematical Association." *Mathematical Gazette* 7 (March 1913): 87–94. Reprinted, under the title "The Mathematical Curriculum," as Chap. IV of *OT* (1917) and Chap. VI of *AE* (1929).

          "Space, Time, and Relativity." *Proceedings of the Aristotelian Society,* N.S., 16 (1915–16): 104–29. Reprinted as Chap. VIII of *OT* (1917) and Chap. X of *AE* (1929).

          "The Aims of Education: A Plea for Reform." *Mathematical Gazette* 8 (January 1916): 191–203. Reprinted as Chap. I of *OT* (1917) and, with omissions, as Chap. I of *AE* (1929).

          "The Organisation of Thought." *Report of the Eighty-sixth Meeting of the British Association for the Advancement of Science* (Newcastle-on-Tyne, 1916), 355–65. Presidential address to Section A (Mathematical and Physical Science) of the Association. Reprinted as Chap. I of *OT* (1917) and Chap. VIII of *AE* (1929).

"La Théorie Relationniste de L'Espace." *Revue de Métaphysique et de Morale* 23 (May 1916): 423–54.

"To the Master and Fellows of Trinity College, Cambridge." Dated July 15, 1916. Cambridge: Printed at the University Press. "Private and Confidential. For Members of the Governing Board of Trinity College only." Reprinted in *Russell: The Journal of the Bertrand Russell Archives,* N.S., 6, No. 1 (1986): 64–70.

OT   *The Organisation of Thought, Educational and Scientific.* London: Williams & Norgate; Philadelphia: J. B. Lippincott Co., 1917.

"Technical Education and Its Relation to Science and Literature." *Technical Journal* 10 (January 1917): 59–74. Reprinted as Chap. II of *OT* (1917) and, with omissions, as Chap. IV of *AE* (1929).

"Graphical Solution for High-Angle Fire." *Proceedings of the Royal Society of London,* Ser. A, 94 (1918): 301–7.

PNK   *An Enquiry Concerning the Principles of Natural Knowledge.* Cambridge: Cambridge University Press, 1919; 2d ed., 1925.

"Fundamental Principles in Education." *Report of the Eighty-seventh Meeting of the British Association for the Advancement of Science* (Bournemouth, 1919), 361.

"A Revolution in Science." *Nation,* November 15, 1919, 232–33. Reprinted in *Educational Review* 59 (1920): 148–53.

"Symposium: Time, Space, and Material: Are They, and If So in What Sense, the Ultimate Data of Science?" With Sir Oliver Lodge, J. W. Nicholson, Henry Head, Mrs. Adrian Stephen, and H. Wildon Carr. *Proceedings of the Aristotelian Society,* Suppl. 2 (1919), pp. 44–108. For Whitehead's contribution, see pp. 44–57.

CN   *The Concept of Nature.* Cambridge: Cambridge University Press, 1920. Tarner Lectures, Trinity College, Cambridge.

"Einstein's Theory: An Alternative Suggestion." *Times* (London) *Educational Supplement,* February 12, 1920, p. 83.

"Report of Committee Appointed by the Prime Minister to Inquire into the Position of Classics in the Educational System of the United Kingdom." With the Marquis of Crewe (Chairman) and other members of the committee. London: His Majesty's Stationery Office, 1921.

"Science in General Education." *Proceedings of the Second Congress of Universities of the Empire,* pp. 31–39. London: G. Bell & Sons, 1921. Reprinted in Pt. III of *ESP* (1947).

"Discussion: The Idealistic Interpretation of Einstein's Theory."
      With H. Wildon, Carr, T. P. Nunn, and Dorothy Wrinch.
      Proceedings of the Aristotelian Society 22 (1921–22): 123–38. For
      Whitehead's contribution, see pp. 130–34.
"The Philosophical Aspects of the Principle of Relativity." In *Pro-
      ceedings of the Aristotelian Society* 22 (1921–22): 215–23.
R   *The Principle of Relativity, with Applications to Physical Science.*
      Cambridge: Cambridge University Press, 1922.
      The Rhythm of Education. London: Christophers, 1922. Reprinted
      as Chap. II of *AE* (1929).
"Uniformity and Contingency," *Proceedings of the Aristotelian So-
      ciety* 23 (1922–23): 1–18. Reprinted in Pt. II of *ESP* (1947).
"The First Physical Synthesis." Chap. VI of *Science and Civiliza-
      tion,* edited by F. S. Marvin, pp. 161–78. London: Oxford Uni-
      versity Press, 1923. Reprinted in Pt. IV of *ESP* (1947).
"Letter to the Editor." *New Statesman,* February 17, 1923, p. 568. A
      reply to C. P. Sanger's review of *The Principle of Relativity.*
"The Place of Classics in Education." *Hibbert Journal* 21 (1923):
      248–61. Reprinted as Chap. V of *AE* (1929).
"The Rhythmic Claims of Freedom and Discipline." *Hibbert Jour-
      nal* 21 (1923): 657–68. Reprinted as Chap. III of *AE* (1929).
"Symposium—The Problem of Simultaneity: Is There a Paradox
      in the Principle of Relativity in Regard to the Relation of Time
      Measured to Time Lived?" With H. Wildon Carr and R. A.
      Sampson. *Proceedings of the Aristotelian Society,* Suppl. 3 (1923),
      pp. 15–41. For Whitehead's contribution, see pp. 34–41.
"The Importance of Friendly Relations Between England and the
      United States." *Phillips Bulletin* 19, No. 3 (April 1925): 15–18.
      Address delivered at Phillips Academy, Andover, Mass.
"Religion and Science." *Atlantic Monthly* 136 (1925): 200–207. Re-
      printed as Chap. XII of *SMW* (1925).
SMW   *Science and the Modern World.* New York: Macmillan Co., 1925;
      Cambridge: Cambridge University Press, 1926.
"The Education of an Englishman." *Atlantic Monthly* 138 (1926):
      192–98. Reprinted in Pt. I of *ESP* (1947).
"Principia Mathematica." *Mind,* N.S., 35 (1926): 130. A note on
      the second edition of *Principia Mathematica.*
RM   *Religion in the Making.* New York: Macmillan Co.; Cambridge:
      Cambridge University Press, 1926. Lowell Lectures, 1926.
"England and the Narrow Seas." *Atlantic Monthly* 139 (1927): 791–
      98. Reprinted in Pt. I of *ESP* (1947).
S   *Symbolism: Its Meaning and Effect.* New York: Macmillan Co.,
      1927; London: Cambridge University Press, 1928. Barbour-
      Page Lectures, University of Virginia, 1927.

"Time." *Proceedings of the Sixth International Congress of Philosophy,* pp. 59–64. New York: Longmans, Green & Co., 1927.

"Universities and Their Function." *Atlantic Monthly* 141 (1928): 638–44. Reprinted in *Harvard Business School Alumni Bulletin* 5, No. 1 (November 1, 1928): 9–14, and as Chap. VII of *AE* (1929).

AE   *The Aims of Education and Other Essays.* New York: Macmillan Co.; London: Williams & Norgate, 1929.

FR   *The Function of Reason.* Princeton: Princeton University Press, 1929. Louis Clark Vanuxem Foundation Lectures, Princeton University, March 1929.

PR   *Process and Reality: An Essay in Cosmology.* New York: Macmillan Co.; Cambridge: Cambridge University Press, 1929. Corrected ed., edited by David Ray Griffin and Donald W. Sherburne, New York: Free Press, 1978. Gifford Lectures, University of Edinburgh, 1927–28.

"An Address." *Radcliffe Quarterly* 14, No. 1 (January 1930): 1–5. Delivered at the celebration of the fiftieth anniversary of the founding of Radcliffe College. Reprinted as "Historical Changes" in Pt. III of *ESP* (1947).

Prefatory Note to *The Practice of Philosophy,* Susanne K. Langer. New York: Henry Holt & Co., 1930.

"On Foresight." Introduction to *Business Adrift,* by W. D. Donham. New York: McGraw-Hill; London: George Routledge & Sons, 1931. Reprinted, with additions, as Chap. VI of *AI* (1933).

"Objects and Subjects." *Proceedings and Addresses of the American Philosophical Association* 5 (1931): 130–46. Reprinted in *Philosophical Review* 41 (1932): 130–46 and as Chap. XI of *AI* (1933).

Symposium in Honor of the Seventieth Birthday of Alfred North Whitehead. Cambridge, Mass.: Harvard University Press, 1932. Printed for private circulation only. Partial publication of Whitehead's reply, under the title "Process and Reality," appears in Pt. II of *ESP* (1947).

AI   *Adventures of Ideas.* New York: Macmillan Co.; Cambridge: Cambridge University Press, 1933.

"The Study of the Past: Its Uses and Its Dangers." *Harvard Business Review* II (1933): 436–44. Reprinted in *Educational Record* 14 (1933): 454–67 and in Pt. III of *ESP* (1947).

Foreword to *The Farther Shore: An Anthology of World Opinion on the Immortality of the Soul,* edited by Nathaniel Edward Griffin and Lawrence Hunt. Boston: Houghton Mifflin Co., 1934.

Foreword to *A System of Logistic,* by Willard Van Orman Quine.

Cambridge: Mass.: Harvard University Press; London: Oxford University Press, 1934.

"Indication, Classes, Numbers, Validation." *Mind* 43 (1934): 281–97. For corrigenda to this article see ibid., p. 543.

NL   *Nature and Life.* Chicago: University of Chicago Press; Cambridge: Cambridge University Press, 1934. Reprinted as Chaps. VII and VIII of *MT* (1938).

"The Aim of Philosophy." *Harvard Alumni Bulletin* 38 (1935): 234–35. Reprinted, with the omission of the first paragraph and the addition of a final paragraph, as the Epilogue to *MT* (1938).

"In Memoriam." In *Bernard Bosanquet and His Friends,* edited by J. H. Muirhead, p. 316. London: George Allen & Unwin, 1935.

"Harvard: The Future." *Atlantic Monthly* 158 (1936): 260–70. Reprinted in Pt. III of *ESP* (1947).

"Memories." *Atlantic Monthly* 157 (1936): 672–79. Reprinted in Pt. I of *ESP* (1947).

"Remarks." *Proceedings and Addresses of the American Philosophical Association* 10 (1936): 178–86. Reprinted in *Philosophical Review* 46 (1937): 178–86 and, without the first paragraph, under the title "Analysis of Meaning," in Pt. II of *ESP* (1947).

MT   *Modes of Thought.* New York: Macmillan Co.; Cambridge: Cambridge University Press, 1938. Six lectures delivered at Wellesley College, Mass., and two lectures given at the University of Chicago.

"An Appeal to Sanity." *Atlantic Monthly* 163 (1939): 309–20.

"John Dewey and His Influence." In *The Philosophy of John Dewey,* edited by Paul A. Schilpp, pp. 477–78. Evanston: Northwestern University Press, 1939.

"The Issue: Freedom." *Boston Daily Globe,* December 24, 1940, p. 12. A letter to the editor.

Abiog.   "Autobiographical Notes." In *The Philosophy of Alfred North White-*
Notes   *head,* edited by Paul A. Schilpp, pp. 1–14. Evanston: Northwestern University Press, 1941; Cambridge: Cambridge University Press, 1943; New York: Tudor Publishing Co., 1951. Reprinted in Pt. I of *ESP* (1947).

"Immortality." In *The Philosophy of Alfred North Whitehead,* edited by Paul A. Schilpp, pp. 682–700. Evanston: Northwestern University Press, 1941; Cambridge: Cambridge University Press, 1943; New York: Tudor Publishing Co., 1951. The Ingersoll Lecture for 1941, this sermon was originally delivered at the Harvard Memorial Church on April 22, 1941. Reprinted in *Harvard Divinity School Bulletin* 39 (1941–42): 5–21.

"Mathematics and the Good." In *The Philosophy of Alfred North Whitehead,* edited by Paul A. Schilpp, pp. 666–81. Evanston:

Northwestern University Press, 1941; Cambridge: Cambridge University Press, 1943; New York: Tudor Publishing Co., 1951.

"Statesmanship and Specialized Learning." *Proceedings of the American Academy of Arts and Sciences* 75 (1942): 1–5. A shortened version, "The Problem of Reconstruction," was published in *Atlantic Monthly* 169 (1942): 172–75.

Preface to "The Organization of a Story and a Tale," by William Morgan. *Journal of American Folklore* 58 (1945): 169.

ESP   *Essays in Science and Philosophy*. New York: Philosophical Library, 1947; London: Rider & Co., 1948.

IS   *The Interpretation of Science*. Edited by A. H. Johnson. Indianapolis: Bobbs-Merrill, 1961.

Index

Victor Lowe, widely recognized as the preeminent authority on the life and work of Alfred North Whitehead, died in 1988, his two-volume Whitehead biography not quite completed. He was Emeritus Professor of Philosophy at the Johns Hopkins University. Volume II of the biography was edited and seen through publication by J. B. Schneewind, chairman of the Philosophy Department at Johns Hopkins.

The Johns Hopkins University Press
Alfred North Whitehead: The Man and His Work, Vol. II

This book was composed in Bembo text and display by The Composing Room of Michigan, Inc., from a design by Chris L. Smith. It was printed on S. D. Warren's 50-lb. Sebago Antique Cream paper and bound in Holliston Roxite A by The Arcata Graphics Company.